CLINICAL THERAPEUTIC APPLICATIONS OF THE
KINESIO TAPING® METHOD
3RD EDITION

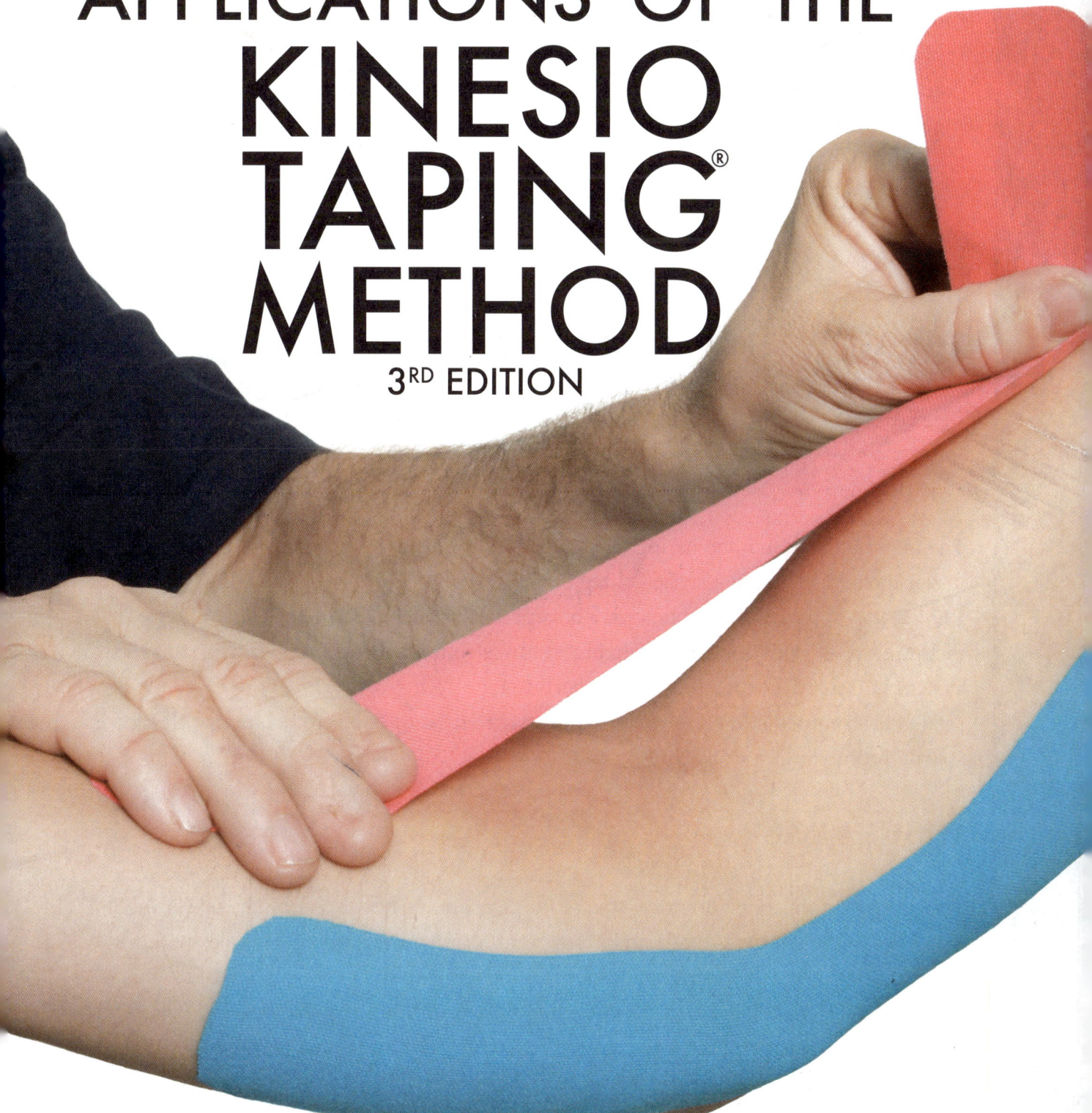

DR. KENZO KASE
Founder of the Kinesio Taping Method

JIM WALLIS
MS, ATC, CKTI

TSUYOSHI KASE
Licensed Judo Therapist, AT, CKTI

DISCLAIMER

The authors of this book do not dispense medical advice nor prescribe the use of the Kinesio Taping® Method as a form of treatment for medical problems with or without the advice of a physician. The intent of the authors is only to offer information of a general nature to help you cooperate with your doctor in your mutual quest for good health. In the event you use any of the information in this book for yourself, you are prescribing for yourself. The authors and publisher assume no responsibility for your actions.

DR. KENZO KASE,
FOUNDER OF THE KINESIO TAPING METHOD

- Born in 1942
- After he graduated from Meiji University, he attended and graduated from National College of Chiropractic in Chicago.
- 1975: opened Kase Chiropractic Clinic in Albuquerque, NM.
- 1976: became an instructor at the University of New Mexico.
- 1978: opened Kase Chiropractic Clinic in Tokyo.
- 1984: Founded Kinesio Taping® Association International
- Chairman of KTAI
- Published author of over 90 books
- He is the President of Kinesio Taping Association and National Chiropractic College Japan.
- He is a certified DC in the United States and one of the best Chiropractors in Japan. He invented and developed the Kinesio Taping® Method 30 years ago.

JIM WALLIS, MS, ATC, CKTI

- Born in 1958
- 1983: graduated from Washington State University and became a certified athletic trainer by **NATA.**
- 1984: earned MS from University of Arizona.
- 1997: became a Certified Kinesio Taping Instructor.
- 2010: inducted in the Oregon Athletic Trainers Hall of Fame.
- 2010: awarded the National Athletic Trainers Association Outstanding Service Award.
- 2012: Northwest Athletic Trainers Association District Directors Award.
- Board Member of the Kinesio Taping Association
- Currently, he is the Assistant Athletic Director for Sports Medicine at Portland State University.

TSUYOSHI KASE, LICENSED JUDO THERAPIST, AT, CKTI

- Born in 1968
- 1991: graduated from Dokkyo University, Foreign Language Department
- 1992: became a Certified Kinesio Taping Instructor
- 1992: graduated from Natural Chiropractic Academy
- 1999: became an instructor for Continuing Education courses at the University of New Mexico.
- 2000: graduated from University of New Mexico, Athletic Training Department
- 2011: graduated from Japan Judo Therapy and Acupuncture College
- Director of the Kinesio Treatment Center
- Currently serves as the Director of Kinesio bone setting clinic in Tokyo and teaches at Hosei University, Sports and Health Department.

Jim Wallis:

When the first edition was written my mother, Nancy, was instrumental in editing and encouraging me to "put in the work". The second edition was corrections due to inexperience in writing or editing a textbook. For the third edition I would like to honor my late wife Julene for allowing me the opportunity to risk the unknown with the security of knowing she would always be there for me. With her passing her presence is still a part of my soul and will always be so.

For all editions a special thank you to my son "Master Kyle" for being patient with me that I could not always be there for him at all times but knowing I would be there for him for all time.

Special thanks to Dr. Gracie Forrester, Itzik Friedman and Kim Stockheimer.

This Kinesio Taping Clinical Textbook could not be written without the gift of Dr. Kase trusting me to explain his ideas and his friendship.

TABLE OF CONTENTS

TABLE OF CONTENTS

TABLE OF CONTENTS

TABLE OF CONTENTS

SECTION 9:

Ankle & Foot - *continued*

SECTION 10:

INTRODUCTION

The Kinesio Taping® Method was first conceptualized in 1973 by Dr. Kenzo Kase. He was treating his patients and one of the primary complaints was pain. He was able to provide therapy to his patient's complaints but was trying to find a method to reduce his patient's pain inbetween office visits. He was not allowed to prescribe pain medication but believed if he could affect a change through the skin he could reduce his patients pain.

The initial concept was to reduce the build up of fluids between and within the layers of the soft tissue (edema) and decrease the increased temperature that results from edema. He felt that if he could lift the skin the interstitial and interstitial fluids would be allow normal movement through the superficial lymphatic vessels. The decrease in fluid pressure would then allow for improvement in muscle function, since muscle dysfunction is generally associated with pain and edema. Muscle function or the function of movement is kinesiology. This led to the original naming of Kinesio Taping.

Kinesio Taping has over time become the Kinesio Taping Technique and more recently Kinesio Taping Method as Dr. Kase has incorporated evaluation techniques and complimentary therapeutic treatment methods. The Kinesio Taping Method is an ongoing journey into the total treatment of each patient as an individual.

Dr. Kase originally experimented with already existing prophylactic tapes and found they were too thick; adhesive was to caustic and were not able to lift the skin. He then began to design a therapeutic tape. Today's Kinesio® Tex Tape is designed with elastic qualities of 40-60% of resting length. Has a 100% heat activated acrylic adhesive. The adhesive is applied in a wave pattern to mimic the waves of fingerprints. The Kinesio Tex Tape is made of 100% cotton fibers. These components mimic the qualities of the skin and when applied properly lift the skin that is demonstrated by convolutions in the skin.

One of the original concepts was to attempt to use an elastic therapeutic tape to replicate what you could do with your hands. The Kinesio Tex Tape is applied as if you have placed your hands upon the patient and as they move you are assisting your patient in a therapeutic treatment.

Since patients visit a clinic a limited number of times each week it was important that the Kinesio Tex Tape be able to be worn for multiple days. The cloth material is coated with a water resistant protectorate to resist moisture penetration. The wave like acrylic adhesive and 100% cotton fibers allows the Kinesio Tex Tape to be worn for 3-5 days.

KINESIO TAPING METHOD

One of the unique qualities of the Kinesio Taping Method is that it can be used from initial injury (acute), sub-acute, chronic to rehabilitation stages of clinical presentations. The method can be used for prevention and in combination with manual therapies as well as other therapeutic treatments. It can be used with, but not limited to: cryotherapy, hydrotherapy, electro-stimulation, acupuncture, chiropractic, osteopathic, massage therapy and ultrasound.

The Kinesio Taping Method first gained recognition outside of Japan in the 1988 Summer Olympics in Seoul, South Korea. Introduction to the USA occured in March 1995 in Portland, Oregon at the Northwest Athletic Trainers Association Annual Clinical Symposium. Europe was next to follow in 1996. With the 2008 and 2012 Olympics it has become the world leader in elastic therapeutic taping. The technique is used by Physical Therapists, Occupational Therapists, Certified Athletic Trainers, Doctors of Chiropractic, Medical Doctors, Acupuncturists' and Massage Therapists just to mention a few.

Dr. Kase believed the elastic therapeutic tape, Kinesio Tex Tape, needed to mimic the qualities of the superficial layer of the skin: the epidermis. The tape is designed to stretch between 40 and 60% of its resting length (a 10" strip of Kinesio Tex Tape will stretch from 14 to 16" in total length). This is approximately the stretch capability of the skin in areas such as the knee, low back and cervical region. The Kinesio Tex Tape only stretches along the longitudinal axis and has a 100% acrylic heat activated adhesive applied in a wave pattern. There is no latex in the product.

The Kinesio Taping Method began with the application of the Kinesio Tex Tape and is now striving to incorporate a total therapeutic treatment system. Currently there are 6 primary assessments with 2 additional assessments described on the Kinesio Taping Association International Database. These assessments provide a framework to assist the Kinesio Taping practitioner in their evaluation of the clinical presentation of their patients. Dr. Kase continues to develop therapeutic treatments and as they are better defined they will be included in future workshops and texts.

PROPERTIES OF KINESIO TEX TAPE

Kinesio Tex Tape has been modified since its' inception to mimic the qualities of the skin. To more easily understand the concepts of the Kinesio Taping Method, it may be helpful to understand the qualities of the Kinesio Tex Tape.

Kinesio Tex Tape has been designed to allow for a longitudinal stretch, of 40% of its resting length, normal stretch length based upon using 2" width. The Kinesio Tex Tape can stretch up to 60%, this is the result of using narrower strips of Kinesio Tex Tape, such as ¼". This degree of stretch approximates the elastic qualities of the human skin. The Kinesio Tex Tape is not designed to stretch horizontally. The Kinesio Tex Tape is applied to the paper substrate with approximately 10% of available tension. The elastic qualities of the Kinesio Tex are effective for 3-5 days before the elastic polymer diminishes.

The thickness of the Kinesio Tex Tape is approximately the same as the epidermis of the skin. This was intended to limit the body's perception of weight and not give a sensory stimuli that there was something on the skin when properly applied. After approximately 10 minutes, the patient will generally not perceive there is tape on their skin.

The Kinesio Tex Tape is comprised of a ureter polymer elastic strand wrapped by 100% cotton fibers. The cotton fibers allow for evaporation of body moisture and following application of water allows for quick drying. The cotton fibers are treated with a water resistant coating assisting the Kinesio Tex Tape resist moisture.

There is no latex in the Kinesio Tex Tape. The adhesive is 100% acrylic and is heat activated. The skin must be free of oils and moisture prior to application. The acrylic adhesive becomes more adherent, the longer the Kinesio Tex Tape is worn. The acrylic adhesive is applied in a wave-like pattern to mimic the qualities of the fingerprint on the fingertip. This not only assists in the lifting of the skin but also allows for zones in which moisture can escape.

Upon removal of the Kinesio Tex Tape, there will be no adhesive residue remaining. This normally allows for multiple taping technique applications without skin irritation. If the patient has sensitive skin, it is recommended that the practitioner apply a small strip of tape and evaluate prior to full use.

The combination of the stretch capabilities, thickness, and adhesion allow the Kinesio Tex Tape to approximate the qualities of the skin. The design of the Kinesio Tex Tape, in combination with proper evaluation of the clinical condition and the unique application technique, create the Kinesio Taping Method.

KINESIO TAPING METHOD VS. OTHER TAPING TECHNIQUES?

Since the inception of the Kinesio Taping Method in 1973 there has been three commonly practiced taping techniques: prophylactic athletic taping, McConnell® Taping Technique and the Kinesio Taping Method. Each are appropriate when used properly for their intended purpose.

Prophylactic ahtletic taping is traditionally used to either assist or limit a movement by applying high tensil strength non-elastic white and elastic tape. It is used to protect acute injuries, prevent excess movement at a joint and protect a joint from further injury just to name a few. It is usually worn for a limited amount of time, can cause skin irritations due to latex and or rubber base adhesives and causes compression of tissues. It is very effective in limiting joint movement but has limited therapeutic purpose.

McConnell® Taping Technique, invented by Jenny McConnell an Australian Physiotherapist, is primarily a bracing or strapping purpose and has limited therapeutic function. There are two types of tape applied: a brown rigid tape is placed over a white cotton mesh tape. Is primarily used for orthopedic injuries such as patellofemoral dysfunction, shoulder subluxation, lumbar, foot and hip pain. It has a limited wear time of approximately 18 hours due to adverse skin reactions. It is widely accepted as an effective technique to provide an external brace or positional stimulus.

Kinesio Taping Technique is an elastic therapeutic taping method that allows for treatment for all types of clinical conditions for acute, sub-acute, chronic, rehabilitation and prophylactic tapings. It allows for and assists in normal circulation/lymphatic flow, decreases pain, assists muscle function, affects fascial tissue, and can improve joint function. The Kinesio Taping Method is designed to have a gentle long term assistance to the body returning to homeostasis. The Kinesio Tex Tape is uniquely designed to not be restrictive, heavy on the skin, and allows full range of motion.

APPLICATION ESSENTIALS

The success of the Kinesio Taping Method is dependant upon two areas. One, proper evaluation technique to allow for application of Kinesio Tex Tape on appropriate tissue. Two, proper application of the Kinesio Taping Technique. When the two are combined, an effective therapeutic modality is available to the practitioner. Early in the learning process of the Kinesio Taping Method, many practitioners believe they can utilize the method with little practice. Generally, this is true. However, success is usually a more hit and miss situation. Consistent successful application is limited by the practitioner's ability to evaluate the patient's condition and possible mistakes in tape application, specifically tension levels. As stated previously, it is recommended that for the Kinesio Taping Method a tape with elasticity from 40-60% be used. Using a tape that has different adhesive, is thicker, does not breath, and has different elastic qualities will not produce the same results.

Primarily, the practitioner needs to "unlearn" tape application methods which have been previously "learned". During conventional athletic taping proper application requires that using all of the stretch is better. The concept is that by taking all of the stretch out of the tape, it will limit or assist a motion and provide for protection from injury/re-injury.

With the Kinesio Taping Method, the practitioner needs to begin to conceptualize that the Kinesio Tex Tape will assist the body's return to normal function through the application of the tape onto the skin. The primary effect of tape application is generally superficial and by applying the Kinesio Tex Tape with undue tension, effectiveness will be limited.

BASIC TERMS USED IN THE KINESIO TAPING METHOD:

Anchor: The beginning of the tape application. It is applied to the tissue in neutral posture with no tension.

Ends: The last portion of tape that is laid down. It is applied with no tension.

Base: The portion of Kinesio Tex Tape between the anchor and the end, regardless of application or cut.

Tails: The portion of tape following the split in either the Y, X, or fan cuts.

Target Tissue: Tissue that has been selected for therapeutic treatment.

Therapeutic Zone: Section of tape applied over the target tissue with a % of stretch.

Tension: The amount of stretch applied to the Kinesio Tex Tape as it is applied to the skin, specified as a percentage of the total available stretch in the tape.

Tissue Stretch: The elongation of Target Tissue. May be active, passive or with manual assistance. Tissue is stretched to maintain normal Range of Motion and expose skin sensors for best stimulation.

Proximal/Origin: Tissue attachment closest to the midline of the body, follows standard anatomical textbook guidelines.

Distal/Insertion: Tissue attachment furthest from the midline of the body follows standard anatomical textbook guidelines.

Inhibition: Stimulus to relax and elongate the muscle.

Facilitation: Stimulus to activate and shorten the muscle.

Therapeutic Direction: The direction of recoil in the applied Kinesio Tex Tape toward the anchor.

SKIN PREPARATION

The target tissue skin should be dry and free of perfumes, oils and lotions. Anything that limits the acrylic adhesive's ability to adhere to the skin will limit both therapeutic benefit and longevity of the application. After evaluation of the patient's skin integrity, the skin should be cleansed. The use of an astringent or rubbing alcohol will work to clean most lotions, natural body oils or any artificial barrier.

For best results, oils used in conjunction with

Manual Therapy and conductive agents applied with Ultrasound treatments should be removed prior to Kinesio Tex Tape applications.

For a limited number of patients, body hair may limit adhesion of the tape directly to the skin. As the Kinesio Tex Tape recoils it will pull and lift the body hair. The result will decrease therapeutic effectiveness through the skin and limit wear time. Most patients will not tolerate tape applied over hair at the nape of the neck, at the axilla or through the groin. If the amount of body hair limits adhesion, the practitioner may ask the patient for permission to trim the hair over the target tissue.

If the patient has sensitive skin, is a pediatric or geriatric client, it is recommended that the practitioner apply 1/2" to 1" block of Kinesio Tex Tape as a "Test Patch". The Test Patch should be applied with "paper-off tension" to the skin of the target tissue. For example: the Test Patch should be applied over the anterior shoulder/chest if evaluation suggests that the Pectoralis Major should be treated with Kinesio Tex Tape. If no skin irritation develops, the tape may be removed after 15 minutes to 24 hours dependent upon the practitioner's recommendations. Kinesio Tex Tape should be removed immediately if the Test Patch is positive, resulting in itching, pain, or any skin irritation. If irritation does occur apply milk of magnesia (external application not internal), aloe vera gel, or mineral oil.

TISSUE STRETCH

For basic Kinesio Taping Applications, the muscle or target tissue is placed in a position of stretch after anchor placement, prior to applying tension. The patient is moved through as much range of motion as pain, strength and tissue extensibility will allow. Tissue stretch, in combination with the stretch capabilities of Kinesio Tex Tape, creates convolutions in the skin. Skin convolutions may be present following the basic application or may appear during normal joint motion. It is believed that even if convolutions are not visible, they are present on a microscopic level. The creation of the convolutions aids in the normal blood and lymph dynamics and tissue remodeling.

TAPE STRETCH AND OR TENSION LEVEL

Proper tension is one of the most critical factors in application success. The elastic qualities of Kinesio Tex Tape range from 10%, "paper-off tension" - 15% to a maximum of 40-60% stretch. Generally, the terms stretch and tension are used interchangeably and for the Kinesio Taping Method have the same meaning. The term stretch is applied to the amount of elasticity in the Kinesio Tex Tape or movement of a body part. Tension is the term used when applying Kinesio Tex Tape to the skin within the therapeutic guidelines. Each Kinesio Tex Tape Application requires a specific range of tensions to be most beneficial. If too much tension is applied, the effects are diminished and may cause non therapeutic tissue compression, and even shearing and irritation to the skin. In initial applications it is wise to apply Kinesio Tex Tape with slightly lower tension than indicated to the skin. When taped using appropriate tension guidelines, patients most often report "a difference" or a positive change such as pain reduction, increased muscle function, and increased range of motion. If during any application there is too much tension, a negative response may occur such as pain increase and skin irritation.

Each Kinesio Taping Application, including basic muscle applications, corrective techniques, and clinical conditions applications require proper tensions for consistent positive results.

Tape tensions are listed both as a percentage of available tension and descriptively. Percentages are listed as the percentage of stretch to be applied based upon 100% of the available tension. For example: 15-25% tension. This translates as 15-25% of the available stretch from the tape's resting length. If you cut a 10" strip of Kinesio Tex Tape, and you stretch it to its maximum available tension (40-60% of overall length), it would be 14-16" long. During a therapeutic application, if the technique requires 25% of the available tension, this would actually be 25% of the total available tension, or 1 to 1.5" for a total length of 11 to 11.25".

STANDARD RANGES AND DESCRIPTORS

0% or none	---	no tension: anchor and/or end
Paper-off	---	10 - 15%
Light	---	15 - 25%
Moderate	---	25 - 35%
Severe	---	50 - 75%
Full	---	100%

> **i** The manufacturer of Kinesio Tex Tape applies the tape to the paper backing with approximately 10% of available stretch. As the Kinesio Tex Tape pulls away from the paper backing during a therapeutic application, the tension increases by approximately 5%. The 10% tension applied during manufacturing plus the resistance as the Kinesio Tex Tape is removed from paper backing totals approximately 15% and is considered "paper-off tension".

RECOIL EFFECT

When Kinesio Tex Tape is applied with tensions at or below 50% of available tension, the tape will recoil or "pull back" towards its anchor. Once the tension level rises above 50%, the elastic polymer is not strong enough to recoil or "pull back". For Kinesio Taping Muscle Applications tension levels are at or below the moderate 35% of available tension. For corrective techniques, tension levels range from 10% to 100% depending upon the patient population, flexibility and turgor of the target tissue.

TAPE DIRECTION

Overview: The appropriate combination of tension and direction of tape/tissue recoil provides the stimulus required to improve muscle function. The tape is applied directly over the targeted muscle parallel to the muscle fibers. When a muscle is overused the muscle shortens and the motor point draws closer to the center of the muscle. By applying the Kinesio Tex Tape from the insertion toward the origin with paper off to light, 15-25% of available tension, the recoil effect of the tape stimulates the muscle to elongate to more normal length. When a muscle is weak, the motor point is distant from the center of the muscle. By applying Kinesio Tex Tape from origin toward the insertion with paper off to moderate, 15-35% of available tension, the recoil effect of the tape stimulates the muscle to shorten to more normal length.

For acutely over used or shortened muscles: Kinesio Tex Tape is applied from INSERTION to ORIGIN (Distal to

Proximal) with paper off to light, 15-25% of available tension. This will offer a calming stimulus for muscle inhibition or rest. To begin the application, the anchor, with rounded edges, is placed with the split in the Y or anchor of the I Strip with no tension approximately 2" below the insertion. The target tissue is stretched by active or passive motion into the largest range of motion as tolerated. Apply the Kinesio Tex Tape by placing it on the muscle, parallel to the muscle fibers as it comes off of the paper backing (paper-off tension) up to 25% of available tension. The end of the tape should then be applied without tension. If, following tape application, the practitioner can see any depression in the skin under the tape; the tape is applied with too much tension. The texture of the Kinesio Tex Tape should be similar to texture of the adjacent skin.

Applying too much tension decreases desired results, not enhance them.

INSERTION to ORIGIN
(Distal to Proximal)

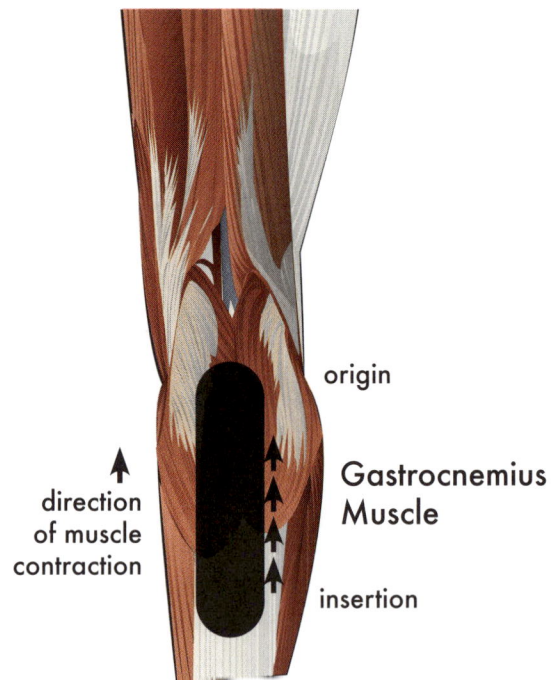

origin

Gastrocnemius Muscle

↑ direction of muscle contraction

insertion

**For chronically weak muscles, or an elongated muscle:** Kinesio Tex Tape is applied from ORIGIN to INSERTION (Proximal to Distal) with paper off to moderate, 15-35% of available tension. This offers a more dynamic stimulus for muscle work or facilitation. The anchor is applied, with rounded edges, with no tension in a neutral posture. The target muscle is stretched and paper off to moderate, 15-35% of available tension is applied parallel to the muscle fibers. The tape application ends with no tension. With taping from INSERTION to ORIGIN it is important to remember that "less is better".

For muscle facilitation applications, there is a large tension range available to the practitioner. The amount of tension applied is related to the number of muscle spindles in the tissue and sensitivity of the skin. In muscle tissue that produces fine motor control (cervical, hand and wrist) there are a higher number of muscle fibers requiring lower tension levels for effective applications. In muscle tissue that functions in weight bearing or has large, multiple muscle bellies, (quad, hamstring, adductor, abductor) there are a lower number of muscle spindles and higher tension levels should be used. When applying Kinesio Tex Tape with proper techniques for ORIGIN to INSERTION, the practitioner should be able to see slight separation of the elastic fibers within the therapeutic zone of the tape after application. The texture of the Kinesio Tex Tape should be slightly rougher than the texture of the adjacent skin.

ORIGIN to INSERTION
(Proximal to Distal)

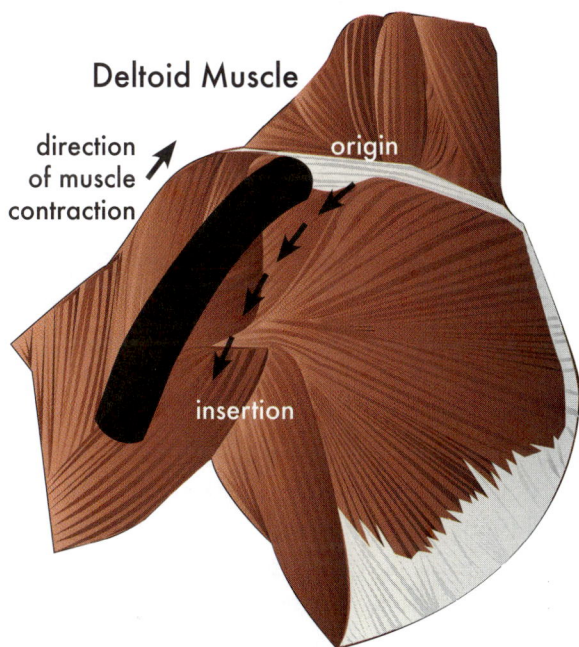

Deltoid Muscle

direction of muscle contraction

origin

insertion

BASICS OF THE KINESIO TAPING METHOD
Evaluation: Screening Assessments

Every practitioner is encouraged to use the evaluation skills that are appropriate within his or her professional scope of practice. Upon completion of the practitioner's assessment, he or she will choose modalities that fit within the treatment plan to reach the patient's goals. A central component of the Kinesio Taping Method is properly identifying the tissue(s) involved in pathologic dysfunction. Dr. Kase developed these Screening/Assessments to encourage the practitioner to look at multiple tissues as they function with directed movement. The effectiveness of the Kinesio Taping Method is directly affected by the proper evaluation of the clinical presentation, appropriate selection of the Kinesio Tex Tape Application(s) including proper tension level and cut. If following the initial Kinesio Taping Method, the results were not as effective as hoped; the practitioner should reevaluate the patient. The practitioner should evaluate - apply appropriate Kinesio Taping Application and re-evaluate.

There are 6 Kinesio Taping Screening/Assessments regularly used to evaluate the overall condition of the involved tissue(s). There are two additional screening assessments in the Kinesio Taping Association International Database. **If during the evaluation process the patient's symptoms are exacerbated, end the evaluation and if appropriate, refer the patient to their primary care provider immediately.**

1. **Kinesio Taping Cervical Flexion Assessment:** demonstrates limitations in movement in the anterior cervical region
2. **Kinesio Taping Cervical Spine Extension Assessment:** demonstrates limitations in movement in the posterior cervical region
3. **Kinesio Taping Trunk Flexion Assessment:** demonstrates limitations in movement in lumbar region of the low back
4. **Kinesio Taping Hip Rotation Assessment:** demonstrates limitations in movement in the pelvis and lumbar region
5. **Kinesio Taping Pectoral Girdle Assessment:** demonstrates limitations in movement in the anterior pectoral region
6. **Kinesio Taping Straight Leg Assessment:** demonstrates limitations in movement in the anterior pectoral region

7 & 8. Kinesio Taping Database: Kinesio Taping Abdominal Pressure Test and Kinesio Taping Bulge in an Artery Test

ANCHOR APPLICATION

Measure and cut the appropriate Kinesio Tex strip for the desired application. (For Kinesio Taping muscle applications, the practitioner my determine the origin or insertion of the desired muscle using manual resistance/muscle testing.) The anchor is applied approximately 2" below/above the target tissue with no tension in neutral position. If the anchor is laid down with any tension in either the Kinesio Tex Tape or in the skin, skin irritation, undesired proprioceptive input, or lifting of the anchor may result. The location of the anchor does not vary with the cut of the Kinesio Tex strip; however practicality may dictate a slight variation due to anatomical limitations, sensitive tissue, body hair or professional decorum. If it is not anatomically possible (adductor in the groin), or if placement of the anchor would be placed in a location which may cause irritation to the patient (axillary or popliteal fossa), place the anchor as close to the anatomical landmark as possible. The anchor must be long enough to ensure that the tension applied in the base of the tape does not transfer to the edges to irritate the skin and the anchor does not lift off the skin. Appropriate tension is applied immediately after the anchor application. Activate the adhesive by rubbing to generate slight friction/heat prior to any movement.

END APPLICATION

Following the application of the proper Kinesio Tex Tape strip over the target tissue, the ends or the last one to 2" of tape are laid down with no tension. In basic Kinesio Tex Tape applications, the patient will be in a stretched position so laying down the end with no tension is all that is required. In the application of the end(s) in the corrective technique the patient may need to be re-positioned to ensure there is no stretch in the skin. If the end is laid down with any tension either in the skin or the Kinesio Tex Tape, skin irritation, limited wear time and undesirable proprioceptive input may result.

KINESIO TEX TAPE APPLICATION STRIPS

Y STRIP APPLICATION - *for use when light to moderate global or multidirectional stimulus is required. Tape width and length should mirror the target tissue.*

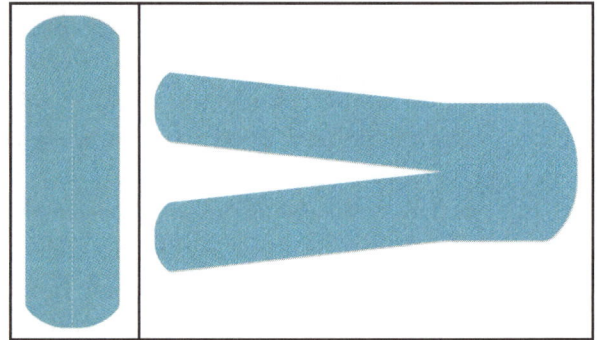

The Y strip is the most commonly selected application strip. It can be used to inhibit or facilitate muscle function as well as with Corrective Kinesio Taping Applications through all phases of the injury/rehabilitation cycle.

With the skin properly prepared, begin by measuring the appropriate length of the Kinesio Tex Tape. Cut one end of the tape through the center leaving about 2" uncut, the uncut section will become the anchor. Round both the anchor and ends. Apply the anchor one to 2" below/above the origin or insertion with no tension. With the muscle in a stretch position it is now time to apply the Kinesio Tex Tape tails. Apply the proper degree of tension: for inhibition paper off to light, 15-25% or for facilitation light to moderate, 15-35%. Surround one edge of the muscle with the first tail. The outermost edge of the muscle in an attempt to "tape your hands around the muscle". The tension is applied parallel to the muscle fibers and evenly along the entire length of the tail until the last one to 2". As the tape is being laid down, follow behind with the pads of your fingers to ensure adhesive attachment to the skin. The final one to 2" of tape is applied with no tension. Next pat the Kinesio Tex Tape to initiate adhesive activation then rub the tape until you feel warmth under your fingers to initiate adhesive prior to any further patient movement. Movement prior to adhesive activation will compromise convolutions, recoil and wear time. Multiple attempts to place the tape are ineffective because the adhesive cannot re-stick once it has been activated and collected dead surface cells on the adhesive.

Where appropriate, place the muscle in an alternate stretched position to stretch muscle fibers at a different angle: for instance the clavicular and sternal fibers of the Pec Major.

A three Strip Y technique may also be selected. The third tail is applied directly through the center of the muscle belly.

I STRIP APPLICATION - *For use when a higher level of focused stimulus is required. Tape width and length should mirror the target tissue.*

Begin by measuring the appropriate length of the Kinesio Tex Tape strip. The application of the I technique follows the same basic principles as the Y technique. Instead of surrounding the muscle belly, the Kinesio I Strip is applied directly over the area of injury, pain or muscle center. When applying the I strip with directional recoil the anchor is applied with no tension in neutral posture. Apply appropriate tension for inhibition or facilitation as described in Y technique. The end is applied as the final 1-2" of tape with no tension. Rub to initiate adhesive prior to any further patient movement. This technique has been found to be effective following acute muscle injuries and some muscles clinically respond better to an I strip than a Y strip (e.g.: Anterior Scalenus). Initially following a muscle injury, the I technique should be applied. Then after the acute injury phase, the practitioner may find increased results by choosing another Kinesio Tex Tape application and cut. The practitioner either by experience of description in this clinical applications book may choose between the Y and I technique.

X STRIP APPLICATION - *For use over a muscle with more than one muscle belly and those muscles with broad insertions and origins. Offers focal stimulus with greatest tension dissipation.*

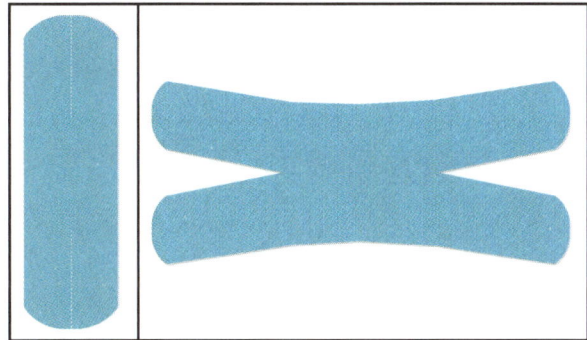

The X strip was one of the first Kinesio Taping Method Application techniques. It was initially felt that having the tension directly over the muscle belly would provide the desired stimulus. As the Kinesio Taping Method developed, taping muscles from origin to insertion and insertion to origin were found to be more consistently effective. The original technique is still commonly used for muscles that cross two joints with a traditional anchor and end application method (e.g.: rhomboid major).

Begin by measuring the appropriate length of the Kinesio Tex Tape strip with the muscle in a stretched position. This is important since an X technique is generally used for muscles that cross two joints. Maximal stretch may greatly increase muscle length and to measure the muscle in an anatomical position will cause the cut strip to be too short.

The X is created by cutting a minimum of two tails on each end of the Kinesio Tex Tape strip. Tear the center of the paper backing and apply the appropriate tension level to the middle 1/3 of the X strip. Place the patient in a stretched position applying the center of the X strip over the muscle belly to the skin. Initiate the adhesive in the center 1/3 and lay down the tails with no tension. Rub to initiate adhesive prior to any further patient movement.

FAN STRIP APPLICATION - *The*
Fan Strip is primarily used for edema or lymphoedema.

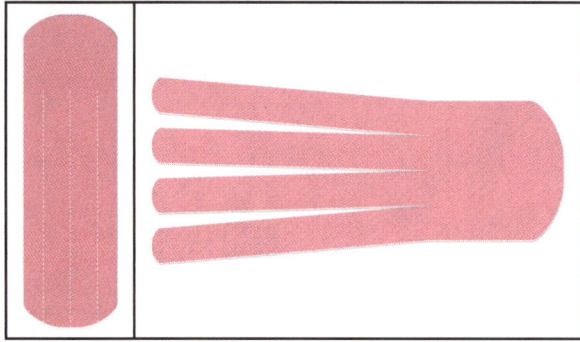

The Kinesio Tex Tape strip is cut into 4, 5 or 6 tails. Generally 4 or 5 strips are most effective and easy to handle. The length of the anchor remains 1-2" and is laid down on or above a healthy, uncompromised lymphatic duct proximal to the region of congestion. The fan strips are applied to the patient with the limb in an elevated, gently stretched position. For lymphatic correction 0-20% of available tension is added to the Kinesio fan tails. The fan tails are laid over the area of edema or swelling in a crisscross pattern. The ends are laid down without tension and patting or gently rubbing ends will initiate adhesive prior to any further patient movement.

WEB STRIP APPLICATION

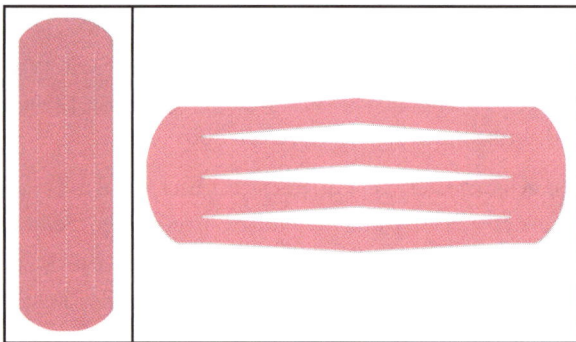

Measure a Kinesio Tex I Strip. Fold in half. Cut the Kinesio Strip on the fold into 4, 5 or 6 strips ending each cut 1-2" from the ends. This allows the strips to separate in the center of the tape keeping the ends solid and uncut. Begin by placing the patient in as much of a stretched position as possible as pain or edema allow. At a minimum a mid joint position. The web is applied by applying one anchor, removing the web's paper backing and applying 10-20% of available tension through the center of the tape. Then apply the end with no tension. Pat or rub to initiate adhesive

prior to any further patient movement.

DONUT HOLE APPLICATION

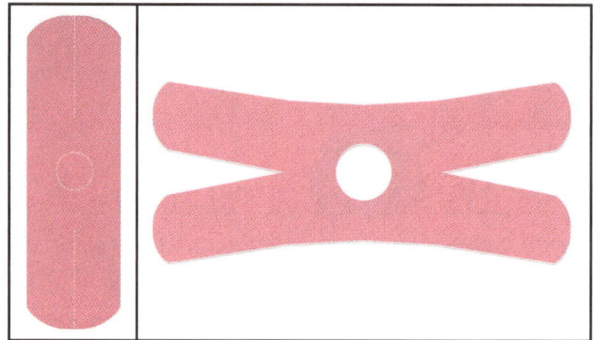

Measure and cut a Kinesio Tex I strip, 6-8" in length is common. Fold in half and cut a dime size hole on the fold. The hole should be slightly smaller than the area to be treated but should never be larger than 50% of the Kinesio Tex Tape width. If the hole is too large, the elastic recoil of the strip is ineffective and cannot pull back to the center to lift the skin and decompress the tissues. The center of the donut is placed directly over the localized area of pain or inflammation with paper off to light, 15-25% of available tension. One strip can be used or a series of up to three strips applied as a "star". If a series of donut strips is required, decrease tension level for each strip. The donut hole can be either applied as an I strip or with tail like an X strip. If using an I strip, lay down the ends with no tension. If using an X strip, splay the tails and lay them down with no tension.

BASKET WEAVE APPLICATION
- for use when multi directional recoil is needed and for pitting edema.

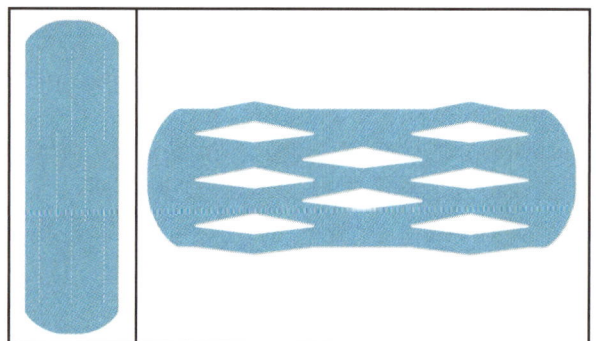

Measure an appropriate length of a Kinesio Tex Tape I strip, usually 6-8" in length. Fold down 2" at one end of the I strip and cut three 1" evenly spaced cuts.

Unfold the end and then fold the tape in half. Cut two evenly spaced 1" cuts then unfold the tape. Fold over the last 2" of the I strip at the opposite end from the first cuts. Cut three evenly spaced 1" cuts. Apply proximal anchor to target tissue with no tension. Gently spread cut sections while applying 25-50% of available tension. Apply the distal end with no tension. Pat or rub to initiate adhesive prior to any further patient movement.

TAPE REMOVAL

The longer the Kinesio Tex Tape is worn the more difficult it will be to remove. If the patient has had irritation from other tapes, the removal of the Kinesio Tex Tape may cause an irritation as well. Use caution and remove tape slowly. There are three basic tape removal techniques.

ROLL METHOD:

Begin by curling up the proximal anchor. Roll off the Kinesio Tex Strip in the direction of hair growth, proximal to distal.

SKIN FROM TAPE METHOD:

Peel back the proximal anchor and apply gentle pull to the Kinesio Tex strip with one hand. With the other hand gently press on the skin to pull the skin away from Kinesio Tex Tape.

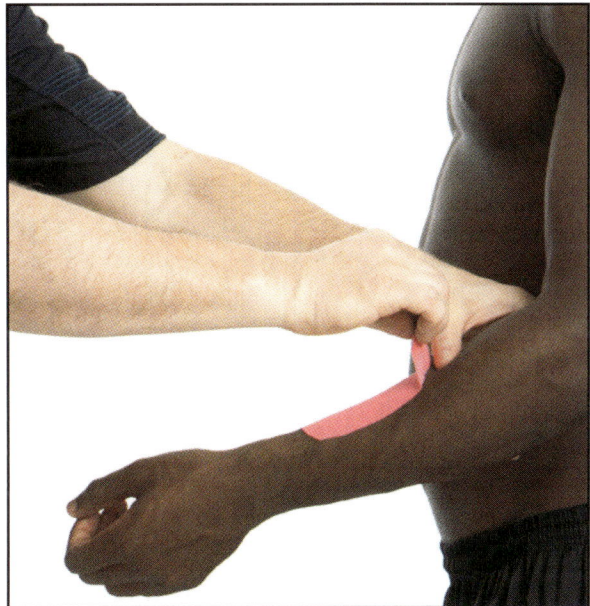

PRESSURE METHOD:

Curl the proximal anchor from the skin. Place one finger directly onto the tape. With the hand holding the anchor apply pressure in an upward direction, pulling the Kinesio Tex Tape from the skin. At the same time with the second hand and one or two fingers on the Kinesio Tex Tape and press down onto the tape and skin. Keeping an even "pulling" with one hand, and even "pressure down" with the other hand, remove the Kinesio Tex Tape.

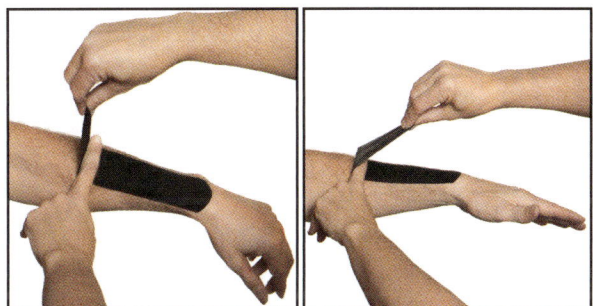

If the patient has sensitive skin or the Kinesio Tex Tape has been worn for the 3-5 day period, apply baby oil, mineral oil or 100% aloe vera lotion to the tape. Allow it to saturate the cotton fibers then remove with either the Roll, Skin from Tape Method, or Pressure Method.

If Kinesio Tex is applied during physical activity an

adhesive may be needed to prepare the skin. Once a spray adherent is used, the removal of the Kinesio Tex Tape will be difficult. Use extreme caution. Commonly available tape adherent adhesive removers will not affect the Kinesio Tex adhesive since it is not a rubber base like most athletic tapes. Use of mineral, baby or olive oil have been found to work best for removal.

Prior to Kinesio Tex Tape applications over sensitive skin, Milk of Magnesia can reduce acidic reaction of salts and chemical exudates of normal skin. Apply to clean unbroken skin (over the target tissues) with a cotton ball. Allow liquid to dry. Gently brush off "chalk" residue and apply Kinesio Tex Tape as indicated. The use of an alternative Kinesio Tex Tape cut may also reduce skin irritations.

PATIENT EDUCATION

Once the basic application is complete it is important to instruct the patient about a few areas of concern. Educate the patient with regards to therapeutic purpose, and management of the tape as it may be worn for multiple days. During the first few days, if an edge of the tape has begun to lift, it can be trimmed. The patient needs to be comfortable wearing Kinesio Tex Tape. Changing the color, cut, or placement of the tape may be necessary to help the patient become more receptive to wearing tape that is visible in public. The tape needs approximately 20 minutes to gain full adhesive strength. Exercise or activities which may initiate perspiration should not occur until the adhesive is well set.

The tape can be worn for 3-5 days and bathing or swimming is allowed. It is important to pat the tape dry. Do not use a blow dryer either to initiate adhesive or to dry Kinesio Tex Tape after bathing. The use of any form of heat will cause the acrylic adhesive to become very difficult to remove.

If the patient experiences skin irritation, pain, localized reaction to the adhesive or any negative symptom after the Kinesio Tex Tape Application, instruct the patient to remove the Kinesio Tex Tape application using safe methods.

POSSIBLE LIMITATIONS OF THE KINESIO TAPING METHOD

A limited number of patients may have excessive body hair and may require shaving or clipping. A limited number of patients may not allow the application of the Kinesio Taping Method due to their resistance to shaving.

Approximately 20-30 minutes is required for the adhesive to become fully activated before the patient can become physically active. If activity occurs prior to this time the tape may come off.

Patient willingness and understanding of the three to four day application of the technique. The patient must be aware that the tape is to remain on for several days and can be worn while bathing or swimming. The tape does not have to be removed if it has become wet, only towel off excessive moisture and allow to air dry.

INITIAL DIFFICULTIES IN APPLICATION

One must begin to think differently about the possible therapeutic use of tape instead of assisting or limiting a movement.

A proper evaluation is required to ensure the correct tissue involved is being treated. If the involved tissue was not properly taped, an incorrect corrective technique was applied patient success may be limited. If a patient has not worn Kinesio Tex Tape before, they may not be willing to wear the tape out in public. The patient needs to be informed of the 3-5 days of application and that even after the Kinesio Tex Tape has become wet it will remain effective.

SIZES AND TYPES OF KINESIO TEX TAPE

Kinesio® Tex Tape, commonly referred to as Kinesio® Tape, may be purchased in various widths, lengths and colors. The 2" wide Kinesio Tex Tape is available in two different lengths with the standard length being 16.4' and a bulk length that is 103.3', making it ideal for clinical or regular use.

Kinesio Tex Tape is also available in a 1" and 3" width. Both the 1" and 3" widths are only available in the beige color and can only be purchased at the standard length of 16.4'. The 1" wide Kinesio Tex Tape is commonly used for finger or neurological taping while the 3" wide Kinesio Tex Tape may be required for larger individuals and/or athletes.

The 2" Kinesio Tex Tape is available in five colors;

beige, blue, red, black and white. The red is a darker color on the light spectrum and will absorb more light slightly increasing the temperature under the Kinesio Tex Tape Strip. The blue is a lighter color on the light spectrum and will reflect more light slightly decreasing the temperature under the Kinesio Tex Tape Strip. Black absorbs all light and has the highest temperature increase under the skin. There are no differences in the manufacturing of the tape, except the dye for color.

If the practitioner determines an increase in temperature is appropriate in the injury site the use of red or black Kinesio Tex Tape could be selected. If the practitioner believes that a reduction in tissue temperature is important, as in tendonitis, the use of the blue Kinesio Tex Tape could be selected. Patients may have a preference to a color and this may affect their perception of the effectiveness of the treatment, unless the color of tape the patient wants is applied.

CONSIDERATIONS

The Kinesio Taping Method is not appropriate for all clinical conditions or for all patients. It is important to remember that prior to any application of the Kinesio Taping Method you should complete a thorough evaluation within the scope of your professional practice. This may include, yet is not limited to, skin health and turgor, range of motion, strength, and postural analysis of the clinical condition, medical social and psychological risk factors and the overall health of their patient. If the patient's health systems are compromised, consult with their physician prior to any application of the Kinesio Taping Method. If Kinesio Tex Tape and the Kinesio Taping Method are utilized by any practitioner and either directly or indirectly "frees up" fluids and returns them into the circulatory/lymphatic system care needs to be taken to not exacerbate any clinical conditions.

CONTRAINDICATIONS

- Consult with physician any time there is a "precaution" or concern about using Kinesio Tex Tape on a patient.
- Do not tape directly over or just proximal to active malignant areas due to the risk of spreading the cancer to another area. However, you can treat a different part of the body that is cancer free with Kinesio Tex Tape.

- Do not apply Kinesio Tex Tape directly on fragile or healing tissue. However, consider taping proximal or around the tissue in question.
- Do not apply Kinesio Tex Tape on or around an area with active cellulitis or infection for the risk of spreading the infection.
- Do not apply Kinesio Tex Tape directly on open wounds. However, consider taping proximal or around the tissue in question.
- Do not apply Kinesio Tex Tape in the area of deep vein thrombosis (DVT).
- Do not tape a patient with known allergies to the tape or medical adhesive bandages.

In cases of controlled cancer and terminal cancer, the doctor may request treating with Kinesio Tex Tape to make the patient more comfortable. In these cases, make sure that both the doctor and patient are aware of the risk factors. Also, make sure that it is documented that the doctor and patient gave permission to proceed with the treatment. Do not treat during a time when the white blood count is too low.

If the patient has gone through series of antibiotic treatments with no changes in swelling or indurated tissue, then it is possible that the tissue is in a state of inflammation. In this case, try Kinesio Tex Tape proximal to the area and check within 24 hours for changes. If the patient improves, continue with treatment. If there is no change, do not continue treatment.

PRECAUTIONS

- Be aware if an individual has had a previous skin reaction to the tape. This may have been a temporary reaction due to medication the person was taking at the time.
- It is recommended you consult with a physician any time there is a concern about using Kinesio Tex Tape on a client.
- Use caution treating diabetic patients with Kinesio Tex Tape.
- Use caution when taping a patient with kidney disease.
- Movement of fluid to the trunk may put patients with asthma and other respiratory problems at risk. Check with the doctor to see if the patient is medically stable enough prior to treatment. Never treat during an acute respiratory problem.
- Patients with congested heart failure can also have

difficulties controlling excessive fluid movement to the trunk.

- For pregnant clients: Always get prior physician approval before Kinesio Taping a pregnant client in the abdomen or lower back. Also be cautious of moving fluid to the abdominal area and over acupuncture sites for uterine contraction.
- In cases of diabetes, the skin may be too fragile, especially in the lower extremities. Also be careful if the patient has a lack of, or diminished, sense of sensation in the extremities.
- In cases of kidney disease, Kinesio Tex Tape can move fluid toward the trunk. The kidneys may not be able to handle the increased fluid load. With these patients, fluid should be moved slower to allow the kidneys more time to process the excess fluid. Consult the doctor prior to treatment. In case of kidney failure, stop all treatment that moves fluid until a doctor gives written orders to proceed.
- Kinesio Tex Tape is excellent for the Lymphedema/ Chronic Swelling population. Due to significant cardiac and renal risk factors, only practitioners with formal training should treat and Kinesio Tape these conditions.
- In cases of congested heart failure, Kinesio Tex Tape can be used if the doctor states that the patient is medically stable enough to handle the fluid movement.
- Never use Kinesio Tex Tape in the area of hardening/ thickening of the arteries of the neck.

KINESIO TAPING METHOD ALWAYS

Assess, Apply Kinesio Taping Technique, Re-assess: Prior to determining the proper Kinesio Taping Application it is important to assess all tissues that might be involved, then apply the appropriate technique and always finish by re-assessing the patient.

Round Edges of Ends: Tape ends are rounded to limit the square edge of the tape from being caught or lifted by contact with clothing. Rounding the edges will lengthen wear time and improve esthetics resulting from fewer edges coming off.

Anchor to skin whenever possible: the Kinesio Tex Tape is designed to adhere to clean skin. If one strip of Kinesio Tex Tape is applied, ending on top of another Kinesio Tex strip, the wear time of the technique will be diminished.

No Tension on Anchors and Ends: When applying Kinesio Tex Tape, always lay down the anchor and ends with no tension. Tension outside the therapeutic zone will promote skin receptor activity and unwanted proprioceptive input. If Kinesio Tex Tape is applied in a sensitive area, such as: face, nape of neck or axillary region it may be helpful to gently stretch the skin under the anchor or ends to ensure no tension is under the Kinesio Tex Tape.

Appropriate tension is applied between the anchors of the Kinesio Tex Tape: This region of tension is called the therapeutic zone. Tensions range from 0% to 100%. Follow Kinesio Taping application guidelines for appropriate tension ranges. Only apply the appropriate tension level for each application and patient population. Do not add additional tension to the application to account for limits in the range of motion. Adding tension does not assist in the therapeutic treatment, it generally only irritates the skin.

Joint is moved through as much range of motion as allowed: Prior to application of the Kinesio Taping Technique move the patient through as much range of motion as tolerated. If range of motion or a particular plane of movement is contraindicated by virtue of pathology or surgery then it is contraindicated for Kinesio Taping Applications as well.

After application of Kinesio Tex Tape pat then rub to activate adhesive: Once the anchor is applied lightly rub to activate adhesive, then apply base of I, Y or X strip, tails or fan. Finish ends then pat and activate adhesive prior to any movement. Without activation of the adhesive movement will lift the tape from the skin. Any further attempt to activate the adhesive will result in limited adhesion and effective wear time.

Apply 20-30 minutes or more before activity: The 100% acrylic adhesive is heat activated and it requires the initial patting then rubbing to begin adhesion. The Kinesio Tex Tape a slow warm up to complete adhesion. If applied to cold, wet or oily skin the adhesive qualities are compromised.

KINESIO TAPING METHOD NEVERS

Avoid sensitive skin areas: Application to sensitive areas of the skin such as: the nape of the neck, axilla, groin anti-cubital or popliteal fossae may cause skin irritation/rash to develop.

Do not "pull patient" in desired position: Using the Kinesio Tex Tape to pull the skin or anatomical joint into a desired position is too aggressive. Place the target tissue in an appropriately stretched posture then apply the Kinesio Tex Tape. Generally, skin irritation or pain will result if tape is used to pull tissue into position.

Remove if undesired effect is experienced: Following even the gentlest application, if the patient experiences a skin reaction, itching or pain, the Kinesio Tex Tape must be removed. You as the practitioner may remove the tape or instruct the patient to remove the tape safely.

Avoid unnecessary contact with adhesive: Limit contact with the acrylic adhesive prior to therapeutic applications. Any contact will decrease the adhesive quality of the Kinesio Tex Tape.

ADVANCED APPLICATION ESSENTIALS

When applying the corrective techniques, the practitioner must always follow the basic essentials of the Kinesio Taping Methods. When applying multiple applications, incorrect muscle applications may limit the success of the corrective techniques. Attention to each element is important in the overall success of the Kinesio Taping treatment protocol: skin preparation, selection of tape width and cut, removal of tape from paper backing, safe tissue stretch, appropriate tape tension and direction and adhesive activation, followed by safe tape removal.

When applying more than one layer of Kinesio Tex Tape, the practitioner should first apply the Kinesio Tex strip that will provide the primary therapeutic effect desired. As successive layers of Kinesio Tex Tape are applied, their effect on the sensory receptors may create interference instead of clear specific stimuli.

If the primary therapeutic goal is pain reduction, the practitioner may use a basic muscle technique from insertion to origin, with a space correction or lymphatic correction. The practitioner may determine that the application of the lymphatic correction should be applied for the first 24-72 hours, and then apply a space correction technique. After 72 hours, application of the basic muscle with a mechanical

correction may be appropriate. One should progress the Kinesio Taping Applications as each symptom/function changes.

The best outcomes generally come from a "less is more" approach. Fewer layers of tape, less tension, and moderate downward pressure are examples of subtle changes transmitted from the Kinesio Tex Tape to the superficial layers of the tissue.

During initial applications of the Kinesio Taping Method, it would be better if the patient returned with a report that the tape was "somewhat effective". In this case, the tape application can be modified for possible improvement in results. If the patient returns with more discomfort and believes the tape application exacerbated the symptoms, the ability of the practitioner to successfully treat the patient is limited.

The descriptions provided for the clinical conditions are not intended to be the only method of tape application for any condition.

Special thanks to Dr. Gracie Forrester for reviewing this chapter.

SECTION 1

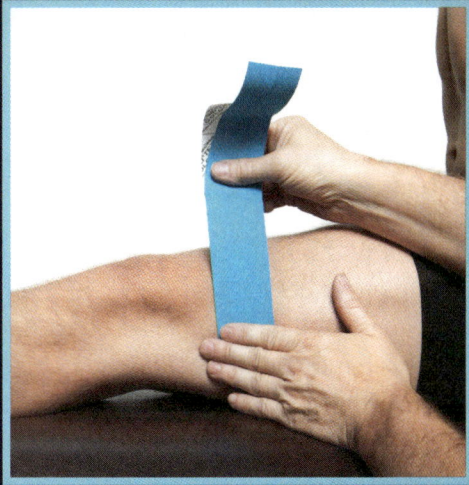

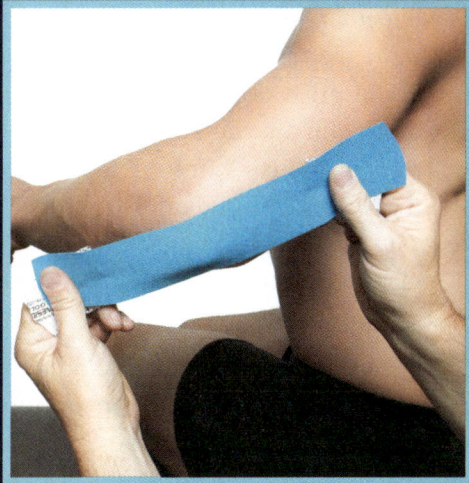

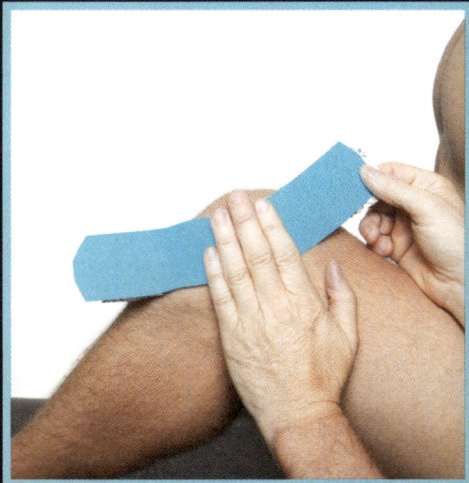

Introduction to Corrective Techniques

Introduction to Corrective Techniques

The Corrective Application Techniques are a continuation in the development of the Kinesio Taping Method. Since 1973 when the original concept of the Kinesio Taping Technique was begun, the technique has continued to evolve. This continuing development has added not only to the theoretical application, but also practical application of the technique. Kinesio Taping Practitioners have developed their skills both by learning during seminars and also practical application. The corrective techniques have been formalized to assist the Kinesio Taping Practitioner gain application and theoretical knowledge in a more systematic fashion.

During Kinesio Taping seminars practitioners desiring to learn the Kinesio Technique have traditionally followed a similar pattern; first, basic concepts of the technique, second, basic application techniques are taught, third, practice and practical application on patients, fourth, additional seminar on advanced concepts, and fifth, sometimes general frustration with application of the advanced concepts without really understanding the theoretical background of the concepts.

Difficulties have risen when a practitioner has completed a course and been introduced to clinical applications without receiving advanced training (corrective techniques). Many practitioners have perceived that each clinical application technique was unique. This required the practitioner, in their mind, to learn each clinical application separately with little or no interconnection. In reality, this is not true.

The clinical application of the Kinesio Taping Method is the systematic application of several layers of the Kinesio Technique with each layer having a specific function. The practitioner initially evaluates the patient's condition and determines which muscles are involved and initiates treatment to the muscles involved (basic concepts and application). Once the involved muscles are taped, the practitioner then needs to apply a clinical corrective technique to assist the body in correcting the condition.

There are 6 current correction application techniques: mechanical, fascia, space, ligament/tendon, functional, and lymphatic. Several of the correction techniques have an overlap of application methods between each other. The Kinesio Taping Practitioner determines the proper application.

Mechanical Correction – utilizes the stretching qualities of the Kinesio Tex Tape to provide for a positional stimulus through the skin. The degree of stimuli is determined by the percentage of stretch applied to the tape during application and degree of downward/inward pressure. Three techniques are used: 1) tails of the Y, 2) base of the Y, 3) tension in the middle of an I strip.

Mechanical correction generally uses 50-75% of available tension.

Fascia Correction – Is applied with an "oscillation" or "jiggling" to create a micro-massage of the fascial tissue. The technique can be applied using a "side to side" or "long and short" oscillation. Tension levels are between 10 and 50%. For superficial fascia 10-25% of available tension is used. For deep fascia 25-50% of of available tension is used.

Space Correction – to create more space directly above the area of pain, inflammation, swelling or edema. This is accomplished by applying the tension into the center of the Kinesio Tex Tape strip and having the recoil affect pull back to the center lifting the skin. The increased space reduces pressure by lifting the skin. Three techniques are used: 1) the center of an I Strip 2) donut hole, and 3) web cut.

Space correction, generally, uses 10-35% of available tension.

Ligament/Tendon Correction – to create increased stimuli over the area of the ligament and/or tendon, resulting in increased stimulation of the mechanoreceptors. The increased stimulus is believed to be perceived as proprioceptive stimuli that simulates more normal tissue. Ligament technique: Kinesio Tex Tape is placed over the ligament with severe to full, 75-100% of available tension. Tendon technique: tape over tendon is applied with 50-75% of available tension.

Functional Correction – used when the practitioner desires a sensory stimulation to either assist or limit a motion. The Kinesio Tex Tape is applied to the skin with 50+% of available tension during active movement. The increased mechanoreceptor stimuli are believed to act as a pre-load during end of motion positions and to stimulate an opposite movement.

Lymphatic Correction – used to assist in the removal of edema by directing the exudate towards a lymph duct. Creating areas of decreased pressure under the Kinesio Tex Tape and acting as channels to direct the exudate to the nearest lymph duct. Tape is applied with the anchor near the lymph node the exudate is to be directed towards. The fan cut tape is applied in a fan like pattern with 0-20% of available tension.

The desired outcome, following a course in the corrective techniques, the practitioner will be able to select the technique appropriate for their patients condition, thus not being limited to what they have seen in a photo or was demonstrated in a seminar.

The practitioner should recognize that for each clinical condition they may use a series of corrective techniques depending on the patients condition and therapeutic goal of the practitioner. Pain reduction may be the first primary therapeutic goal, and application of a space or lymphatic correction may be selected. After pain has decreased, a mechanical correction or fascia correction might be selected. The corrective technique allows the practitioner the opportunity to design a therapeutic course of treatment for each patient based upon the patients needs and not a pre-determined formula.

MECHANICAL CORRECTION

The Mechanical Correction should be thought of as positional in nature and not as an attempt to fixate the tissue. This technique uses the properties of the Kinesio Tex Tape through the application of moderate to severe tension to provide a stimulus perceived by the mechanoreceptors. The degree of stimuli is accomplished as the result of the combination of tension levels above 50% and downward/inward pressure that provides stimulus to deeper tissue. Remember that the degree of stretch and downward pressure will determine the degree of stimulus and depth of penetration. You, as a practitioner, will need to adjust your application technique to the needs of the patient.

This technique can be used to assist in the positioning of muscle, fascia tissue or joint position to stimulate a sensation which results in the body's adaptation to the stimulus. Functional support can be maintained without losing active range of motion or inhibiting circulation. The Mechanical Correction can be used to either, position the tissue in the desired position, provide stimulus in which the body will adjust position to minimize the created tension, or provide a "blocking" action of joint or tissue movement.

There are three methods used to place the tissue in the desired position: 1) tension in tails, 2) tension in the base, and 3) tension in the middle of the base.

Tension in the tails provides a low level of stimulus and is generally used in pediatrics and geriatrics. With tension applied to the generally 1" wide tail it is difficult to create downward/inward pressure. The corrective effectiveness is minimal. Basically you are applying tension in the skin to provide a minimal stimulus to the mechanorecptors.

Tension on the base is a moderate level of stimulus and can be used on all patients. Tension in the base, usually a minimum of 2" in width, allows for a greater degree of stimulus to multiple layers of tissue. With the wider Kinesio Tex Tape the downward/inward pressure will create more stimulus with a greater number of mechanoreceptors being affected.

Tension in the middle of the base provides a high level of stimulus. It is more positional in its function and acts to block pathological movement. It can be used on all patients but use caution as this technique is aggressive.

A 2" wide strip of Kinesio Tex Tape is generally used. This application can provide the highest degree of inward/downward pressure providing stimulus to the greatest number of mechanoreceptors. It is important to have longer anchors since there is a higher degree of tension in the middle of the I strip. Use the rule of 1/3s: 1/3 anchor, 1/3 therapeutic zone and 1/3 anchor. Using shorter anchors may result in the anchors coming off.

When selecting one of the three methods, the intent of the tape is to go past the point of recoil of the elastic polymer. The tape application is completed so that when the tape is applied with tension higher than 50% it creates tension upon the skin and downward/inward pressure which stimulates a sensory stimuli.

The application of downward/inward pressure provides for a deeper stimulus to mechanoreceptors affecting deeper layers of tissue. The combination of higher tension and downward pressure are the primary components of the mechanical corrective technique.

Mechanical Correction Application Techniques
Application of Y Technique, Tension on Tails

Application of Y Technique with tension on tails. This technique overrides the "recoil" effect of the elastic qualities of the tape. Since the width of the tail is generally 1" in width the primary effect is superficial. The amount of stretch applied to the Kinesio Strip and degree of downward pressure determines the depth and perception of skin movement. Tension in the tails applies the lowest degree of mechanical correction.

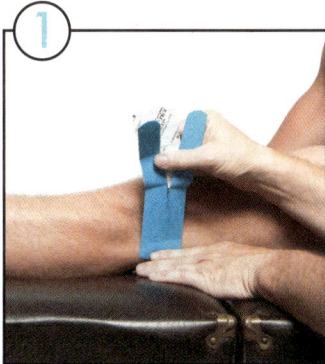

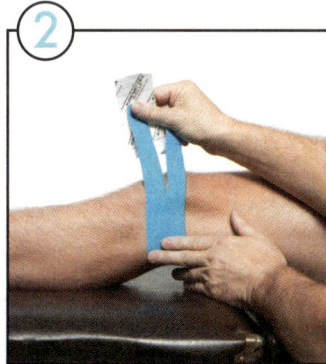

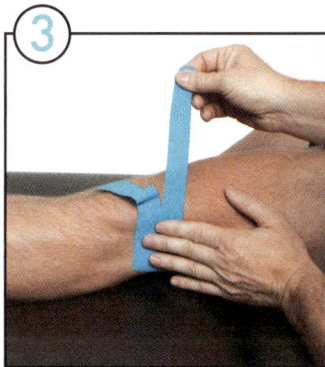

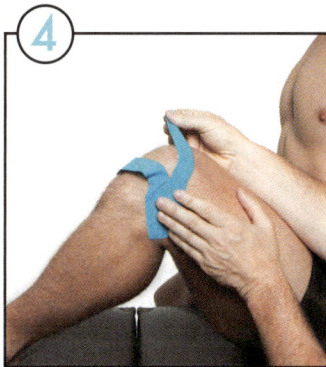

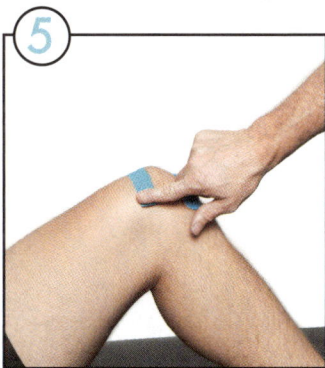

1. Start tape with no tension at the beginning. Image shown has an approximately 2-3" anchor. The length of the anchor is determined by the tension level. If the anchor is too short it will limit the effectiveness of the technique. The split in the Y should be located prior to the treatment zone.

2. With one hand hold the anchor to ensure no tension will be added.

3. Apply 50-75% of available tension to one tail. Tension is applied both in the longitudinal direction and with downward/inward pressure.

4. When the desired tension has been applied slide the hand, which is holding the anchor up to the point of end tension. Have the patient move into a stretched position as indicated. Lay down the tails of the Y with either: no tension, or with 15-25% of available tension to the last 1-2".

5. The tails should be splayed out to dissipate the tension created over as large an area as possible. Lay down the final approximately 1" of remaining tape with no tension. Rub to initiate adhesive prior to any further patient movement.

Mechanical Correction Application Techniques
Application of Y Technique, Tension on Base

Application of Y Technique with tension on base of Y. This technique uses the base of the Y cut to apply tension to the skin. The amount of stretch applied to the Kinesio Strip and degree of downward pressure determines the depth reception of skin movement. The tension will provide a moderate tension effect.

1. Apply anchor with no tension. The higher the tension level and the longer the tension is applied over the therapeutic zone determines the length of the anchor.

2. With one hand hold the anchor to ensure no tension will be added. Apply 50-75% of available tension. Tension is applied both in the longitudinal direction and with downward/inward pressure. Prior to tape application the practitioner may want to place the patients joint in a position which may either stimulate or limit motion.

3. When the desired tension has been applied slide the hand which is holding the anchor of the Y up to the point of end tension. This will initiate adhesive prior to any further patient movement. The patient can move into a stretched position at this time or wait till the next step.

4. Have the patient move into a stretched position. Lay down the tails of the Y with either: no tension, or with 15-25% of available tension to the last 1-2". The tails should be splayed out to dissipate the tension created over as large an area as possible.

5. Medial view of completed mechanical correction. Note tails are splayed out to dissipate force.

   This technique can be applied using the above description using a Kinesio I strip. All steps remain the same except there is only one end, instead of two when using tails.

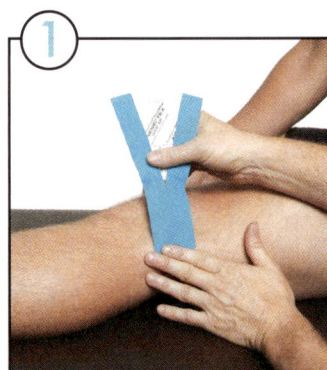
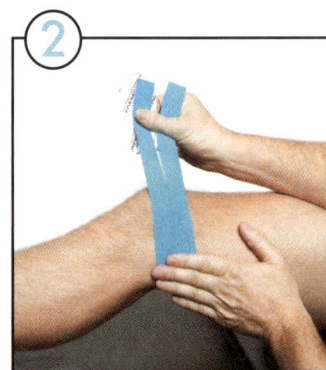
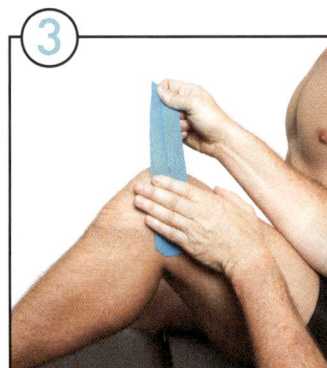
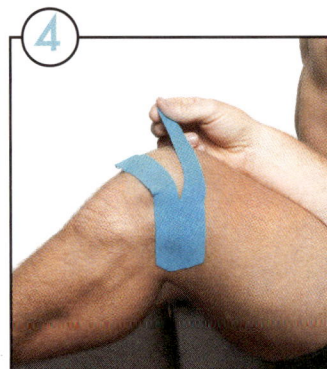
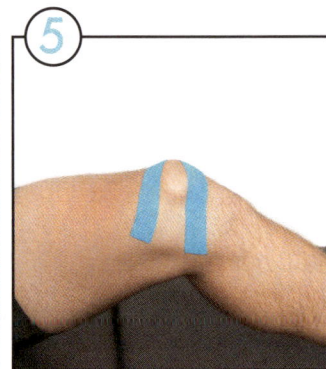

Mechanical Correction Application Techniques
Application of I Technique, Tension in Center

Application of I Technique with tension in middle of Kinesio strip. This technique uses the application of tension in the middle of the Kinesio I strip and downward pressure to provide a "blocking" of movement. The amount of tension and downward pressure determines the degree of "blocking". The tension in the middle of an I strip applies the highest degree of mechanical correction.

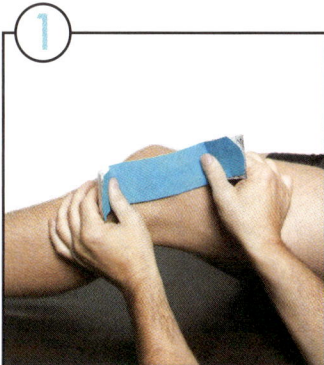

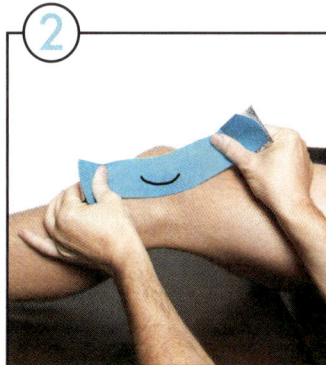

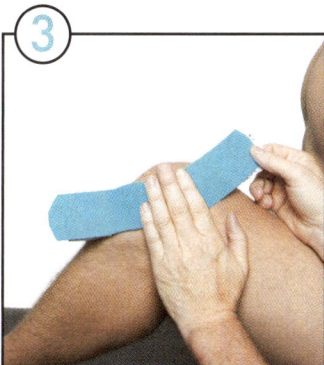

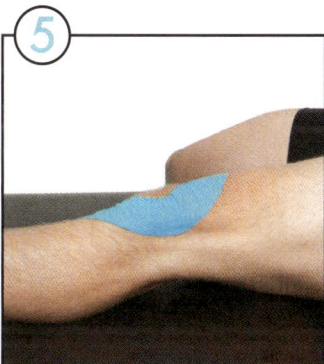

1. Begin by tearing the center of a Kinesio I Strip of approximately 6-8", or appropriate length for the area being treated.

2. Apply moderate to severe, 50-75% of available tension to the middle (center) of the I strip Place the center of the I strip with tension directly over the tissue to be treated. Place the Kinesio strip over the treatment area with tension and downward/inward pressure.

   Use the Kinesio strip to create a "block" to limit movement of a joint or tissue.

3. Have the patient move into position which places the joint, or tissue being treated in a stretched position.

4. Normally during application of this technique the zone of tension applied is longer than desired or greater than the therapeutic zone. The practitioner may need to "peel back" the tension zone so tension is only being applied to the desired therapeutic zone. Lay down the tails of the Y with either: no tension, or with 15-25% of available tension to the last 1-2".

5. Lay down the ends of the Kinesio I Strip with no tension. Rub to initiate adhesive prior to any further patient movement. The photo shown has approximately ½ of the Kinesio I Strip over the lateral border of the patella to limit lateral tracking.

FASCIA CORRECTION

Tape is applied using the "recoil effect" of the Kinesio Tex Tape. This technique is intended to be gentle and effect the body through the breaking down of limitations of fascia movement by the movement of the skin and elastic qualities of the Kinesio Tex Tape. Oscillations or jiggling is applied to the Kinesio Tex Tape during the application attempting to break down the elastic polymer fibers by micro-massage. Allowing the Kinesio Tex Tape to "hold" the fascia in a desired direction. Following the breaking down of the fibers they will be able to realign themselves in a more organized position.

The fascia technique is applied in two basic application methods and one advanced method. For basic application methods there is tension in the base or tension in the tails. Tension in the base, generally 2" wide, will provide a wider and higher degree of stimulus with a deeper penetration. If the fascial adhesion is more focal or localized the use of the tension in the base is the best choice. Tension in the ends, generally 1" wide, will provide a lower degree of stimulus and is more superficial. If the fascial adhesion or tissue movement limitation is over a larger area use of the tension in the tails is the best choice.

The proper application technique for using the elastic qualities of the Kinesio Tex Tape involves the "oscillation" or "jiggling" of the Kinesio strip. After applying the anchor of the Y, the anchor is held to limit adding tension, The practitioner "oscillates" or "jiggles" the Kinesio Tex Tape. The "oscillations" or vibration is gentle and may include a slight downward pressure if the effects are required to be felt in deeper tissues. The hand holding the anchor can apply gentle oscillation to the skin as it follows the hand applying oscillation to the Kinesio Tex Tape strip. You are trying to create various zones of tension within the Kinesio Tex Tape strip. This is felt to limit the "recoil" effect of the tape of returning to its original position towards the base. The tension level is 10-50% of available tension The oscillations should be applied as close to the skin as possible so the Kinesio Tex Tape can adhere to the skin with various degrees of tension within the application. There are two methods of application of the "oscillations". Long and short and side to side.

The "side to side "is applied in a horizontal direction to the anchor. This technique has been found to be more effective in wider limitations of fascial movement. Following the application of the anchor the desired tension level is applied to the Kinesio Tex Tape Strip, 10-50%, with this tension being maintained during application, and the tape is then oscillated in a "side to side" fashion.

The" long and short" is applied in perpendicular direction to the anchor. This technique has been found to be more effective in localized limitations of movement. Following the application of the anchor the tape is oscillated in a "long and short" fashion. The practitioner is trying to have various tension zones within the Kinesio Base Application as the Kinesio Tex Tape is applied to the skin.

Downward and inward pressure can be applied during application if the Practitioner is wanting deeper penetration. Higher tension levels and downward/inward tension can provide fascia correction to deeper fascial layers. Be careful to not use too high a degree of tension or downward/inward pressure or you may cause shearing forces.

FASCIA CORRECTION ADVANCED: MANUAL GLIDE

A more aggressive fascial treatment is to manually position the fascia and apply the Kinesio Tex Tape at higher than 50% of available tension to maintain a constant tension on the tissue. The higher degree of tension over a long period of time can cause shearing forces breaking down adhesions.

THE FASCIA

In this chapter you will learn how fascia is defined, as well as what defines it, sorts of fascia, properties biological and mechanical. How can fascia be modified, how it is influencing our physical realm and why in essence we are now in the fascia era?

DEFINITION

The term fascia is used in anatomical literature for the envelopes and separating layers of musculature that are composed of connective tissue. In a narrower sense, fasciae consist primarily of collagen connective tissue, the fibers of which intersect in a latticed pattern (at 45 degrees). The tough collagen fibers are also combined with true elastic fibers to varying degrees (Waldeyer and Mayet 1993: 29; Benninghof 1994: 169).

Strictly using a dictionary definition fascia stands for covering in Latin.

We are able to differentiate between two types of fascia due to their physical appearance. Superficial fascia looks like a cloud under the skin and extends ad infinitum. Works as a sort of a matrix and actually used to shape our body, extends all over our body from head to toes and considered by some researchers to be the communication network of the body since it is the only one tissue that is all over continuously.

The second type is deep fascia as some call it we reach a different story. If in the former matrix it was all loose as clouds and loose packs then the deep fascia appears very orderly sometimes transparent sometimes opaque material.

In essence every single muscle fiber is wrapped with fascia as well as every group and the whole is looking like a three dimensional set of envelopes going on forever.

ARCHITECTURE OF THE FASCIA

Contrary to what is found via dissection, when we describe the fascia we are referring to two major characteristics. One will be the continuity of the fascial planes and the other refers to the fascial proprioception. Both enable the continuous transfer of information about location and tension at all-times everywhere in the musculoskeletal system, this means that the transfer of forces along the muscle tendon bone structure depends mainly on the flawless movement within the fascial body (Van der Wal et al, The architecture of the connective tissues/ 2008)

FASCIAL BIOMECHANICS & PHYSIOLOGY

Various research articles from the years 2006-2008 has shown that the majority of the pathologies we have learned based on muscle, bursa, tendon and ligaments are in most cases dysfunctions of the superficial fascia or deep fascia. For that we can count the Ilio Tibial band syndrome, ankle strain, trochanter bursitis and frozen shoulder and more. Evidence shows that further to dysfunction in proprioceptive abilities the muscle tendon bone unit function is disrupted due to the same reasons. (Stecco et al, 2008. Franklyn-Muller et al, 2008 and many more)

CYTOLOGY & HISTOLOGY

Fascia provides mechanical support and framework for the other tissues of the body. Type 1 collagen is the major portion component of the fascia.

The fibroblasts are the cell type primarily responsible for its biosynthesis and remodeling. (Grinnell, 2008)

CONTRACTIBILITY OF THE FASCIA

Dense connective tissue sheets, commonly known as fascia, play an important role as force transmitters in human posture and movement regulation. Fascia is usually seen as having a passive role, transmitting mechanical tension that is generated by muscle activity or external forces. However, there is some evidence to suggest that fascia may be able to actively contract in a smooth muscle-like manner and consequently influence musculoskeletal dynamics. General support for this hypothesis came with the discovery of contractile cells in fascia, from theoretical reflections on the biological advantages of such a capacity, and from the existence of pathological fascial contractures.

Further evidence to support this hypothesis is offered by in vitro studies with fascia which have been reported in the literature (Schleip et al, 2005).

Special thanks to Izik Friedman for assistance with the Fascia section.

Fascia Correction Application Technique
Tension on the Tails

Use of fascia correction technique with tension in the tails. In this technique the practitioner is going to use the elastic qualities of the Kinesio Tex Tape to stimulate a manual therapy technique. The elastic qualities of the Kinesio Tex Tape will be applied using a "oscillation" motion in an attempt to reduce tension and adhesions between and within layers of the fascia. Tension in the tails is a more superficial technique. Tape width and tension level determines the depth of penetration.

Introduction to
Corrective Techniques

1. Begin by placing the anchor of an appropriate length Kinesio Y strip approximately ½ to 1" from the area of fascia movement limitation.

2. Long Short: With one hand hold anchor to ensure no tension will be added. Apply 10-50% of available tension to one tail by "oscillating" the tape with various degrees of tension. Stretch should be applied using the "long and short" technique. Higher tension levels and using optional downward pressure during application will determine the depth of the treatment effect.

3-4. Side to Side: With one hand hold anchor to ensure no tension will be added. Apply 10-50% of available tension to one tail. Tension is applied using the "side to side" technique(images shown are an exaggeration of the side to side method). Higher tension levels and using optional downward pressure during application will determine the depth of the treatment effect.

5. Lay down the tails of the Kinesio Y Strip with no tension and also splay them out. Rub to initiate adhesive prior to any further patient movement.

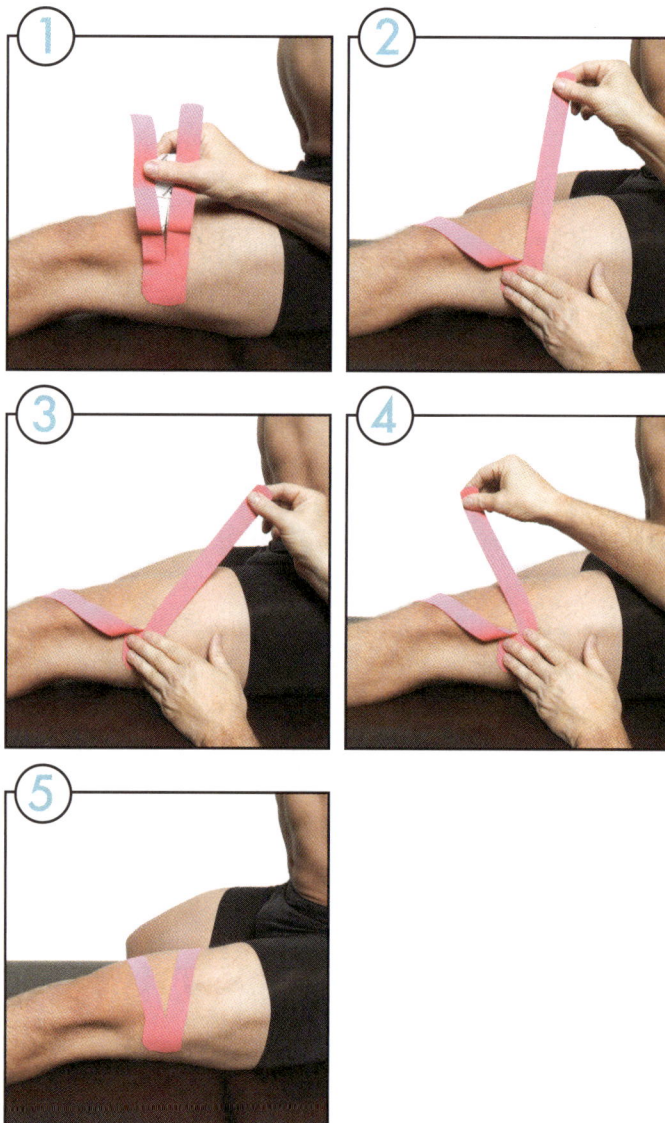

Fascia Correction Application Technique:
Tension on the Base

Use of fascia correction technique with tension on the base. In this technique the practitioner is going to use the elastic qualities of the Kinesio Tex Tape to stimulate a manual therapy technique. The elastic qualities of the Kinesio Tex Tape will be applied using an "oscillation" motion in an attempt to reduce tension and adhesions between and within layers of the fascia. Tension in the base is a more aggressive technique than tension in the tails. With the wider width of the Kinesio Tex Tape and higher tension level deeper tissues or a larger/more specific fascia limitation can be treated.

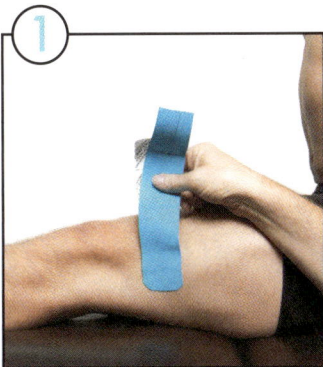

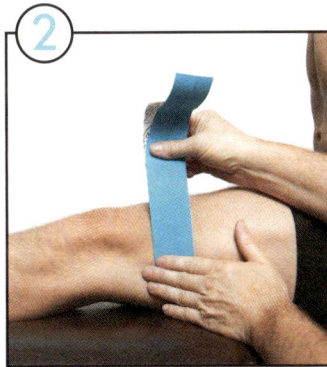

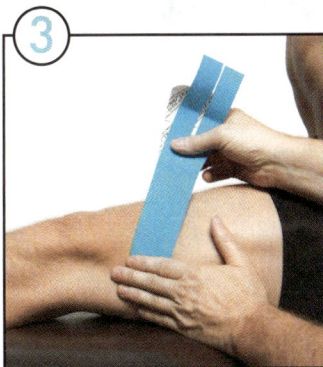

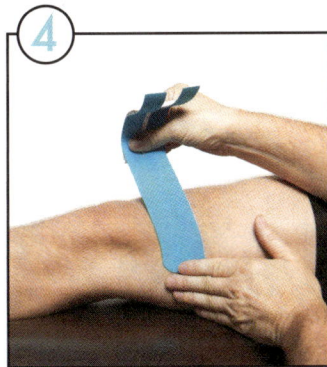

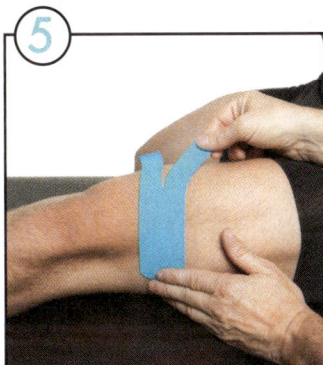

1. Begin by placing the anchor of an appropriate length Kinesio Y strip approximately ½ to 1" from the area of fascia movement limitation.

2. Long Short: With one hand hold anchor to ensure no tension will be added. Apply 10-50% of available tension to the base by "oscillating" the tape with various degrees of tension. Stretch should be applied using the "long and short" technique. Higher tension levels and using optional downward pressure during application will determine the depth of the treatment effect.

3-4. Side to Side: With one hand hold anchor to ensure no tension will be added. Apply 10-50% of available tension to the base. Tension is applied using the "side to side" technique (images shown are an exaggeration of the side to side method). Higher tension levels and using optional downward pressure during application will determine the depth of the treatment effect.

5. When the desired facia correction tension ends, the practitioner can apply either no tension or paper off to light, 15-25% of available tension. Lay the ends of the Kinesio Y Strip down with no tension and also splay them out. Rub to initiate adhesive prior to any further patient movement.

Fascia Correction Application Technique:
Manual Glide

Use of fascia correction technique manual glide. In this technique the practitioner is going to use a manual method to place the fascia in the desired position and use the recoil effect of the Kinesio Tex Tape to maintain desired position. This technique is usually used when the practitioner has a higher level of skill in manual therapy techniques. It can also be used when the practioner desires a more aggressive fascia application.

Introduction to Corrective Techniques

1. After assessing the fascia, position patient in a neutral postion. Measure and cut a Kinesio Tex Y strip and apply the anchor with no tension.

   In this example the tissue at lateral thigh does not glide inferiorly toward knee.

2. Place hand on anchor and apply gentle inward/downward pressure to capture the most superficial tissues and glide tissue inferiorly.

   Maintain hand placement on anchor and apply 10-15% tension through the base.

   Up to 25% tension may be applied for subsequent applications as needed.

3. Slide hand gently onto base of the tape while maintaining tissue position and the gentle downward/inward pressure.

4. End the tails of the Y strip without tension. Rub to initiate adhesive prior to any further patient movement.

5. Completed Manual Glide application.

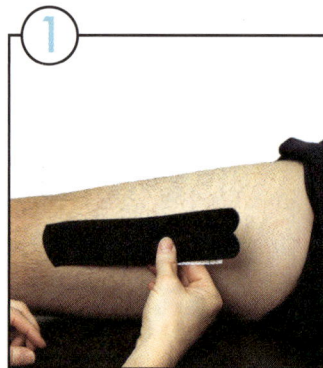
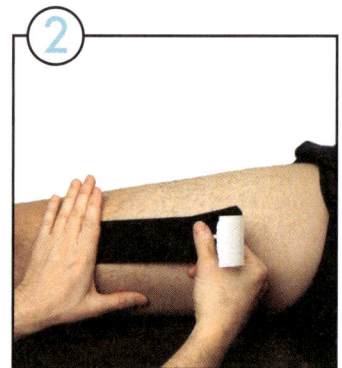
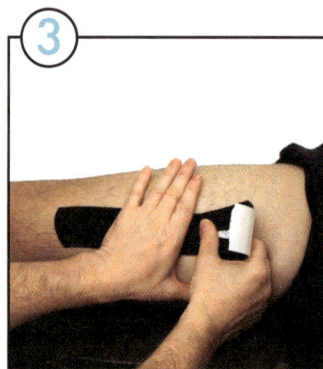
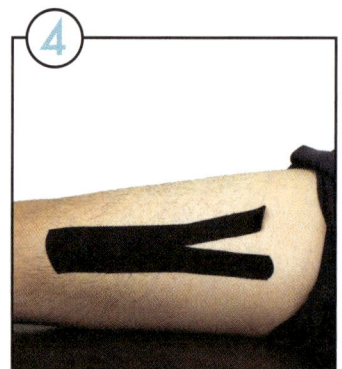

SPACE CORRECTION

The space correction is applied to create more space directly above an area of pain, inflammation, swelling or edema. The increased space that is created decreases the pressure in the area treated by "lifting" the skin directly over the treatment area. The recoil affect "creates" the space directly over the therapeutic zone in a specific location.

The result of the decreased pressure assists in reducing the amount of irritation on the chemical receptors, and nociceptors, thus decreasing pain. An increased level of lymphatic/circulation is also felt to occur in the area allowing for increased removal of exudate. Stimulation of the mechanoreceptors may also aid in decreasing pain. By increasing sensory stimulation the gate control theory of pain may be initiated.

Space is created by using the elastic qualities of the Kinesio Tex Tape by lifting skin, fascia and soft tissue over the area of pain or inflammation. Tape application needs to be performed slowly and the practitioner should not allow the skin to bunch (can cause a blister) under the Kinesio Tex Tape or allow the technique to be applied with too much tension (causing irritation to the skin).

The space correction technique may be selected by the practitioner as a primary therapeutic goal following initial evaluation of the patients condition. The patient may initially receive the greatest benefit from reduction of inflammation and pain during initial visits. Following initial reduction in inflammation and pain the practitioner may select another therapeutic goal such as fascia correction or mechanical correction.

There are three main techniques used with space correction: 1) the center of an I strip 2) web cut, and 3) donut hole.

Space correction, generally, uses light to moderate tension, 10-35% of available tension. If using multiple strips or in an area that has significant skin movement (eg: elbow, knee, low back and neck) the use of as little as paper off tension, 10-15% of available tension may be effective.

The elastic qualities of the Kinesio Tex Tape can be used to pull the connective tissue toward the desired area by applying the Kinesio strip with tension in the center of the strip with no tension on the ends and use the Kinesio Tex Tape to maintain the tissue over the desired area.

This technique uses the elastic qualities of the Kinesio Tex Tape to lift the skin and create space. This is accomplished by applying tension to the middle 1/3 section of the Kinesio Strip, application of tension area strip to skin, and laying down both the end 1/3 with no tension. A single strip or a series of overlapping strips (star technique) can be applied. With this method a "pocket" is formed under the tape decreasing pressure and pain.

1. Generally a Kinesio Tex Tape I Strip of 6-8" is used. Remember the "rule of thirds". Anchor, treatment zone and anchor - each approximately the same length, 1/3 of the total for each.

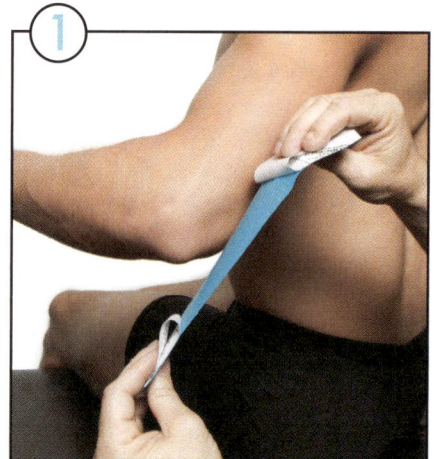

2. Place the joint in an appropriate position, for the elbow in as much flexion as the patient is able to actively move. Full range of motion may not be possible due to pain or edema.

   Begin by tearing the middle of the Kinesio I Strip through the paper backing. Apply light to moderate, 25-35% of available tension to the Kinesio I Strip in the middle 1/3 of the strip. Place the center of the Kinesio Tex Tape I Strip over the region of the desired space correction. Lay down each end 1/3 of the Kinesio Strip with no tension. Rub to initiate adhesive prior to any further patient movement.

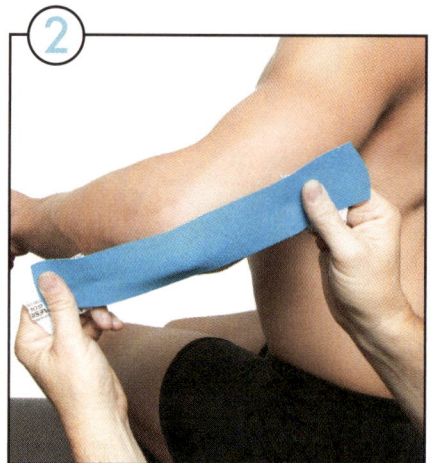

3. With the elbow, knee, and low back convolutions of the skin should be evident. For areas that do not have as much "loose skin" the convolutions may only be present during joint range of motion. If too much tension is applied convolutions may not be present resulting from the Kinesio Tex Tape "pushing down" on the skin.

   A series of strips can be applied with the intersection of each strip located over the desired space correction location (area of desired "pocket"). With more than one strip apply less tension on each strip counting on the accumulation of tension of each strip to create the space. For complete description see "star technique" in low back section.

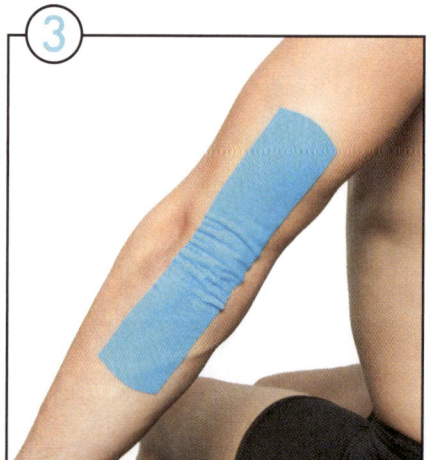

The web cut is used to lift the skin over an area of edema: eg: inflamed bursa. The web cut creates channels of lower pressure under the strips. As the lymph fluid is removed from under the strips the exudate between the strips (higher pressure) will flow to the area of lower pressure that has been created under the strips. A series of two or three strips can be used depending upon the size of the area to be treated.

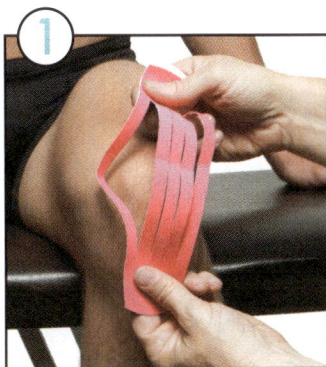

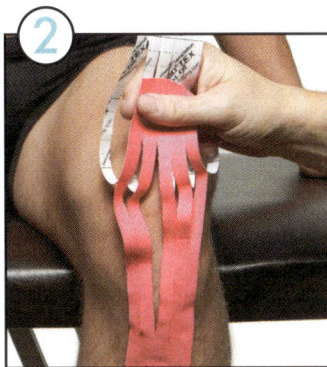

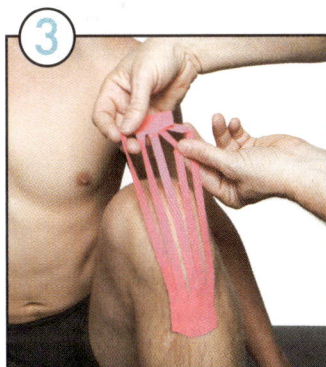

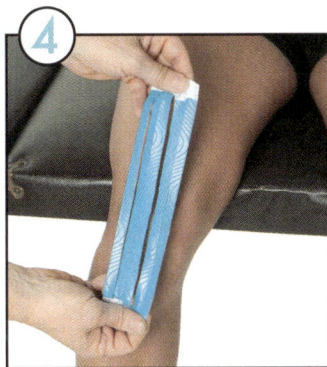

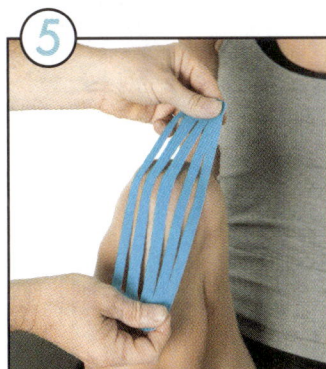

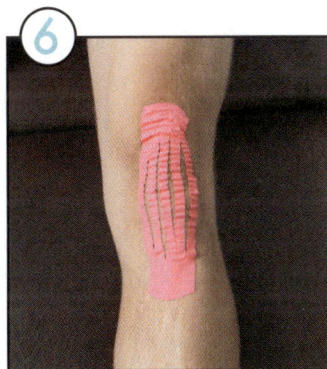

1. Measure and cut an appropriate length of a Kinesio Tex Tape I strip. Fold the I strip in half and cut 4-6 strips ending a minimum of 1" on each end.

2. Have the patient move into as much active motion as pain and edema allows.

   Method One: Images 2-3-6. Tearing one end, peel back paper backing from one end. Apply anchor proximal or distal to area of edema with no tension. Peel back paper backing and separate fan strips. Apply 10-20% of available tension. Apply strips with slight separation over target tissue. Apply end with no tension and activate adhesive.

   Method Two: Image 4-5-6. Tear the paper backing leaving approximately 2" one anchor. Peel away the paper backing from the web cut strip leaving approximately 2" on the second anchor. Apply 10-20% of available tension to the strips. Separate the strips and apply over target tissue. Lay down the ends with no tension and pat or rub to initiate adhesive prior to any further patient movement.

3. When activating adhesive make sure to gently pat the web strips down and only rub a minimal amount in one direction to activate the adhesive. With multiple thin strips the more you rub the more likely it is that the edges of the strips roll. It is easy to "overpower" the narrow web strips during application, so care should be given to only apply 10-20% of available tension.

Space Correction Application Techniques
Donut Hole Technique

This technique uses a hole cut in the center of the Kinesio I Strip slightly larger than the area to be treated. The donut hole technique is used to lift the skin surrounding the localized/focal point of pain the patient has presented with. By lifting the skin surrounding a focal point of pain it will decrease pressure directly over the pain. Generally a series of two or three strips are used. When using multiple strips the technique works best to use slightly narrower strips so there is exposed skin between the strips.

1. Begin by cutting a hole in the center of an approximately 6-8" Kinesio I Strip. Be careful to not cut more than ½ of the available width of the Kinesio Tex Tape keeping the hole to about the size of a dime or slightly smaller than the area to be treated. A hole cut too large will reduce the effectiveness of the technique and may reduce its ability to adhere to the patients skin. Too large of a hole may also reduce the ability of the Kinesio Tex Tape strip to have enough tape to recoil.

   Cut the distal approximately 1 ½ - 2" of each end into two or three tails.

2. Have the patient actively move through as much range of motion as possible, at a minimum to a mid joint position. In the center of the Kinesio Strip tear the paper backing and peel back exposing the middle 1/3 to allow for tension to be applied to the center of the Kinesio Tex Tape. Apply paper off to light, 15-25% of available tension to the Kinesio Strip and place the hole directly over the area of desired space.

3. Lay down the tails on both ends with no tension. Splay the ends to dissipate tension which was created in the area of the donut. Rub to initiate adhesive prior to any further patient movement.

   A series of two to three strips can be used. When using multiple strips the technique works best to use slightly narrower strips so there is exposed skin between the strips and each strip should be applied with slightly lower tension. For example see Lateral Epicondylitis.

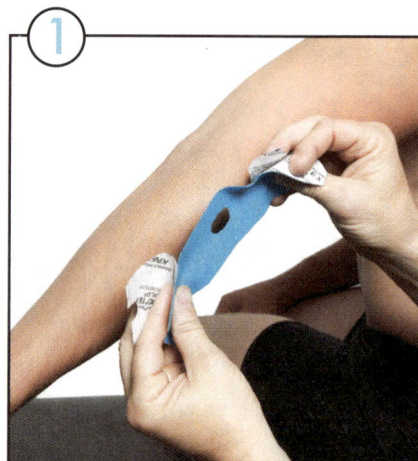

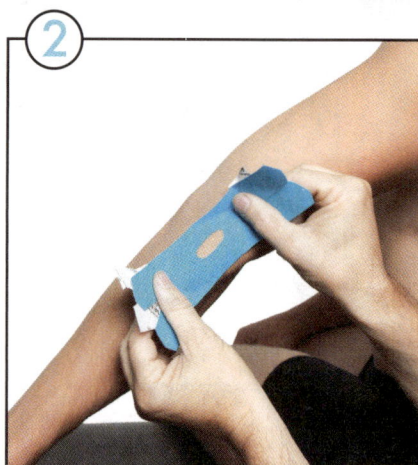

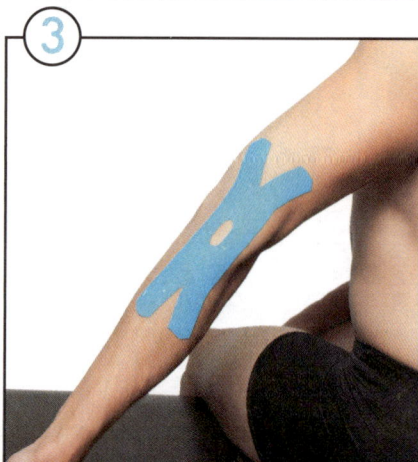

LIGAMENT / TENDON CORRECTION

Ligament Correction: Is applied to create increased stimuli over the area of a ligament that results in increased stimulation to the mechanoreceptors in the skin and joint capsule. This increased stimulus is believed to be perceived as proprioceptive stimuli that are interpreted by the brain as more similar to normal tissue tensions.

Kinesio Tex Tape is applied for ligaments with 75-100% of available tension with the tape directly over the area of the ligament. Maximum or full, 100% of available tension may also be used if the practitioner determines it appropriate. However if 100% of available tension is used the acrylic adhesive, and limited tensile strength, may not be able to adhere to the skin for an extended period of time or provide the desired limitation of tissue movement. The ends as always have no tension at the start or end of the tape application.

It can either be applied from proximal to distal or distal to proximal, as best determined by the practitioner. Generally, the tape should be applied from distal to proximal, in this manner the tension of the tape will be limiting the allowable movement of the ligament. It may be desirable to have the patient move the area being taped through a limited or full range of motion if appropriate for function. The joint is generally placed in a position of function, as an example the knee will be 20-30 degrees of flexion.

The length of the Ligament Correction should adhere to the "rule of thirds". The two anchors should be at least the same length as the center of the strip. If the anchors are too short the high tension in the center of the strip will apply tension to the anchors and cause premature pulling away from the skin.

Two methods of application for the ligament tendon can be used. One: Preferred method: begin by applying the Kinesio I Strip with no tension at the beginning, apply desired tension over the length of the ligament, end by laying down the end of the strip with no tension. Second: begin by tearing the paper backing in the middle of the I strip, apply desired tension to the middle 1/3 of the strip, with tension held in the Kinesio Strip apply the strip over the length of the ligament, end the application by having the patient move the body part through as much range of motion as possible and complete by applying ends of strip with no tension.

The use of the ligament correction is not intended to replace the use of a protective brace or provide protection from joint instability. If the patient or athlete has a ligament instability the use of the Kinesio Taping Technique Ligament Correction is not to be used as a replacement for more protective methods.

Tendon Correction:

The tendon correction is applied to create increased stimuli over the area of the tendon and tendon sheath that results in increased stimulation to the golgi tendon organ. The golgi tendon organ is the primary receptor that provides the required stimuli to the CNS informing the brain about the tension level of the muscle tissue.

Tape application for the tendons is similar to the Ligament Correction except uses less tension 50-75% of available tension applied directly over the area of the tendon. The ends have no tension at the start or end of the tape application. Tension can be increased directly over the area of the tendon. When the tape crosses over the musculotendonous junction the tension should be adjusted for either an origin to insertion: light to moderate, 15-35% of available tension, or insertion to origin: light to moderate tension, 15-25% of available tension.

Ligament Correction Application Techniques

Use of ligament correction technique applied to create increased stimuli over the area of a ligament resulting in increased stimulation to the mechanoreceptors in the skin and joint capsule. Generally, the base of the corrective strip should be started below the proximal attachment of the ligament. This should ensure the tension being created by the Kinesio Strip is having a shortening effect on the skin and joint.

Introduction to Corrective Techniques

1. Begin the anchor of tape with no tension. The anchor length should be approximately the same length as the area of tension. If the anchor is too short the high tension zone will "pull" on the anchors. Hold the anchor to ensure that no tension will be added. Practitioner may want to practice the placement of the Kinesio Strip prior to anchor placement to limit error on initial application.

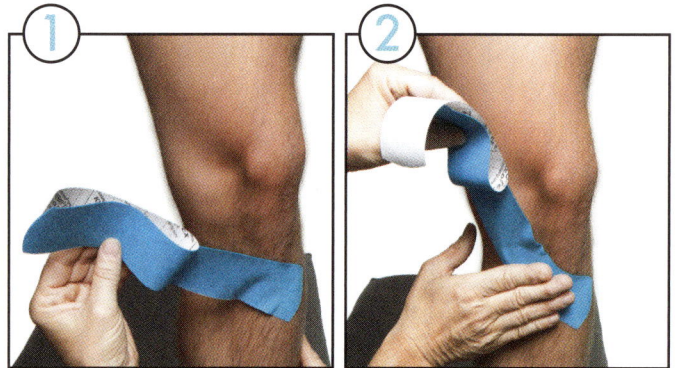

2. Images shown are for MCL of the knee. In this example the anchor is being placed in a position to assist the anchor to adhere better. From the area of the anchor apply paper off to light, 15-25% of available tension to the beginning of the ligament.

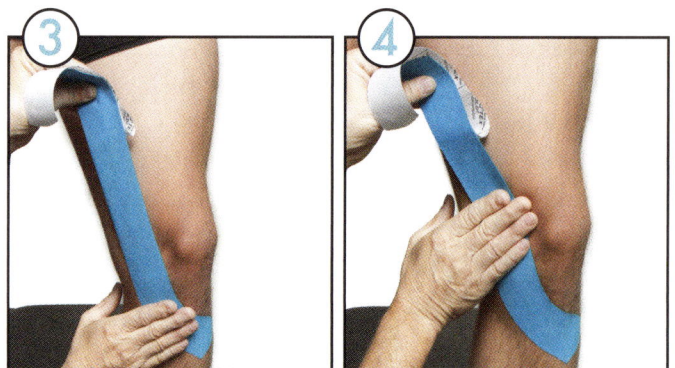

3. Apply severe to full, 75-100% of available tension along the approximate position of ligament, with patient in a functional position (e.g.: knee 20-30 degrees of flexion). The center of the I strip should be placed directly over the ligament. 100% of available, or full tension can be used for this technique. However the ability of the acrylic adhesive and lack of tensile strength of the Kinesio Tex Tape will limit the length of application and effectiveness of the technique.

4. Slide the hand that was holding tension at the base up to the end of tension position at approximately the proximal end of the ligament. Lay down the next section of tape with paper off to light, 15-25% of available tension to the anchor.

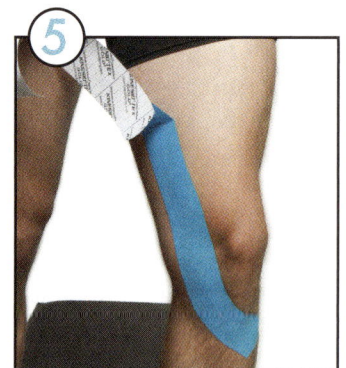

5. Lay down end with no tension and vigorously rub to initiate adhesive prior to any further patient movement. Prior to completion of the Kinesio Strip application the joint may need to be moved through a full range of motion prior to laying down end of application.

Tendon Correction Application Techniques

Use of tendon correction technique applied to create increased stimuli over the area of a tendon that results in increased stimulation to the golgi tendon organ. The proper application of the tendon correction technique will have an increased tension, 50-75% of available tension over the length of the tendon. Prior to the tendon and following the musculotendonous junction the tape tension should be appropriate for an O to I or I to O application.

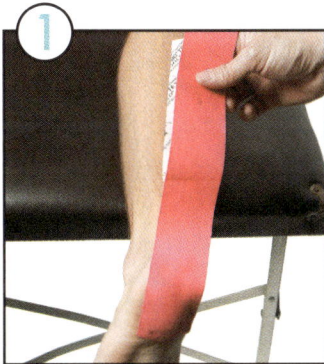

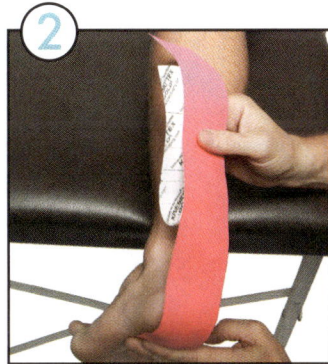

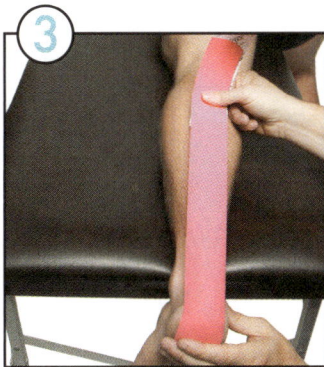

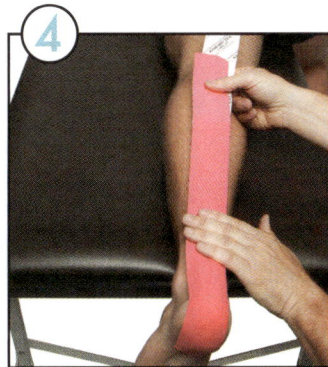

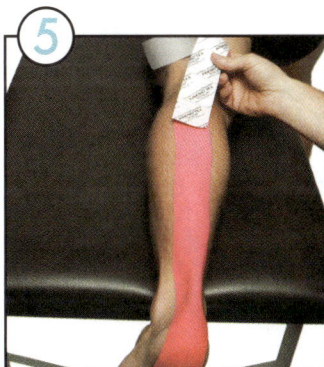

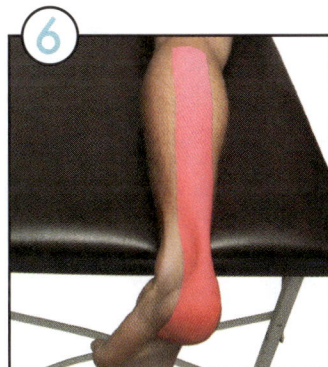

1. Begin anchor of tape with no tension.

2. Hold the tape end to ensure that no tension will be placed on the anchor of the tape.

3. Place the patient in a position of stretch. Apply 50-75% of available tension along the length of the tendon.

4. Slide the hand that was holding the anchor up to the end of tension position, this will initiate adhesive. Remember to reduce tension at musculotendonous junction for either origin to insertion or insertion to origin application.

5. Apply paper off to light, 15-25% of available tension to the next section of Kinesio Tex Tape. Lay down the end with no tension. Rub to initiate adhesive prior to any further patient movement. If the patient moves prior to adequate adhesive activation the tape will "pull away" from the skin. Reapplication of the Kinesio Tex Tape will be ineffective.

6. Completed Tendon Correction for Achilles Tendon.

FUNCTIONAL CORRECTION

The functional correction is used when the practitioner desires a sensory stimulation to either assist or limit a motion. The Kinesio Tex Tape is applied to the skin with the tension removed during active movement. The tension created by the increased stimuli during active movement is believed to provide stimulation to the mechanoreceptors. The perceived stimuli are believed to be interpreted as proprioceptive stimuli, which acts as a pre-load during end of motion positions.

The Kinesio Tex Tape is applied by cutting the appropriate length of an "I" strip. Length should be approximately 4" above and below the joint or a length appropriate for the joint chosen. Place the joint, or muscle to be taped in the appropriate position. Example: if assisting flexion and resisting extension place the joint in flexion. Begin tape application at the distal end of selected joint with a minimum of three to 4" of tape with no tension as the anchor. Apply appropriate tension from light, moderate, severe or full then adhere the second anchor, of approximately 3-4".

The above description will create a "tent" or "bridge". The practitioner needs to hold both anchors and instruct the patient to move into a stretched position. Rub vigorously to initiate adhesive prior to any further patient movement.

When first using the functional correction the most difficult part is determining the proper tension during this phase of application. The first time a practitioner applies this technique do not be surprised if either to much or to little tension is applied. Initially the practitioner should use 50+ tension of available tension for the total technique.

Following the functional tape application as described above, the patient will perceive stimuli, which will assist with flexion and resist the end position of extension (as described in practical application on the following page). This is accomplished by the stimuli perceived from the mechanoreceptors, in the skin and joint capsule, interpreting the stimuli as normal joint position. During extension the increased tension on the skin will provide a stimulus being perceived as reaching the end of normal joint position. This perception is created through increased skin tension which would normally occur at end of motion. Flexion will be assisted by the perception of increased tension in positions of extension that cause the repositioning of the joint to normalize perceived skin tension.

The high degree of tension will cause the sensory input resulting in a change in joint position to "normalize" the tension. The effect will also assist in limiting over stretching of a muscle, limit joint hyper-mobility and re-injury.

It is important that on the first application that the practitioner uses the minimal tension level to accomplish the therapeutic goal. It is better to need to increase tension level on subsequent treatments than to have a negative reaction from the initial treatment.

Functional Correction Application Techniques

Use of functional correction technique to assist or restrict a motion (e.g. flexion or extension). It is believed this is accomplished by changing the perception of joint position through increased tension in the skin. The body will adjust joint position to normalize the increased tension on the skin in an attempt to return to normal tension levels.

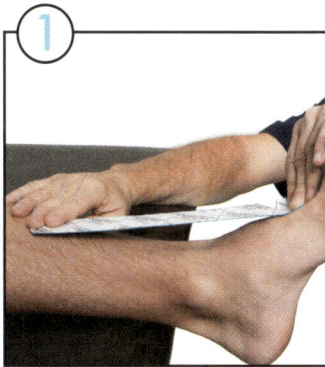

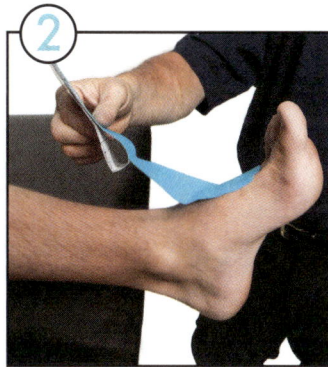

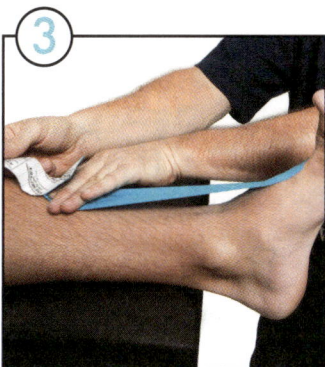

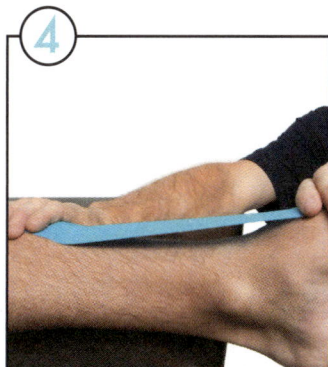

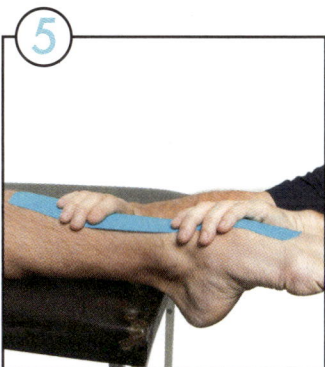

1. The Kinesio Tex Tape is applied by cutting the appropriate length of an "I" Strip. Length should be approximately 4" above and below the joint (or a length appropriate for the joint chosen).

2. Place the joint, or muscle to be taped in the appropriate position. Example: if assisting dorsiflexion and limiting plantar flexion place the joint in neutral or slight dorsi flexion. Begin tape application by placing anchor at the distal end of selected joint with a minimum 3-4" of tape with no tension.

3. With one hand hold the distal anchor so no tension will be added during further application. Apply an appropriate degree of tension, 50+% of available tension and adhere the second anchor of the tape at the proximal end of the selected joint. Initially it may be difficult to determine the appropriate amount of tension, several applications may be needed prior to establishing proper tension. This anchor should also be 3-4" of tape with no tension. This creates the "bridge or tent".

4. With one hand placed on each anchor, both proximal and distal, have the patient actively move the joint into the opposite end range of motion. Example: if assisting dorsiflexion and limiting plantar flexion have the patient now actively move into plantar flexion.

5. To finish the tape application move both hands towards the middle of the joint and apply remaining tape to the skin. Vigorously rub to initiate adhesive prior to releasing tension, otherwise the Kinesio I Strip will have limited adherence.

CIRCULATORY/LYMPHATIC CORRECTION

Circulatory/ lymphatic correction help provide a directional pull of the tape to guide the exudate to less congested areas, through superficial tissues. This in turn helps to reduce symptoms due to inflammation and/or swelling. When the tails of the circulatory/ lymphatic correction are overlapped, multi directional changes of tension occur in the soft tissue as a person moves. This multi directional change in tension helps encourage the opening and closing of the initial lymphatics. This helps decrease the congestion in the interstitial space. The multi directional change in tension also encourages the pumping of the valves of the collector lymphatics. It encourages the uptake of fluid through the valves of deeper lymphatics.

There is a close relationship between the venous system and the lymphatic system. Lymphatic system is an overflow control system. The lymphatic system is a network of the superficial to deep lymphatic. It works in conjunction with the venous system to control fluid movement back to the body. The lymphatic system assists the venous system when it is over extended. This is when there is too much internal venous pressure causing swelling in the interstitial space or when there is trauma to the soft tissue causing pain and/ or swelling.

The circulatory/lymphatic correction can be used for acute and chronic swelling and inflammatory conditions. The anchor is place in a less congested area that is free from swelling. The therapeutic direction of pull is toward the anchor. Typically the anchor is positioned proximal, toward the trunk area.

The tails are positioned over the congested area, distal to the anchor. Fluid is routed from the tails to the anchor area. The less congested area can then assist the congested swollen areas in the routing of fluid back to the body.

Ultimately, the circulatory/lymphatic correction can:

• Enhance fluid exchange between tissue layers

• Reduce edema

• Equalize inflamed soft tissue temperature

• Remove Congestion of Lymphatic Fluid and Hemorrhages under the Skin.

• Promote natural fluid flow between layers of soft tissue.

• Reduce pain and discomfort

• Promote soft tissue healing

The lymphatic system is a blind system that begins with capillaries, to angions, to lymph vessels, to lymph nodes with collector lymph nodes leading to larger lymph vessels that empty into the venous system at the right venous arch.

There is a significant amount of fluid filtrated and diffused per day when the body is working normally. During a 24 hour period between 50 and 100% of plasma proteins leave the blood steam and are taken up by the lymph system and returned to the venous system. The sum of the capillary diameters is 1,000 times larger than the aorta, this results in the blood flowing 1000 times faster in the aorta than the capillaries. Within the average adult there is a blood volume of 5-6 liters, during an average day up to 70 liters of filtration is normal. Between 20,000 and 60,000 liters of diffusion is normal per 24 hours.

Lymphatic fluids are initially collected in pre-lymphatic vessels that allow for water bound with proteins to enter. Endothelial cells located within the vessel matrix function as flap valves for filling. The endothelial cells are connected to the fascia via filaments that open the flap valve when movement occurs. The lymph system works on a negative pressure gradient, meaning that less pressure must be inside the vessel to allow for fluid to enter and then move up to larger vessels. The lymph vessels flap valves open and create an obligatory load: an obligatory load is the amount of pressure which must exist at the ends of the system to create higher distal pressures that causes the collected fluid to move to a region of lower pressure further up the system. When the obligatory load occurs the flap valves close the system and the fluid within the system moves to an area of lower pressure.

Pre-lymph collectors (vessels) are located in subcutaneous layers connected to superficial arterial capillary networks. These are connected to a deeper network of the arterial system. They are efferent vessels of the deep lymph capillaries where valves within vessels begin. There exists an interconnected web like anastomosis that creates an overlapping drainage or watershed. The watershed allows for the lymphatic system to create multiple connections within interconnected areas to allow for drainage over a larger area.

The lymphatic fluid moves from the pre-lymph collectors (subcutaneous) at the most distal entrance location to angions (epi-fascial) that are linked like a pearl necklace. A valve between each of the "pearls" prevents back-flow of fluid movement. The movement of the lymphatic fluid from areas of higher pressure distally to areas of lower pressure proximally is provided by muscular contractions. Like the pre-lymph collectors, the angions and the connected lymph capillary network contain many cross connections to similar vessels. The fluid is moved toward lymph nodes via lymph vessels that contain musculature which contracts to move the fluid along.

The lymph nodes are located sub-fascia and are connected to the deep lymph vessels. The deep lymph vessels flow along long bones to the respective lymph nodes. The lymphatic fluids move from lymph node to lymph node and eventually dump into the venous system at the right or left venous arch.

Edema, a local or generalized condition in which the body tissues contain an excessive amount of fluid, occurs when there is an interruption or overloading of the lymph system. Edema may occur when the transport capacity of the lymph system is not sufficient to transport the lymph obligatory load from the tissues. When the lymph volume exceeds the transport capabilities edema will occur and as a result the "bathtub overflows".

The lymphatic correction is applied using a fan cut. The Kinesio Tape can easily be cut into 4 strips. Clinically, cuts of 5 or 6 strips have been shown to be most effective in edema reduction. It is however more difficult to make and apply cuts of 5 or 6 strips, it may be best for the practitioner to initially use a fan of 4 cuts. The anchor of the Kinesio Fan Strip is placed above the lymph node the edema is to be directed. The patient is placed in a stretch position and the fans strips are applied with 0-20% of available tension. The fan strips is applied in an overlapping, crisscross pattern to further assist with edema reduction.

If the edema or lymphedema is located in a region in which the closest lymphatic duct is either non-existent or dysfunctional then apply the Kinesio Tex Tape fan strips towards a viable node or working lymphatic field. The lymphatic system has redundancy built in, anastomosis, and attempting to drain lymphatic fluid to dysfunctional or missing lymph duct will not reduce edema. Use the lymphatic fan strips to re-direct the edema towards a viable lymph node or nodes. Example: if the axillary lymph node has been removed due to surgery then direct the lymph fluid to the posterior region of the shoulder, neck and back.

Special Assistance by: Kim Rock Stockheimer

Circulatory/Lymphatic Correction Application

The Kinesio Strip is applied using a fan cut. The crisscross pattern of the technique is applied over the area of the edema and is adjusted as needed in subsequent applications. If the lymph duct nearest to the edema is non-existent or dysfunctional then re-direct the lymphatic fluid towards a viable duct using the anastomosis present in the lymphatic system.

1. Place anchor of fan cut slightly above the lymph node to which lymph drainage is being directed. Have the patient move into a stretch position if appropriate for area to be treated. In example shown, the knee is in extension and the ankle in dorsi flexion.

2. Apply the tails of the fan with 0-20% of available tension over area of edema.

3. The placement of the lymphatic strips are directed over the area of edema. The photo shows drainage from the area of the calf to posterior medial aspect of knee, location of the lymph node.

   After the first fan strip application pat or gently rub to initiate adhesive prior to any further patient movement.

4. The second fan is placed in such a position as to create a crisscross pattern over the area of edema. Fan tails are applied using 0-20% of available tension.

5. Following the application of the second fan strip gently pat to initiate adhesive prior to any further patient movement. Rubbing will cause the fan strips to roll or curl limiting wear time and effectiveness. The use of a tape adherent, bees wax and a non-compressive tape placed on the ends may lengthen wear time.

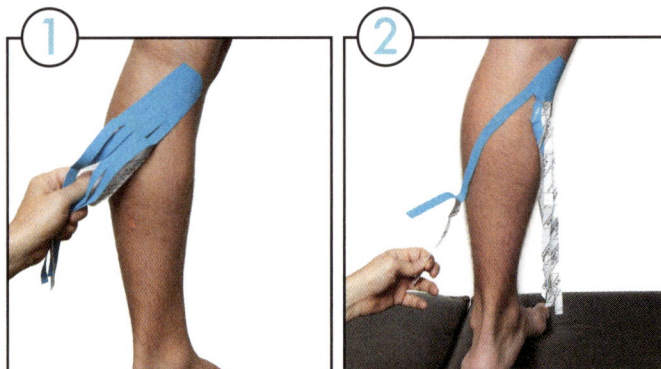

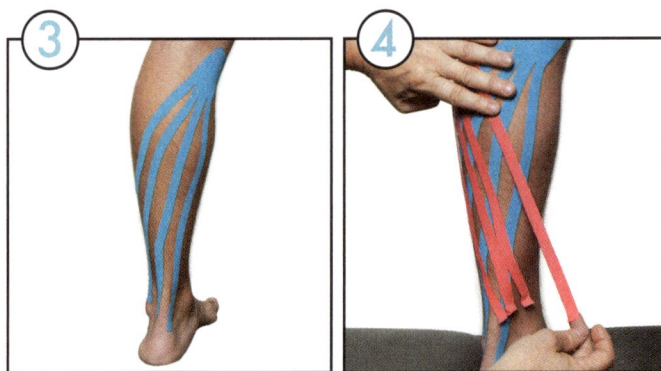

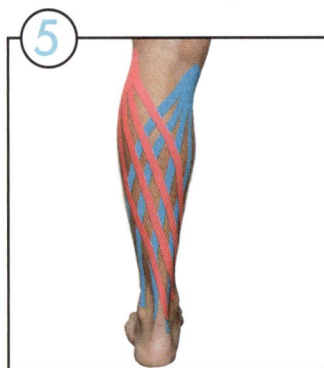

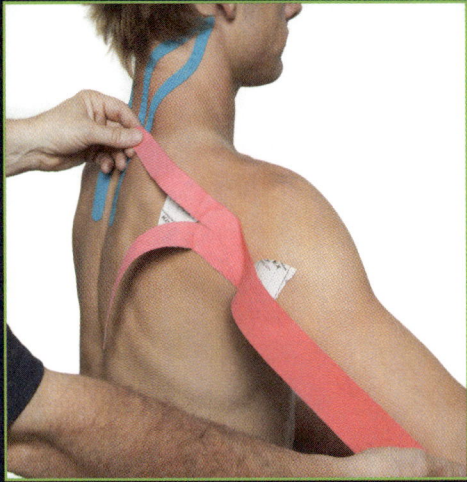

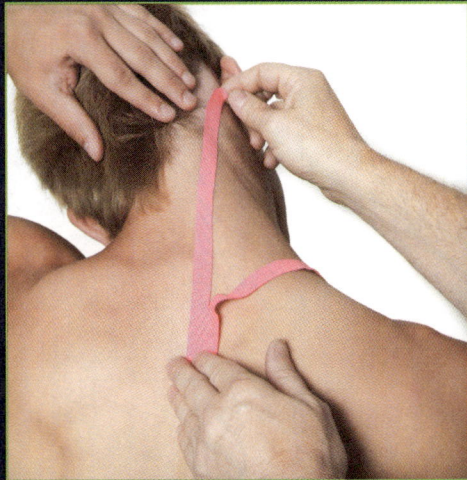

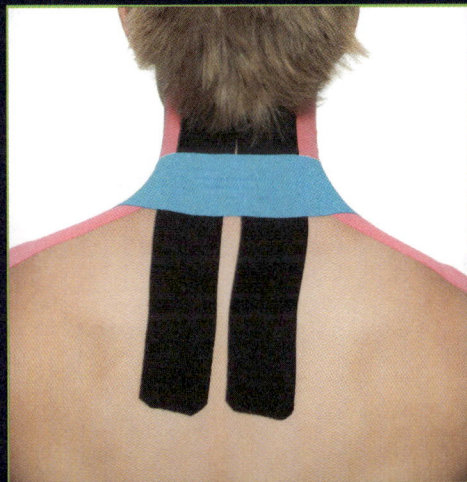

SECTION 2

Head and Neck

Section 2

Muscle-Contraction Headache

A muscle-contraction headache may develop from forward flexion of the head during work, or from excess stress during activities of daily life. The example provided has been shown in clinical practice to have a high rate of success.

The Kinesio Taping Method will assist with reduction in muscle tension. Clean the forehead area to be treated removing oils prior to application.

Muscle-Contraction Headache

1. Prior to any application technique make sure the skin is clean of oils. The forehead and neck region generally are areas in which it is difficult to adhere the Kinesio Tex Tape unless properly cleaned.

   Two strips are applied, one above each eyebrow at approximately 45 degrees.

   Begin strip one slightly lateral to the medial aspect of the eyebrow. Place one hand directly over the eye in the region of the hair line. Apply tension to the skin, located above the eyebrow in the direction of the hair line.

   Lay down the Kinesio I strip with paper off, 10-15% of available tension. Initiate adhesive activation prior to any further patient movement.

2. Begin strip two slightly lateral to the medial aspect of the eyebrow. Place one hand directly over the eye in the region of the hair line. Apply tension to the skin located above the eyebrow in the direction of the hair line.

   Lay down the Kinesio I strip with very paper off, 10-15% of available tension. Initiate adhesive activation prior to any further patient movement.

3. Basic Kinesio Taping Method application of splenius capitis and semispinalis capitis inhibition technique.

   Begin by measuring the Kinesio Y Strip from thoracic 3-5 to occiput of skull.

   Place the anchor of the Kinesio Y Strip over the spinous process of the T 3-5 with the neck in neutral position, and no tension on the base.

   Be careful not to add tension to the tape. The nap region of the neck is very sensitive to tension, less is better in this region of the body.

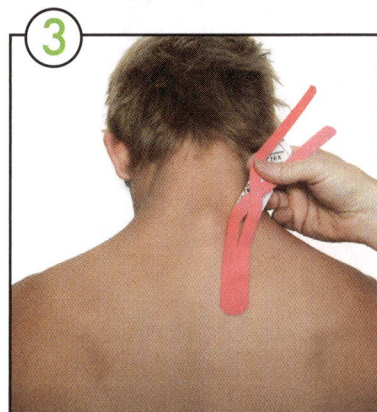

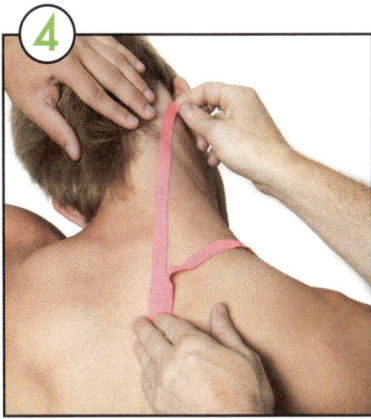

4. Have the patient move into neck flexion with rotation to the same side. Apply the medial tail along the spinous process, with paper off to light, 15-25% of available tension, from T 3-5 to C 5-6. Then begin to angle the tail towards the mastoid process.

If the patients hair line is low, be careful not to apply the Kinesio Y strip tail onto the hair. This may cause an increase in symptoms. If possible, clip the hair in this region.

Rub to initiate adhesive prior to any further patient movement.

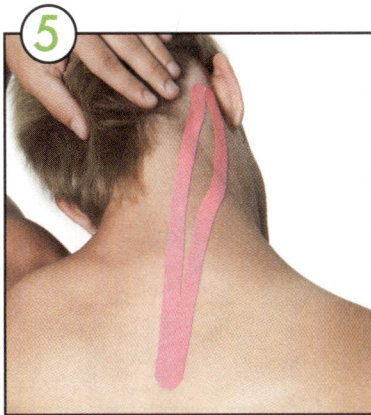

5. Have the patient move into neck flexion with lateral rotation to the opposite side. Apply paper off to light, 15-25% of available tension and direct the lateral tail to angle towards the mastoid process.

Rub to initiate adhesive prior to any further patient movement.

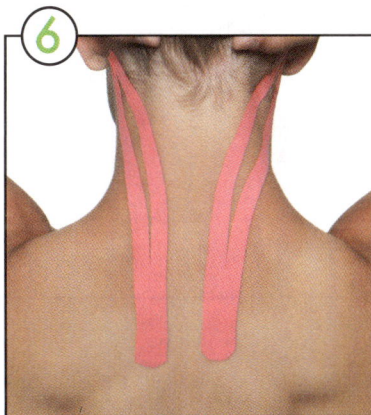

6. This technique is repeated to provide relief on both sides of the neck.

Temporomandibular Joint (TMJ)

TMJ is a joint comprised of the condyle of the mandible and the mandibular fossa of the temporal bone. It may become injured from direct trauma or degenerative changes may occur. Pain may be constant or be felt when movement of the jaw occurs.

The Kinesio Taping Method will assist in reducing pain and edema. Prior to tape application the practitioner should have the patient open and close their jaw to locate the TMJ joint or location of pain. If this region is experiencing hypersensitivity, the tape should be applied with tension removed from skin prior to tape application.

Temporomandibular Joint

Prior to any treatment the skin should be cleaned removing any oils that may limit the adhesive qualities of the adhesive.

1. Place anchor of the Kinesio Y strip slightly posterior to the TMJ, with no tension. The split in the Y should be placed over the TMJ joint or location of pain. The width of the Kinesio Y strip should be adjusted to the size of the patient, eg: a smaller patient may require 1" or 1 ½" width.

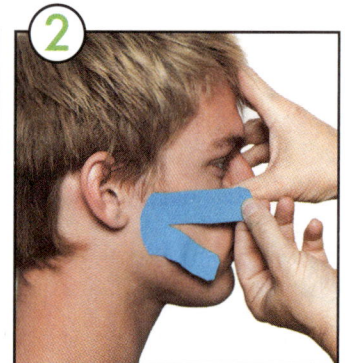

2. Determine the path of the superior tail of the Kinesio Y strip, prior to application: pull skin from the TMJ region in the direction of the nose. This will limit the addition of excess tension of the Kinesio Y strip.

   Once tension has been removed from the skin, apply the Kinesio Y strip superior tail with paper off , 10-15% of available tension. Lay down the end without tension. Rub to initiate adhesive adhesion.

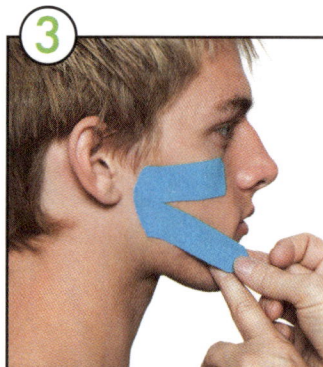

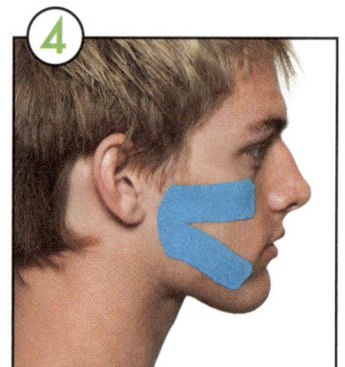

3. Once tension has been removed from the skin, apply the Kinesio Y strip inferior tail with paper off , 10-15% of available tension. Lay down the end without tension. Rub to initiate adhesive adhesion.

4. Completed application.

Trigeminal Neuralgia

Trigeminal Neuralgia is an inflammation of the 5th cranial nerve, or Trigeminus. The patient will experience a hypersensitivity in the lateral aspect of the face. This can be painful and care must be taken to not exacerbate symptoms.

The Kinesio Taping Method will assist by decreasing area of senstivity and pain. The technique should be left on as long as possible, so as not to cause an increase in nerve sensitivity. Each time the Kinesio Tex Tape is removed, it will remove the superficial layer of dead skin cells, possibly making the skin sensitivity to increase.

Four strips of Kinesio Tex Tape will be applied. The strip located by the TMJ is placed upon the skin with tension going from the TMJ to the nose region. Prior to any treatment the skin should be cleaned removing any oils that may limit the adhesive qualities of the adhesive.

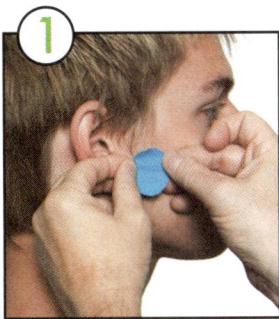

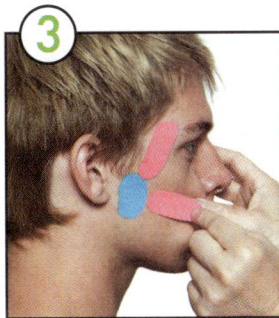

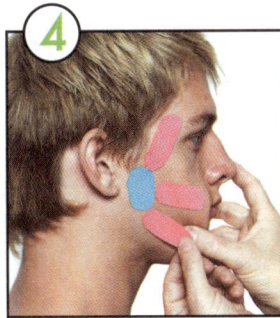

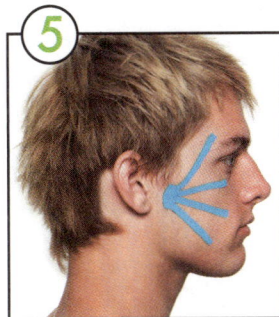

1. The first strip of Kinesio Tex Tape is applied with the tension going from the TMJ to the nose region. For this application each of the three Kinesio Tex Tape I strips need to be cut so the stretch is applied in the horizontal, instead of the normal vertical direction. This is done by cutting the Kinesio Tape of the desired width. Before placing the tape on the patient, rotate the Kinesio Tape apply 0 to very light, 0-15% available tension.

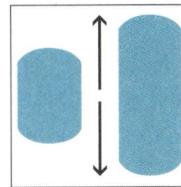

Normal Tension   Tension for this Application

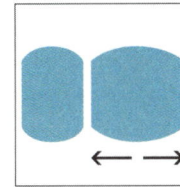

2. Place the base of second strip anterior and superior to the first strip, in the direction from the TMJ to the superior aspect of the brow. Apply the anchor with no tension. Place the other hand in the region of the brow, and pull the skin towards the brow. Apply 0 to very light, 0-15% available tension.

3. Place the second strip from the TMJ to the space between the nose and upper lip. Apply the anchor with no tension. Place the other hand in the region of the nose, and pull the skin towards the nose. Apply 0 to very light, 0-15% available tension.

4. Place the second strip from the TMJ toward the mandible. Apply the anchor with no tension. Place the other hand in the region of the mandible, and pull the skin towards the mandible. Apply 0 to very light, 0-15% available tension. Rub all strips prior to activate adhesive prior to any further patient movement.

5. Alternative method of application. Cut the 2" wide Kinesio Tex I strip into 4 tails. Apply anchor on or near the TMJ. Stretch skin under each fan tail prior to application. Apply 0-15% of available tension and end with no tension. Rub to activate adhesive prior to any further patient movement.

Cervical Spondylitis

Cervical Spondylitis is an inflammation of one or more vertebrae in the cervical region. It is generally associated with degenerative joint disease and arthritis.

The Kinesio Taping Method will assist in the reduction of edema, and pain.

1. Basic Kinesio Taping Method application of muscle taping for the Splenius Capitis and Semispinalis Capitis Inhibition technique. Begin by measuring the Kinesio Y strip from thoracic 3-5 to occiput of the skull.

   Place the anchor of the Kinesio Y strip over the spinous process of T3 - T5 with the neck in neutral position, and no tension on the base.

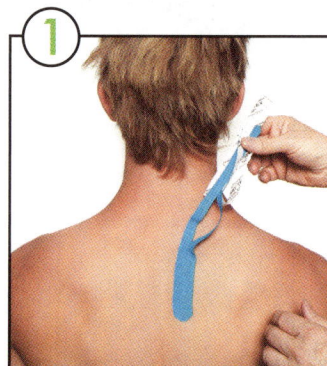

2. Have the patient move into neck flexion. Apply the medial tail along the spinous processes with, paper off - light, 15-25% of available tension, from T 3-5 to C 5-6. Then begin to angle the tail towards mastoid process of the skull along the hair line of the patient.

   If the patient's hair line is low, be careful to not apply Kinesio Y strip tail onto the hair, this may cause an increase in symptoms. If possible, clip the hair in this region. Initiate adhesive activation prior to any further patient movement.

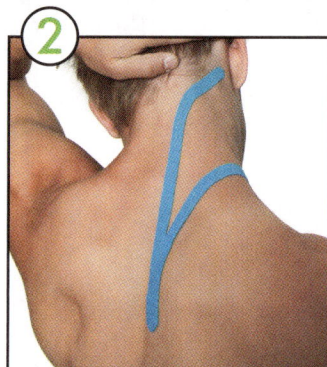

3. Have the patient move into neck flexion with lateral rotation to the opposite side. Aim the lateral tail towards the mastoid process with paper off to light, 15-25% of available tension. Initiate adhesive activation prior to any further patient movement.

   This technique can be applied bilaterally, depending upon the patient's symptoms.

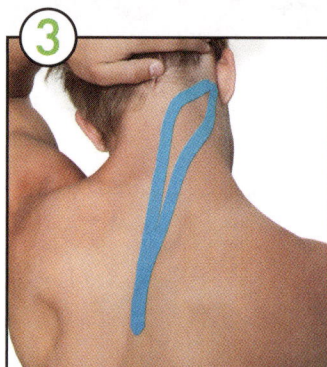

4. Example of Bilateral Application Splenius Capitis.

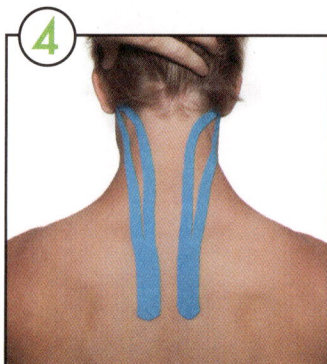

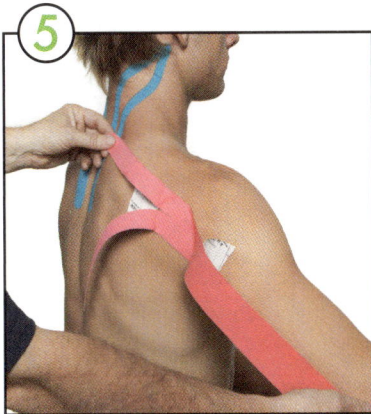

5. Application of the brachial plexus neurapraxia Kinesio Taping Method.

Measure a length of tape from just past the most distal point of paresthesia, to the occiput of the skull. Cut a Y in the proximal end to approximately the musculotendonous junction of the teres minor and major.

Tear the paper backing at the anchor of the Y cut and apply approximately a 2" area with no tension to the musculotendonous junction of the teres minor and major.

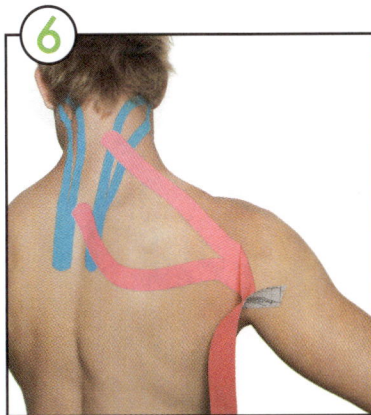

6. Have the patient move into shoulder flexion with horizontal flexion, lateral flexion with neck rotation to the opposite side of the injury.

Apply the upper tail along the upper trapezius to the occiput of the skull with paper off to light, 15-25% of available tension. The lower tail is placed either over any detectable trigger point or along the teres minor and major to approximately the axillary border of the scapula. These two strips should be placed "surrounding" any patient pain. or paraesthesia. Rub to initiate adhesive prior to any further patient movement.

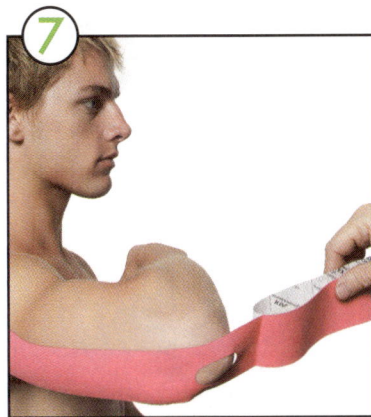

7. Have the patient flex their wrist and elbow, shoulder abduction and horizontal flexion. Apply the Kinesio I Strip with paper off to light, 15-25% of available tension along the paraesthesia.

At the elbow either adjust the Kinesio Strip to miss the olecranon process, to avoid placing pressure over the olecranon bursa, cut a hole in the middle of the Kinesio Strip directly over the olecranon process. This is done to limit any negative affects on the olecranon bursa. Continue over the dorsum of the forearm and to the dorsum of the hand.

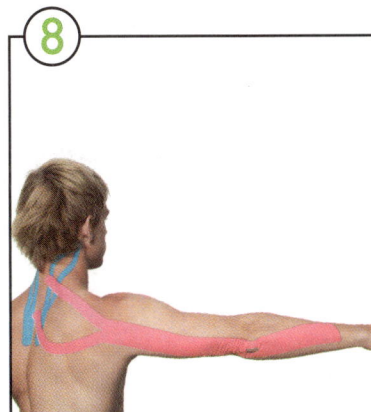

8. The brachial plexus nerve strip only needs to be applied as far down the arm as the radiating pain is felt by the patient.

Completed application of the Kinesio Taping Method for cervical spondylitis.

Neck Sprain or Whiplash

A sprain to the neck generally occurs as the result of a quick snapping of the head into forward flexion followed by possible extension. It may be associated with a strained neck, since the same motion may cause an over stretching to the cervical paraspinal muscles.

The Kinesio Taping Technique will assist with reduction in edema, muscle spasm and with the application of a ligament correction limit painful neck movement.

The lymphatic technique as demonstrated is draining the inflammation to the lymphatic duct in the cervical region. You can also apply the anchor near the insertion of the upper trapezius or more anteriorly to draw the fluid further away from the inflamed tissue.

ACUTE: FIRST 24 - 72 HOURS

Initial treatment for inflammation or edema is provided by applying two Kinesio lymphatic correction techniques.

1. Begin by placing the base of the Kinesio fan strip at approximately the insertion of the upper trapezius. Have the patient move into forward flexion with rotation to the opposite side. Apply the tails with 0-20% of available tension. Tails are angled at approximately 45 degrees over the injured cervical segment.

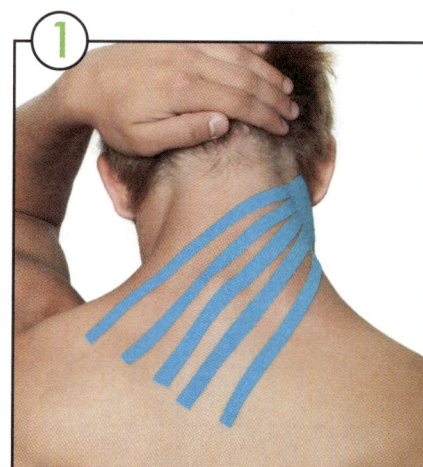

2. The second Kinesio fan strip is placed at approximately the insertion of the upper trapezius opposite the first Kinesio fan strip, in neutral spine position. Have the patient move into forward flexion with rotation to the opposite side. Apply the tails with 0-20% of available tension. The two lymphatic correction strips should form a crisscross pattern over the injured cervical segment.

Pat or rub the lymphatic tails to initiate adhesive prior to any further patient movement.

An alternative Kinesio Lymphatic Fan Pattern can be applied by placing the anchors approximately in the middle aspect of the upper trapezius with no tension. Angle the lymphatic strips at a 45 degree angle over the are of edema with paper off, 10-20% of available tension.

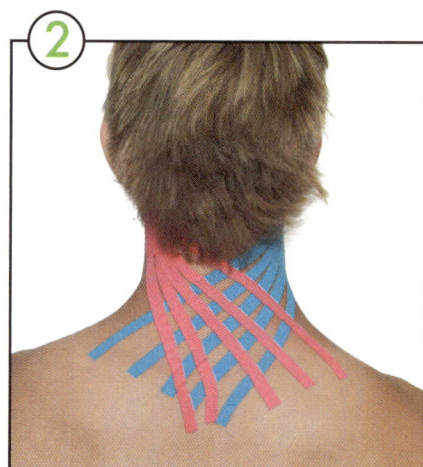

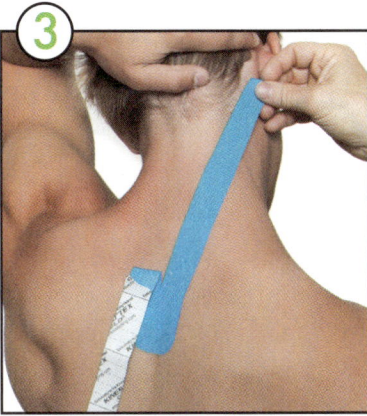

POST ACUTE: AFTER 72 HOURS

3. Begin with the patient in a neutral neck position. Apply the anchor of the Kinesio Y strip with the cut of the Y at approximately T 3 or T 4 spinous process, or below the area of pain with no tension.

Have the patient move into neck flexion with rotation to the opposite side. Apply the tails towards the occiput of the skull on each respective side. Tension should be paper off to light, 15 -25% of available tension, less tension is better tolerated in the neck region as a result of the increased sensitivity of the region.

Lay the ends down with no tension. Rub to initiate adhesive prior to any further patient movement.

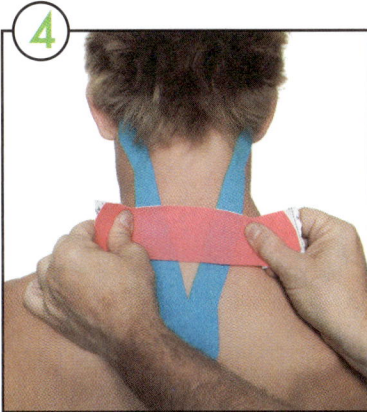

4. Application of a ligament correction technique.

Place the patient in slight neck flexion. Begin by tearing the middle of an approximately 4-6" Kinesio I strip through the paper backing. Apply severe to full, 75-100% of available tension to the Kinesio strip. Place the Kinesio strip with the center of the 2" wide Kinesio Tex Tape over the region of the ligament requiring correction.

Have the patient then rotate to one side lay down the end down with no tension. Repeat for the second end. Rub to initiate adhesive prior to any further movement.

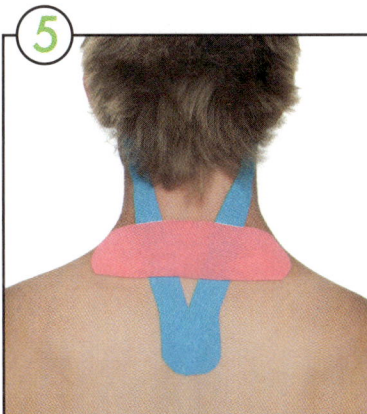

5. Completed Neck Sprain - Whiplash application technique.

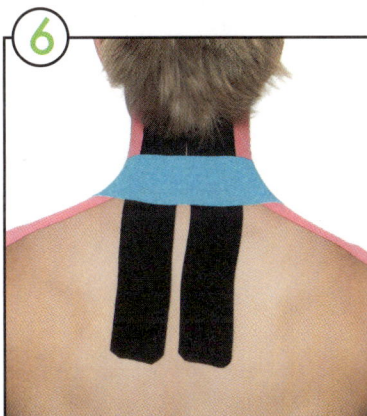

ALTERNATIVE METHOD FOR PATIENTS IN NEED OF MORE SUPPORT:

6. Apply an I strip along each upper trapezius from proximal to distal for facilitation. Apply a 2″ I strip along the cervical erector spinae muscles from proximal to distal for facilitation. Apply a 2 or 3″ Kinesio ligament correction strip directly over the area of pain.

If during acute stages this technique may be applied using a inhibition technique, distal to proximal. The width of the Kinesio Tex Tape is adjusted depending upon the size of the patient. For larger patients a 3″ I strip may be appropriate, for smaller patients 1 ½″ or 1″ strips may be used.

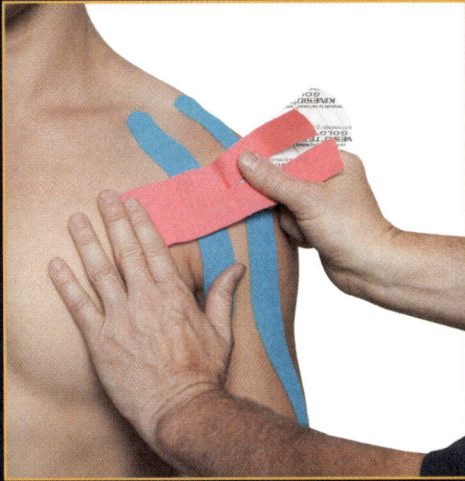

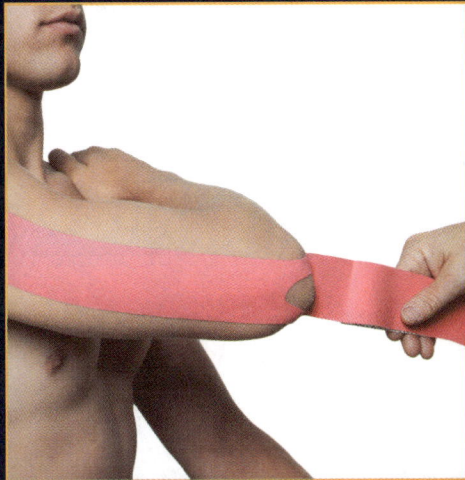

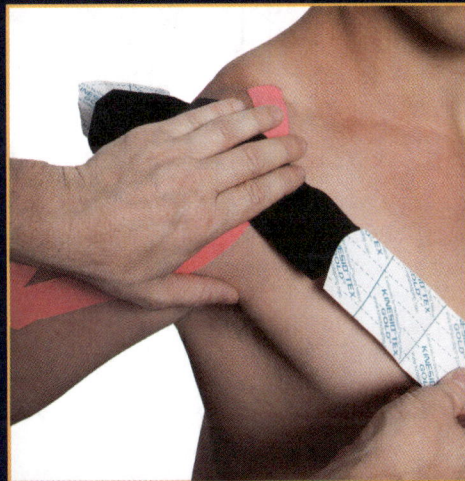

SECTION 3
Shoulder

Section 3

Rotator Cuff Impingement or Tendinosus

Rotator Cuff Impingement is a term which refers to a compression of a specific tissue or a combination of the supraspinatus, long head of the biceps tendon, or the subacromial bursae on the bony coracoacromial arch. When inflammation develops the soft tissue is compressed against the bony arch causing an increase in edema and possibly over time a partial thickness injury. This condition may also be seen in combination with shoulder instability.

The Kinesio Taping Method will assist in reduction of edema and pain, with an increase in muscle activity to provide increased joint stability.

Rotator Cuff

Application of the inhibition technique to the supraspinatus muscle this should be applied first as it is the primary tissue to be treated.

1. Begin by placing the anchor of the Kinesio Y strip approximately 2" below the greater tuberosity of the humerus, with no tension.

2. Have the patient move into shoulder adduction behind the back, with lateral neck flexion to the opposite side. Apply paper off - light, 15-25% of available tension to the Kinesio Y strip. The superior tail should follow superior to the spinous process of the scapula, approximately the junction between the upper and middle trapezius muscles and ending at the supraspinous fossa on the superior medial border of the scapula.

   The inferior tail should be applied just superior the spinous process of the scapula. Lay the distal 1 to 2" down with no tension.

   Rub to initiate adhesive activation prior to any further patient movement.

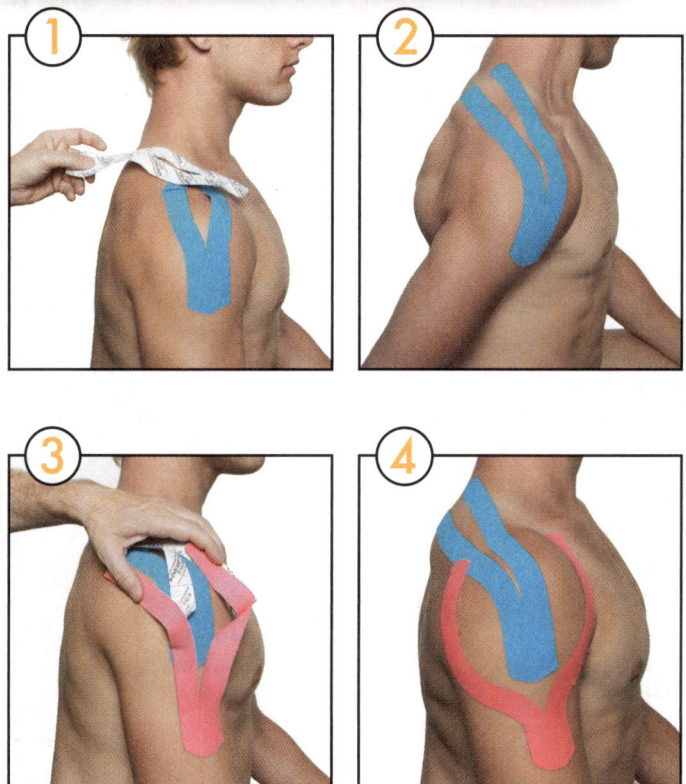

3-4. Inhibition application of the deltoid muscle taping, insertion to origin, as demonstrated all three portions are being taped as a group. The practitioner may select to tape the muscles separately.

   Place the anchor of the Kinesio Y strip approximately 2" below the deltoid tuberosity of the humerus with no tension. Have the patient move into shoulder abduction to approximately 45 degrees with external rotation.

   Apply paper off - light, 15-25% of available tension to the tails of the Kinesio Y strip. Anterior tail should follow the curvature of the anterior deltoid muscle. Lay down the end with no tension and rub to initiate adhesive prior to any further patient movement.

   Have the patient move into shoulder adduction with horizontal flexion. Apply paper off - light, 15-25% of available tension to the tails of the Kinesio Y strip. Posterior tail should follow the curvature of the posterior deltoid muscle, ending at approximately the acromioclavicular joint. Lay down the ends with no tension, rub to initiate adhesive prior to any further patient movement.

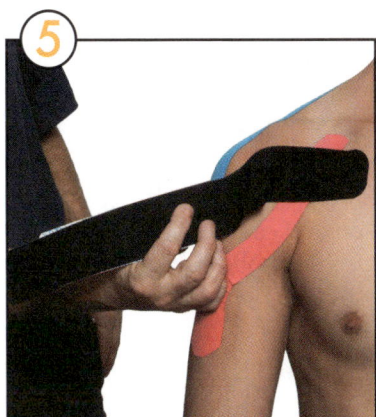

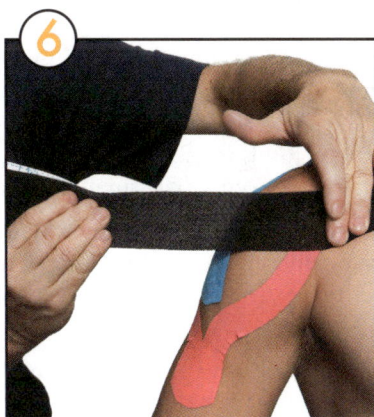

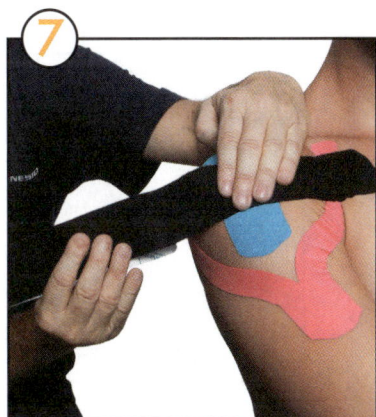

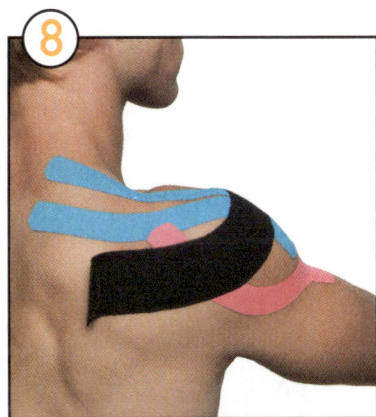

5. Application of mechanical correction technique tension in I strip to limit anterior translation of the humeral head.

Anchor an approximately 6-8" Kinesio I strip on the anterior aspect of the shoulder medial to the coracoid process with no tension. Ensure the anchor to accommodate the high degree of tension with the mechanical correction technique.

6. Place the humerus in a neutral position with slight internal rotation. One hand should hold the anchor to ensure no tension is added. Apply moderate to severe, 50-75% of available tension with downward/inward pressure to the middle of the lateral aspect of the humeral head.

7. When the I strip has reached the middle of the humeral head on the lateral aspect of the shoulder, slide the hand which was holding the anchor up to the point of end tension on the Kinesio Tex Tape. This initiates adhesive activation prior to any further patient movement.

8. Have the patient move into horizontal flexion and apply the remaining I strip with paper off to light 15-25% of available tension. Lay down the end with no tension and rub to initiate adhesive prior to any further patient movement.

9. Completed Rotator Cuff Impingement or Tendinosous Kinesio Taping Application.

On optional taping to "depress the humeral head" in the subacromial arch would be a mechanical correction as described in Anterior Shoulder Instability.

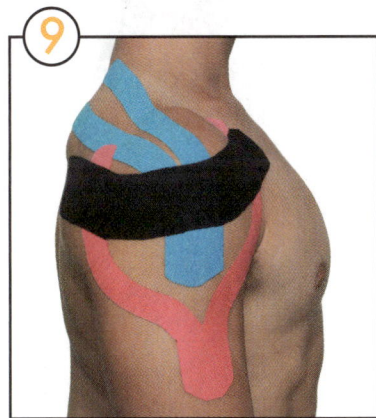

Scapulohumeral Dysfunction

Movement of the scapula in relation to the humerus during normal range of motion is referred to as scapulohumeral rhythm. In order for normal shoulder range of motion there must be a coordination of the humerus, scapula, and clavicle with the acromioclavicular and sternoclavicular joint. When there is excess joint motion of the glenohumeral joint, inadequate scapular movement, and or decreased motion allowed at the acromioclavicular joint, a dysfunctional movement pattern occurs.

The Kinesio Taping Method assists in decreased pain, improved muscle function and can provide proprioceptive stimulus to facilitate a more normal movement pattern. The specific application technique can not be described for the practitioner, this will need to be determined by the patients symptoms.

The following are examples of application techniques the practitioner may want to select, the correct application technique will be a combination that fits with the patient's symptoms.

GLENOHUMERAL LAXITY - ANTERIOR:

1. Application of the Kinesio Taping Method for anterior glenohumeral laxity. For review, see glenohumeral laxity.

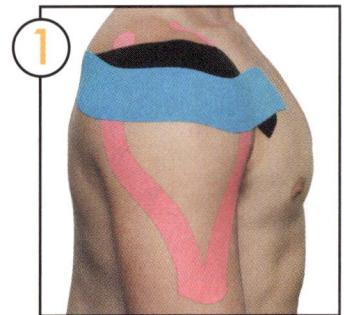

IMPINGEMENT OF THE ROTATOR CUFF:

2. Application of the Kinesio Taping Method for impingement of the rotator cuff. For review, see impingement of the rotator cuff.

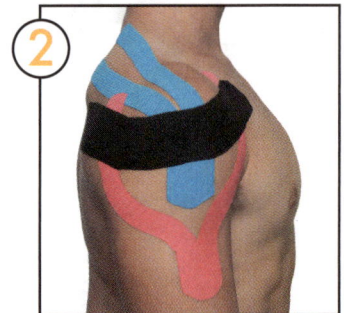

MULTI-AXIAL INSTABILITY OF GLENOHUMERAL JOINT:

3. Application of the Kinesio Taping Method for multi-axial instability of the glenohumeral joint. For review see multi-axial instability of the glenohumeral joint.

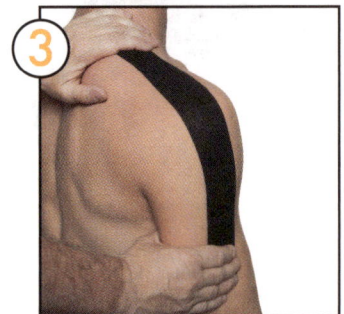

TAPING FOR SCAPULAR ABDUCTION AND UPWARD ROTATION DYSFUNCTION:

4. Functional Correction. For complete description see multi-axial instability. Place 3-4" anchor 2-3" below deltoid tubercle with no tension. Place the shoulder in abduction between 90-120 degrees. Apply 50+% to I strip and anchor on superior fibers of trapezius with no tension. Hold both anchors and have patient move into adduction. Vigorously rub to initiate adhesive prior to any further patient movement.

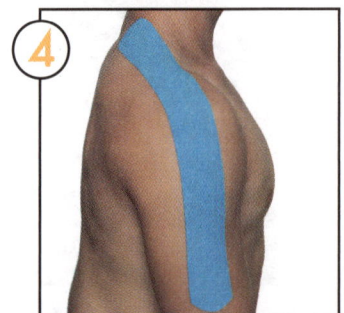

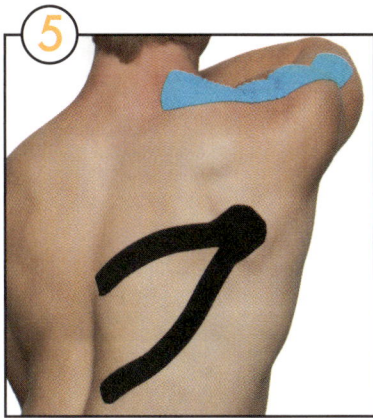

5. Lower trapezius facilitation, to increase muscle contraction, if the scapula is abducted and in upward rotation.

Place the anchor of the Kinesio Y strip at a 45 degree angle, from the inferior angle of the scapula with no tension.

Have the patient move into shoulder abduction and horizontal flexion, apply paper off - moderate, 15-35% of available tension, surrounding the lower trapezius muscle. Lay the tails down with no tension. Rub to initiate adhesive prior to any further patient movement.

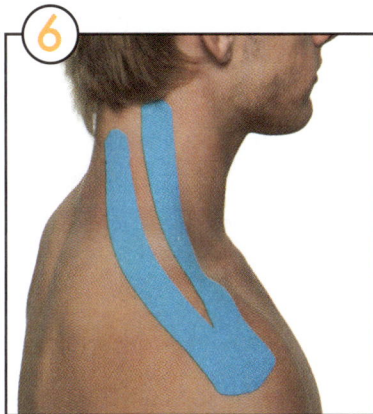

TAPING FOR FORWARD SHOULDER:

Additional Optional Tape Applications: apply an upper trapezius and rhomboid facilitation in conjunction with a pectoralis major inhibition technique.

6. Upper trapezius inhibition, place the anchor on the posterior border of the lateral third of the clavicle with no tension.

Have the patient move into adduction behind their back with lateral neck flexion to the opposite side, apply paper off - light, 15-25% of available tension, surround the upper trapezius, lay upper tail to the occiput and the lower tail to the C3-4 vertebrae. Rub to initiate adhesive prior to any further patient movement.

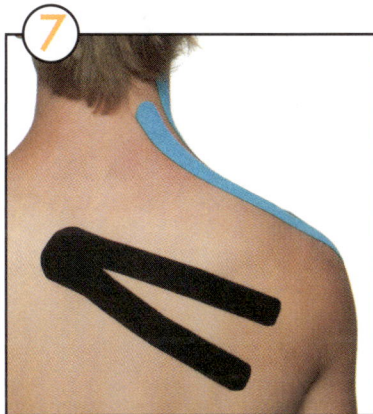

You may determine that the upper trapezius may need to be facilitated.

7. Rhomboid Major facilitation, Option 1 - Y technique. Place the anchor in the middle of T2-T5 vertabrae with no tension. Place patient in horizontal adduction. Apply the upper tail with 15-35% tension to the middle of the medial spine of the scapula. The lower tail should be directed to the inferior angle of the scapula. Ends should be laid down with no tension, and rub to activate adhesive prior to further patient movement.

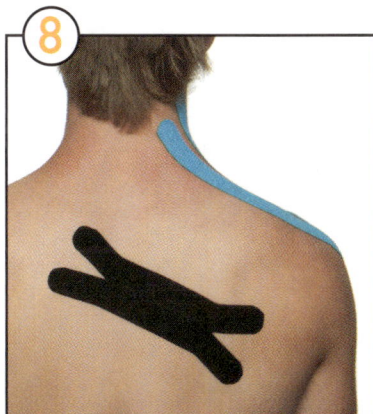

8. Rhomboid Major facilitation, tear the center of the paper backing of the X cut. Place the patient in horizontal adduction. Apply 15-35% of available tension to the exposed Kinesio Tex Tape and lay down at approximately a 45 degree angle from the middle of T2-T5 vertebrae towards the lower 1/3 of the inferior angle of the scapula. Splay the ends, to dissipate tension in the center of the X technique, and lay down with no tension, rub to initiate adhesive prior to further patient movement.

9. Pectoralis Major inhibition will be shown, an option may be to apply tape to the Pectoralis Minor, to reduce shortening and tension.

Begin by placing the anchor of a Kinesio Y strip at crest of the greater tubercle with no tension. Apply paper off - light, 15-25% of available tension. Have the patient move into abduction to 90 degrees and external rotation of the shoulder, for the upper tail, place just inferior to the clavicle to the sternocostal joint. Have patient move into 120 degrees of abduction, with the lower tail, place along the inferior aspect of the muscle to the fifth sternocostal joint. Ends are laid down with no tension, rub to initiate adhesive prior to movement.

OPTIONAL TECHNIQUE:

10. Inhibition of supraspinatus. For complete review see bicipital tenosynovitis.

11. Facilitation of rhomboid major. For complete review see previous page.

12. Serratus Anterior Support. Tear the center in the paper backing of an 8-10" Kinesio I strip. Expose the Kinesio Tex Tape and apply light to moderate, 15-35% of available tension. Have the patient exhale and place shoulder in maximum abduction. Place the center of the I strip over the lateral border of ribs 5-6. Lay down the ends with no tension. Rub to initiate adhesive prior to any further patient movement.

13. Repeat the above description. The I strip should be approximately 1" longer than the first strip to allow for Kinesio Tex Tape to skin adhesion of ends. Place the second I strip covering approximately ½ of the first strip. Rub to initiate adhesive prior to any further patient movement.

14. Repeat the above description. Again, cut the I strip approximately 1" longer than strip two, which would be 2" longer than strip one. Place the third I strip covering approximately ½ of the second strip. Rub to initiate adhesive prior to any further patient movement.

With three layers of Kinesio Tex Tape the adhesion time will be decreased.

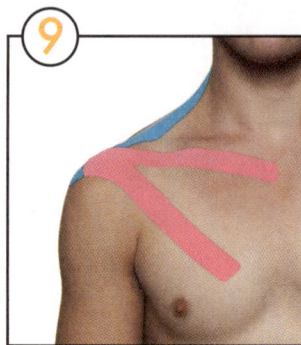
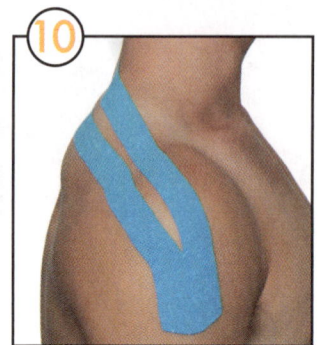
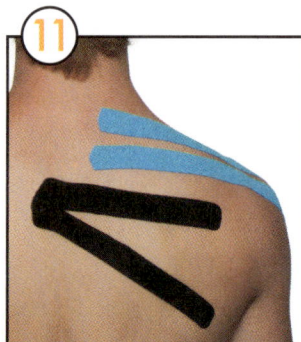
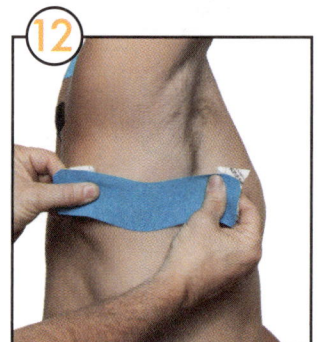
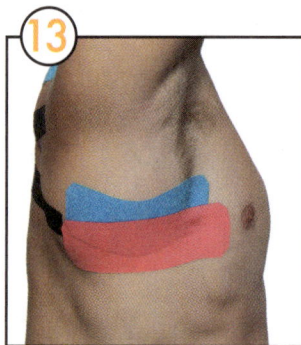
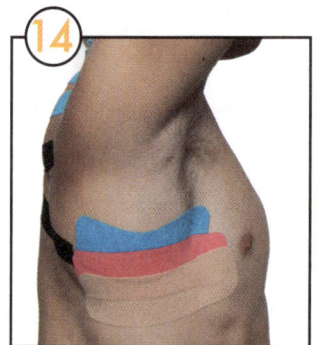

Shoulder Instability, Anterior or Multiaxial

Shoulder instabilities can develop after acute dislocations, chronic subluxation, or long term overuse activities which stretch the shoulder capsule (baseball pitchers, tennis, javelin). In most cases, the instability is the result of an acute injury to the anterior region of the shoulder capsule.

Kinesio Tex Tape is not designed to mechanically stop a motion or movement of a body tissue. It does not have the tensile strength to stop the humeral head from dislocating, it can provide a proprioceptive stimulus to the joint capsule through the skin that will cause the body's tissues to adjust to the tension or mimic normal joint capsule tension stimuli to the CNS.

The Kinesio Taping Technique will assist in reducing edema, pain and provide proprioceptive stimulus.

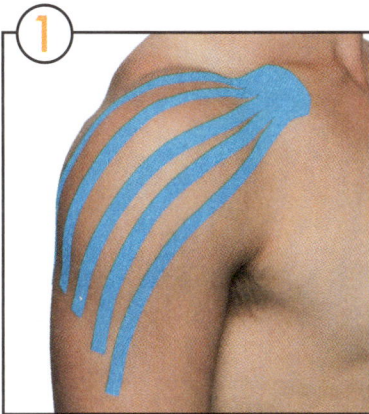

ACUTE PHASE:

Application of the lymphatic corrective technique, two lymphatic correction strips will be applied.

1. Place shoulder in abduction and external rotation, apply anchor of the Kinesio fan strip near the middle one third of the clavicle, direct the tails of the fan over the AC joint towards the posterior deltoid region with 0-20% of available tension. Pat the strips or rub to initiate adhesive prior to any further patient movement.

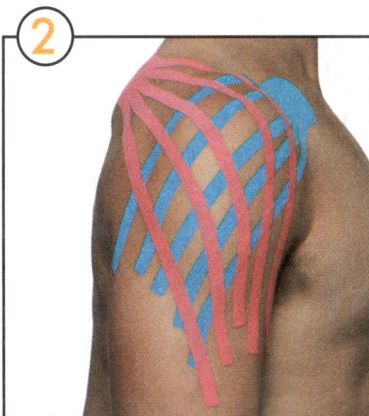

2. Place the shoulder in horizontal adduction and place anchor of the second Kinesio fan strip near the middle one third of the spine of the scapula. Direct the tails towards the anterior deltoid region with 0-20% of available tension. The two strips should form a crisscross pattern. Pat the fan strips to initiate adhesive, be careful to not rub the tails as this may cause them to roll and limit adhesion.

   The position of the lymphatic strips can be altered with one anchor being placed near the SC joint on the anterior aspect and one anchor being placed near the superior medial angle of the scapula.

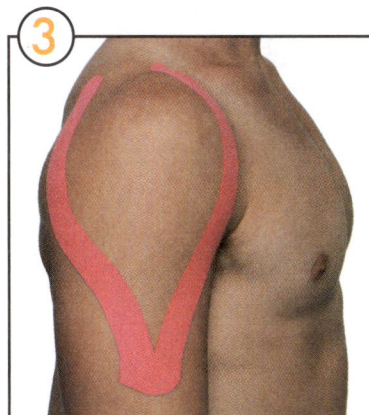

3. Depending upon the evaluation by the practitioner, an inhibition deltoid muscle taping technique may be applied. This may assist in pain reduction by decreasing spasm in the deltoid in it's attempt to splint the shoulder. Upper trapezius, pec major and minor, and rhomboid are additional muscles which may require inhibition application to assist with shoulder pain or weakness.

   The inhibition, insertion to origin technique is demonstrated for early symptoms. For later applications facilitation, origin to insertion technique can be used to provide stability. For complete description see Rotator Cuff Impingement.

SHOULDER INSTABILITY - ANTERIOR:

Application of humeral head depression mechanical correction technique.

4-5. Tear the Kinesio I strip in the middle of the paper backing, and peel the middle 1/3rd of the paper backing away. Apply the Kinesio I strip with moderate to severe, 50-75% of available tension and downward pressure, approximately between the AC joint and the lateral edge of the humeral head with the center of the Kinesio strip.

Have the patient move into abduction and external rotation and lay down the anterior end with no tension. Next have the patient move into adduction and horizontal flexion and lay down the posterior end with no tension. Rub to initiate adhesive prior to any further patient movement.

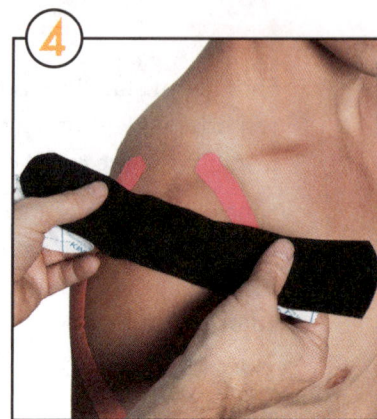

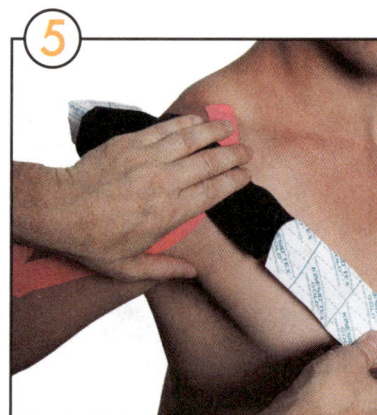

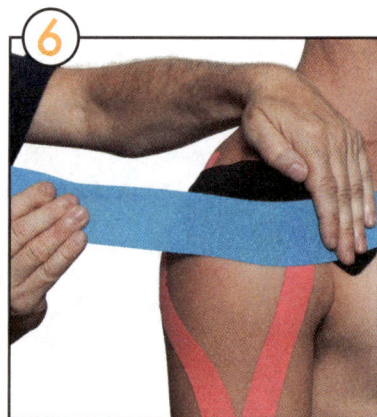

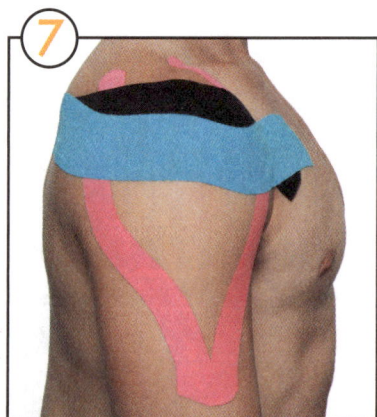

APPLICATION OF MECHANICAL CORRECTION TO LIMIT ANTERIOR TRANSLATION OF HUMERAL HEAD. See Rotator cuff Tendonosus for more photos.

6. Place the patients shoulder in slight internal rotation for anterior instability. Place the anchor of a mechanical correction strip between the anterior fibers of the anterior deltoid and the SC joint with no tension. Aim the base of the Kinesio I strip towards the central region of the humeral head. If applying this technique for posterior instability, apply this technique in the reverse direction and the shoulder should be placed in external rotation. Place one hand on the anchor to ensure no tension is added during the technique. Apply moderate to severe, 50-75% of available tension and downward pressure as the Kinesio I strip is pulled around the anterior, and middle deltoid region, ending tension approximately in the middle of the lateral head of the humerus. Slide the hand which has been holding the anterior anchor of the Kinesio strip to the end point of tension. Rub to initiate adhesion prior to any further patient movement.

7. Have the patient move into shoulder adduction with horizontal flexion. Then apply the posterior end with no tension, try not to apply the end on any other Kinesio Taping Technique applications. The Kinesio Tex's adhesive is not as effective in adhering to itself as it is to the skin. Initiate adhesive adherence prior to additional shoulder movement.

Image shown has an inhibition for the deltoid as described in Rotator Cuff Tendonosous. Facilitation may be more appropriate to assist in humeral head stability. An additional facilitation application might be upper trapezius and rhomboid major.

Completed example of possible Kinesio Taping Technique for shoulder instability - anterior.

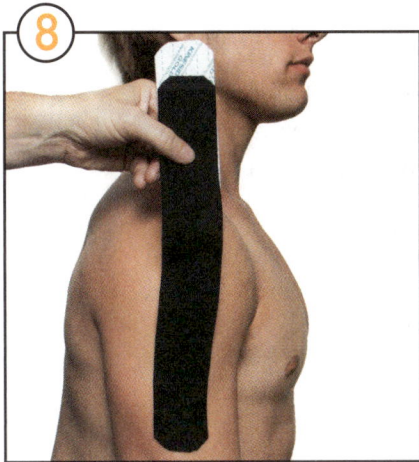

SHOULDER INSTABILITY - MULTIAXIAL

Application of functional correction technique for multiaxial instability. This concept may also be used for anterior instability. The practitioner may determine that facilitation of one or more of the following muscles may assist in limiting unwanted pathological movement: deltoid, upper trapezius, rhomboid, and levator scapulae are just a few examples.

8. Begin by placing the distal anchor of the Kinesio I strip approximately 3 - 4" inferior to the deltoid tubercle, with no tension. The described technique can be modified by the practitioner for instability in more than one plane. This technique can also be applied from proximal to distal.

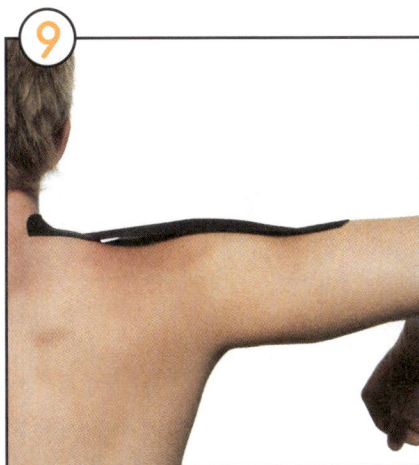

9. Have the patient move into shoulder abduction to minimum of 90 and maximum of 120 degrees. Apply tension to the Kinesio I strip, for initial application, 35-75% tension is an appropriate range. The degree of tension is determined by the amount of perceived limitation in range of motion desired. This will form a "bridge or tent" over the shoulder joint. Apply the proximal anchor of approximately 4" with no tension.

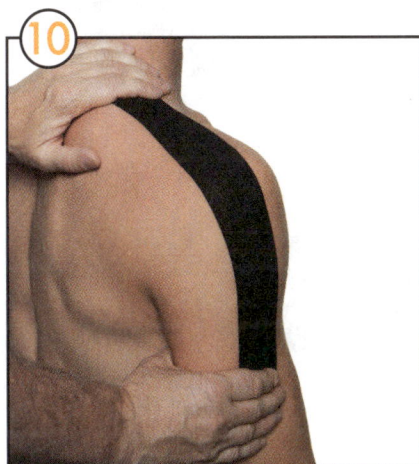

10. Place one hand on each of the anchor locations of the Kinesio I strip. Have the patient move into shoulder adduction. When the patient is in anatomical position, move the two hands together and initiate adhesive activation prior to any further movement.

Shoulder Instability, Anterior or Multiaxial

Bursitis of the Shoulder

Bursitis of the shoulder most commonly occurs to the subacromial bursa, or subdeltoid bursae as it is also named. Inflammation of the bursae may result from chronic overuse, shoulder impingement, falling on the point of the shoulder, or direct trauma. Once the bursae becomes inflamed it compresses surrounding soft tissues.

The Kinesio Taping Method assists in reducing edema, and pain. The practitioner may determine that following their evaluation of the bursitis, basic Kinesio Taping Applications of possible affected muscles may also be indicated. Suggested muscles are: supraspinatus, deltoid and biceps brachii.

Bursitis of the Shoulder

ACUTE PHASE - 24 TO 72 HOURS:

During the first 24 to 72 hours of an acute trauma to a subacromial bursa the primary goal is to limit inflammation.

1. Strip one, place the shoulder in abduction and external rotation. Place the anchor of the Kinesio fan strip from the SC joint or near the anterior inferior angle of the anterior deltoid, direct the tails of the fan over the AC joint and inferior to the acromion process over the area of edema. Applying paper off - lymphatic correction tension, 10-20% of available tension. Lay down the ends with no tension. Pat the fan strips to activate adhesive.

2. Strip two, place the shoulder in horizontal flexion. Place the anchor of the Kinesio fan strip superior to the posterior deltoid, direct the tails of the fan over the area of edema. Applying paper off - lymphatic correction tension, 10-20% of available tension. Lay down the ends with no tension. Pat the fan strips to activate adhesive.

   The two strips should form a crisscross pattern.

3. Web Cut Application is an optional space/lymphatic correction. One or two Web Cut strips can be applied. For complete description please see Web Cut correction in the Space Correction section.

POST-ACUTE PHASE - PAST 72 HOURS

Two Space Corrections will be shown for post-acute or chronic pain. Application of space correction I strip, star technique and donut hole.

This star technique creates space between the skin and bursae to allow for edema reduction. The donut hole creates space surrounding a specific area of pain or inflammation. With the donut hole technique pain is reduced directly below the "donut hole".

4. Have the patient move into shoulder adduction behind the back. Tear the paper backing in the center of the Kinesio I strip and hold directly over the area of inflammation or pain. Apply paper off - light, 25-35% of available tension. Lay down the end with no tension.

   Rub to activate adhesive prior to any additional movement by the patient.

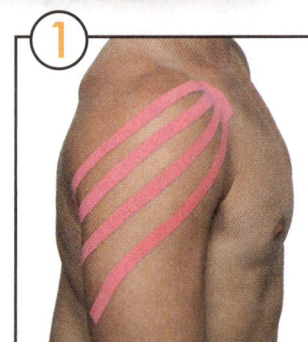

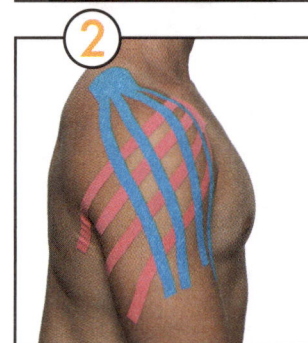

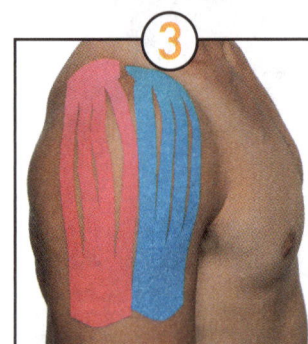

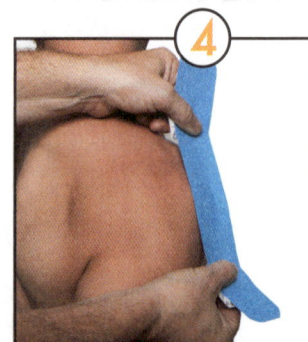

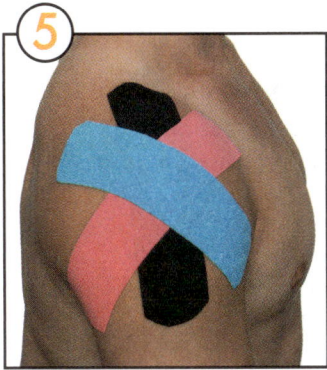

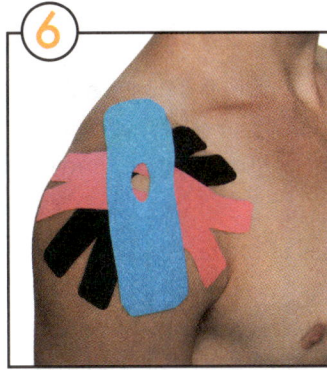

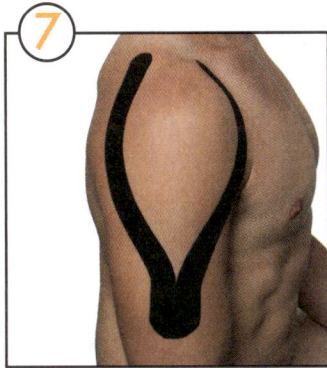

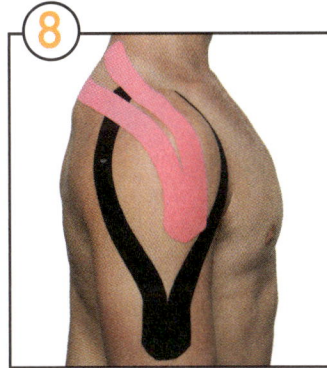

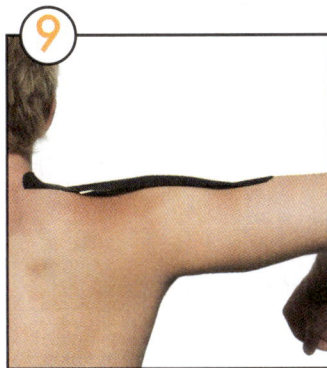

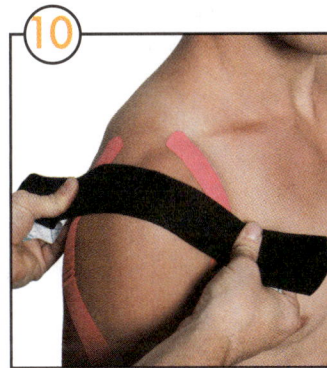

5. Completion of Star Technique: a series of 3 I strips tension in the middle space corrections complete the star technique. When applying more than one I strip, tension in the middle space correction is applied lower the tension level of each I strip to approximately 15-25% allowing for the accumulative affect to cause the lifting effect desired.

6. Donut hole application the above procedure is repeated except a Donut Hole is cut into the center of each strip. The donut is placed directly over the area of pain. The donut hole strip is generally applied with two tails to dissipate tension created in the center of the donut hole strip. For more detailed description see AC Joint Sprain.

Following the acute or post-acute phase the practitioner may apply inhibition techniques to appropriate muscles. Application of a functional correction or humeral head depression correction may also be appropriate.

OPTION 1: Inhibition of Deltoid Muscle.

7. For complete description of deltoid muscle taping, see Rotator Cuff Impingement or Tendonitis.

OPTION 2: Inhibition of supraspinatus muscle.

8. For complete description of supraspinatus muscle taping, see Rotator Cuff Impingement or Tendonitis.

OPTION 3: Application of functional correction to provide support.

9. For complete review see Shoulder Instability

OPTION 4: Application of Humeral Head Depression to decrease impingement of the humeral head on the subacromial arch.

10. For complete review see Shoulder Instability

Acromioclavicular Joint Sprain

A sprain in the Acromioclavicular (AC) joint is a very common injury resulting from falling on an outstretched hand, landing on the point of the shoulder, or landing on the shoulder from the side. Pain and inflammation are generally felt on the "point" of the shoulder and can be felt during active shoulder movements.

The Kinesio Taping Technique uses the elastic qualities of the tape to hold down the clavicle near its formation of the AC joint with the acromion process of the scapula. The Kinesio strip will be applied using the ligament correction, using significant tension and downward pressure. In the acute phase a lymphatic correction technique may also be used to reduce edema as a result of the injury.

OPTION 1 - ACUTE PHASE:

Two lymphatic correction strips will be applied.

1. Place one anchor of the Kinesio fan strip near the middle one third of the clavicle. Apply 0-20% of available tension and direct the tails of the fan over the AC joint towards the posterior deltoid region. Pat or rub to initiate adhesive prior to any further patient movement.

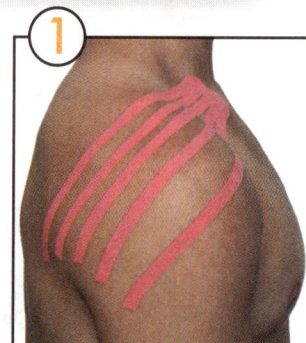

2. A second strip begins by placing the anchor of the Kinesio fan strip near the middle one third of the spine of the scapula. Apply 0-20% of available tension and direct the tails of the fan over the AC joint and towards the anterior deltoid region. Pat to initiate adhesive prior to any further patient movement.

   The two strips should form a crisscross pattern.

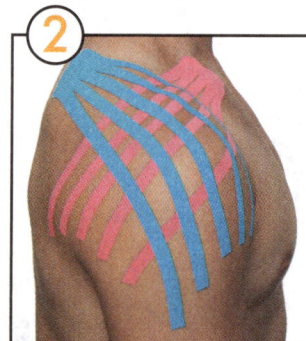

OPTION 2 - ACUTE PHASE:

3. Application of the Donut Technique for reduction of inflammation and pain. Begin by cutting a "donut" hole, approximately the size of a dime, in the center of a 6-8" Kinesio I strip. Tear the center of the paper backing and apply paper off - light, 15-25 % of available tension. Apply the donut directly over the AC joint, laying the ends down without tension. Two tails are normally used to splay out the tension of the center of the donut hole, it is an option to apply without tails. Rub to initiate adhesive prior to any further patient movement.

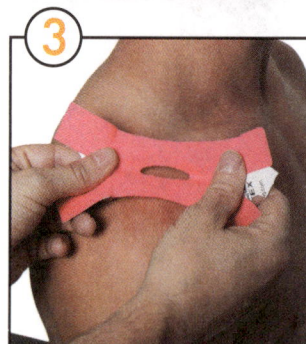

4. A series of two to three strips can be applied to maximize the lifting effect of the donut hole technique. When using a series of two or three donut holes less tension can be applied to each strip, the accumulative effect of the strips provides a more effective result. Also make sure to move the shoulder when applying the ends of each donut hole strip to ensure no limitations of movement due to "pulling" by the ends.

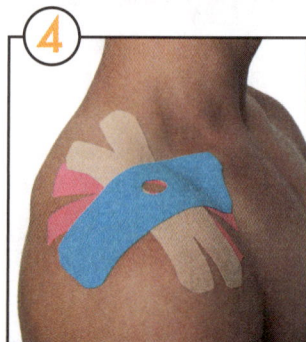

Acromioclavicular Joint Sprain

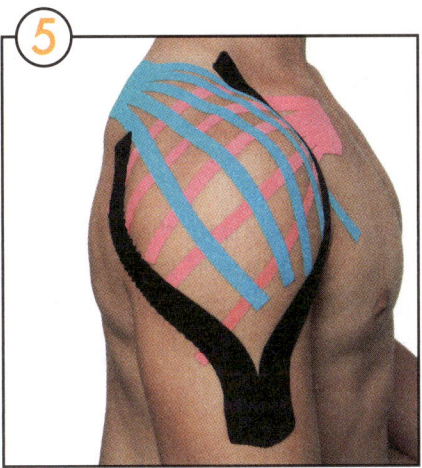

5. Depending upon the evaluation by the practitioner, a deltoid muscle inhibition taping to reduce spasm resulting from splinting of the shoulder can be applied.

The practitioner may also determine that additional muscles ,upper trapezius, pectoralis major or minor as examples, may require muscle inhibition application to assist with shoulder pain or splinting.

Begin by placing the anchor of the Y strip 2-3" below the deltoid tubercle. Move the patient into abduction and external rotation. Apply 15-25% of available tension and apply the anterior tail on the medial fibers of the anterior deltoid. Lay down end with no tension and rub to initiate adhesive prior to any further patient movement. Apply 15-25% of tension to the posterior tail and have the patient move into adduction and horizontal flexion. Apply the posterior tail along the medial fibers of the posterior deltoid. Lay down end with no tension and rub to initiate adhesive prior to any further patient movement.

POST ACUTE:

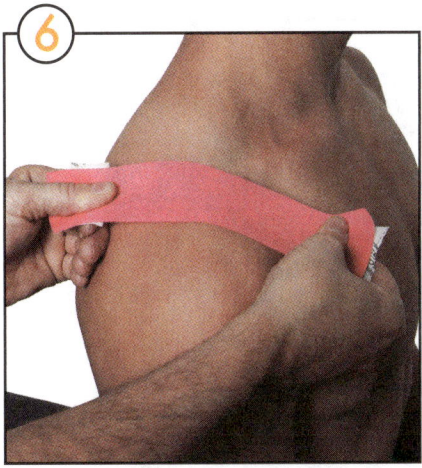

6. Application of ligament correction technique. Begin by tearing the Kinesio I strip in the middle of the paper backing, and peeling back the middle third. Apply the Kinesio I strip with 75-100% of available tension and downward pressure with the center of the Kinesio strip directly over the AC joint. Rub to initiate adhesive of tape applied prior to any further patient movement. Have the patient move into shoulder horizontal flexion and apply posterior end with no tension. Next have the patient move into abduction and external rotation and apply the anterior end with no tension. Rub vigorously to initiate adhesive prior to any further patient movement.

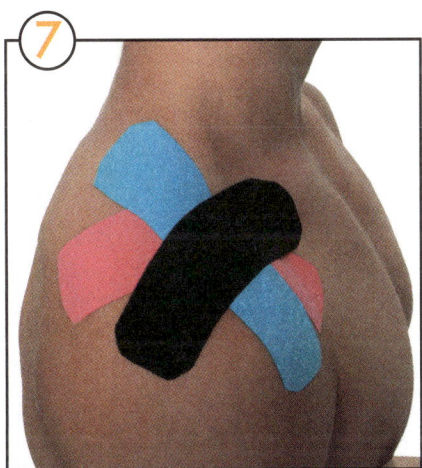

7. A series of two or three ligament corrections strips should be applied to provide appropriate ligament correction. For each strip the practitioner will need to have the patient move prior to end application. This will limit any "pulling" on the ends during patient movement.

The intent of the Kinesio Tex Tape strip is to provide stability to the acromioclavicular ligament. The downward pressure is to assist with the "holding down" of the clavicle in it's proper placement next to the acromion process.

Completed example of possible Kinesio Taping Technique for Acromioclavicular sprain, with three ligament correction strips applied.

Frozen Shoulder - Adhesive Capsulitis

Frozen shoulder is generally considered to be rare in a young healthy individual, it is much more common in an older patient. The cause of frozen shoulder is not clear, it does involve a thickening and contraction of the capsule which surrounds a joint. Adhesive capsulitis can occur in any joint, it is most common in the shoulder. The muscles, which surround the shoulder, become shortened and weak adding to the difficulty of shoulder motion.

The Kinesio Taping Technique will assist in reducing edema, pain and assist in normal muscle function. The practitioner will need to determine the appropriate tissues to tape following their evaluation, the muscles used in the demonstrated application have been shown to be successul in clinical practice. With frozen shoulder, remember the patient is limited in their shoulder movement pattern. During tape application, have the patient move through as much range of motion as possible and apply the appropriate tension.

BASIC KINESIO TAPING METHOD APPLICATION OF DELTOID MUSCLE, INSERTION TO ORIGIN.

1. Begin by placing the anchor of the Y strip 2-3" below the deltoid tubercle. Move the patient into abduction and external rotation. Apply 15-25% of available tension and apply the anterior tail on the medial fibers of the anterior deltoid. Lay down end with no tension and rub to initiate adhesive prior to any further patient movement. Apply 15-25% of tension to the posterior tail and have the patient move into adduction and horizontal flexion. Apply the posterior tail along the medial fibers of the posterior deltoid. Lay down end with no tension and rub to initiate adhesive prior to any further patient movement.

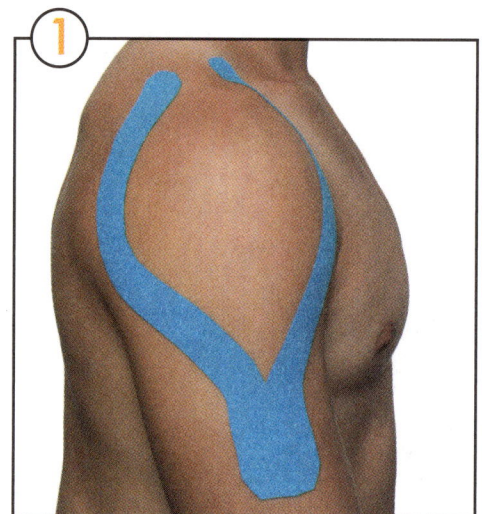

BASIC KINESIO TAPING METHOD APPLICATION OF CORACOBRACHIALIS MUSCLE, INSERTION TO ORIGIN

2. Begin by placing the anchor of the Kinesio Y strip approximately 2" below the mid-medial border of the humerus, with no tension.

   Have the patient move into shoulder abduction, extension, and limited external rotation. Apply paper off - light, 15-25% of available tension to the tails of the Kinesio Y strip. The superior tail should follow superior angle of the muscle belly, aiming for the coracoid process of the scapula.

   The inferior tail should follow along the inferior angle of the muscle belly, aiming for the coracoid process of the scapula. Lay the ends down with no tension.

   Rub to initiate adhesive activation prior to any further patient movement.

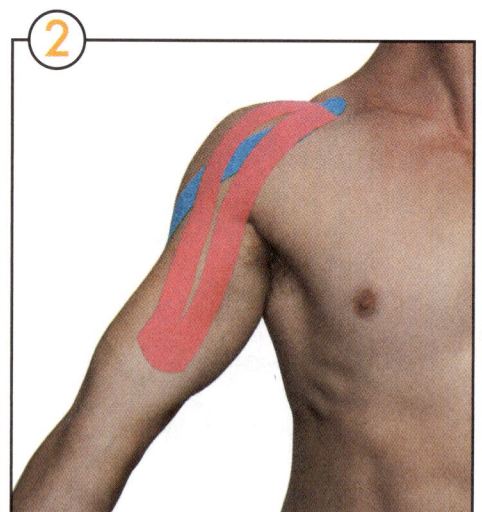

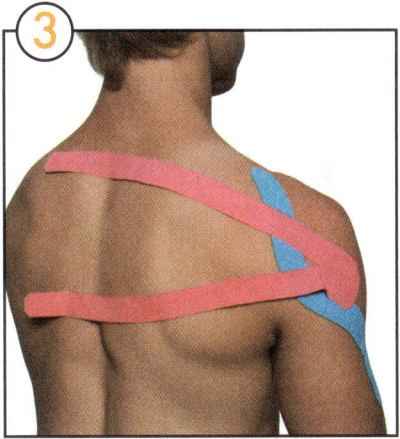

BASIC KINESIO TAPING METHOD APPLICATION INHIBITION OF SUBSCAPULARIS MUSCLE, INSETION TO ORIGIN.

3. Place the anchor of the Kinesio Y strip 2" lateral to the lesser tuberosity of the humerus, with no tension.

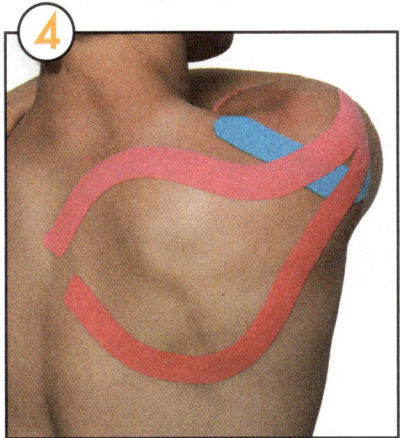

4. Have the patient move into shoulder adduction with horizontal flexion and internal rotation. Apply paper off - light, 15-25% of available tension to the tails of the Kinesio Y strip. The superior tail should follow along the inferior border of the spinous process, aiming for the superior medial tip of the scapula. Lay the end down with no tension. Rub to initiate adhesive prior to any further patient movement.

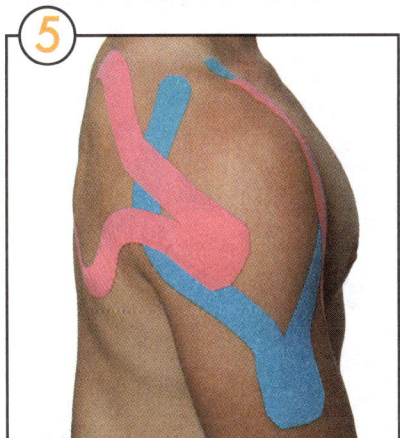

The inferior tail should follow along the inferior border of the scapula, aiming for the inferior medial tip. Lay the end down with no tension. Rub to initiate adhesive prior to any further patient movement.

5. Completed application for Frozen Shoulder technique.

An alternative subscapularis taping is to begin with the anchor of the Kinesio Y strip on the inferior lateral border in the axillary region (which more closely approximates the muscle's origin). Have the patient abduct the shoulder, then internally rotate while applying the Kinesio tails along the muscles path.

Be careful to not irritate the sensitive skin in the axillary region using this application.

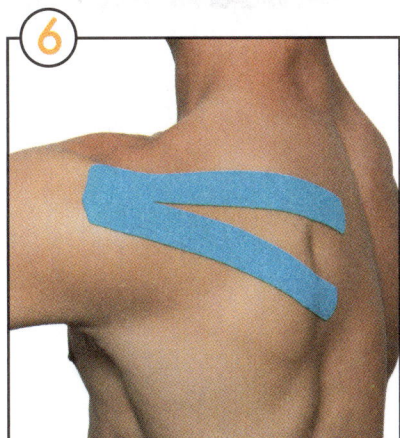

OPTIONAL: BASIC KINESIO TAPING METHOD FOR TERES MINOR, INHIBITION

6. Begin by placing the anchor of a Kinesio Y strip on the inferior aspect of the greater tubercle of the humerus, with no tension. Have the patient move into abduction, horizontal flexion, with internal rotation.

Place the superior tail along the superior edge of the middle (axillary) border of the scapula. Place the inferior tail along the inferior edge of the axillary border of the scapula. Apply paper off - light, 15-25% tension. Rub to initiate adhesive prior to any further patient movement.

OPTIONAL: APPLICATION OF KINESIO Y STRIP AS DERMATOME CORRECTION FOR ASSISTING EXTERNAL ROTATION BY RELEASING THE TENSION OF INTERNAL ROTATION.

7. Place the anchor of the Kinesio Y strip on the posterior lateral border of humerus.

   Place the patient supine with their shoulder in as much abduction and external rotation as patient comfort allows. Providing support to limit patient pain.

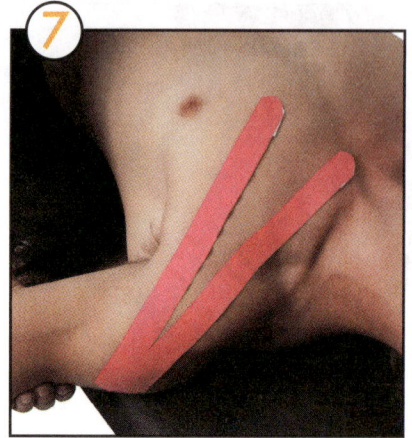

8. Apply paper off - light, 15-25% of available tension to the superior tail of the Kinesio Y strip. The superior tail should follow inferiorly to the clavicle and end on the sternoclavicular joint with no tension. Rub to initiate adhesive prior to an further patient movement.

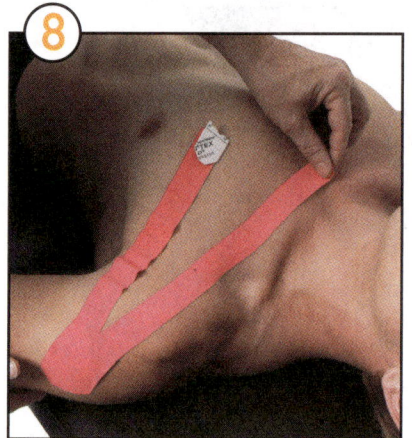

9. Apply paper off to light, 15-25% of available tension to the inferior tail following the lower fibers of the pectoralis major to the costochondral joint and end with no tension. Rub to initiate adhesive prior to any further patient movement.

   The desired effect is to inhibit internal rotation which would then allow for external rotation to occur in a passive movement.

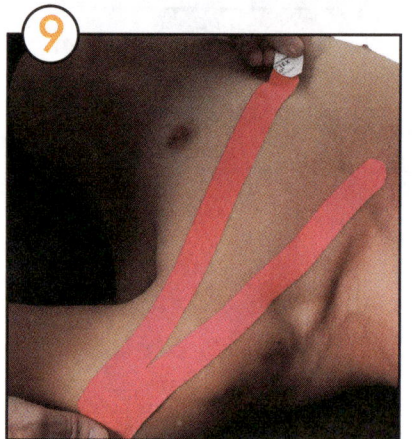

Bicipital Tendinosus

Bicipital Tendinosus is commonly believed to be an inflammation between the long head of the biceps tendon and the sheath which surrounds it. The inflammation most commonly occurs where the biceps tendon crosses under the transverse humeral ligament as it passes through the bicipital groove of the humerus. This condition is most commonly seen in overhead motion activities: tennis, baseball, volleyball, and javelin.

The Kinesio Taping method will assist in reducing inflammation and pain. Bicipital Tendinosus is generally also associated with rotator cuff impingement or tendinosus/tendonitis.

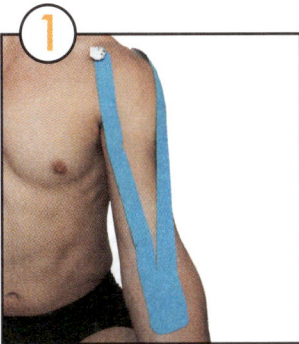

INHIBITION OF BICEPS TENDON. This should be applied first as it is the primary tissue to be treated.

1. Begin by placing the anchor of the Kinesio Y strip 2" below the biceps tuberosity on the radial head. The anchor can also be placed superior to the antecubital space on the humerus, with no tension. Avoid placing the anchor in the antecubital space. Have the patient move into shoulder abduction, extension, and slight external rotation.

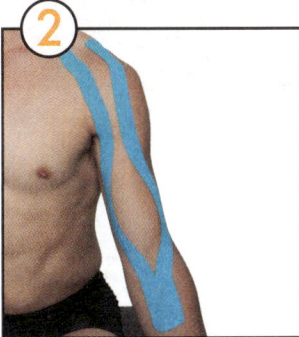

2. Apply paper off - light, 15-25% of available tension to the tails of the Kinesio Y strip. The lateral tail should follow the outside edge of the long head of the biceps, to the supraglenoid tuberosity of the scapula. Lay the end down with no tension. Rub to initiate adhesive prior to any further patient movement.

   The medial tail should follow along the short head of the biceps, to the coracoid process of the scapula. Lay the end down with no tension. Rub to initiate adhesive prior to any further patient movement.

   For an acute tendinosus surround the area of inflammation in the region of the biceps groove this will aid in more focused lymphatic/circulatory fluid reduction.

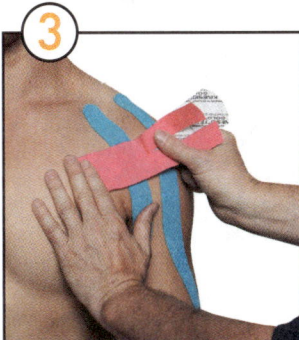

APPLICATION OF MECHANICAL CORRECTION TECHNIQUE TENSION IN BASE.

3. Begin by placing the anchor of a 6-8" long Kinesio Y strip (an I strip can also be applied, see shoulder instability) on the anterior aspect of the shoulder inferior to the coracoid process, with no tension. The anchor should be adjusted so the cut of the Y is directly medial to the region of pain.

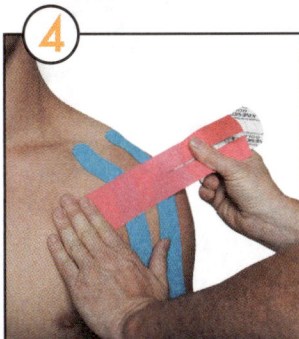

4. One hand should hold the anchor to ensure no tension is added. Apply 50-75% of available tension with downward pressure with the base surrounding the area of pain. Try to have the split in the Y cut to be applied directly prior to the region of pain.

5. When the split in the Kinesio Y strip has reached the area of pain, slide the hand which was holding the anchor up to the point of end tension on the Kinesio Y strip. Rub to initiate adhesive activation prior to any further patient movement. The mechanical correction is intended to limit movement of the biceps tendon in the bicipital groove during movement.

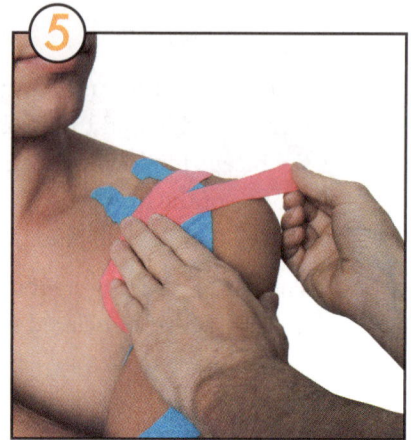

6. Have the patient move into shoulder adduction with horizontal flexion. Apply 15-25% of available tension to the next section of the tail, ending tension approximately 1-2" before the end. Lay down the end with no tension and rub to initiate adhesive prior to any further patient movement. Initiate adhesive activation prior to any further patient movement. Apply the second tail in a similar fashion, the tails of the Kinesio Y strip in a splayed out pattern to dissipate the created force. Lay down second end with no tension and rub to initiate adhesive prior to any further patient movement.

Completed rotator cuff tendinosus Kinesio Taping Method application.

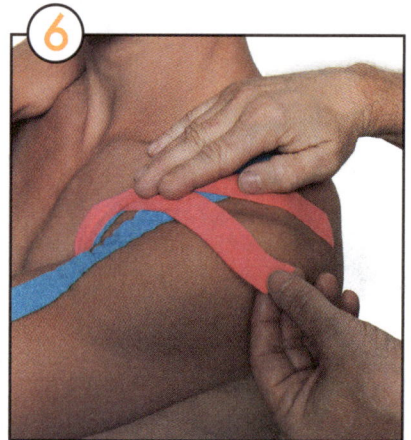

OPTIONAL: APPLICATION OF MODIFIED SPACE CORRECTION TECHNIQUE WITH TENSION ON TAILS, IN ACUTE INFLAMMATION.

7. Begin by placing the anchor of a 6-8" long Kinesio Y strip on the anterior aspect of the shoulder inferior to the coracoid process, with no tension. The anchor should be adjusted to place the cut of the Y several inches below the region of pain.

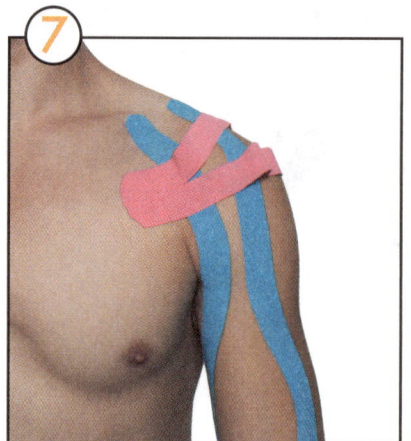

8. One hand should hold the anchor to ensure no tension is added. Apply paper off to moderate, 15-35% of available tension onto the superior tail, having the tail above the area of pain. Decrease tension as you are one to 2" superior (above) the area of pain. The hand holding the anchor should move to the end point of tension to initiate adhesive prior to any further patient movement.

The tension is added to the tails to create a "recoil" effect with the Kinesio Tape. This will gather skin directly over the area of inflammation, resulting in decreased lymphatic edema. The tension in the tape will have a secondary effect of limiting shoulder external rotation and abduction limiting some of the causing factor of tendinosus.

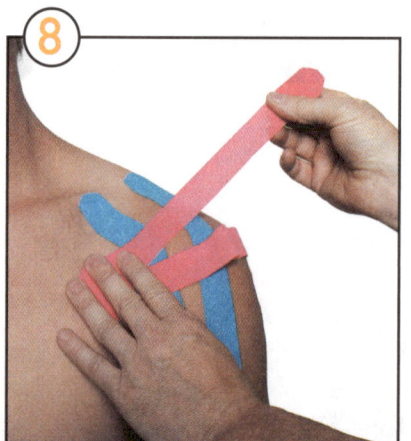

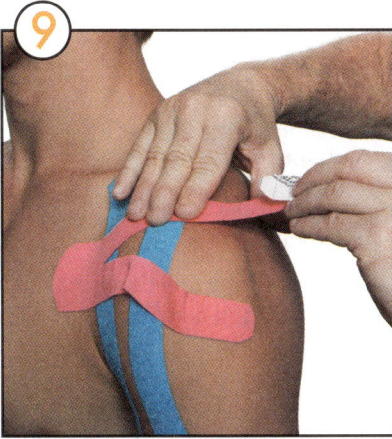

9. Have the patient move into shoulder adduction and horizontal flexion. Apply the end with no tension to the Kinesio Y strip. Rub to initiate adhesive prior to any further patient movement.

10. Apply the second tail in the same manner as described above. The tails should be applied in a splayed out pattern to dissipate the created force.

    Creating a "box" around the area of inflammation. The area of pain should not have any Kinesio Tex Tape applied, this might cause a downward or compressing force increasing the patient symptoms.

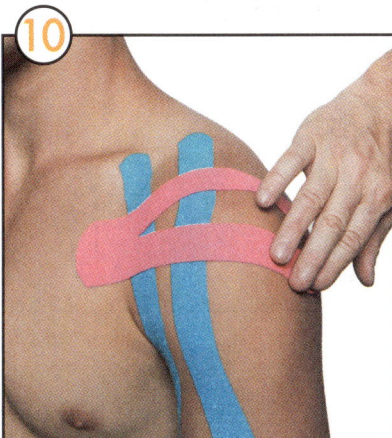

OPTIONAL: APPLICATION OF DONUT HOLE TECHNIQUE

Biceps Brachii Inhibition is applied as primary muscle involved.

11. Application of the Donut Technique for reduction of inflammation. Technique as shown is using a 1 ½" width I strip of Kinesio Tex Tape. Due to the width of the area an adjustment in width of the I strip used is appropriate. The Donut Hole technique is more effective with space between the strips. The space creates areas of higher and lower tension on the skin enhancing pressure reduction.

    Begin by cutting a "donut" hole, approximately the size of a dime, in the center of a 6-8" Kinesio I strip of 1 ½" width. Tear the center of the paper backing and apply paper off - light, 15-25% of available tension. Apply the donut directly over the area of pain. Pat or rub the center area of the donut hole strip to initiate adhesive adhesion. For the anterior tail have the patient move into abduction and external rotation and lay the end down without tension. Rub to initiate adhesive prior to any further patient movement.

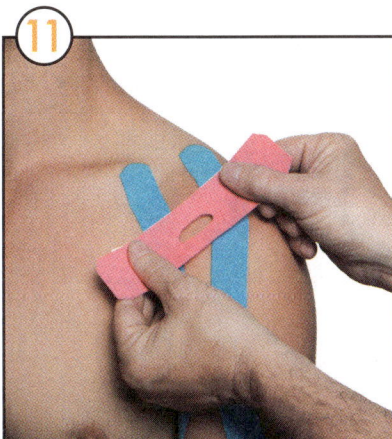

    For the posterior tail have the patient move into horizontal flexion and lay down the end with no tension. Rub to initiate adhesive prior to any further patient movement.

12. A series of two to three strips can be applied to maximize the lifting effect of the donut hole technique. When laying down the ends repeat the above application technique, in particular laying down the ends with the shoulder in a stretched position to ensure a full range of motion. When using a series of two or three donut holes less tension can be applied to each strip, the accumulative effect of the strips provides a more effective result.

    Two tails are normally used to splay out the tension of the center of the donut hole, it is an option to apply without tails. Rub to activate adhesive prior to any further patient movement.

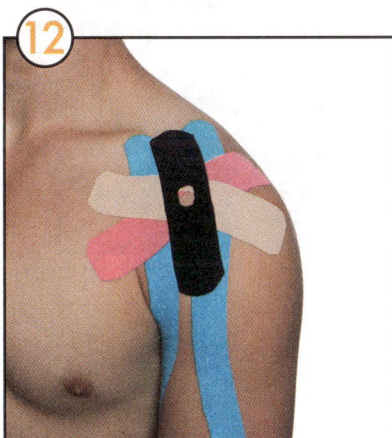

Brachial Plexus Neurapraxia (Burner)

Brachial plexus neurapraxia, decrease in function of a peripheral nerve without degenerative changes occurring, is a common injury resulting from stretching or pinching of a cervical nerve root. General terms used commonly in reference to this condition are: stinger, burner, or pinched nerve. If the neck is forced laterally and has a load placed upon it, the cervical nerve root can be affected.

The Kinesio Taping Technique will assist by reducing effusion, inflammation, pain, and paresthesia. The length of the affected cervical nerve root involved will be taped along its dermatome.

The brachial plexus nerve strip can be initiated from either the neck or hand. The importance is that with each segmental application of the brachial plexus nerve strip the segment be placed in a stretch position.

1. Measure a length of tape from just past the most distal point of paresthesia, to the occiput of the skull. Cut a Y in the proximal end to approximately the insertion point of the teres minor and major.

   Tear the paper backing at the base of the Y cut and apply approximately a 2" area with no tension to the insertion point of the teres minor and major.

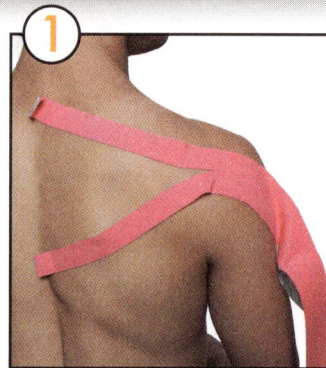

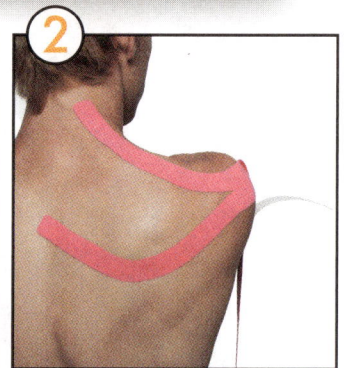

2. Have the patient move into shoulder horizontal flexion, and neck rotation with lateral flexion to the opposite side of the injury.

   Apply the upper tail with paper off to light, 15-25% or available tension along the upper trapezius to the occiput of the skull. The lower tail is placed either over any detectable trigger point or along the teres minor and major to approximately the axillary border of the scapula. The ends are laid down without tension and rub to activate adhesive prior to any further patient movement.

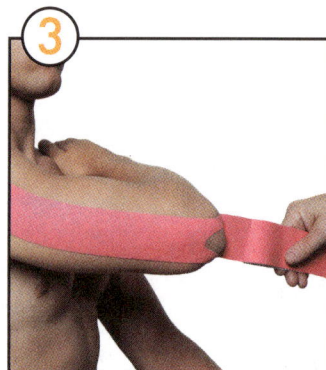

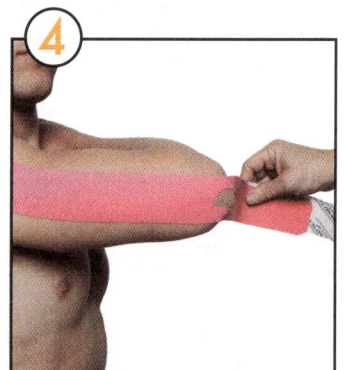

3. Have the patient flex their wrist and elbow and maintain shoulder horizontal flexion. Apply the Kinesio strip with paper off to light, 15-25% of available tension along the paraesthesia.

4. At the elbow either adjust the Kinesio strip to miss the olecranon process, to avoid putting pressure on the olecranon bursa, or cut a hole in the middle of the Kinesio strip directly over the olecranon process.

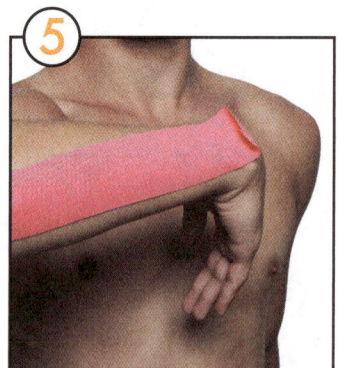

5. Continue along the forearm and to the dorsum of the hand. Lay down the end with no tension and rub to initiate adhesive prior to any further patient movement.

   The brachial plexus nerve strip only needs to be applied as far down the arm as the radiating pain is felt by the patient.

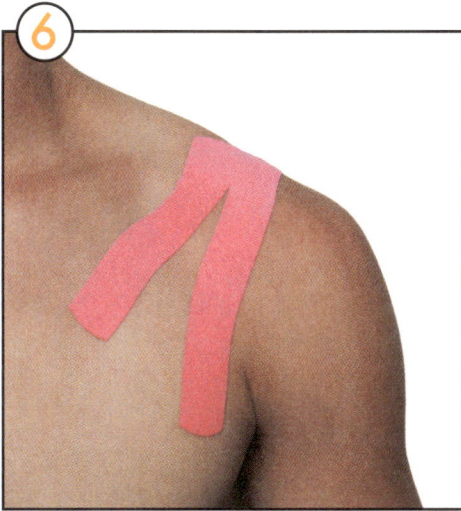

OPTIONAL INHIBITION TAPINGS:

6. Application of pectoralis minor inhibition, application technique.

Begin by placing the anchor of the Kinesio Y strip, superior to the coracoid process of the scapula, with no tension. Have the patient move into shoulder abduction above 90 degrees and as much external rotation as possible.

Apply paper off - light, 15-25% of available tension to the Kinesio Y strip. The superior tail should aim for the anterior surface of the sternal end of the 3rd rib. The inferior tail should aim for the anterior surface of the sternal end of the 5th rib. Lay the distal 1-2" down with no tension.

Rub to initiate adhesive prior to any further patient movement.

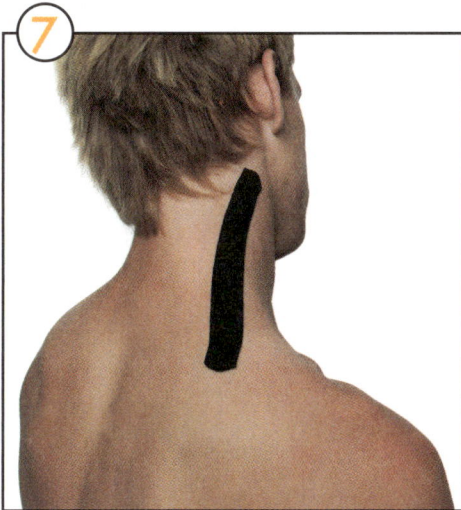

7. Basic inhibition muscle application levator scapula technique. Begin with the patient in a neutral position. Place the anchor of the 1" Kinesio strip at the medial border of the scapula between spine and superior angle. Have the patient move into neck flexion, rotation to the opposite side, and lateral flexion of the neck (chin on opposite shoulder). Apply paper off - light, 15-25% of available tension. Direct the 1" strip to the transverse processes of C 1-4. Rub to initiate adhesive prior to any further patient movement.

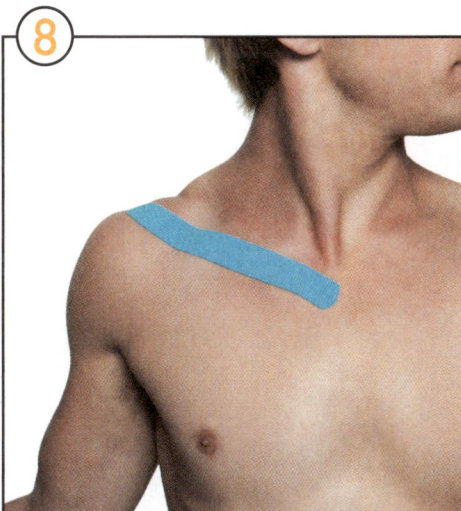

8. Basic inhibition application subclavius. Begin with the patient in neutral position. Place the anchor near the inferior surface of the clavicle at the subclavian groove - the inferior surface of the middle third of the clavicle with no tension. Apply paper off - light, 15-25% of available tension. Direct the 1" strip to the junction of the first rib with its costal cartilage. Rub to initiate adhesive prior to any further patient movement.

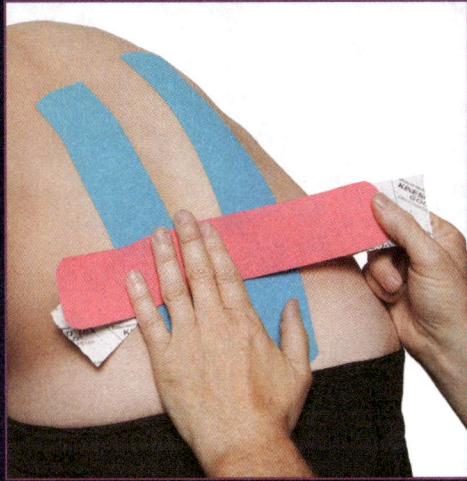

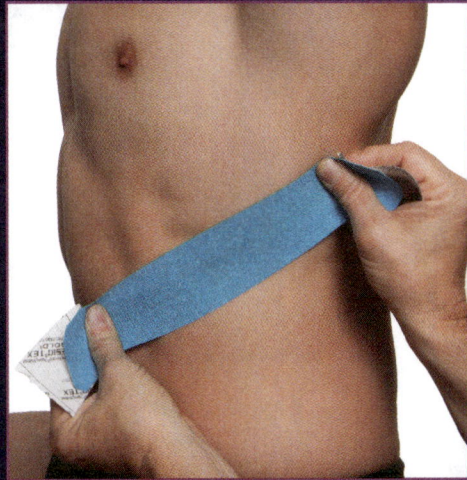

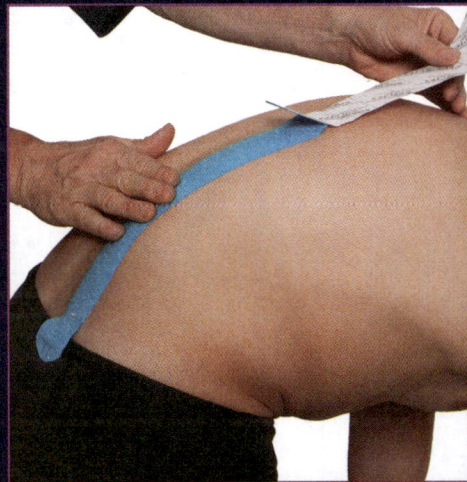

SECTION 4

Trunk
and
Back

Section 4

Thoracic Outlet Syndrome

Thoracic outlet syndrome is a compression of the neurovascular bundle in the neck and shoulder. Structures which are commonly involved include; subclavian artery, subclavian vein, and brachial plexus. Compression may occur in the areas of the pectoralis minor, first rib and clavicle, space between the anterior and middle scalene muscles.

The Kinesio Taping Method will assist in reducing tension in the regions in which compression occurs. Following the practitioner's evaluation, they will be able to determine the specific compression causing the thoracic outlet syndrome. The Kinesio Taping Technique demonstrated includes the most clinically effective.

1. Basic Kinesio Taping Method application of subclavius muscle inhibition technique.

   Begin with the patient in neutral position. Place the anchor near the inferior surface of the clavicle at the subclavian groove - the inferior surface of the middle third of the clavicle with no tension.

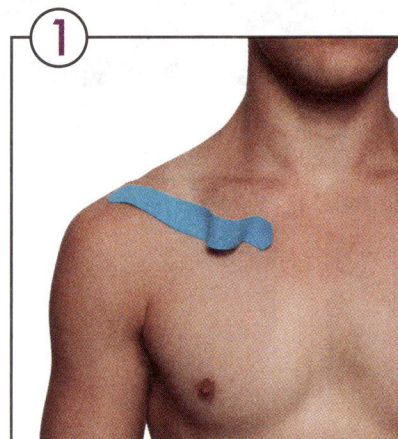

2. Have the patient move into shoulder abduction and external rotation with neck rotation to the opposite side. Apply paper off to light, 15-25% of available tension to the Kinesio I strip. Follow along the inferior aspect of the clavicle to the sternoclavicular joint. Lay the end down with no tension. Initiate adhesive activation prior to any further patient movement.

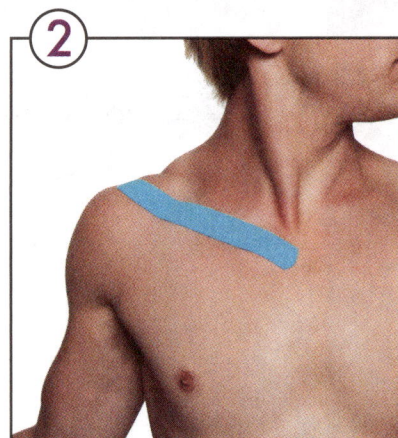

3. Basic Kinesio Taping Method application of pectoralis minor muscle inhibition.

   Begin by placing the anchor of the Kinesio Y strip, superior to the coracoid process of the scapula, with no tension. Have the patient move into shoulder abduction above 90 degrees and as much external rotation as possible.

   Apply paper off - light, 15-25% of available tension to the Kinesio Y strip. The superior tail should aim for the anterior surface of the sternal end of the 3rd rib. The inferior tail should aim for the anterior surface of the sternal end of the 5th rib. Lay the end down with no tension. Rub to initiate adhesive prior to any further patient movement.

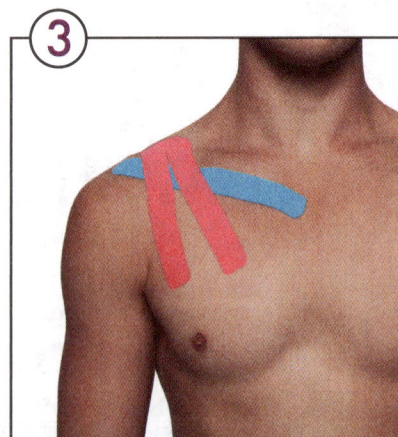

④

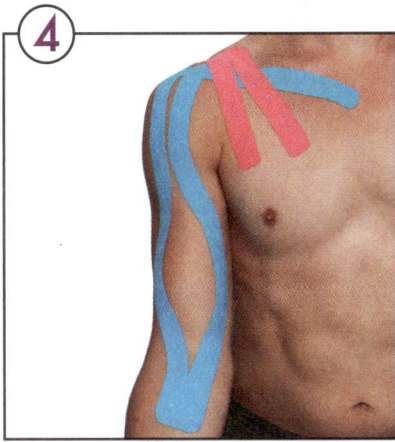

4. Basic Kinesio Taping Method application of biceps brachii muscle inhibition.

Place the anchor inferior to the anti-cubital fossa with no tension. Place the patient in extension and external rotation. Apply the tails with paper off to light, 15-25% of available tension. Direct the medial tail to surround the short head of the biceps to the coracoid process. Direct the lateral tail to surround the long head of the biceps to the supraglenoid tubercle. Lay down ends with no tension. Rub to initiate adhesive prior to any further patient movement.

5. Basic Kinesio Taping Method application of scalenes anterior.

⑤

With the patient's neck in neutral, begin by placing the anchor of the Kinesio Y strip at the scalene tubercle of 1st rib (medial 2/3), with no tension.

Have the patient move into lateral flexion to the opposite side of pain with rotation to the same side (ear on opposite shoulder, and chin in the air on the same side of injury). Apply paper off to light, 15-25% of available tension to the 1" Kinesio I strip. Direct the I strip to the anterior tubercles of the transverse process of C 3-6. Lay down end with no tension.

Initiate adhesive activation prior to any further patient movement.

With the high number of spindles in the cervical muscles use lower tension for initial application. The use of too much tension may cause an allergic reaction or result in a negative response.

⑥

6. Completed scalenes anterior application.

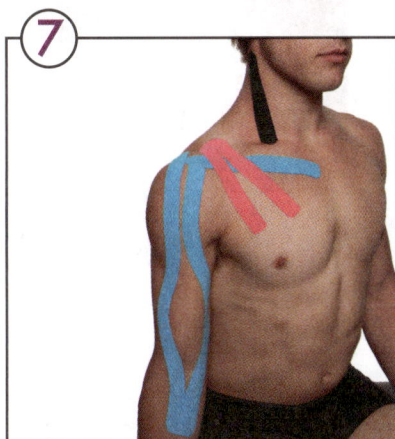

⑦

7. Completed Thoracic Outlet Syndrome Application

Sternoclavicular Joint Sprain

The Sternoclavicular Joint is an uncommon injury, which is generally caused by a force transmitted through the shoulder to the clavicle. The joint is moveable, and is the primary joint allowing for motion during the initiation of shoulder abduction to 90 degrees. It has a history of taking a long time to heal.

The Kinesio Taping Method assist by reducing edema, and pain with the use of space correction technique.

Sternoclavicular Joint Sprain

LYMPHATIC CORRECTION:

1. Place anchor with no tension superior to the SC joint. Apply 0-20% of available tension with the fan strips over the area of edema. Pat to initiate adhesive prior to any further patient movement.

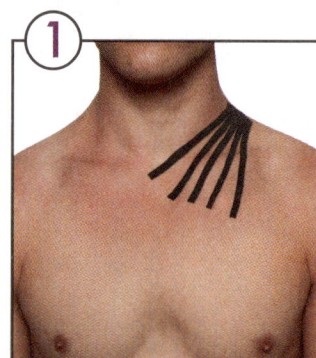

2. Place anchor inferior to the AC joint. Apply 0-20% of available tension with the fan strips over the area of edema. Pat to initiate adhesive. The two strips should form a crisscross pattern.

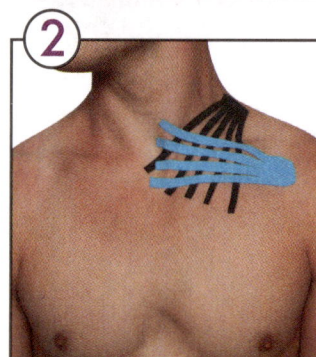

SPACE CORRECTION: TWO OPTIONS

3. Space correction tension in center of I strip

   Begin by tearing the middle of an approximately 4-6" Kinesio I strip through the paper backing. Strip shown is 1" wide. Apply paper off to light, 15-25% of available tension to the exposed I strip. Place the Kinesio I strip with the center of the strip directly over the SC joint and lay down the tails without tension. Initiate adhesive prior to any further strip applications. Repeat this strip application 2-3 times to create space directly over the SC joint.

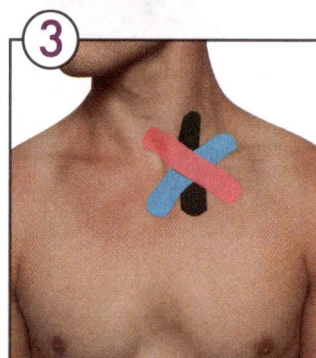

4. Space correction donut hole. Application is the same as space correction tension in I strip, except a hole is cut in the center of the I strip approximately the size of a dime. The donut hole is placed directly over the SC joint.

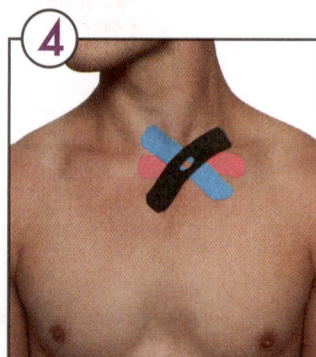

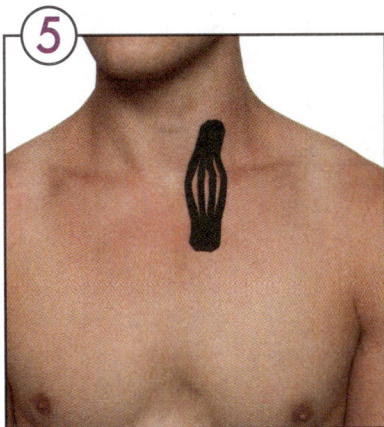

OPTIONAL WEB CUT:

5. Cut 4-5 slits into an approximately 6" I strip, leaving at least a 1" anchor at each end. Tear the paper backing just above the start of the slits. Peel off the paper backing and tear prior the second anchor. Apply 10-20% tension to the slits and spread them slightly. Apply the web strips over the SC joint. Lay down the ends with no tension. Pat to initiate adhesive prior to any further patient movement.

POST ACUTE:

6. Ligament correction technique. 1" I strips will be used.

Begin by tearing the center of the paper backing of a 4-6" Kinesio I strip. Peel back the paper backing and apply, severe to full, 75-100% tension to the center of the I strip. Apply the center of the I strip directly over the SC joint with downward pressure.

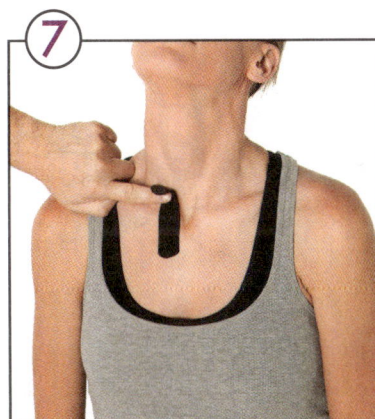

7. If appropriate have the patient move into neck extension so when ends are laid down they will not "pull" on the ends. Lay the ends down without tension. Rub to initiate adhesive prior to any further patient movement.

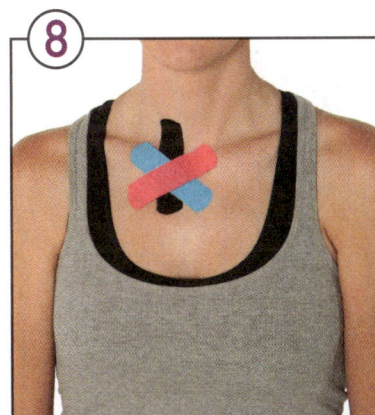

8. Normally a series of three I strips are applied to provide support. Leave a space between I strips to maximize tape adherence.

Scoliosis

Scoliosis is a lateral curvature of the spine, with an associated rotation of the vertebral bodies most commonly in the thoracic region,. The condition can be functional or structural in cause. An unequal leg length and unequal muscle development are examples of a functional cause. Structural causes may result from a bony defect in the spine.

The Scoliosis Technique demonstrated should only be used as an example. The practitioner following their evaluation will need to determine the location of the curvature and degree and direction of rotation to the spine.

The Kinesio Taping Method will assist by either facilitating or inhibiting muscle function, and create tension through the skin to facilitate an "unwinding" of the spinal rotation.

Example shown is for right thoracic curvature with left lumbar curvature causing right shoulder to be forward and left shoulder to be back.

For this application the recoil effect of the tape will be used to create a proprioceptive stimulus to "reposition" the patient. With the anchor placed in the direction of desired positioning of the tissue the tendency of the elastic polymers to "recoil" or "pull back" to the anchor will transfer the desired stimulus through the epidermis and dermis via sensory receptors.

It is not a true mechanical correction or functional correction, but the stimulus perceived through the skin will mimic their effects.

1. For the anterior superior region begin by placing the anchor of the Kinesio Y strip with no tension 2" below the area to be treated. The Y strip should be approximately 6-8" (depending upon the size of the patient). Lay down the anchor with no tension.

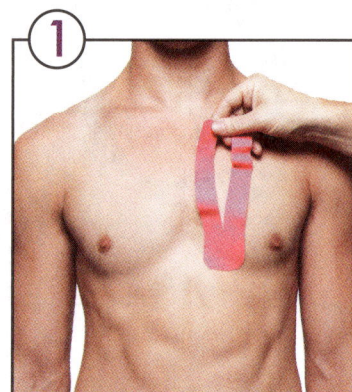

2. Have the patient move into back extension with rotation in the opposite direction of desired correction. With one hand, hold the anchor to ensure no tension is added.

   Apply light to moderate, 15-35% of available tension to the tails of the Kinesio Y strip. Splay the tails to spread the force over a larger tissue area. Lay down the ends with no tension. Rub to initiate adhesive prior to any further patient movement.

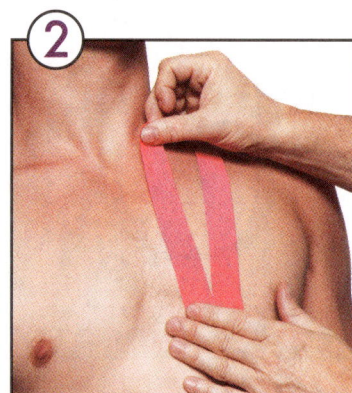

3. Application of a fascia correction technique tension in the tails.

   Begin by placing the anchor of the Kinesio Y strip, of approximately 6-8", 2" medially to the area to be treated, with no tension.

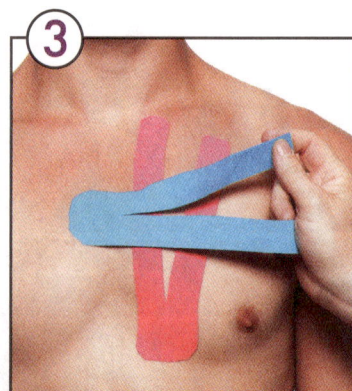

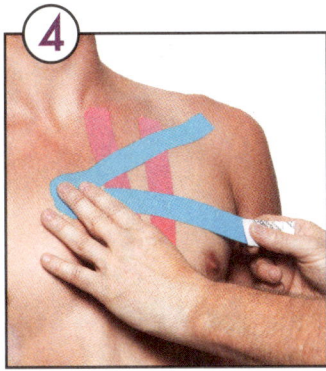

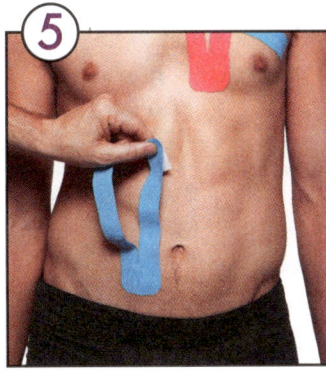

4. Have the patient move into back extension with rotation in the opposite direction of desired correction. With one hand hold the anchor to ensure no tension is added. Apply 15-50% of available tension using either the long and short or side to side technique as described in fascia correction. Apply the ends with no tension. Rub to initiate adhesive activation prior to any further patient movement.

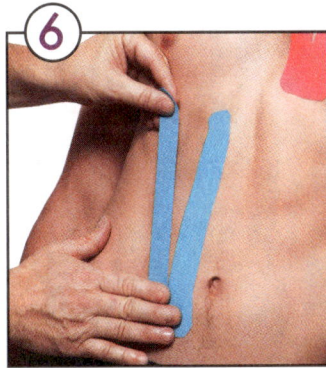

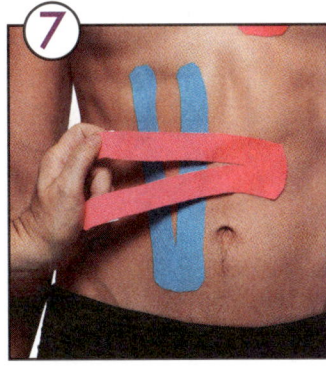

FOR THE ANTERIOR LOWER REGION THE MOTIONS WILL BE REVERSED TO PROVIDE STIMULUS IN AN OPPOSITE DIRECTION, THAN THE SUPERIOR REGION. THE DESIRED EFFECT IS TO "UNWIND" THE SPINE BY CREATING TENSION IN OPPOSITE DIRECTIONS.

5. Anchor is applied with no tension below area to be treated.

6. Place patient in low back extension and rotation to the opposite side. Apply light to moderate, 15-35% of available tension to the tails of the Kinesio Y strip. Splay the tails to spread the force over a larger tissue area. Lay down the ends with no tension. Rub to initiate adhesive prior to any further patient movement.

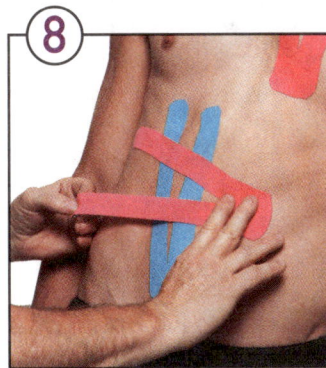

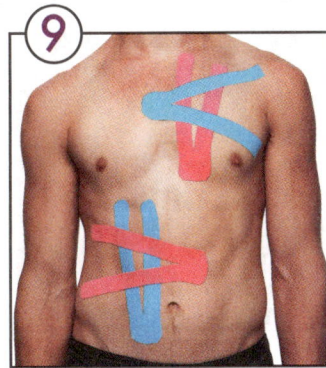

7. Application of a fascia correction technique tension in the tails. Begin by placing the anchor of the Kinesio Y strip, of approximately 6-8", 2" medially to the area to be treated, with no tension.

8. Have the patient move into back extension with rotation in the opposite direction of desired correction. With one hand hold the anchor to ensure no tension is added. Apply 15-50% of available tension using either the long and short or side to side technique as described in fascia correction. Apply the ends with no tension. Rub to initiate adhesive activation prior to any further patient movement.

9. Completed anterior Scoliosis taping for left lumbar curvature causing right shoulder to be forward and left shoulder to be back.

10. For the posterior superior aspect, tape should be applied on the opposite side of the anterior superior aspect. The desired effect is to "unwind" the spine.

Posterior view with corrections applied to the opposite sides as applied on the anterior. The combination stimulates a "derotational" affect of the spine.

OPTIONAL APPLICATION:

11. Patient is demonstrating a scoliosis with left shoulder anterior rotation.

12. Functional Correction Application to stimulate derotation. Apply and anchor of an I strip without tension from the anterior aspect of the shoulder near the middle region of the anterior deltoid. Place the patients shoulder into extension with rotation to the opposite side. Apply 50+% of available tension (less is always better to start) in an approximately 45 degree angle. Apply the second anchor inferior to rib 12.

13. Hold both anchors and have the patient move into shoulder flexion with rotation to opposite side. Slide two hands together and rub vigorously to initiate adhesive prior to any further patient movement.

14. Finished Functional Correction for rotation.

15. Functional Correction to stimulate shoulder elevation. Apply the anchor with no tension from the anterior aspect of the shoulder near the central 1/3 of the upper trapezius. Place the patient in shoulder extension with rotation to the opposite side. Apply 50+% of available tension (less is always better to start) apply over the medial border of the scapula ending inferior to rib 12.

16. Hold both anchors and have the patient move into shoulder flexion with rotation to opposite side. Slide two hands together and rub vigorously to initiate adhesive prior to any further patient movement.

17. Anterior view of anchor placement.

Be careful to not "overcorrect" during first application. Use a lower tension level for first several applications and increase as patient is able to tolerate.

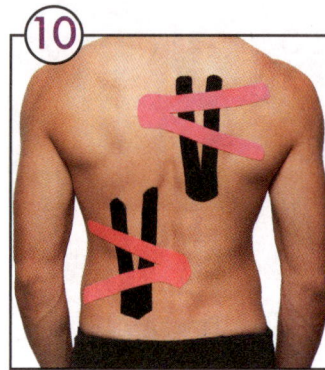
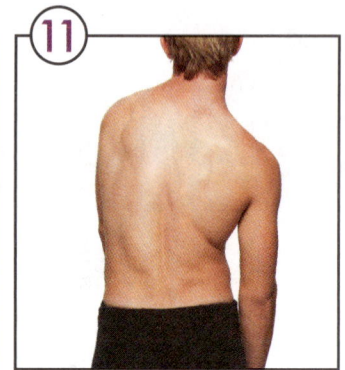
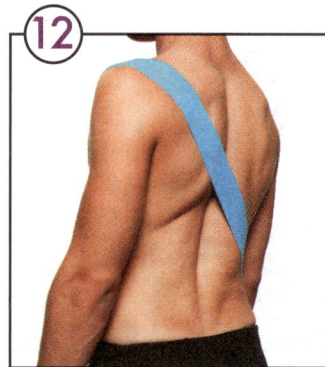
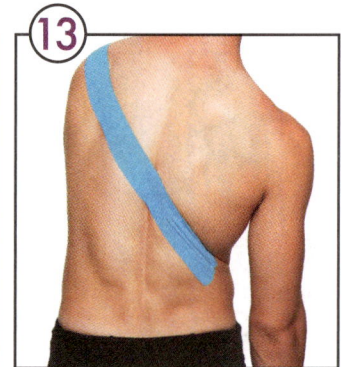
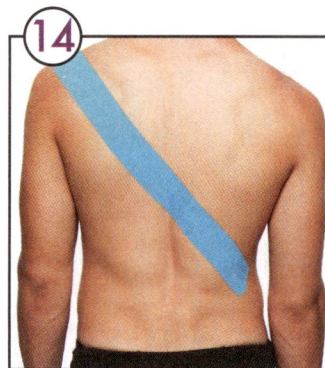
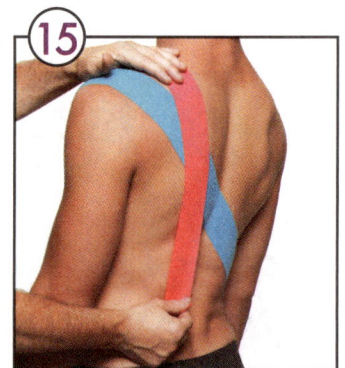
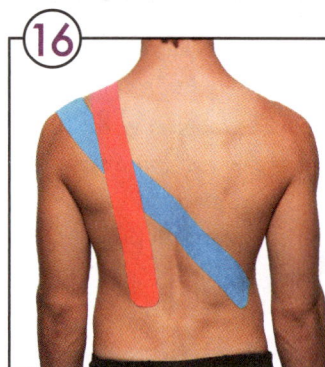
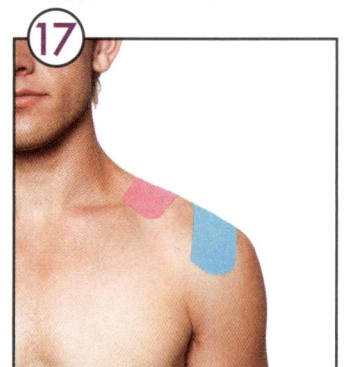

Rib Fracture or Contusion

A fracture or contusion of a rib is usually associated with direct blunt trauma. They are common in collision sports and it can be difficult to differentiate between a fracture or a contusion. Ribs 5 - 9 are the most commonly injured. Caution must be used in allowing a patient to participate with a fractured rib, if the fracture is pressed posterior, it may cause damage to a lung.

The Kinesio Taping Method assists by reducing edema, pain and provides stabilization of the fracture site. This technique has been found to be preferred by patients as it does not apply further pressure to a sensitive area and also allows for easier breathing.

In the acute phase of the injury, the practitioner may select to apply a lymphatic correction in a crisscross pattern over the site of the fracture or contusion.

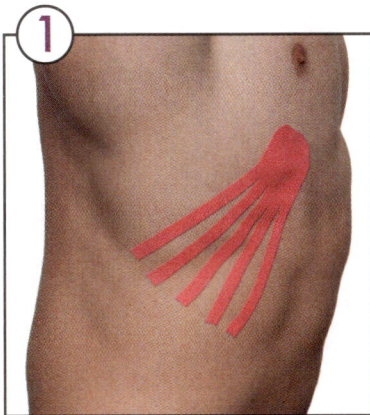

ACUTE PHASE FIRST 24 - 72 HOURS:

Application of lymphatic correction technique to reduce inflammation and pain.

1. Begin by applying the anchor of the first fan strip superior to the fx site or contusion with no tension. The patients should be placed in as much shoulder abduction as possible. Apply the tails of the fan strip at approximately a 45 degree angle with paper off, 0-20% of available tension. Lay down the ends with no tension. Pat to initiate adhesive prior to any further patient movement.

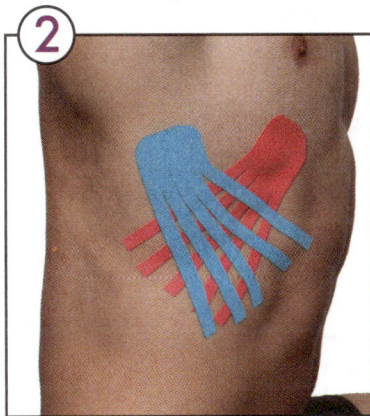

2. The second strip is applied superior to the fx site of the rib fracture or contusion as to allow for the two strips will form a crisscross pattern. The patients should be placed in as much shoulder abduction as possible. Apply the tails of the fan strip at approximately a 45 degree angle with paper off, 0-20% of available tension. Lay down the ends with no tension. Pat to initiate adhesive prior to any further patient movement.

POST ACUTE:

3. The first strip applied is a mechanical correction technique.

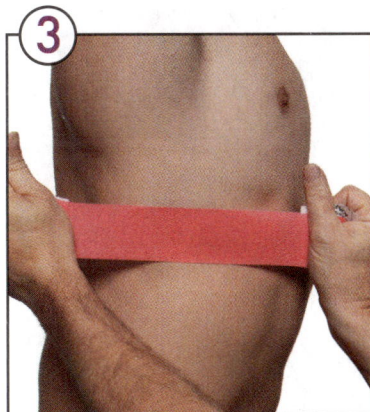

Have the patient abduct their shoulder to approximately 90 degrees, or as far as pain allows. Tear the center of the paper backing of an approximately 6-8" Kinesio I strip. Apply 50-75% of available tension (or as much tension as the patient pain allows).

Place the center of the Kinesio I strip over the fracture or contusion site with downward pressure. Make sure to not apply too much downward pressure as to increase pain.

Have the patient take in a full breath and lay down the two ends of the Kinesio I strip with no tension. Rub to initiate adhesive prior to any further patient movement. A second corrective strip may be appropriate depending upon the size of the patient.

4. Apply one mechanical correction strip anterior to the suspected fracture or contusion site.

With the arm still in an abducted position, tear the center of the paper backing of an approximately 6" Kinesio I strip and apply 50-75% of available tension with downward pressure.

Have the patient take in a full breath and lay down the two ends of the Kinesio I strip with no tension. Rub to initiate adhesive prior to any further patient movement.

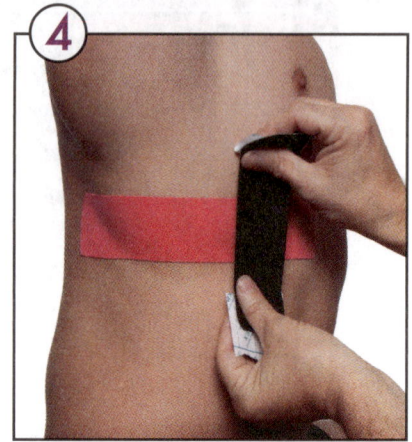

5. Apply one mechanical correction strip posterior to the suspected fracture or contusion site with downward pressure.

With the arm still in an abducted position, tear the center of the paper backing of an approximately 6" Kinesio I strip and apply 50-75% of available tension with downward pressure.

Have the patient take in a full breath and lay down the two ends of the Kinesio I strip with no tension. Rub to initiate adhesive prior to any further patient movement.

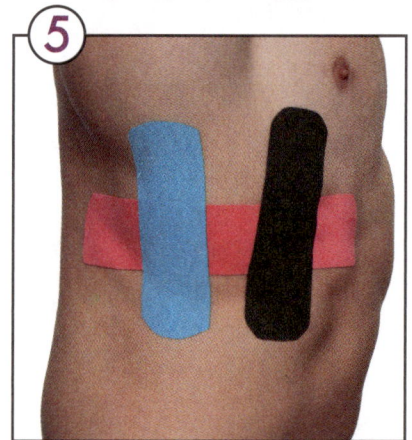

OPTIONAL SPACE CORRECTIONS:

6. Donut Hole technique. Begin by cutting a hole of approximately the size of a dime in all three 4-6" Kinesio I strips. Tear the middle of the paper backing. Peel back the paper backing and place the patient in as much shoulder abduction as pain allows. Apply paper off to light, 15-25% of available tension to the I strip. Place the Kinesio Strip with the center of the donut hole directly over the rib fx. Have the patient take in a full breath and lay down the tails without tension. Rub to activate adhesive prior to any further patient movement. Repeat this strip application 2-3 times to create space directly over the fracture or contusion site.

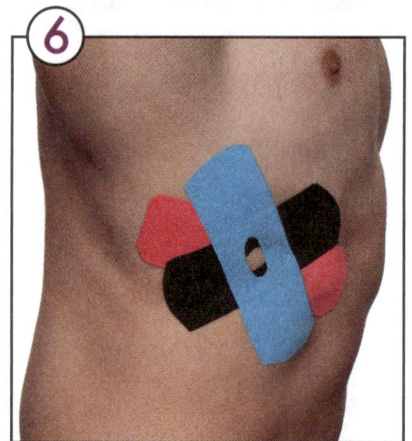

7. Web Cut technique. Begin by cutting 4-5 slits into an approximately 6-8" Kinesio I strip, leaving a 1-2" anchor on each end. Begin by placing the patient in as much shoulder abduction as pain allows. Apply 10-20% of available tension to the center of the web cut directly over the fx site. Lay down the ends with no tension. Pat to initiate adhesion prior to any further patient movement.

The practitioner may also select to apply a tension in the center of the I strip as described in the donut hole technique.

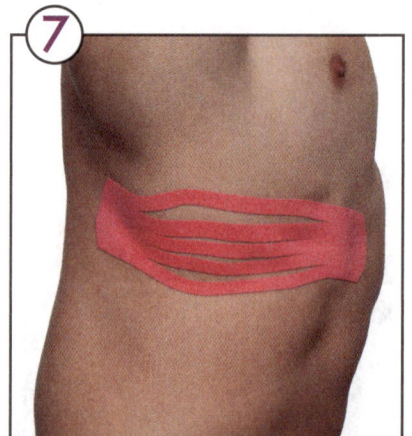

Intercostal Neuralgia

Intercostal neuralgia is seen as severe sharp pain along the course of the nerves located in the intercostal region. It may exhibit itself during cases of prolonged coughing.

The Kinesio Taping Method will assist by reducing edema, and pain along with the neural pathway.

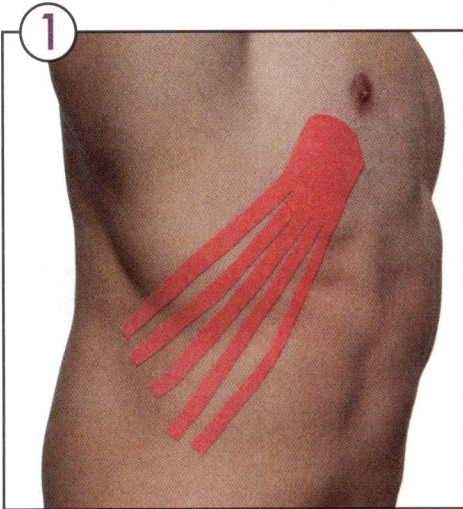

TREATMENT FOR INFLAMMATION IS PROVIDED BY APPLYING TWO KINESIO LYMPHATIC CORRECTIVE FAN STRIPS.

1. Have the patient move into shoulder abduction and lateral flexion towards the non painful side. Place the first lymphatic Kinesio fan anchor approximately 3-4″ superior and medial to the area of pain with no tension. Angle the fan tails at 45 degrees in an inferior and posterior direction with 0-20% of available tension. Pat to initiate adhesive prior to any further patient movement.

2. Have the patient maintain shoulder abduction and lateral flexion towards the non painful side. The second lymphatic fan anchor is approximately 3-4″ superior and posterior to the area of pain with no tension. Angle the fan tails at 45 degrees in an inferior and anterior direction with 0-20% of available tension. Pat to initiate adhesive prior to any further patient movement.

The fan strips should form a crisscross pattern.

Completed application of the Kinesio Taping Method for Intercostal Neuralgia.

The practitioner may select to apply a Web Cut in place of the Lymphatic Technique. For example see Fractured or Contusion to Rib.

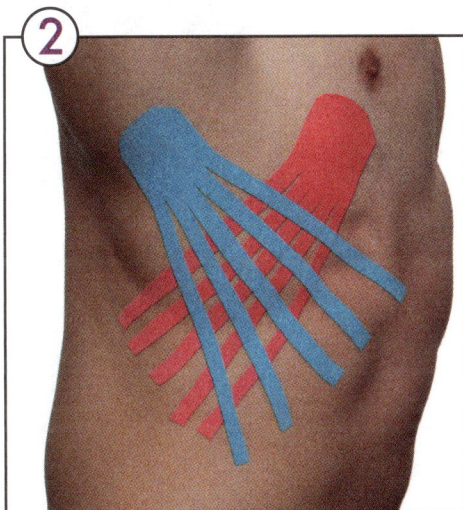

Costochondral Separation or Sprain

A separation or sprain to the junction of the costochondral cartilage and rib is a common injury, even more common than rib fractures. It is generally caused by rotation to the rib cage or direct blunt trauma (such as landing on a ball). Pain and possible separation can be palpated on the junction of the castocartilage and the ribs. There will be difficulty with breathing and rotation movements of the thoracic spine.

The Kinesio Taping Method will assist in reduction of edema, or pain and provides stabilization of the injury site. This technique has been found to be preferred by patients as it does not apply further pressure to a sensitive area and also allows for easier breathing.

In the acute phase of the injury, the practitioner may select to apply a lymphatic correction in a crisscross pattern over the site of the separation or sprain.

ACUTE PHASE, FIRST 24-72 HOURS:

In the acute phase two lymphatic correction strips will be applied.

1. Place the patient in as much shoulder abduction as pain allows. Apply the anchor of the Kinesio fan strip with no tension superior and posterior to the costochondral joint. Apply 0-20% of available tension over the injured costochondral joint at approximately a 45 degree angle. Lay down the ends with no tension. Pat to initiate adhesive prior to any further patient movement.

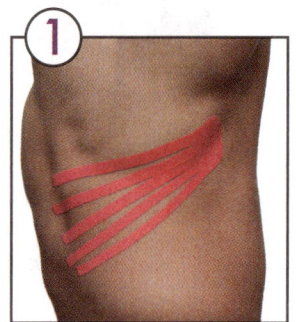

2. A second strip begins by placing the anchor of the Kinesio fan strip superior and medial to the costochondral joint. Apply 0-20% of available tension over the injured costochondral joint at approximately a 45 degree angle. Lay down the ends with no tension. Pat to initiate adhesive prior to any further patient movement.

   The practitioner may also select to use the donut hole or star techniques for complete description see Sterno Clavicular joint.

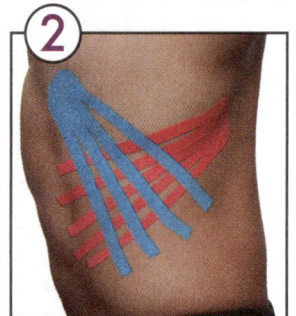

POST-ACUTE:

3. Apply a mechanical correction technique. For complete description see Rib Fracture.

   Have the patient abduct their shoulder to approximately 90 degrees, or as far as pain allows. Tear the center of the paper backing of an approximately 6-8" Kinesio I strip. Apply 50-75% of available tension. Place the center of the Kinesio I strip over injured costochondral site with downward pressure. Make sure to not apply too much downward pressure as to increase pain. Have the patient take in a full breath and lay down the two ends of the Kinesio I strip with no tension. Rub to initiate adhesive prior to any further patient movement. A second corrective strip may be appropriate depending upon the size of the patient.

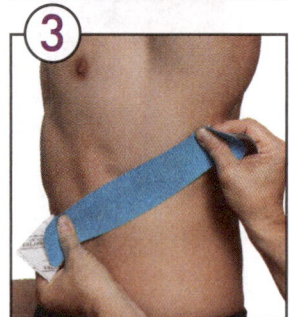

4. Apply two mechanical strips as described above. One anterior and one posterior to the costochondral injury.

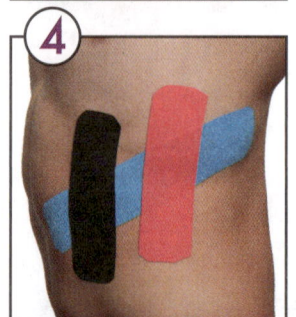

Erector Spinae Muscle Strain, Lumbar Region

This muscle group provides vertebral stabilization and can become injured as the result of sudden overload possibly in extension, weak muscles, trunk rotation, and may be associated with lumbar intervertebral disk herniation.

The Kinesio Taping Technique will assist by reducing acute or chronic muscle spasm, edema, and pain. Several application techniques will be demonstrated, these are not the only options available to the practitioner. Following a complete evaluation, the practitioner may select variations of the described techniques.

An option which is not shown is the star technique which is demonstrated in the lumbar disk herniation.

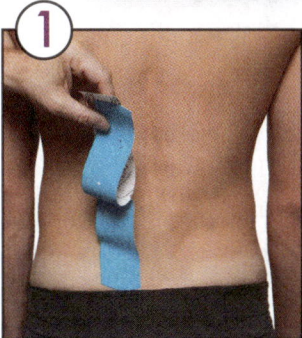

APPLICATION OF INHIBITION KINESIO TAPING METHOD FOR THE ERECTOR SPINAE MUSCLE GROUP WITH AN I STRIP.

1. Place the patient in a neutral spine position and apply the anchor of the Kinesio I strip a minimum of 2" below the area of pain. Apply the anchor below the pant line. The practitioner may find that this strip is more effective by placing the anchor below the SI joint and as low as the mid gluteal region. If the pain is located in the thoracic or cervical region, apply the base approximately 2" below the initiation of pain.

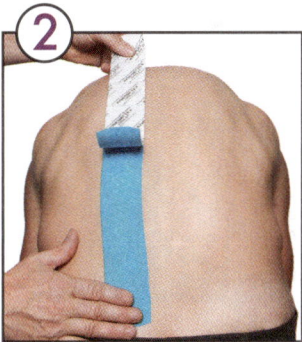

2. Have the patient move into as much hip flexion as they are able to with rotation to the opposite side. Apply the tail with paper off to light, 15-25% of available tension over the central region of the erector spinae muscle.

   Due to spasm or limitation of movement the patient may keep a "flat back" and have limited hip flexion.

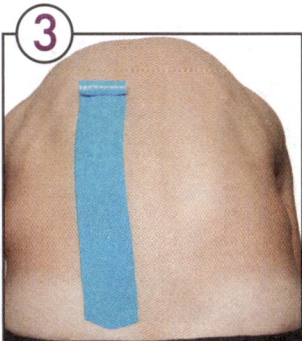

3. For the last approximately 2", lay down the end with no tension. Initiate adhesive activation prior to any further patient movement.

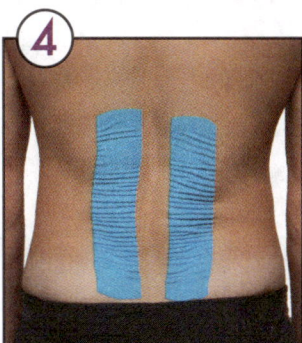

4. Either have the patient return to neutral posture position, or have the patient move into forward flexion with rotation to the opposite side. This will allow the second Kinesio I strip to be properly applied. Repeat the application steps as described above.

5. This technique can use the Kinesio Y strip unilaterally, or bilaterally. For application technique please see Kinesio I strip on previous page.

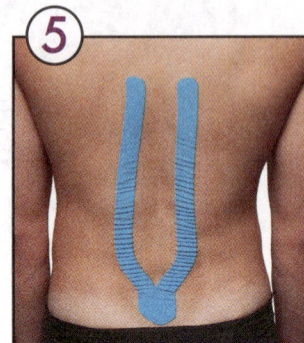

H TECHNIQUE APPLICATION

Application of inhibition Kinesio I strip bilaterally for Erector Spinae muscle strain or spasm.

6. First begin by applying a bilateral I strip erector spinae application as described on the previous page. The third strip is a space correction technique, or if desired a corrective technique may be used in acute muscle spasm or strain.

Measure a Kinesio I strip long enough to extend approximately 2" on either side of the previously applied Kinesio I strips.

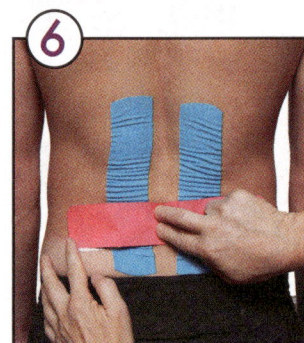

7. Have the patient move into as much flexion as pain allows. Tear the center of the paper backing and apply the center of the mechanical I strip between the two I strips and in the center of the region of greatest pain or spasm with no tension. One had holds the central anchor to ensure no tension is added during the next step. Next apply paper off to moderate, 15-35% tension to the space correction I strip across the vertical Kinesio I strip. Slide the hand holding the central anchor over the applied I strip to initiate adhesive. Apply the remaining tape with no tension. Rub to initiate adhesive prior to any further movement. Repeat for opposite side.

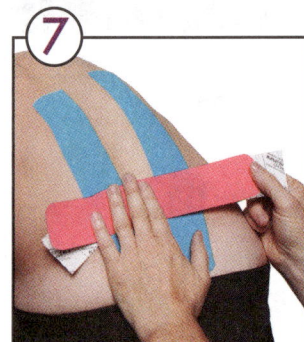

8. Completed Erector Spinae Muscle Strain, H Technique

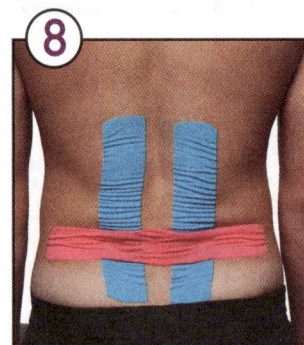

OPTIONAL: LONGER I STRIP LENGTH APPLICATION

9. The practitioner may choose to apply the I strips to the mid gluteal region for additional support and proprioceptive stimuli. Longer I strips minimizes the rubbing of pants or undergarments on the ends and improves the length of time the technique is able to be worn.

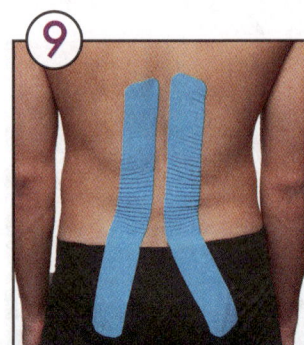

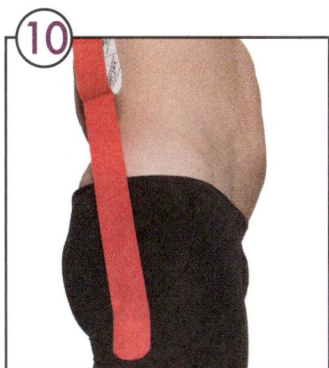

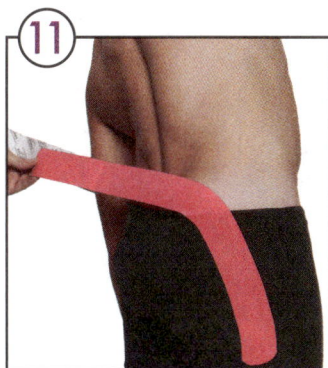

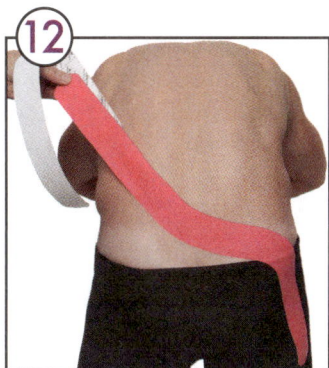

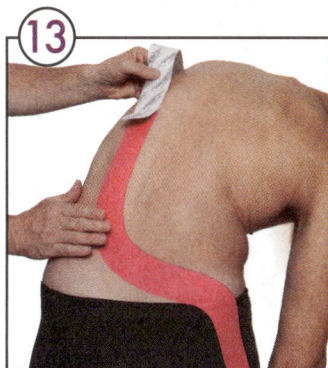

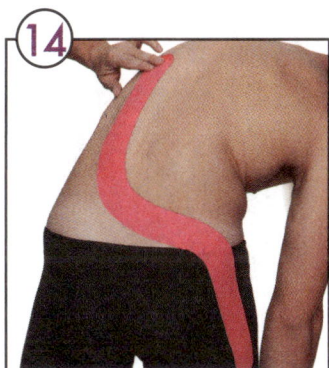

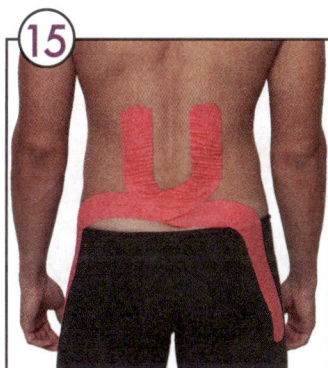

OPTIONAL X TECHNIQUE

10. Begin by measuring a length of 2" wide Kinesio Tex Tape from approximately the femoral greater trochanter, across lumbar region, and ending at the posterior inferior angle at the ribs.

    Apply the anchor of the Kinesio I strip inferior to the greater trochanter with no tension. The anchor can also be placed in the mid gluteal region.

11. Have the patient move into lateral flexion to the opposite side. Apply the Kinesio I strip, with paper off to light, 15-25% of available tension, over the tensor fascia latae and over the PSIS. Rub to initiate adhesive prior to any further patient movement

12. Have the patient move into as much hip flexion as the patient tolerates. Apply the Kinesio I strip across the area of pain with paper off to light, 15-25% of available tension.

    As the Kinesio I strip reaches the lateral border of the erector spinae muscle group, end this section of tape application. Rub to initiate adhesive prior to any further patient movement

13. With the patient remaining in flexion have them also move into lateral flexion to the side in which the tape was initially started. Angle the remaining Kinesio I strip along the erector spinae and end at posterior inferior angle of the thoracic ribs. Rub to initiate adhesive prior to any further patient movement

14. End the last approximately 2" of the Kinesio I strip with no tension. Rub to initiate adhesive prior to any further patient movement

15. For the opposite side, repeat the above steps.

16. Measure a strip of 2" wide Kinesio Tex Tape approximately the same length as used in the first layer. Begin by placing the base slightly medially and inferior to the first strip.

    Repeat steps as described in photos 12-16. Initiate adhesive activation prior to any further patient movement.

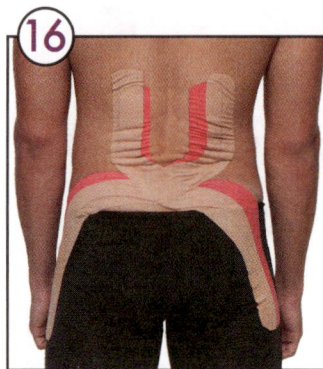

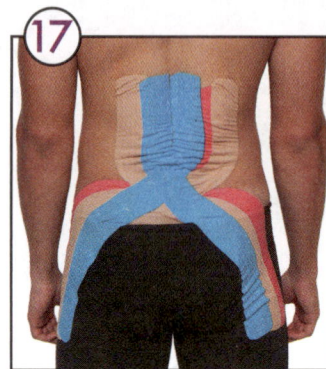

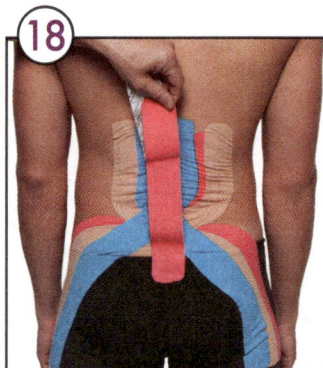

17. Measure a strip of 2" wide Kinesio Tex Tape approximately the same length as used in the first layer. Begin by placing the base slightly medially and superior to the second strip.

    Repeat steps as described in photos 12-16. Initiate adhesive activation prior to any further patient movement.

18. Begin the anchor of 2-3" (depending upon the patient size) Kinesio I strip 10-12" in length in the coccyx region with no tension.

19. Have the patient move into as much hip flexion as possible. Apply paper off to light, 15-25% of available tension to the Kinesio I strip over the area of pain. Lay down the last 2-3" with no tension.

    This strip may be applied as a space correction. See description below for image 20.

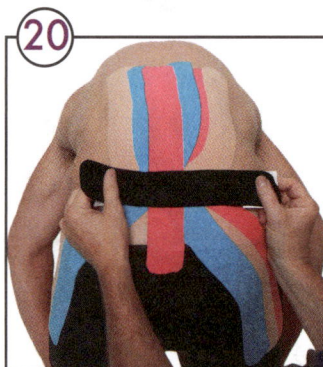

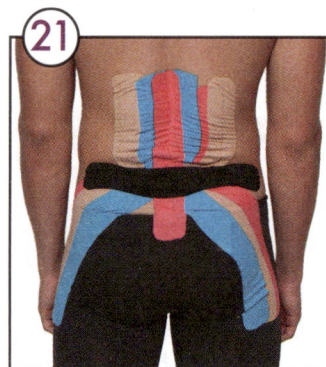

20. Apply a space correction tension in the center of the I strip. Tear the center of the paper backing and apply 25-35% of available tension to the center of the I strip. Place the center of the I strip over the area of pain and apply. Lay down the ends with no tension. Rub to initiate adhesive prior to any further patient movement.

    This strip may be applied as described in photos 20-21.

21. Completed Taping for Erector Spinae Muscle, X Technique

    The practitioner may determine that one, two, three, or all four strips are appropriate. Size, activity, patient strength level, and clinical condition along with practitioner experience will determine the appropriate taping application.

    For smaller patients you may want to apply steps in photos 10-14 add the steps in photos 18-21. For a slightly larger patient apply the steps in photos 10-14 then photo 16 then add photos 18-21. For larger patients you may need to apply the steps in photos 10-14, add photo 17 then add photos 18-21.

Sacroiliac Sprain or Inflammation

The Sacroiliac Joint is formed by the sacrum and ilium and is held in place with strong ligaments that allow for movement. This joint can become sprained, inflamed and hypomobile as the result of twisting, rotating or motions that load forces to this joint.

For years, many believed this joint did not move and that since it did not move, it could not become injured. When this joint becomes involved, it may lead to changes in posture, pelvic tilt, pelvic rotation, and lumbar spine mobility.

The Kinesio Taping method will assist in reduction of effusion, joint pain and assist in muscular balance associated with pelvic stabilization.

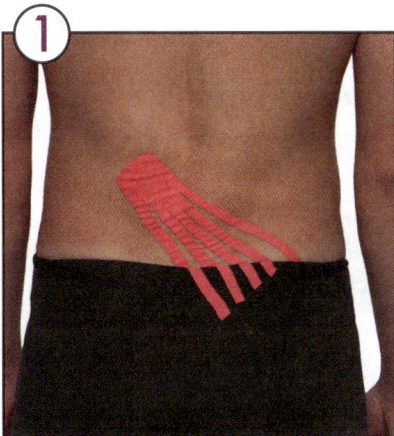

INITIAL TREATMENT FOR INFLAMMATION OR EDEMA IS PROVIDED BY APPLYING TWO KINESIO LYMPHATIC CORRECTION FAN STRIPS.

1. Begin by placing the anchor of the Kinesio fan strip approximately 2-3" superior to the sacroiliac (SI) joint along the spinous processes with the patient in a neutral spine position. Have the patient move into forward flexion with rotation to the opposite side of the injured joint. Apply 0-20% of available tension to the tails. The tails of the fan strip should be angled slightly downward at 45 degrees over the SI joint and ending near the superior aspect of the gluteus maximus. Ends are laid down with no tension. Pat to initiate adhesive prior to any further patient movement.

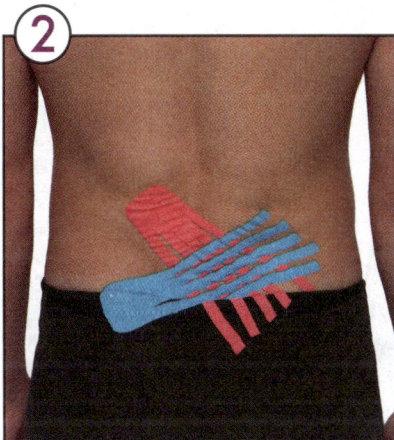

2. The second Kinesio fan strip is placed approximately 2-3" inferior to the SI joint along the spinous processes with the patient in neutral spine position. Have the patient move into forward flexion with rotation to the opposite side of the injured joint. Apply 0-20% of available tension to the tails. The tails of the fan strip should be angled upward at 45 degrees over the SI joint and ending near the superior aspect of the posterior superior iliac spine. Ends are laid down with no tension. Pat to initiate adhesive prior to any further patient movement.

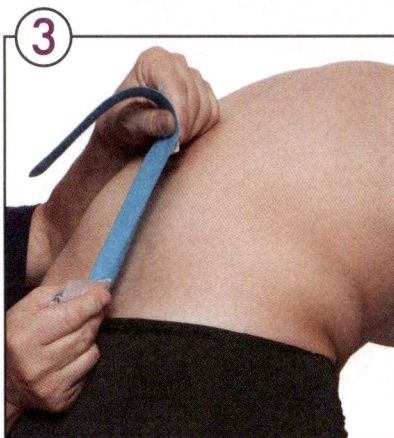

3. Another treatment option is to apply a space correction combined with an inhibition application to the erector spinae muscle. Begin by measuring a Kinesio I strip from 3-4" below the SI joint to approximately the 12th rib. Have the patient move into flexion. Tear the center of the paper backing approximately 5-6" from the inferior anchor. Apply paper off to moderate, 25-35% of available tension to the exposed tape. Apply the I strip with the added tension over the SI joint and lay down on the skin. Rub to initiate adhesive prior to any further patient movement.

4. Lay down the distal end without tension.

5. For the superior tail apply paper off to moderate, 15-35% of available tension. Lay down the end with no tension.

6. Rub the entire length of the I strip to initiate adhesive prior to any further patient movement.

7. Space correction center of I strip: Cut an approximately 6" Kinesio I strip. Tear the paper backing in the middle of the I strip. Apply 25-35% of available tension to the exposed section. With the patient either remaining in flexion, or having the patient move into flexion apply the Kinesio I strip over the area of the SI joint.

8. With one hand press down on the central section just applied to initiate adhesive. Peel of the paper backing on one end and lay down the end with no tension. Repeat this step for the other end. Rub entire I strip to initiate adhesive prior to any further patient movement.

9. For the second strip, which is forming the X over the SI joint, repeat the above steps as shown in photos 7-8.

The combination of a space correction over the SI joint will help to decrease pressure. The addition of the inhibition application for the erector spinae will assist with assisting normal muscle activity possibly assisting in normal function at the SI joint. By laying two additional space corrections over the SI joint there will be an accumulative effect in assisting pain reduction.

During the evaluation the practitioner may determine that one or more muscles are also involved. Possibly a tight iliopsoas, piriformis, gluteus maximus, or quadratus lumborum. If this is present application of an inhibition or facilitation application(s) should be applied.

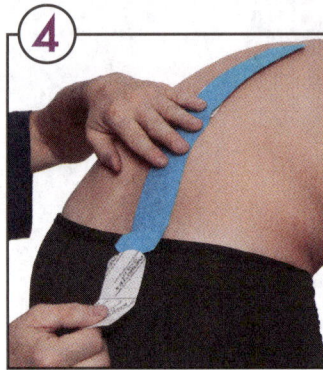

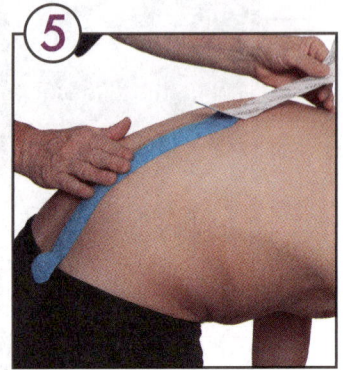

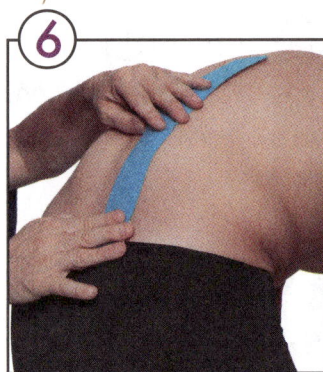

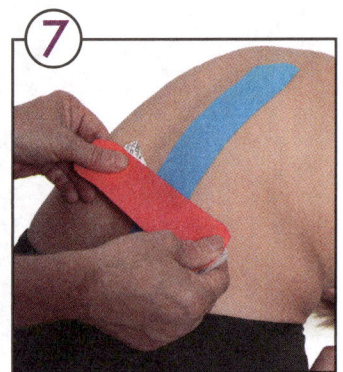

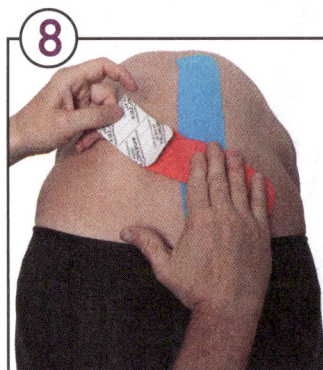

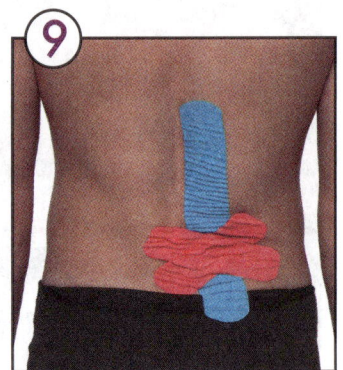

FACILITATION

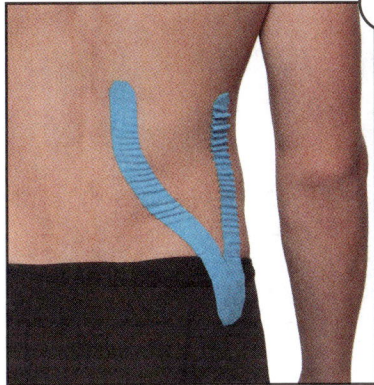

(1)

INHIBITION

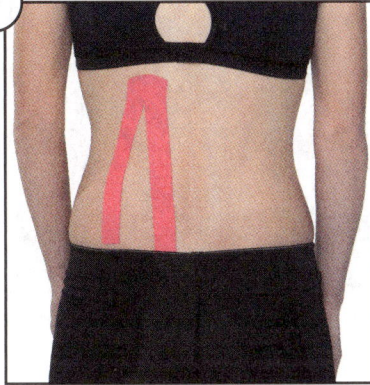

FACILITATION

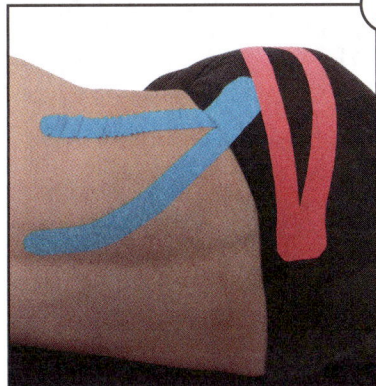

(2)

INHIBITION

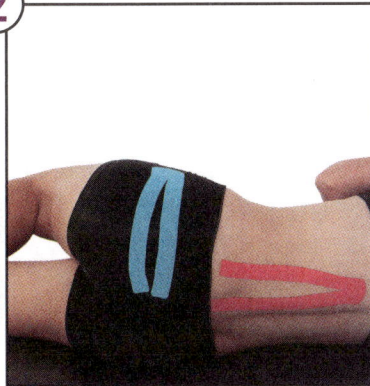

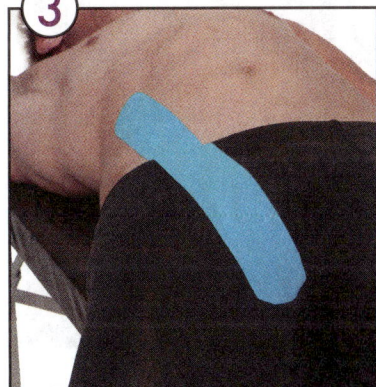

(3)

OPTIONAL MUSCLE APPLICATIONS

1. Application of Quadratus Lumborum facilitation Y strip. Begin anchor Y strip on PSIS with no tension, place the patient in hip flexion with rotation to the opposite side. Apply paper off to moderate, 15-35% of available tension, the medial tail is directed towards the transverse process of L1-2, lay down the end with no tension. The lateral tail is directed towards L3-4 transverse process. Lay down the end with no tension and rub to initiate adhesive prior to any further patient movement.

If appropriate apply a inhibition technique with paper off to light, 15-25% or available tension. Due the shape of the QL you may want to use two 1" I strips to form a Y strip.

2. Application of Piriformis Facilitation Y strip. Begin anchor of Y strip on the sacrum vertebrae 2-4 with no tension, place the patient in hip flexion and adduction. Apply paper off to moderate, 15-35% of available tension and direct the superior tail towards the superior aspect of the greater trochanter, lay down end with no tension. Direct inferior tail towards the inferior aspect of the greater trochanter lay down the end with no tension. Rub to activate adhesive prior to any further patient movement.

If appropriate apply a inhibition technique with paper off to light, 15-25% of available tension. Ends are applied with no tension.

3. Application of External Oblique Abdominus fascilitaiton I strip. Begin anchor of I strip at the external surfaces and inferior borders of the fifth to twelfth ribs with no tension. Have the patient move into back extension with rotation to the opposite side. Apply paper off to moderate, 15-35% of available tension and direct the Kinesio I strip to as close to the pubic symphysis as patient comfort and professional decorum allows. Lay down the end with no tension and rub to initiate adhesive prior to any further patient movement.

If appropriate apply an inhibition technique with paper off to light, 15-25% of available tension.

Spondylolysis and Spondylolisthesis

Spondylolysis is an acute or chronic condition to the vertebrae most commonly in the lumbar 4-5 region that can be either bilateral or ipsilateral. The pars interarticularis region of the vertebrae may be fractured from repetitive trauma or a congenital weakness. Spondylolisthesis is a complication or result of spondylolysis that results in an anterior movement of the vertebral body. These conditions are generally exacerbated by repetitive hyperextension movements.

The Kinesio Taping Method will assist by reducing effusion, pain and assist in muscular imbalance associated with pelvic stabilization.

Options which are not shown: erector spinae strain and lumbar disk.

ACUTE PHASE:

Initial treatment for inflammation or edema is provided by applying two lymphatic correction strips or web cut strips.

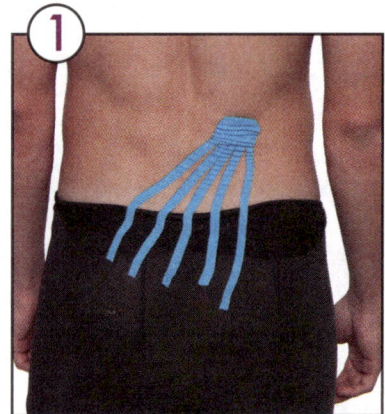

1. Begin by placing the anchor of the Kinesio fan strip approximately 2-3" superior and lateral to the location of the edema along the lateral flank with the patient in a neutral spine position. Have the patient move into forward flexion with rotation to the opposite side of the edema. Apply 0-20% of available tension to the tails angled downward at 45 degrees over the edema and ending near the superior aspect of the sacroiliac joint. Lay down the ends with no tension. Pat to initiate adhesive prior to any further patient movement.

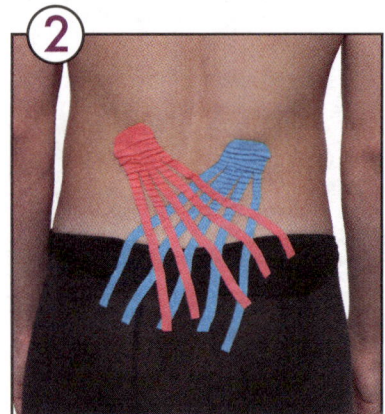

2. The second Kinesio fan strip is placed approximately 2-3" superior to the edema along the opposite lateral flank to strip one in the region. With the patient in neutral spine position. Have the patient move into forward flexion with rotation to the side of the edema. Apply 0-20% of available tension to the fan tails. The tails of the fan strip should be angled at 45 degrees downward over the edema and ending near the superior aspect of the sacroiliac joint. Lay down the ends with no tension. Pat to initiate adhesive prior to any further patient movement.

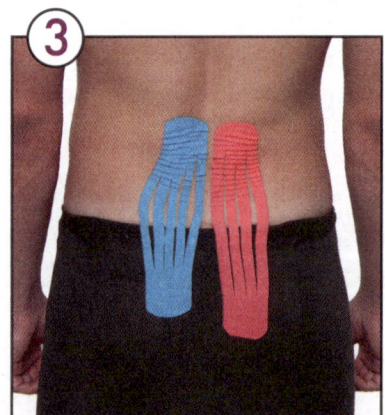

3. Application of two web cut strips. Cut 4-5 slits into the appropriate length Kinesio Tex Tape leaving 1-2" on each end. Tear the center of the paper backing and apply 10-20% of available tension to the center of the web cut. Place the patient in as much flexion and rotation to the opposite side as pain and edema allows. Apply the web cut with the center of the web cut over the central area of the edema. Lay down the ends with no tension. Pat to initiate adhesive prior to any further patient movement. Apply the second web cut in the same method.

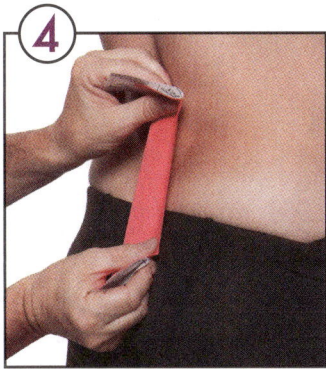

POST-ACUTE:
SPACE CORRECTION APPLICATION OF THE STAR TECHNIQUE

Space Correction application of the star technique.

4. Tear the center backing of a 6" Kinesio I strip. Apply paper off to moderate, 15-35% of available tension to the center of the I strip. Apply the center of the I strip directly over the area of pain with the patient in a neutral position.

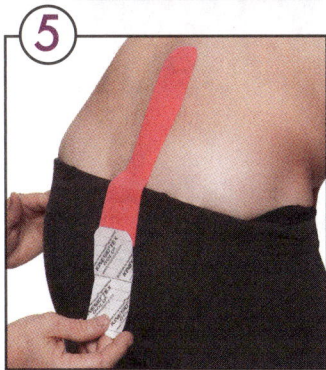

5. After the center is applied hold down the central area with one hand. This will initiate adhesive activation. Lay down the tails with no tension. Rub to initiate adhesive prior to any further patient movement.

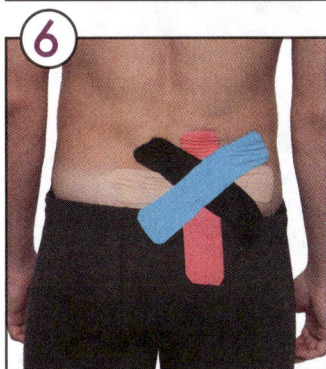

6. Apply 2-3 more space corrections. Repeat the above application technique. With the horizontal I strip the patient can be in a neutral position. With the two angle strips that make an X are applied with the patient in hip flexion and rotation to the opposite side.

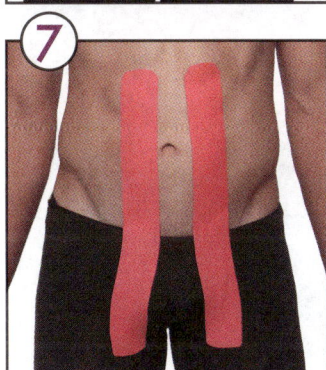

APPLICATION OF ILIOPSOAS INHIBITION

7. Begin anchor of Kinesio I strip, with no tension near the lesser tubercle of the femur, medial aspect of upper 1/3 of femur. Have the patient move into hip extension to place iliopsoas in a stretch position.

   Apply paper off to light, 15-25% of available tension to I strip trying to place the strip between the spinous processes of T12 and L1 and PSIS. Hitting between the insertion of Psoas Major, Psoas Minor and Illiacus. Apply the end with no tension. Activate the adhesive prior to any patient movement.

   Repeat this process for the opposite side.

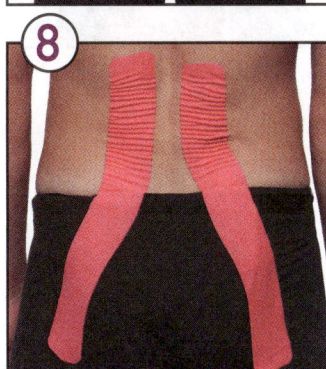

8. Application erector spinae and gluteal combination I strip. Measure an I strip from 3-4" below the ischial tuberosity to the 12th rib. Have the patient move into hip flexion. Place the anchor of the I strip, with no tension, approximately 3-4" below the ischial tuberosity with no tension.

   Have the patient move into hip flexion and flexion at the knees (squatting position). Apply the anchor without tension. Apply paper off to light, 15-25% of available tension and angle I strip over the ischial tuberosity continuing up through the gluteals through the SI joint and up the erector spinae muscle group. Apply the end with no tension. Rub to initiate adhesive prior to any further patient movement. Repeat the above for the opposite side.

   If the patient is limited in hip flexion, begin by placing the patient side lying in maximum allowable hip and knee flexion on the first side to be taped.

Application of an anterior (abdominal) support I strip. The strip should be approximately from the left ASIS to right ASIS plus 4-6" per side.

9. Begin by having the patient move into as much extension as possible. Apply light to moderate 15-35% of available tension to the I strip center between the ASIS and ASIS. Place the tape in an upward, lifting motion approximately 2-3" below a line drawn between the two ASIS. Rub to initiate adhesive prior to any further movement.

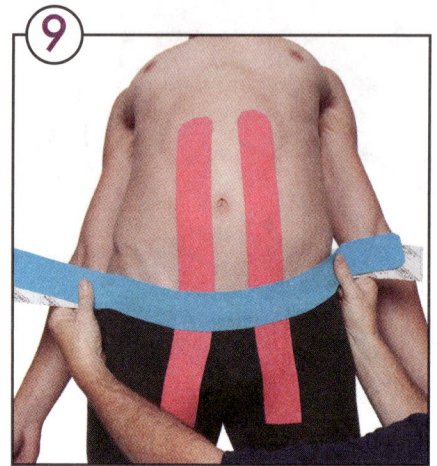

10. Next have the patient move into as much lateral flexion as possible to the opposite side while maintaining extension if possible.

One hand holds the Kinesio strip just lateral to the ASIS. The end of the Kinesio strip is angled up the lateral aspect of the chest and directed towards the axillary area with paper off to light, 15-25% of available tension. Lay down the ends with no tension. Rub to initiate adhesive prior to any further patient movement.

Repeat process for opposite side.

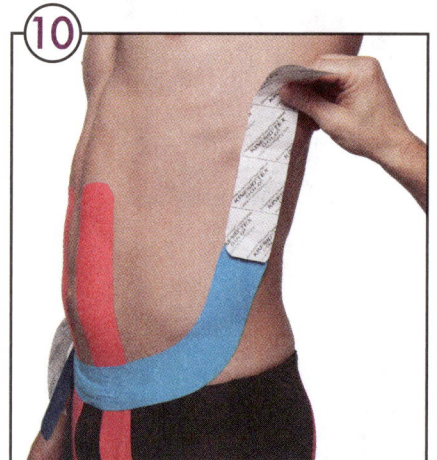

11. Completed anterior application.

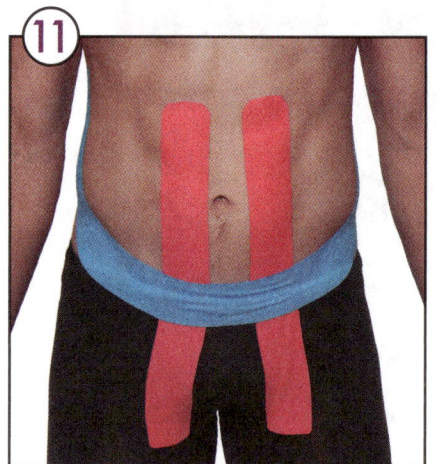

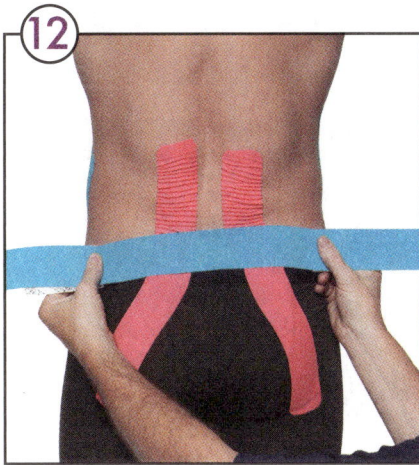

12. Application of a posterior (lumbar) support I strip. The strip should be approximately from the left PSIS to right PSIS plus 4-6" per side.

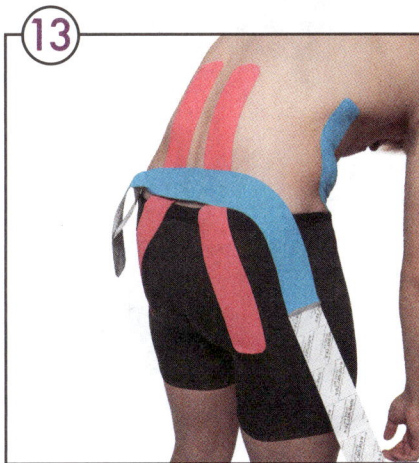

13. Place the patient in as much flexion as possible. Tear the center of the I strip and apply paper off to light, 15-25% of available tension to center of the I strip. Apply the I strip from PSIS to PSIS crossing the area of pain with a slightly downward pressure. Rub the applied Kinesio I strip to initiate activation prior to any further movement. Hold the applied I strip at the PSIS and have the patient move into lateral flexion. Apply the remaining length of tape over the greater trochanter towards the tensor fascia latae with paper off to light, 15-25% of available tension. Lay down the end with no tension. Rub to initiate adhesive prior to any further patient movement.

Repeat for opposite side.

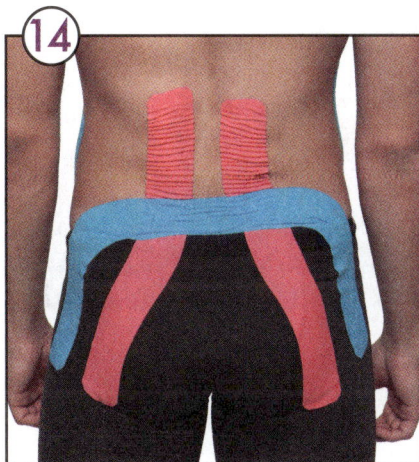

14. Completed posterior application. The portion of the I strip located over the gluteal muscles may be applied using a fascia correction strip. Either long and short or side to side can be used.

Myofascial Low Back Pain

Myofascial low back pain is a syndrome resulting from pressure applied to a trigger point within a muscle. The trigger point is a sensitive area which refers pain to a generally predictable distribution. The pain syndrome has been associated with muscle involvement to the quadratus lumborum and piriformis. The Kinesio Taping Technique also includes the external oblique abdominus with a fascial correction technique. If during the evaluation the practitioner is able to isolate a trigger point within a muscle, the trigger point should also be treated to reduce radiating pain.

The Kinesio Taping Technique will assist in reducing edema, pain, muscle tension and trigger point sensitivity.

FACILITATION   ①   INHIBITION

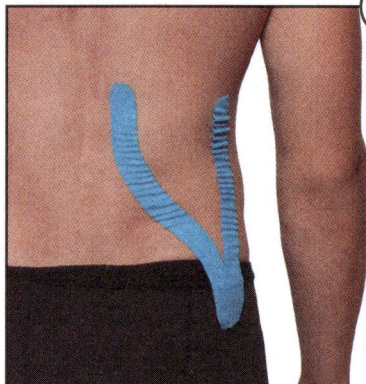
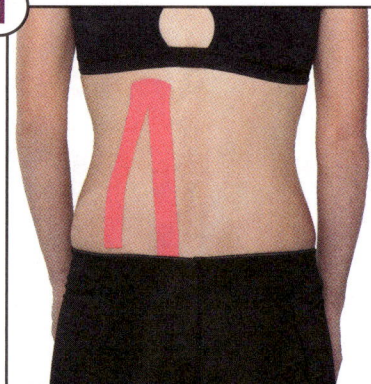

1. Application of Quadratus Lumborum facilitation Y strip. Begin anchor of Y strip on PSIS with no tension, place the patient in hip flexion with rotation to the opposite side. Apply paper off to moderate, 15-35% of available tension, the medial tail is directed towards the transverse process of L1-2, lay down the end with no tension. The lateral tail is directed towards L3-4 transverse process. Lay down the end with no tension and rub to initiate adhesive prior to any further patient movement.

   If appropriate apply a inhibition technique with paper off to light, 15-25% of available tension. Due to shape of the QL you may want to use two 1" I strips to form a Y strip.

FACILITATION   ②   INHIBITION

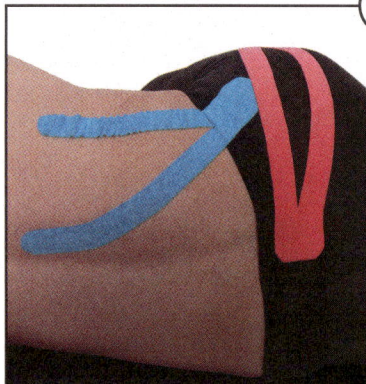
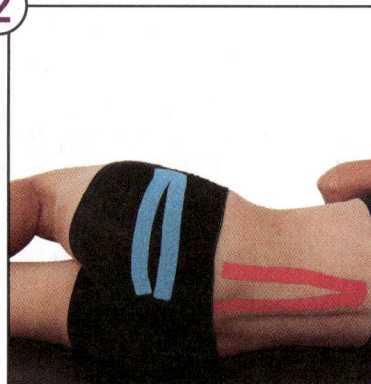

2. Application of Piriformis Facilitation Y strip. Begin anchor of Y strip on the sacrum vertebrae 2-4 with no tension, place the patient in hip flexion and adduction. Apply paper off to moderate, 15-35% of available tension and direct the superior tail towards to superior aspect of he greater trochanter, lay down end with no tension. Direct inferior tail towards the inferior aspect of the greater trochanter lay down the end with no tension. Rub to activate adhesive prior to any further patient movement.

   If appropriate apply a inhibition technique with paper off to light, 15-25% of available tension. Ends are applied with no tension.

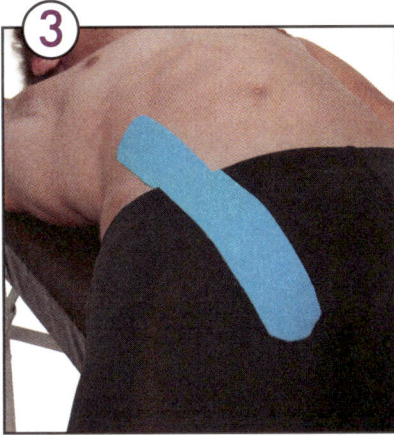

3. Application of External Oblique Abdominus facilitation I strip. Begin anchor of I strip at external surfaces and inferior borders of the fifth to twelfth ribs with no tension. Have the patient move into back extension with rotation to the opposite side. Apply I paper off to moderate, 15-35% of available tension and direct the Kinesio I strip to as close to the pubis symphysis as patient comfort and professional decorum allows. Lay down the end with no tension and rub to initiate adhesive prior to any further patient movement.

If appropriate apply an inhibition technique with paper off to light, 15-25% or available tension.

APPLICATION OF FASCIA CORRECTION

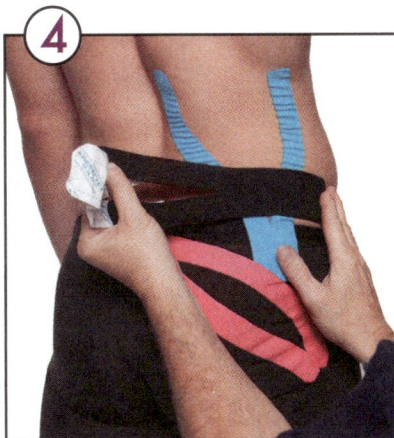

4. Fascia Correction tension in base. Begin by placing the anchor of the Kinesio Y strip with no tension approximately ½ to 1″ from the area of limitation. Apply tension to the tape in the direction fascia correction is desired. With one hand hold the anchor to ensure no tension is added, apply paper off to moderate, 15-50% of available tension. The oscillation can either be "long and short" or "side to side". Lay down the ends with no tension and rub to initiate adhesive prior to any further patient movement.

With this application, the practitioner would apply the fascia correction in the area they believe is limiting normal motion of the low back.

APPLICATION OF SPACE CORRECTION, IF TRIGGER POINT HAS BEEN IDENTIFIED. Apply an I
strip tension in the middle space correction technique directly over the trigger point.

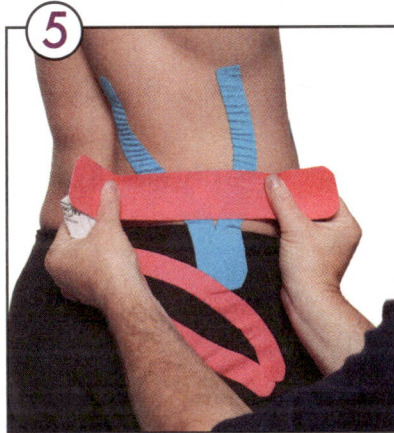

5. Begin by placing the patient in a neutral or slight lateral flexion to the opposite side. Tear the paper backing in the center of 4-6″ Kinesio I strip. Apply paper off to moderate, 15-35% of available tension and apply directly over the area of the trigger point or pain as indicated by the evaluation.

Lay the two ends of the Kinesio I strip down with no tension. Rub to initiate adhesive prior to any further patient movement.

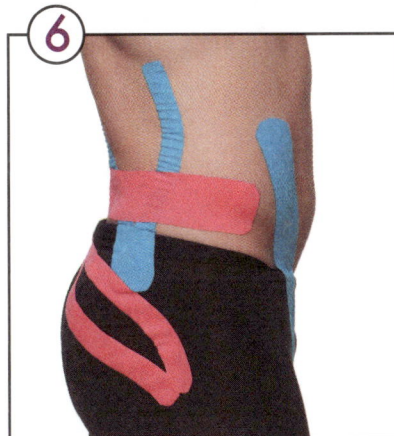

6. Complete application of the Myofascial Low Back pain. The Quadratus Lumborum, Piriformis and External Oblique have been demonstrated as facilitation. Your evaluation may determine all three should be applied as inhibition, or some other combination of inhibition and facilitation. Other muscles may also be involved: illiocostalis, transverse abdominus and iliopsoas are other examples.

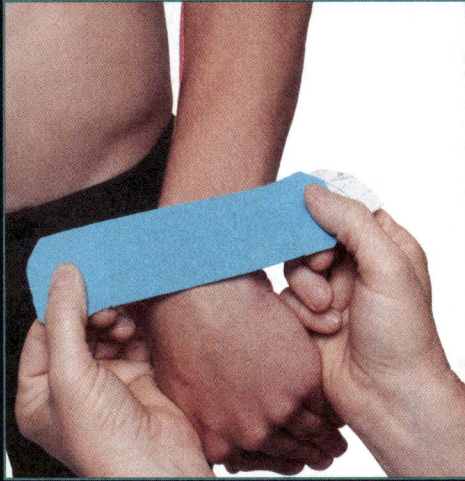

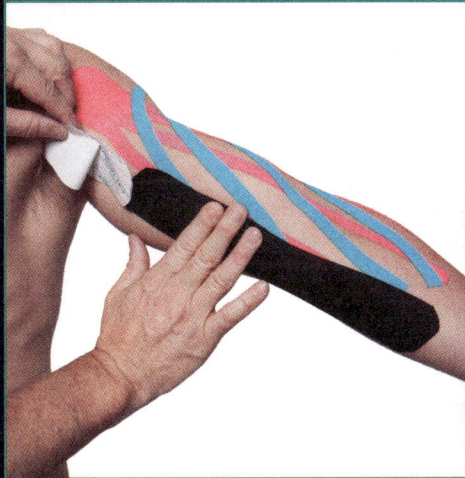

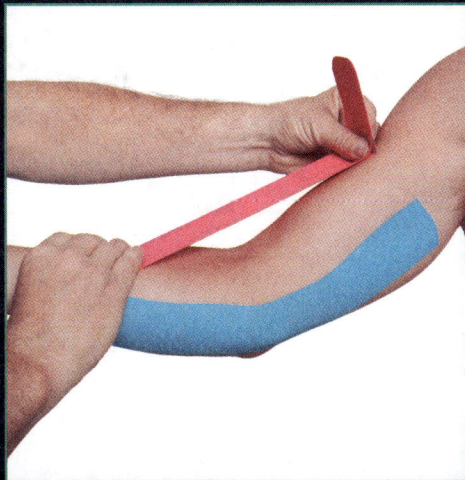

SECTION 5

Elbow and Forearm

Valgus Laxity of the Elbow

A chronic Valgus Laxity of the Elbow may develop from repetitive valgus forces being applied during overhead activities. During overhead motions, such as pitching in baseball, the shoulder is abducted with external rotation, elbow flexion and a valgus force. This causes the ulnar collateral ligament of the elbow to become lax over time, allowing for excessive joint motion at the elbow. Valgus laxity can also occur from a valgus force during hyperextension.

The Kinesio Taping Method will assist in reducing edema, pain and with the application of a ligament correction and functional correction limit excessive valgus motion.

APPLICATION OF A LIGAMENT CORRECTION TECHNIQUE

The distal anchor and proximal end need to be long enough to dissipate the high degree of tension over the UCL of the elbow. If the anchors are too short the high tension will "pull off" the ends, limiting wear time.

1. Begin anchor of ligament correction I strip approximately 4" below the medial epicondyle of the humerus, with no tension. Before application of the corrective strip, first estimate the line of the corrective strip to assist in application.

2. Place one hand on the anchor of the ligament correction strip prior to applying tension to the Kinesio strip. Apply moderate to severe, 75-100% of available tension over the length of the ligament.

3. When the Kinesio strip has passed the origin of the ligament, move the hand holding the base with no tension to the point of end tension above the elbow.

4. Lay the end of the Kinesio strip down with no tension. Vigorously rub to initiate adhesive prior to any patient movement.

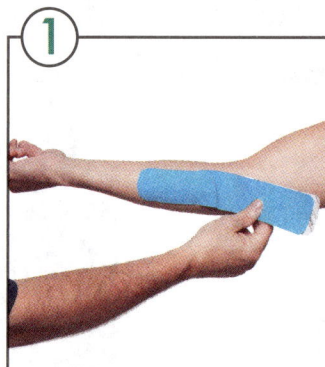

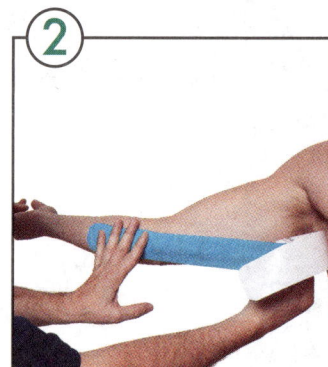

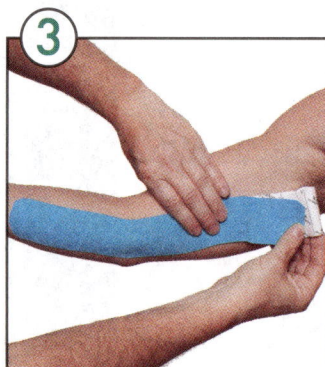

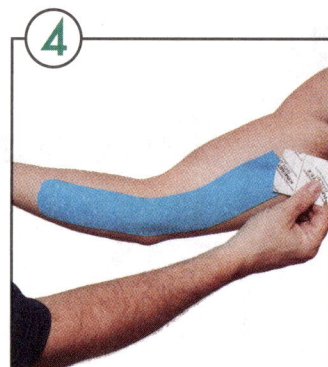

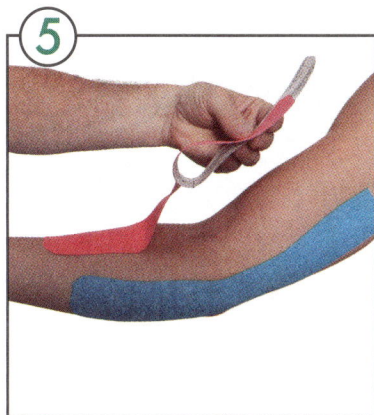

APPLICATION OF A FUNCTIONAL CORRECTION
TECHNIQUE Limiting full extension will reduce stress loading on the UCL.

5. Measure a Kinesio I strip approximately 5-6″ above and below the antecubital space. Begin by placing the patients elbow in approximately 20-30 degrees of elbow flexion, or in slight flexion prior to the point of any pain.

   Apply distal anchor of 3-4″ inferior to the antecubital space with no tension.

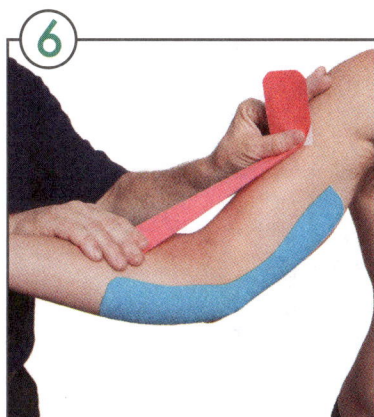

6. With one hand hold the inferior anchor to limit tension being added to the anchor. Apply 50+% of available tension to the body of the I strip. The amount of tension added is determined by the practitioner. The percentage of tension applied to the Kinesio strip is to limit elbow extension and assist with elbow flexion (higher tension limits more movement). Having a lower tension level during initial application is generally suggested.

   Apply the proximal anchor of 3-4″ in length with no tension.

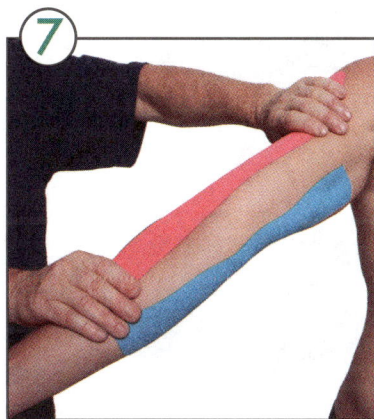

7. Place one hand on each anchor and have the patient move into extension. Next move both hands towards the center of the I strip. Vigorously rub to initiate adhesive otherwise the high tension level of the functional correction will cause the I strip to "pull off" the skin.

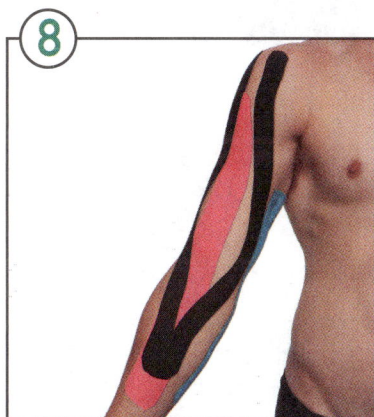

OPTIONAL:

8. Application of basic biceps Kinesio Taping Technique, from insertion to origin is shown. This should be placed prior to the functional correction technique. For complete review, see bicipital tenosynovitis. The Biceps Brachii can also be treated with a facilitation correction in the post-acute stages.

   By applying the anchor of the biceps tendon on the functional correction strip the adhesion of the adhesive will be limited. This will result in the anchor to have limited wear time.

Valgus Laxity of the Elbow

Bursitis of the Elbow

The Olecranon Bursa is the most commonly injured bursa of the elbow. It lies between the skin and the olecranon process of the humerus. A large effusion may be present on the posterior aspect of the elbow with limited range-of-motion in flexion.

The Kinesio Taping Method will assist by reducing edema and pain.

ACUTE PHASE - 24-72 HOURS:

Two lymphatic correction strips will be applied.

1. Strip one: Place the elbow in as much flexion as possible. Apply anchor 4-5" above medial epicondyle. Apply 0-20% of available tension and direct the fan strips at 45 degree angle over the olecranon bursa to the lateral aspect of the radius. Lay down the ends with no tension and pat or rub to initiate adhesive prior to any further patient movement.

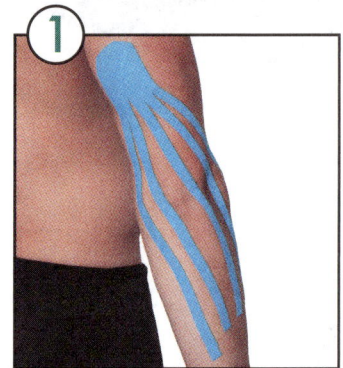

2. Strip two: with the elbow remaining in flexion, place anchor 4-5" above the lateral aspect of the lateral epicondyle. Apply 0-20% of available tension and direct the fan strips at a 45 degree angle over the olecranon bursa to the medial aspect of the ulna. The two strips should create a crisscross pattern over the inflammation. Lay down the ends with no tension and pat or rub to initiate adhesive prior to any further patient movement.

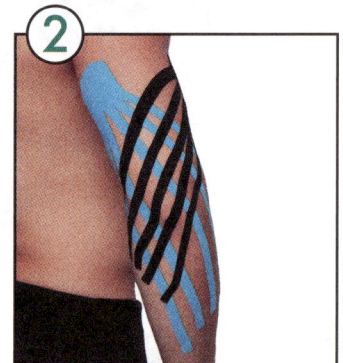

POST-ACUTE PHASE - POST 72 HOURS:
OPTION 1:

Application of a space correction technique tension in center of I strip.

3. Have the patient move into as much elbow flexion as pain or edema allows. Tear the center of an approximately 6-8" long Kinesio I strip through the paper backing. Apply paper off to moderate, 15-35% of available tension to the center of the Kinesio I strip. Place the center of the 2" wide Kinesio I strip over the olecranon bursa. Lay down each end of the Kinesio strip with no tension. Rub to initiate adhesive prior to any further patient movement.

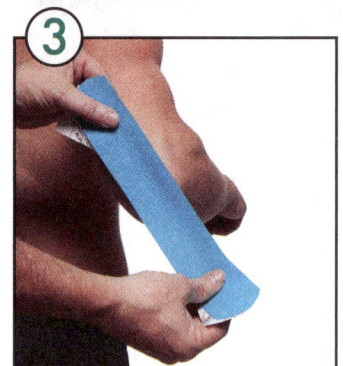

   A series of two to three strips can be applied, with the intersection of each strip located over the desired space correction location (area of desired "pocket").

4. Convolutions of the skin should be evident when in extension. If convolutions are not present the tape was applied with too much tension.

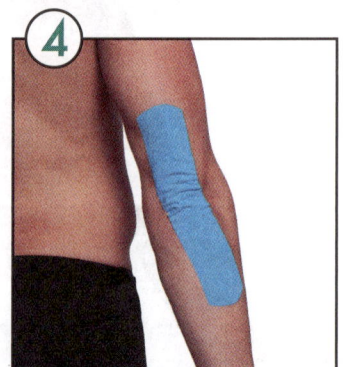

   If a series of strips are used remember to keep the tension level lower so the accumulative affect of the tape lifts the skin and does not "push down".

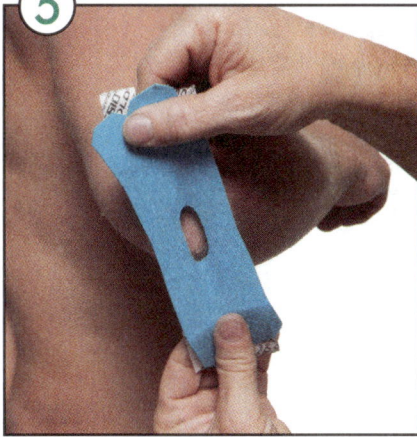

OPTION 2: DONUT HOLE TECHNIQUE

5. Cut a hole about the size of a dime in the center of a 6" Kinesio I strip and the distal 1-2" of each end into two to three tails. Do not cut more than ½ of the available width of the Kinesio Tape. This will reduce its ability to adhere, lift the skin and reduce recoil effect.

Place the elbow in as much flexion as pain or edema allows. Tear the center of the paper backing and peel back, apply paper off to light, 15-25% of available tension, and place the hole directly over the area of desired space.

Lay down the tails on both ends with no tension. Splay the ends to dissipate tension which was created in the area of the donut. Rub to initiate adhesive prior to any patient movement.

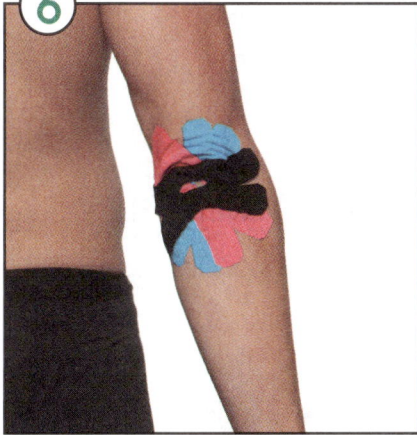

6. Several Donut Hole strips may be used, depending upon the size of the patient and the degree of inflammation. The width of the Donut Strip should be adjusted to the size of the patient. Smaller patients may need a 1 ½" or 1" wide strip instead of a 2" strip.

If a series of strips are used remember to keep the tension level lower so the accumulative affect of the tape lifts the skin.

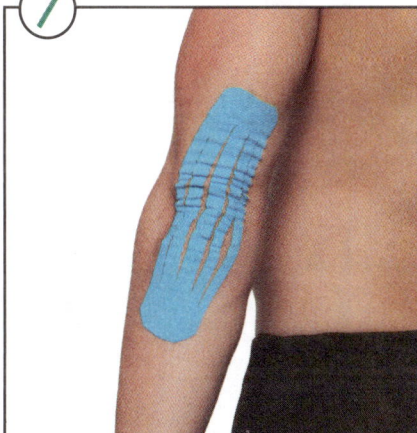

OPTION 3: WEB CUT

7. Cut 4-5 slits in the Kinesio I strip. The Kinesio Tape is cut allowing for each end to remain intact.

Place the patient in as much elbow flexion as pain or edema allows. Apply 10-20% of available tension to the web cut strips during application. The web cut strip can be applied one of two ways. The first option is to begin by anchoring proximally then applying the web slits over the area of desired space and ending with no tension. The second option is to tear the paper backing in the center and peel back. Apply the appropriate tension to the center of the web cut directly over the area of desired space. Lay down the ends with no tension.

Rub to activate adhesive prior to any patient movement.

It is easy to a add too much tension to the narrow strips during application. Too much tension will cause the Kinesio Tex Tape to "push down" instead of lifting the skin.

Elbow Hyperextension

The elbow is a relatively stable joint which may become injured when it is forced past its normal end position of extension. The olecranon process in the olecranon fossa can act as a fulcrum when a force is applied causing a range of motion past normal 0 degrees of extension, females may normally have up to +3 degrees. Generally, the elbow has marked edema and pain in the region of the ulnar collateral ligament.

The Kinesio Taping Technique will include a lymphatic corrective taping to reduce acute edema, ligament correction for the ulnar collateral ligament, basic biceps muscle taping, and if appropriate a functional correction to limit elbow extension during the acute or post acute injury phase.

FIRST 24 TO 72 HOURS:

1. Strip one: place anchor of the Kinesio fan on the anterior deltoid. Place elbow in extension and shoulder extension. Apply 0-20% of available tension and direct the tails over the antecubital fossa to the medial aspect of the mid-forearm. Lay down ends with no tension and pat or rub to initiate adhesive prior to any further patient movement.

2. Strip two: place anchor along border of lateral deltoid. Apply 0-20% of available tension and direct the tails of the fan over the antecubital fossa to the medial aspect of the mid-forearm. Lay down ends with no tension and rub to initiate adhesive prior to any further patient movement. The two strips should form a crisscross pattern over the edema.

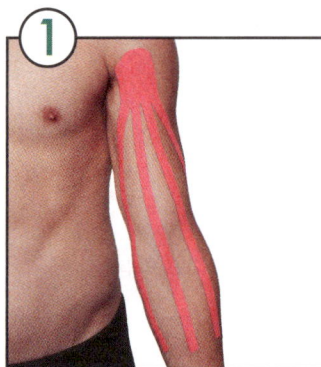

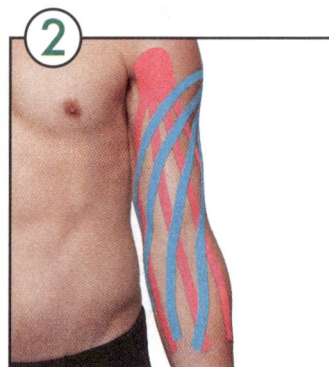

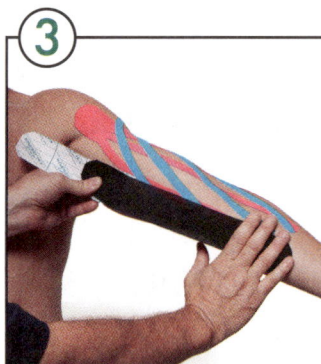

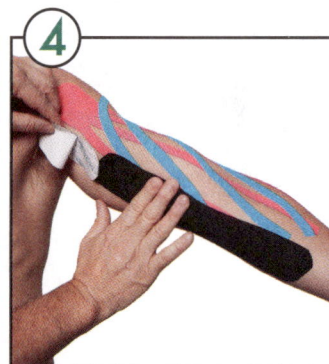

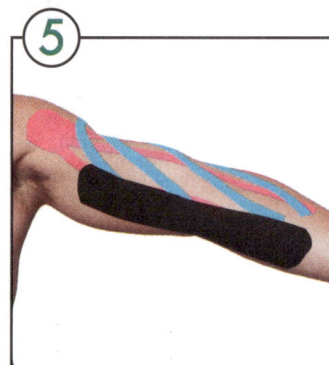

POST 72 HOURS:

Ligament corrective technique application to the ulnar collateral ligament, if indicated as a result of the evaluation of the injury. For a mild hyperextension (no increased ligament laxity), this strip is optional. For moderate to severe (increased ligament laxity), this strip is recommended. For complete review of the ligament correction technique, see valgus laxity of the elbow.

3. With patient's elbow in as much extension as possible, place the anchor of the Kinesio I strip ligament correction technique approximately 4" below the medial joint line of the elbow, with no tension. With one hand, hold the anchor of the Kinesio I strip to limit tension on the anchor during application.

4. Over the length of the ulnar collateral ligament, apply 75-100% of available tension. When the tension reaches the end of the ligament, slide the hand holding the anchor up to this point of end tension. This will initiate adhesive.

5. Lay down remaining Kinesio Tex I strip with no tension and vigorously rub to initiate adhesive prior to any further patient movement.

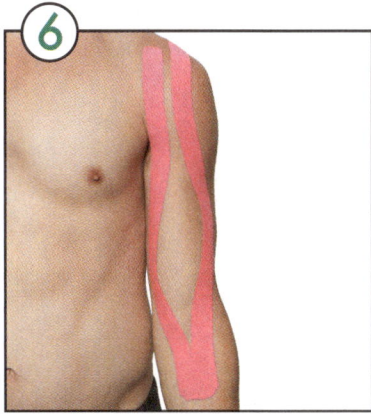

6. Application of the Biceps Brachii muscle inhibition technique. For complete review, see Biceps Tendonitis. The desired result will be decreased muscle spasm in the biceps muscle from over extension during forced elbow hyperextension. Practitioner may choose to apply the biceps brachii with Ligament Correction and or Functional Correction.

Lay down anchor inferior to or above the anticubital fossa with no tension. Apply paper off to light, 15-25% of available tension to the tails. Medial tail along the short head of the biceps, the lateral tail along the long head of the biceps. Lay down the ends with no tension and rub to initiate adhesive prior to any further patient movement.

POST-ACUTE PHASE - 24-72 HOURS:

Application of the Functional Corrective Technique to limit elbow extension.

The degree of elbow extension to be limited is determined by the practitioner during evaluation. The desired result would be limitation of elbow extension just short of a painful position by the patient.

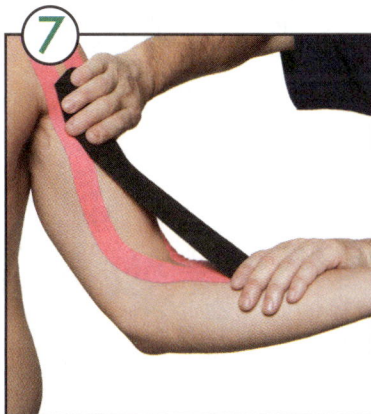

7. Functional correction should be applied with the elbow in flexion, with the superior anchor approximately 5-6" above the joint. The inferior anchor should be 5-6" below the joint. The practitioner determines the appropriate degree of tension to limit joint movement following the application of the first anchor and before the application of the second anchor. Apply the Kinesio I strip with 50+% of available tension.

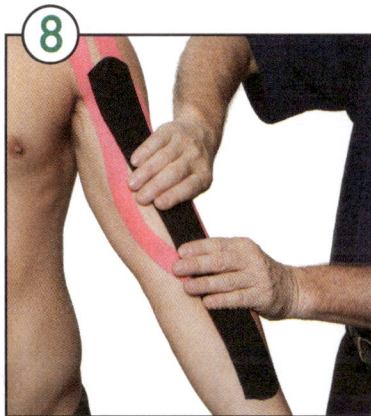

8. Hold both the proximal and distal anchor and have the patient move into as much extension as possible. Move both hands towards the antecubital fossa. Rub vigorously to initiate adhesive activation prior to any further elbow motion.

9. Completed application of the Kinesio Taping Technique for Hyperextension of the Elbow with Biceps Brachii inhibition and Functional Correction. You can also apply the Ligament Correction in addition to the Biceps and Functional Correction.

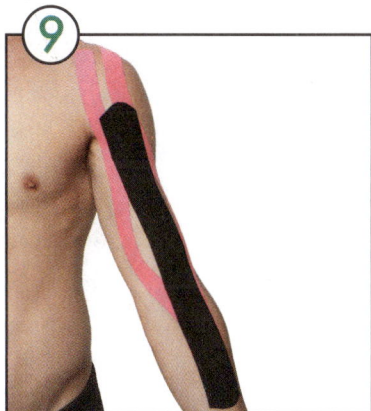

Lateral Epicondylitis of the Elbow

Lateral Epicondylitis results from repetitive extension of the forearm and wrist with excessive pronation. It is generally associated with overhead activities: such as tennis, racquetball, baseball, and javelin. It is associated with pain on wrist extension and may be the result of poor mechanics by the patient.

The Kinesio Taping Technique will assist in reducing edema and pain. The techniques demonstrated are only basic examples of the possible choices available. The practitioner may also add space corrections during acute inflammation, fascia correction for chronic conditions, mechanical correction to apply pressure to an area, select a functional correction to limit a movement, or tape the supinator to assist or limit a motion.

An option which is not shown is a mechanical correction to "hold down" the common flexors of the elbow. An example is shown in Osgood-Schlatter syndrome and medial & lateral epicondylitis combination taping.

APPLICATION OF THE COMMON EXTENSOR MUSCLE INHIBITION TAPING FOR ACUTE INFLAMMATION

1. The elbow should be in extension with wrist in ulnar deviation. Place the anchor of the Kinesio Y strip with the split in the Y near the base of the second and third metacarpal with no tension.

2. Place the patient in elbow extension, wrist ulnar deviation and flexion. Apply paper off to light, 15-25% of available tension to the tails. The medial tail should follow the inferior aspect of the common muscle group. Lay down end with no tension, rub to initiate adhesive prior to any further patient movement.

3. Place the elbow in extension, wrist ulnar deviation and extension. The lateral tail should follow the superior aspect of the common muscle group. Both tails should end surrounding the lateral epicondyle of the humerus. Lay down the end with no tension, rub to initiate adhesive prior to any further patient movement.

4-5-6. Facilitation of common extensor. If the condition is chronic facilitation technique may be appropriate.

For application place anchor superior to the lateral epicondyle with the ends near the base of the second and third metacarpal. Apply the medial and lateral tails in reverse direction as described above applying 15-35% of available tension to the tails.

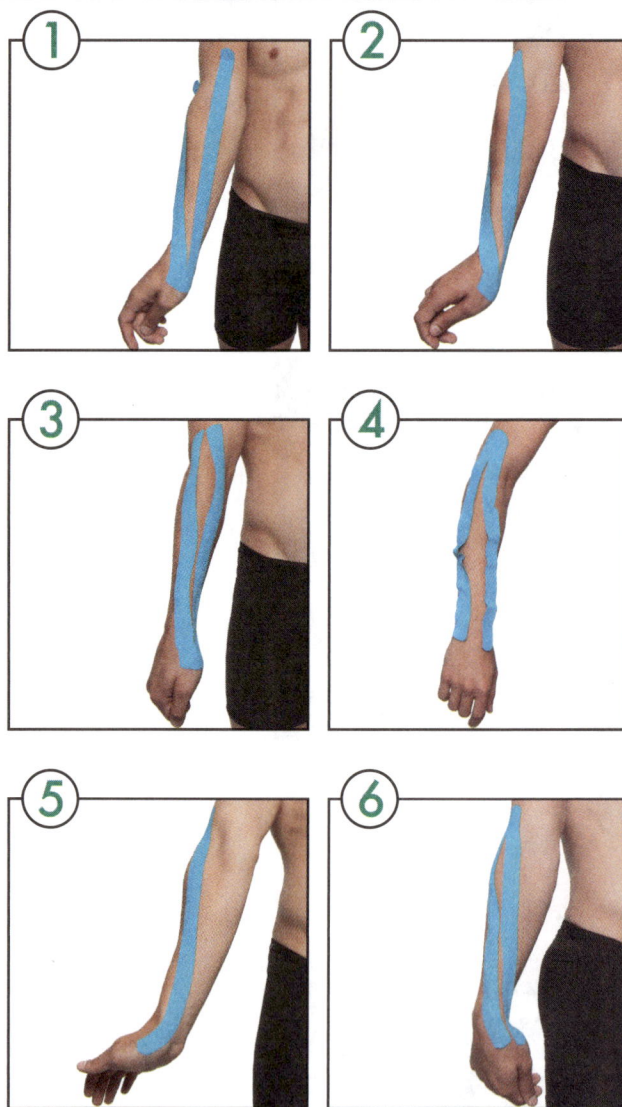

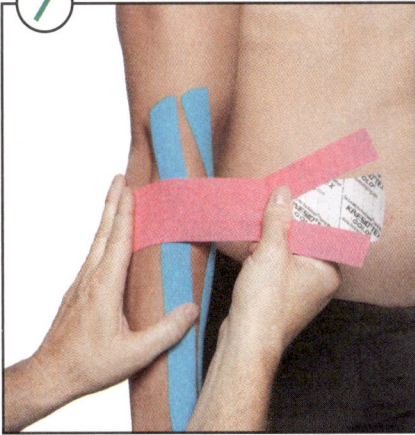

OPTION 1: Y STRIP MECHANICAL CORRECTION TENSION IN BASE

7. Application of a mechanical correction technique, tension on base, to limit tendon movement. May also use tension in tails if less aggressive technique is desired. Place the anchor of the Kinesio Y strip below the area of pain; do not cross over the lateral border of the ulna - this may cause pain in this region, with the elbow in a neutral position.

Before applying the anchor of the Y strip, estimate the proper position, so that when tension is removed from the tape the split in the Y will be placed lateral to the location of pain.

Apply 50-75% of available tension and downward/inward pressure to the base inferior to the point of pain. Slide hand holding anchor to this point. Lay down tails with 15-25% tension, lay down ends with no tension. Rub to initiate adhesive prior to any further patient movement.

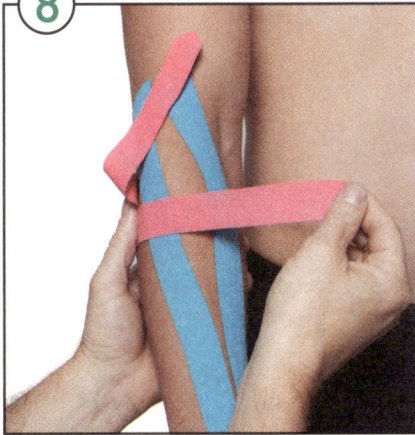

OPTION 2: Y STRIP FASCIA CORRECTION TENSION IN TAILS

8. Apply anchor ½ to 1" below the area of adhesion with no tension. Hold the anchor to ensure no tension is added. Apply 10-50% of available tension to each tail. Using either the side to side or long and short application. As tension is added slide the hand holding the anchor following fascia tension technique application. Lay down the the ends with no tension. Rub to initiate adhesive prior to any further patient movement.

If the technique is applied correctly for both the mechanical and fascia corrections, a "square" will be formed directly over the area of pain.

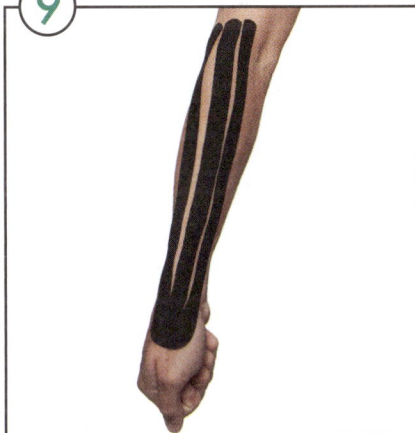

OPTION 3: USE OF THREE TAIL KINESIO STRIP WITH DONUT SPACE CORRECTION.

9. Begin by applying a common extensor inhibition Kinesio strip cut into three equal widths. The tape should be measured from the base of the second and third metacarpal base to the lateral epicondyle of the humerus.

Place the patient in elbow extension and wrist flexion with ulnar deviation. Apply paper off to light tension, 15-25% of available tension. Place the superior tail along the superior edge of the common extensor muscle group. The middle tail along the mid-belly of the muscle, and the inferior tail along the inferior edge. Lay down ends with no tension. Rub to initiate adhesive prior to any further patient movement.

10. Application of the donut space correction technique.

   Begin by cutting a hole approximately the size of a dime in the center of an approximately 6-8" Kinesio I strip. Be careful to not cut more than 50%, ½ of the available width of the Kinesio Tex Tape. Cutting the hole too large will reduce its ability to adhere to the patient's skin and limit the recoil affect of the Kinesio Tex Tape.

   Cut the distal approximately 2" of each end into two or three strips. This is will assist in dissipating force of the donut hole application.

   Place the patient in elbow extension. Tear the center of the paper backing and peel back to allow for tension to be applied to the Kinesio Tex Tape. Apply 15-25% of available tension to the Kinesio Strip and place the hole directly over the area of pain, or desired space.

   Lay down the tails on both ends with no tension. Splay the ends to dissipate tension which was created in the area of the donut. Rub to initiate adhesive prior to any further patient movement.

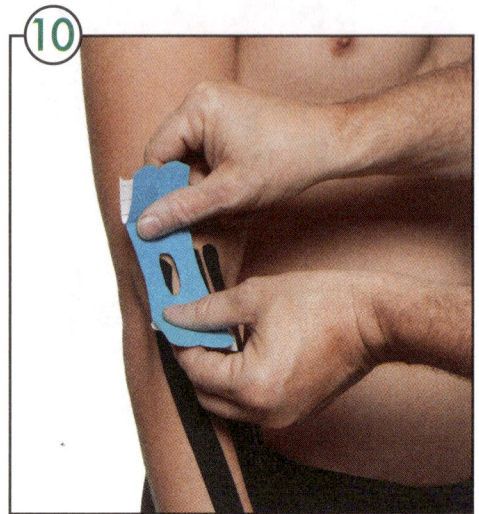

11. A series of two or three donut hole space correction strips may be appropriate. For a smaller patient the donut hole strips should be smaller, image shown is 1 ½" wide. Slightly change the angle, maybe as much as 45 degrees to facilitate the gathering of more tissue. When the technique is applied correctly, skin should fill the donut hole and push above the level of the Kinesio Tex Tape strips.

   Avoid applying any Kinesio Tex Tape strips covering the anti-cubital fossa.

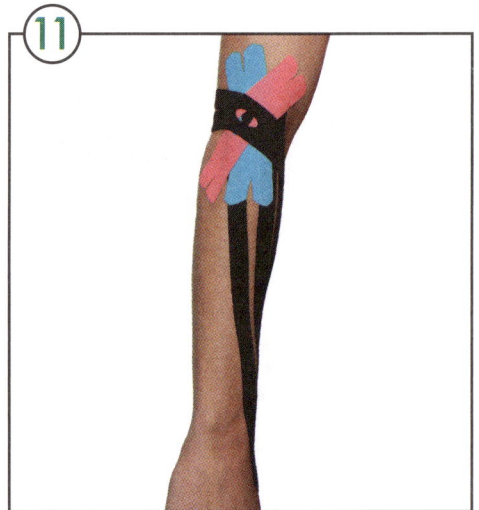

Medial Epicondylitis of the Elbow

Medial Epicondylitis results from repetitive forceful flexion of the wrist and valgus force on the elbow. It has also been called: golfer's elbow, pitcher's elbow, and javelin elbow. It is associated with pain on wrist flexion combined with ulnar deviation and may be the result of poor mechanics by the patient.

The Kinesio Taping Technique will assist in reducing edema and pain. The techniques demonstrated are only basic examples of the possible choices available. The practitioner may also add space corrections during acute inflammation, fascia correction for chronic conditions, mechanical correction to apply pressure to an area, or select a functional correction to limit a movement.

An option which is not shown is a mechanical correction to "hold down" the common flexors of the elbow. An example is shown in Osgood-Schlatter syndrome and medial & lateral epicondylitis combination taping.

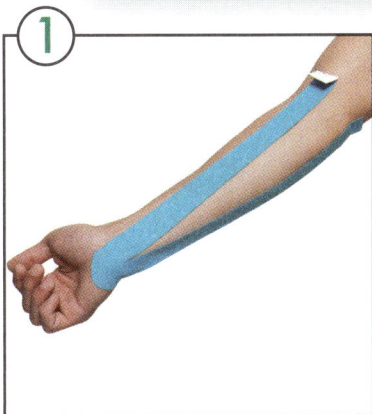

APPLICATION OF THE COMMON FLEXOR INHIBITION FOR ACUTE INFLAMMATION

If the condition is chronic facilitation may be appropriate, see lateral epicondylitis for explanation.

1. The elbow should be in extension with wrist in radial deviation. Place the anchor of the Kinesio Y strip near the base of the 5th metacarpal with no tension.

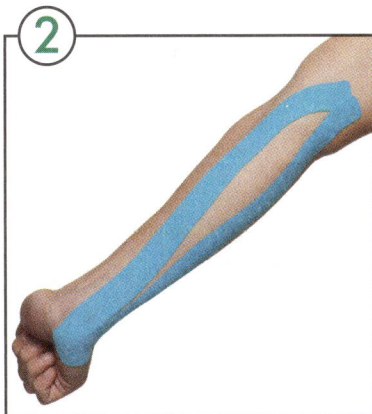

2. Maintain the patient in elbow extension, wrist radial deviation and extension. Apply paper off to light, 15-25% of available tension to the tails. The inferior tail should follow the inferior aspect of the common muscle group. Lay down end with no tension, rub to initiate adhesive prior to any further patient movement.

   Keeping the elbow in the same position. The lateral tail should follow the superior aspect of the common muscle group. Both tails should end surrounding the lateral epicondyle of the humerus. Lay down the end with no tension, rub to initiate adhesive prior to any further patient movement.

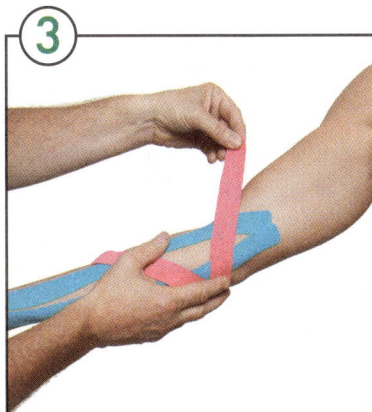

OPTION 1: KINESIO Y STRIP FASCIA CORRECTION TENSION IN TAILS

3. Apply anchor ½ to 1" below the area of adhesion with no tension. Hold the anchor to ensure no tension is added. Apply 10-50% of available tension to each tail. Using either the side to side or long and short application. As tension is added slide the hand holding the anchor following fascia tension technique application. Lay down the ends with no tension. Rub to initiate adhesive prior to any further patient movement.

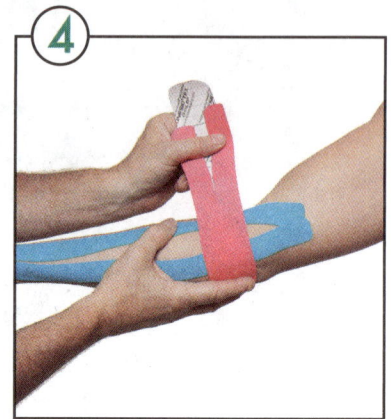

4. Application of a mechanical correction technique, tension on base, to limit tendon movement. May also use tension in tails if less aggressive technique is desired. Please also see Little League Elbow for an alternative mechanical correction.

Place the anchor of the Kinesio Y strip below the area of pain; do not cross over the medial border of the ulna - this may cause pain in this region, with the elbow in a neutral position.

Before applying the anchor of the Y strip, estimate the proper position, so that when tension is removed from the tape the split in the Y will not be over the location of pain.

Apply 50-75% of available tension and inward pressure to the base inferior to the point of pain. Slide hand holding anchor to this point. Lay down tails with 15-25% tension in the next zone and lay down ends with no tension. Rub to initiate adhesive prior to any further patient movement.

If the technique is applied correctly for both the mechanical and fascia corrections, a "square" will be formed directly over the area of pain.

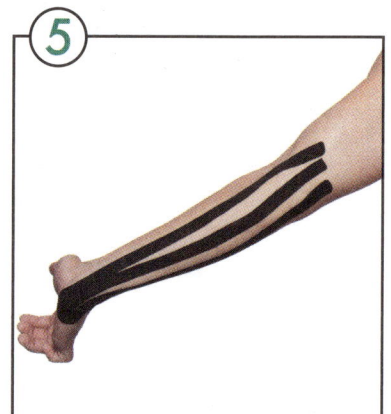

OPTION 2: USE OF A THREE TAIL KINESIO STRIP WITH DONUT SPACE CORRECTION

5. Begin by applying a common flexor inhibition Kinesio strip cut into three equal widths. The tape should be measured from the base of the 5th metacarpal base to the medial epicondyle of the humerus.

Place the patient in elbow extension and wrist extension with radial deviation. Apply paper off to light tension, 15-25% of available tension. Place the superior tail along the superior edge of the common flexor muscle group. The middle tail along the mid-belly of the muscle, and the inferior tail along the inferior edge. Lay down ends with no tension. Rub to initiate adhesive prior to any further patient movement.

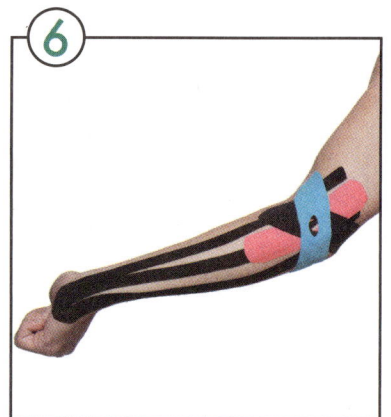

DONUT HOLE APPLICATION:

6. Begin by cutting a hole approximately the size of a dime in the center of an approximately 6-8" Kinesio I strip. Be careful to not cut more than 50%, ½ of the available width of the Kinesio Tex Tape. Cutting the hole to large will reduce its ability to adhere to the patient's skin and limit the recoil affect of the Kinesio Tex Tape.

Cut the distal approximately 2" of each end into two or three strips. This will assist in dissipating force of the donut hole application.

Tear the center of the paper backing and peel back to allow for tension to be applied to the Kinesio Tex Tape. Apply 15-25% of available tension to the Kinesio Strip and place the hole directly over the area of pain, or desired space. Lay down the tails on both ends with no tension. Splay the ends to dissipate tension which was created in the area of the donut. Rub to initiate adhesive prior to any further patient movement.

A second or even a third donut space correction strip may be appropriate.

Little League Elbow

Little League Elbow is a common injury which occurs to the medial epicondyle of the humerus. The cause of this injury is an overuse of the common flexor muscle group during adolescence. It results from repetitive microtrauma of the bony attachment for the common elbow flexors, which during puberty are stronger than the boney attachment.

The Kinesio Taping Technique will assist in reducing edema and pain. There are several Kinesio Taping Techniques which may provide reduced inflammation and pain, the practitioner will need to determine which techniques are best for their patients. If one technique does not provide significant results, another technique may.

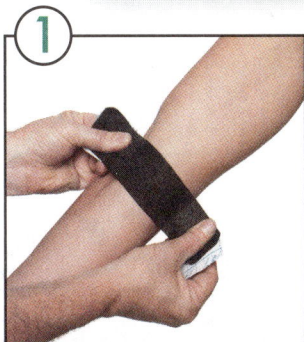

OPTION 1: MECHANICAL I STRIP

A mechanical correction strip may be applied in an attempt to "hold down" the apophysitis of the medial epicondyle of the humerus.

1. Place the patient's elbow in slight flexion. Begin by tearing the center of the paper backing of a 4-6" long Kinesio I strip exposing the central 2". Holding both ends, apply moderate to severe, 50-75% of available tension, with downward pressure to the center of the Kinesio strip over the medial epicondyle of the humerus.

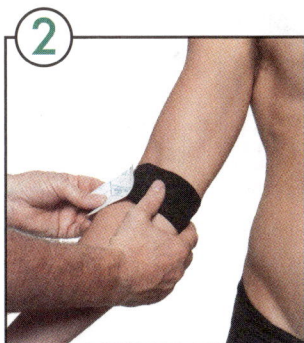

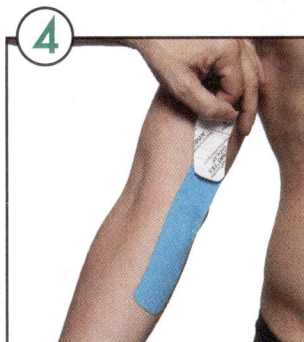

2. Prior to laying down the Kinesio strip ends, have the patient move their elbow into full extension and lay down the ends with no tension. Rub to initiate adhesive prior to any further patient movement.

   A 3" Kinesio Tex Tape I strip may be more effective, or using two 2" Kinesio I strips may also be found to provide more support.

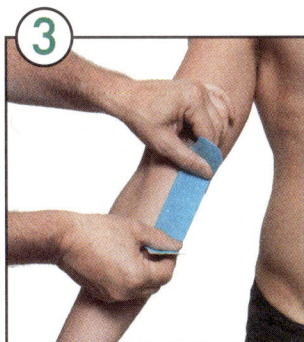

OPTION 2: APPLICATION OF A SPACE CORRECTION TECHNIQUE CENTER OF I STRIP

3. Place the patient's elbow in extension. Begin by tearing the center of the paper backing of a 4-6" long Kinesio I strip exposing the central 2". Holding both ends, apply light to moderate, 15-35% of available tension to the center of the Kinesio strip over the medial epicondyle of the humerus.

4. Lay down the ends with no tension. Rub to initiate adhesive prior to any further patient movement.

5. Two and three strips can be applied using space correction tension in the center of an I strip to more aggressively create a "pocket" above the injured tissue. Make sure that when the ends of the 2nd and 3rd strips are applied the elbow may need to be in flexion, internal or external rotation when the ends are laid down to limit tension added to the ends during active movement.

Other options may be fascia correction or donut hole space correction. See Elbow Medial and Lateral Epicondylitis for complete descriptions.

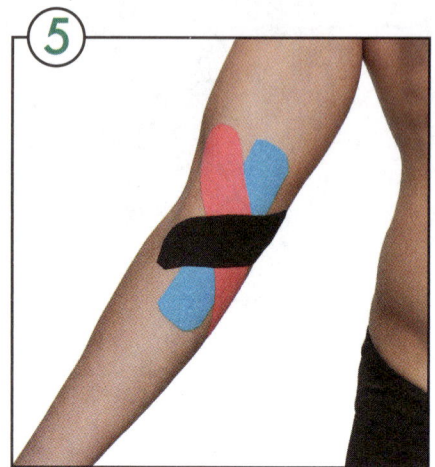

OPTION 3: KINESIO I STRIP WITH FUNCTIONAL CORRECTION FOR LITTLE LEAGUE ELBOW

6. Begin by measuring approximately 4-5" above and below the anti-cubital fossa and cut into an I strip. Image shown has a ligament correction to the UCL, for description see Valgus Laxity of the Elbow.

Place the distal anchor, of approximately 3-4", with no tension 4-5" below the anti-cubital fossa and hold with one hand. Place the elbow in flexion, the degree of flexion is determined by the practitioners evaluation of what degree of elbow extension would benefit the patient. Apply moderate to severe, 50+% of available tension to the I strip. Apply proximal anchor with no tension.

Hold both anchors and have the patient move into extension. Bring both hands together by initiating adhesive prior to any further patient movement. Rub vigorously to initiate adhesive prior to any further patient movement.

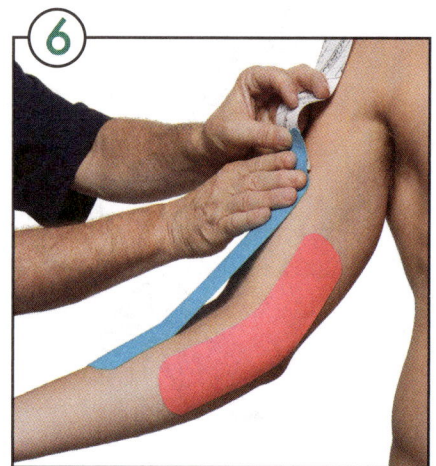

OPTION 4: APPLICATION OF A FOUR TAIL Y TECHNIQUE FOR COMMON FLEXOR MUSCLES, AND THE SUPINATOR MUSCLE.

7. To inhibit the common flexor muscle group and supinator.

Begin by cutting 4 tails into an appropriate length of Kinesio Tex Tape. Begin the anchor near the base of the 5th metacarpal with the patient's elbow in extension and wrist in extension and radial deviation. Apply paper off to light, 15-25% of available tension to the tails. The first two tails surround the common flexor muscle group. For a more complete explanation, see Medial Epicondylitis.

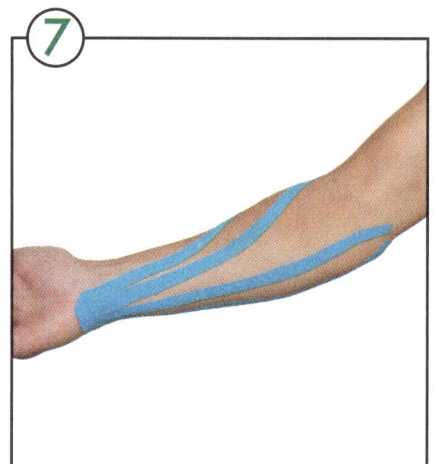

Have the patient move into ulnar deviation, wrist flexion. The first two tails follow along the common extensor muscle group on the lower aspect of the forearm to the medial epicondyle of the humerus. The second set of tails aim from the lateral proximal radial shart towards the lateral epicondyle of the humerus surrounding the supinator muscle in the upper forearm. Lay the ends down with no tension and rub to initiate adhesive prior to any further movement.

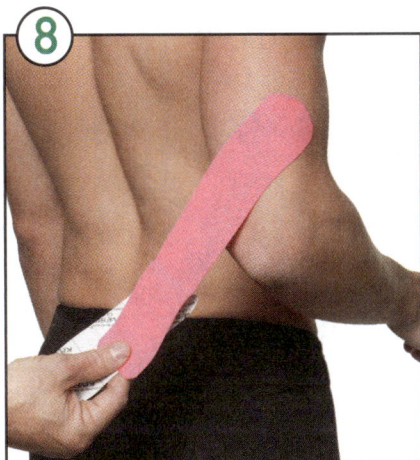

APPLICATION OF A "MODIFIED" FUNCTIONAL CORRECTION TO THE PRONATOR TERES MUSCLE.

8. Place the anchor of the Kinesio I strip slightly superior to the medial epicondyle of the humerus with the elbow in 30 degrees of flexion and forearm in pronated position angled at approximately 45 degrees.

   Apply light to moderate, 25-50% of available tension to the Kinesio I strip. Have the patient move into elbow extension and forearm supination as the Kinesio I strip is being laid down. The strip should be directed towards the junction of the proximal and medial 1/3 of the radius on the lateral aspect.

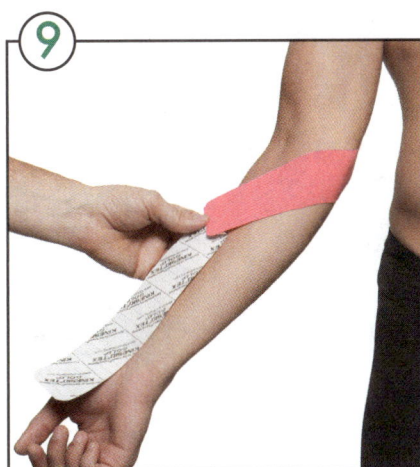

9. Lay down the end with no tension. Initiate adhesive activation prior to any further patient movement.

   This strip is intended to limit supination and assist in pronation, a functional correction. We are not able to create a "bridge or tent" which results in the "modification of the functional correction".

OPTION 5: KINESIO Y STRIP WITH MECHANICAL/SPACE CORRECTION COMBINATION TENSION IN BASE, SPACE OR FASCIA CORRECTION MAY ALSO BE APPLIED

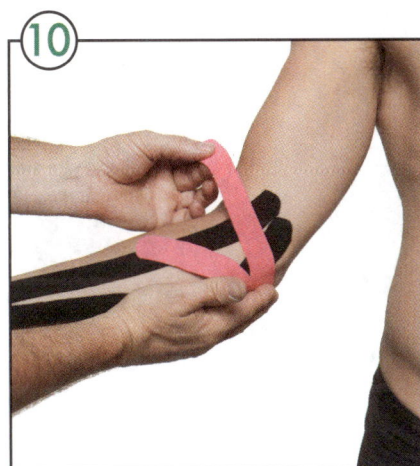

10. The common flexor group is demonstrated by application using the 2 tail technique. The mechanical/space correction combination tension in base begins by applying the anchor with no tension inferior to the area of pain. With one hand holding the anchor, apply downward pressure with this hand and slowly "lift" the gathered skin in the direction of the medial epicondyle. Apply 50-75% of available tension to the base of the Y strip. End tension just inferior to the location of pain. Hand holding the anchor moves up to end tension. Do not let go of this "lifted" skin and mechanical correction tension. With each tail apply paper off to light, 15-25% of available tension on either side of the area of pain. Lay down the end with no tension. Rub to initiate adhesive prior to any patient movement. The mechanical correction lifts the tissue below the lateral epicondyle and space correction in the tail recoils the tissue above the lateral epicondyle to create space.

Carpal Tunnel Syndrome

Carpal tunnel syndrome is a compression between the carpal bones and the transverse carpal ligament. An inflammation may develop or a decrease in ligament elasticity may develop resulting in pressure placed upon the median nerve which lies within the tunnel. The most common cause is repetitive flexion of the wrist.

The Kinesio Taping Method assists by reducing the edema and pain associated with the syndrome. The practitioner may also add space corrections during acute inflammation, fascia correction for chronic conditions, mechanical correction to apply pressure to an area, or select a functional correction to limit a movement.

OPTION 1: SPACE CORRECTION TENSION IN THE MIDDLE OF AN I STRIP

1. Measure a Kinesio I strip from the heads of the metacarpals to the epicondyles of the humerus. Make an X cut in the Kinesio Strip, each ends cuts are approximately 2".

   The palm area must be clean and dry prior to any application of the Kinesio Tex tape.

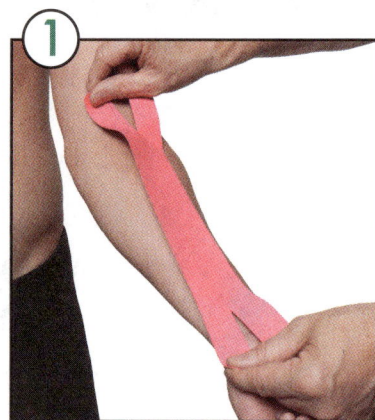

2. Tear the Kinesio paper backing in the center and peel back paper backing to expose the Kinesio Tex Tape to just short of the X's. Have the patient move into wrist and elbow extension. Apply paper off to moderate, 25-35% of available tension to the area in which the paper backing has been peeled back.

   Place the area of tension distally from the insertion of the palmaris longus, over the carpal tunnel region of the lower forearm inferior to the anti-cubital fossa. Rub to initiate adhesive prior to laying down the tails.

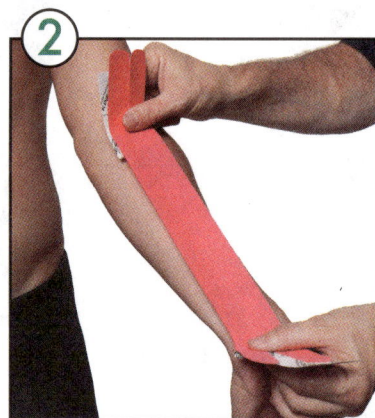

3. Lay down the ends of the X cut with no tension. Rub to initiate adhesive prior to any further patient movement.

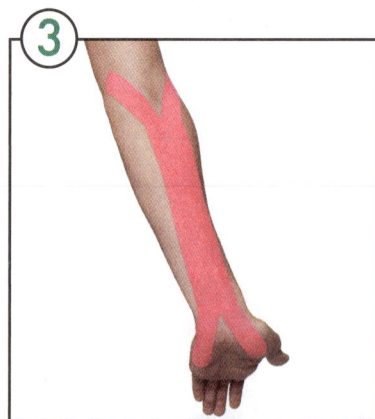

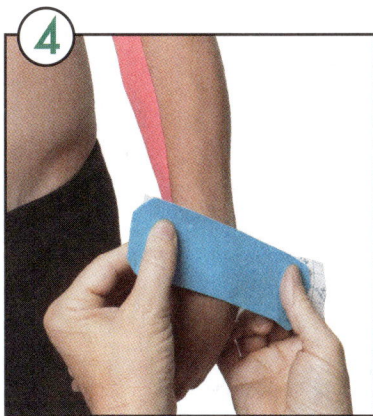

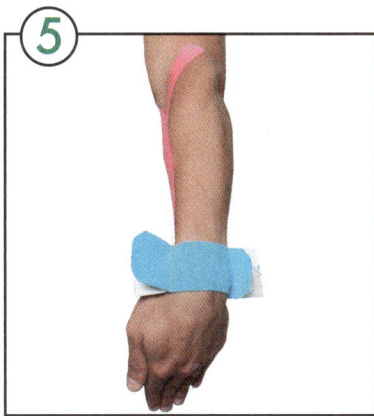

APPLICATION OF A SECOND SPACE CORRECTION TECHNIQUE TO THE DORSUM OF THE WRIST. THE LYMPHATIC NODE IS LOCATED IN THIS REGION.

4-5. Begin by tearing the center of the paper backing of a 4-6" Kinesio I strip. Apply paper off to moderate, 15-35% of available tension to the exposed Kinesio Tex. Place the patients wrist in a slightly flexed position. Place the Kinesio strip with applied tension directly over the distal 2" of the ulna and radius on the dorsum of the hand.

Rub to initiate the adhesive prior to any further movement.

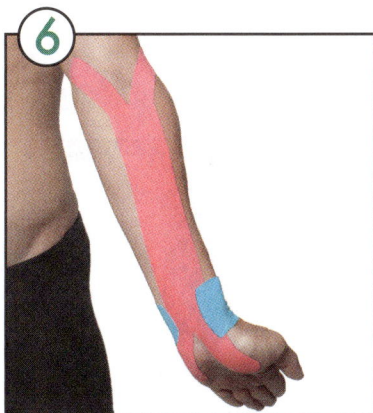

6. Place one hand to hold the Kinesio I Strip on both the radial styloid process and ulnar styloid process, and have the patient move into extension. With the other hand, lay down the ends of the Kinesio I strip with no tension. Make sure to not have the ends of the Kinesio I strip meet, leave a small gap to minimize applying any tension directly over the carpal tunnel.

This space correction can also be applied on the palmar side of the wrist directly over the carpal tunnel to create space directly over the carpal tunnel.

OPTION 2:

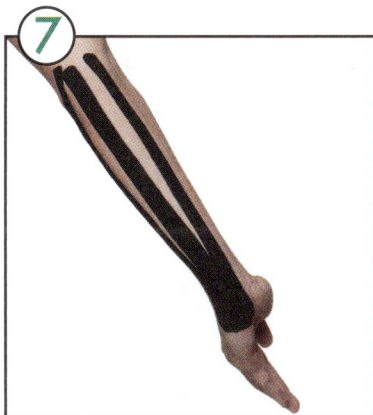

7. Application of the basic Kinesio Taping Method for the common flexor muscle group using a 3 tail Y technique. For review, see medial epicondylitis.

OPTION 3:

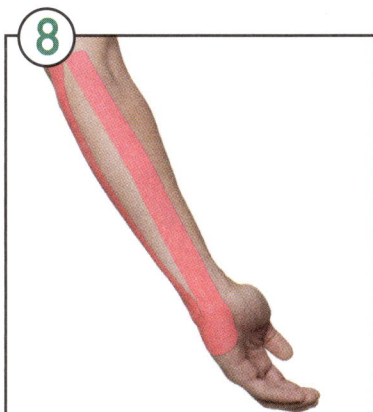

8. Application of the basic Kinesio Taping Method for the common flexor muscle group using a 2 tail Y technique. For review, see medial epicondylitis.

For both option 2 and 3, a space correction strip as described in option one is applied either over the lymphatic node on the dorsum of the wrist or directly over the carpal tunnel.

Carpal Tunnel Syndrome

OPTION 4: BUTTON HOLE TECHNIQUE

9. Measure a Kinesio I strip from the lateral epicondyle to the base of the proximal phalanx, and back to the medial epicondyle.

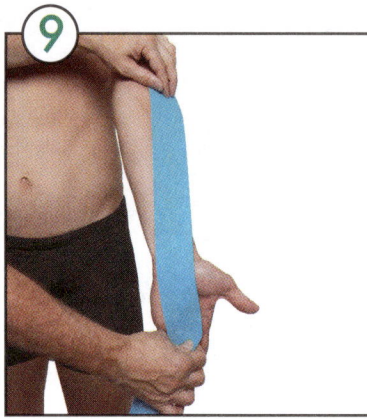

10. Cut two holes (button holes) in the middle of the Kinesio I strip. Make sure to not make the holes too large as to cause this area to tear due to minimal Kinesio Tex Tape between the web of the fingers.

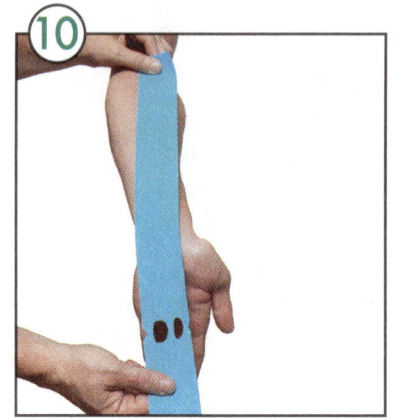

11. Tear the paper backing of the Kinesio I strip in the location of the button holes. Apply the two holes over middle and ring fingers.

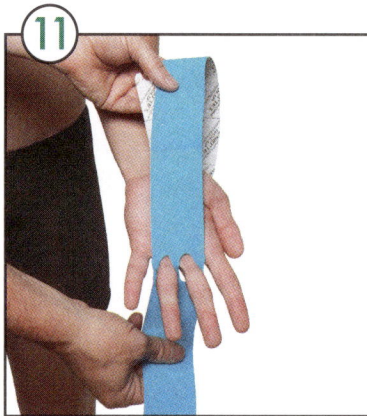

12. Have the patient move into wrist extension with radial deviation and apply the Kinesio I strip with paper off to moderate 15-25% of available tension in the direction of the medial epicondyle of the humerus.

    Lay down the end with no tension. Rub to initiate adhesive prior to any further patient movement.

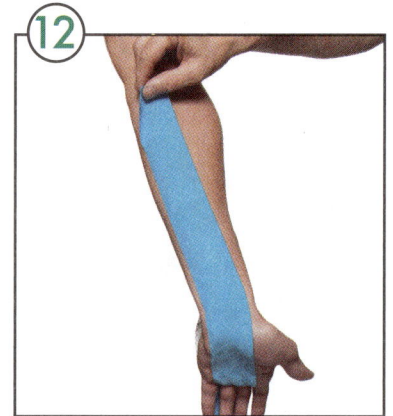

13. Have the patient move into wrist flexion with ulnar deviation. Apply paper off to moderate, 15-25% of available tension in the direction of the lateral epicondyle of the humerus. Lay down the end with no tension and rub to initiate adhesive prior to any further patient movement.

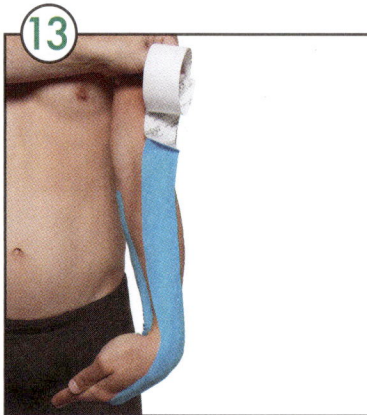

14. The application of the dorsal strip may also be applied ending in the middle forearm region rather than extending to the lateral epicondyle.

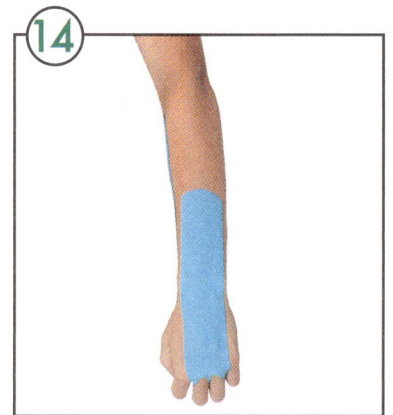

APPLICATION OF A SECOND SPACE CORRECTION TECHNIQUE TO THE DORSUM OF THE WRIST. THE LYMPHATIC NODE IS LOCATED IN THIS REGION.

15. Begin by tearing the center of the paper backing of a 4-6" Kinesio I strip. Apply moderate, 25-35% of available tension to the exposed Kinesio Tex Tape with the wrist in extension.

    Place the Kinesio strip with applied tension directly over the distal 2" of the ulna and radius on the dorsal side of the hand.

    Lightly rub to activate the adhesive prior to any further movement.

16. End the tension of the space correction on the ulnar and radial styloid process.

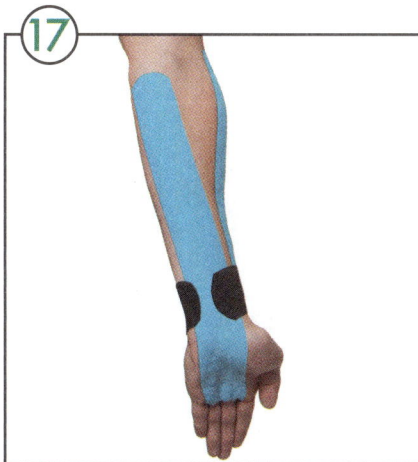

17. Place one hand to hold the Kinesio I Strip on both the radial styloid process and ulnar styloid process, and have the patient move into extension.

    With the other hand, lay down the ends of the Kinesio I strip with no tension. Make sure to not have the ends of the Kinesio I strip meet, leave a small gap to minimize applying any tension directly over the dorsal lymph node.

    This space correction can also be applied on the palmar side of the wrist directly over the carpal tunnel to create space directly over the lymph node.

Lymphedema - Edema of Upper Extremity

Lymphedema of the Upper Extremity is the result of edema that forms from acute or chronic dysfunction. In an acute injury, the degree of edema may be too significant for the lymph system to remove in a short period of time. In a chronic condition, the lymph system is not able to channel the fluid in the normal pathways and edema, or true lymhedema has formed in the dependent extremity.

The Kinesio Taping Method will assist in reducing edema by application of the lymphatic corrective technique. This is accomplished by lifting of the skin which decreases pressure and allows for more normal flow of lymphatic fluids (For more extensive review, see lymphatic corrective technique).

The practitioner will need to determine where the lymphatic system has diminished function and by application of the lymphatic corrective technique channel the fluid to another region of the system which is functioning normally.

Precautions to Kinesio Taping on Lymphedema applications may include: Diabetes, Kidney Disease/ Dynamic forms of Lymphedema, Congestive Heart Failure, Thyroid Disease, and possibly pregnancy with associated medical conditions.

Lymphatic drainage will be demonstrated from the distal to the proximal lymph vessel. During practical application not all sections may be required.

APPLICATION OF LYMPHATIC CORRECTIVE TECHNIQUE FROM THE HAND TO THE ELBOW.

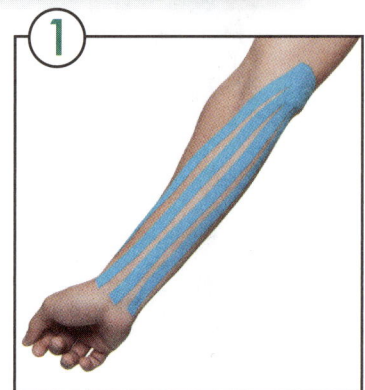

1. Have the patient place their hand in neutral and the elbow in extension. Place the anchor of the Kinesio fan strip superior to the medial epicondyle of the humerus with no tension. Direct the tails across the anterior aspect of the forearm towards the base of the thumb. Apply 0-20% of tension to the tails. The ends are applied with no tension. Pat or rub to initiate adhesive prior to any further patient movement.

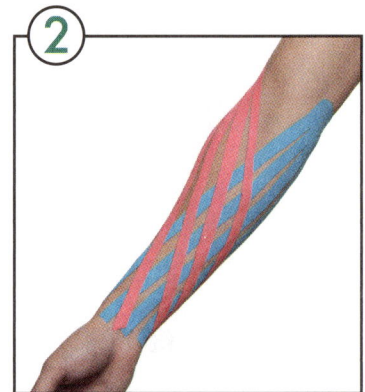

2. Place a second anchor superior to the lateral epicondyle of the humerus. Apply 0-20% of available tension to the tails. Direct the tails across the lymphedema/edema either on the anterior aspect of the forearm or possibly on the posterior aspect of the forearm towards the dorsum of the hand. The ends are applied with no tension. Pat or rub to initiate adhesive prior to any further patient movement.

   For an optional technique for the hand to the elbow see the end of this section.

AXILLARY LYMPH NODE IS FUNCTIONAL: UPPER ARM

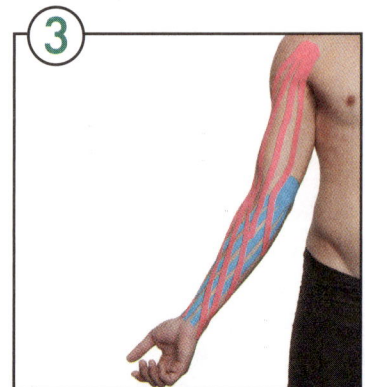

3. Have the patient move into shoulder abduction, extension and external rotation. Place the anchor of the Kinesio fan strip above the axillary lymph node in the region of the middle aspect of the anterior deltoid.

   Apply 0-20% of available tension to the tails. Direct the tails of the Kinesio fan strip towards the medial aspect of the elbow. The ends are applied with no tension. Pat or rub to initiate adhesive prior to any further patient movement.

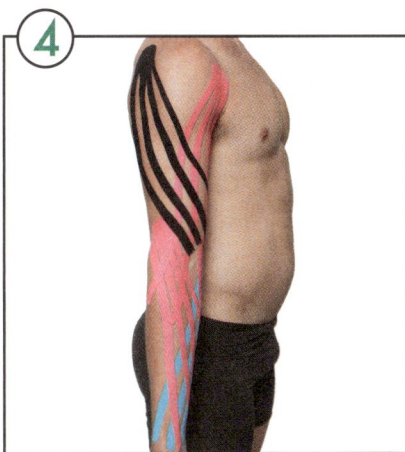

OPTIONAL SECOND FAN STRIP: UPPER ARM

4. Place the anchor of a second Kinesio fan strip in the middle region of the posterior deltoid with no tension.

Have the patient move into shoulder adduction, internal rotation and horizontal flexion. Apply 0-20% of available tension to the tails. Direct the tails of the Kinesio fan strip over the lateral aspect of the humerus and elbow and/or posterior region near the triceps. The ends are applied with no tension. Pat or rub to initiate adhesive prior to any further patient movement.

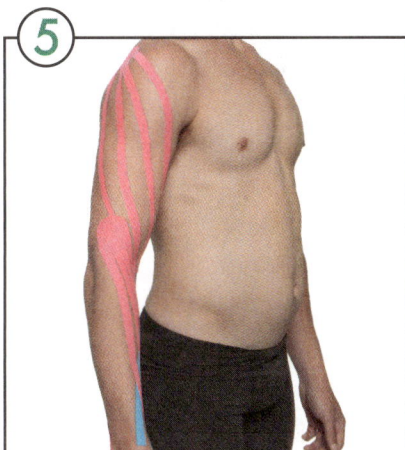

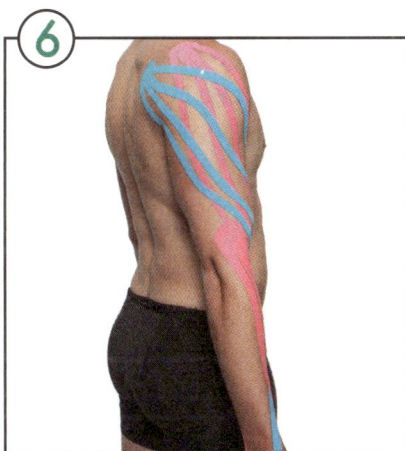

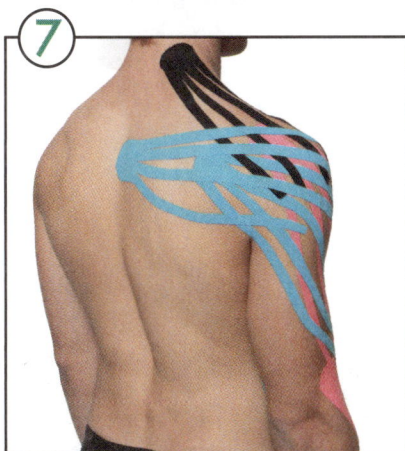

AXILLARY LYMPH NODE IS NOT FUNCTIONAL: UPPER ARM. DO NOT APPLY AXILLARY STRIP

5. Have the patient move into shoulder abduction, internal rotation and horizontal flexion. Place the anchor of the Kinesio fan strip near the insertion of the teres minor and major muscles.

Apply 0-20% of available tension to the tails. Direct the tails of the Kinesio fan strip over the middle deltoid muscle and towards the medial aspect of the elbow. Lay down the ends without tension. Pat or rub to initiate adhesive prior to any further patient movement.

OPTIONAL SECOND FAN STRIP: UPPER ARM LYMPH NODE IS NOT FUNCTIONAL

6. Have the patient move into shoulder adduction and horizontal flexion. Place the anchor of the Kinesio fan strip near insertion of the teres minor and major muscles, either slightly higher or lower than the first strip.

Apply 0-20% of available tension to the tails. Direct the tails of the Kinesio fan strip over the posterior deltoid muscle and towards the posterior aspect of the upper arm in the triceps region and wrapping around and over the biceps brachii. The ends are applied with no tension. Pat or rub to initiate adhesive prior to any further patient movement.

OPTIONAL STRIP TOWARDS NECK OR MID BACK LYMPHATIC NODES.

7. Place anchor of Kinesio fan strip on cervical transverse processes. Have the patient move into horizontal shoulder adduction and neck lateral flexion to opposite side. Apply 0-20% of available tension to the tails. Direct the tails of the fan strip towards the posterior aspect of the shoulder. The ends are applied with no tension.

The second fan strip is applied from the spinous process of T 4-8 and directed over the triceps and posterior deltoid with 0-20% tension. The ends are applied with no tension. Pat or rub to initiate adhesive prior to any further patient movement.

OPTIONAL BUTTON HOLE TECHNIQUE FOR LOWER ARM LYMPHATIC DRAINAGE

8. Measure a Kinesio I strip from the lateral epicondyle to the base of the proximal phalanx, and back to the medial epicondyle.

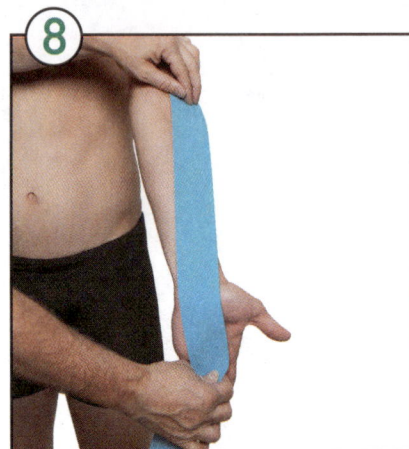

9. Cut two holes (button holes) in the middle of the Kinesio I strip. Make sure to not make the holes too large as to cause this area to tear due to minimal Kinesio Tex Tape between the web of the fingers.

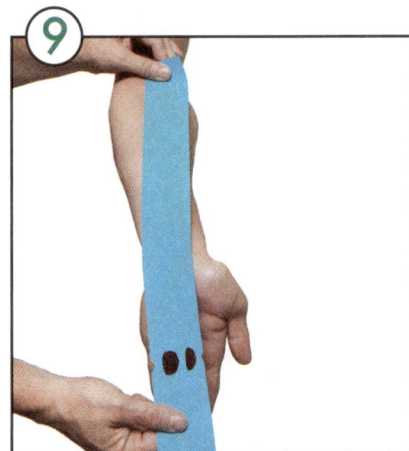

10. Tear the paper backing of the Kinesio I strip in the location of the button holes. Apply the two holes over middle and ring fingers. Have the patient move into wrist extension with radial deviation and apply the Kinesio I strip with moderate 25-35% of available tension in the direction of the medial epicondyle of the humerus.

    Lay down the end with no tension. Rub to initiate adhesive prior to any further patient movement.

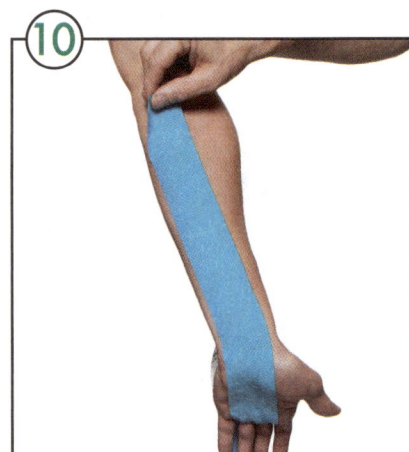

11. Have the patient move into wrist flexion with ulnar deviation. Apply moderate, 25-35% of available tension in the direction of the lateral epicondyle of the humerus. Lay down the end with no tension and rub to initiate adhesive prior to any further patient movement.

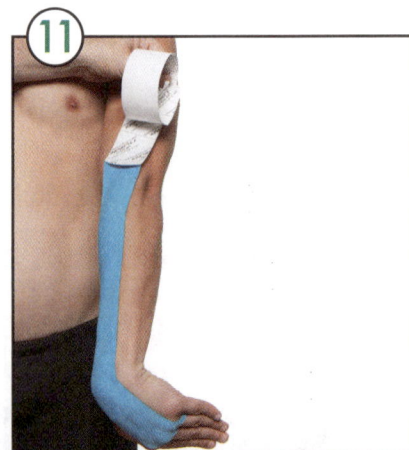

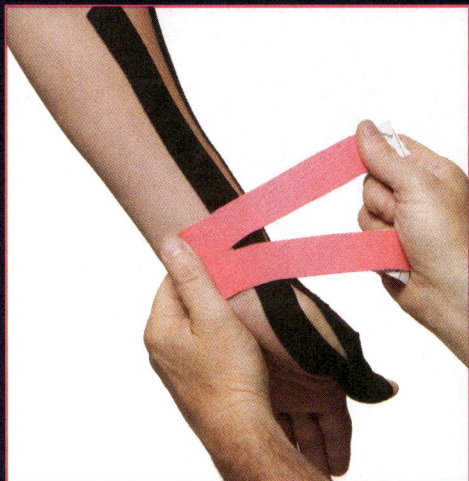

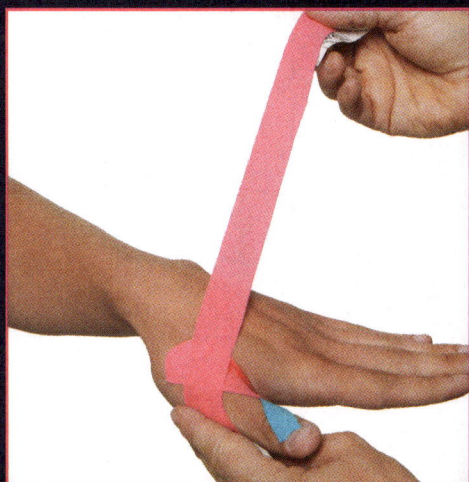

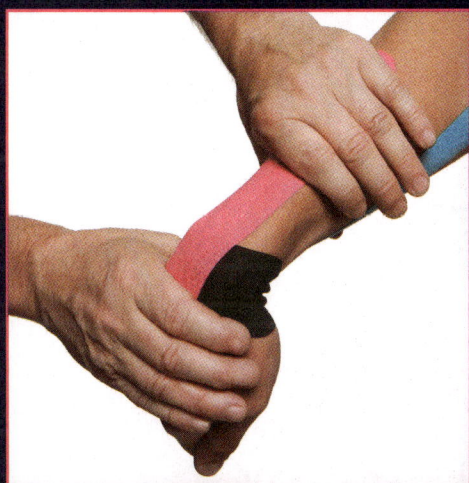

SECTION 6

Wrist
and
Hand

Section 6

Wrist Sprain –Trifibrocartilage (TFC)

Wrist sprains are a common acute and chronic injury which occur as a result of activity. These injuries can either occur from a specific injury or develop from long term overuse (weight lifting, repetitive hyperextension or flexion). Evaluation of wrist sprains may be difficult, pain may result from injuries to the trifibrocartilage, posterior and anterior ligaments. Circulation to the carpal bones may be constricted resulting from wrist sprains.

The Kinesio Taping Technique will include lymphatic correction taping to reduce acute or chronic edema, ligament correction to assist joint laxity, and optional functional taping to limit range of motion.

Wrist Sprain - Trifibrocartilage (TFC)

APPLICATION OF LYMPHATIC CORRECTIVE TECHNIQUE TO THE DORSUM OF THE HAND

The technique is demonstrated for an injury due to excessive wrist flexion. For an injury due to wrist extension this technique can be reversed.

1. Place the anchor of the lymphatic fan cut approximately 3-4" superior to the ulnar styloid process, or area of edema. Have the patient move their hand into wrist flexion with radial deviation angling the tails in approximately 45 degrees over the area of edema. Apply tails with 0-20% of available tension. Pat or rub to initiate adhesive prior to any further patient movement.

2. Place the second fan strip approximately 2" superior to the radial styloid process. Place the patient in wrist flexion with ulnar deviation. Angle the tails in approximately 45 degrees over the area of edema. Apply fan strips with 0-20% of available tension. Pat or rub to initiate adhesive prior to any further patient movement.

3. Completed dorsal application of lymphatic technique for wrist flexion injury.

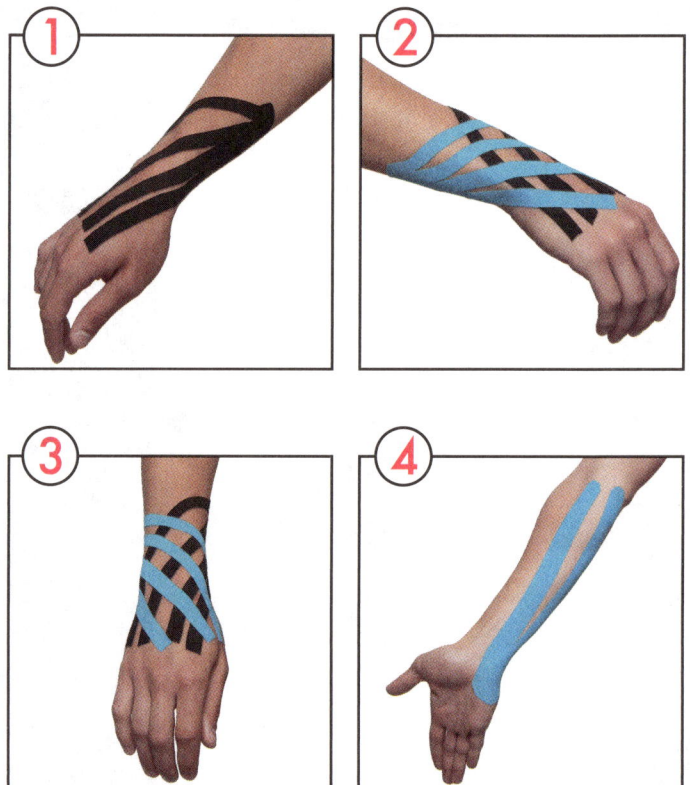

OPTIONAL APPLICATION OF THE BASIC KINESIO TAPING METHOD FOR THE COMMON FLEXOR MUSCLE GROUP USING A Y TECHNIQUE. For review, see medial epicondylitis.

4. This may be applied to reduce spasm in the common flexor muscle group following an injury to the wrist. Apply anchor distal to 5th metacarpal base with no tension. Place wrist in extension and radial deviation. Apply 15-25% of available tension surrounding the common flexor muscle group. End with no tension above the medial epicondylitis. Rub to initiate adhesive prior to any further patient movement.

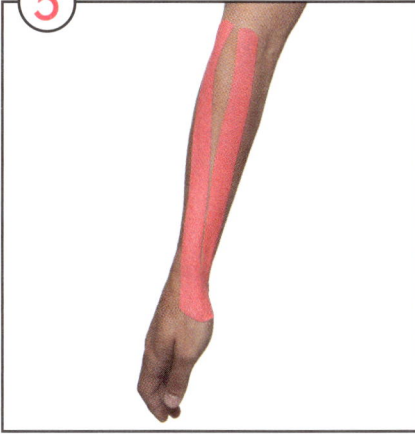

OPTIONAL APPLICATION OF THE BASIC KINESIO TAPING METHOD FOR THE COMMON EXTENSOR MUSCLE GROUP USING A Y TECHNIQUE.

5. This may be applied to reduce spasm in the common extensor muscle group following an injury to the wrist. Apply anchor distal to 2nd and 3rd metacarpal base with no tension. Place wrist in extension and ulnar deviation. Apply 15-25% of available tension surrounding the common flexor muscle group. End with no tension above the medial epicondylitis. Rub to initiate adhesive prior to any further patient movement.

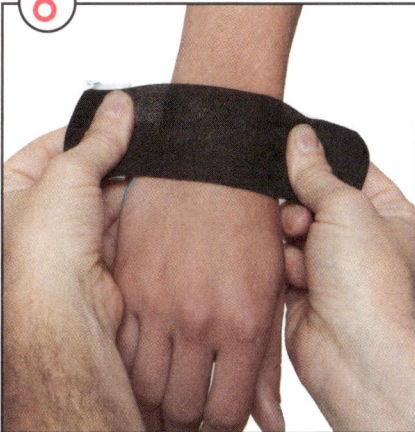

LIGAMENT CORRECTION

6. Application of the ligament corrective technique in the dorsum of the hand for injury due to wrist flexion.

Place the patient's hand in approximately 10 degrees of extension and the fingers splayed. Begin by tearing the center of the Kinesio I strip of approximately 6-8" through the paper backing. Apply 75-100% of available tension and downward pressure directly over the area of pain or ligaments where support is desired. The downward and inward pressure is applied to affect deeper tissues. Rub applied Kinesio I strip to initiate adhesive prior to any further patient movement.

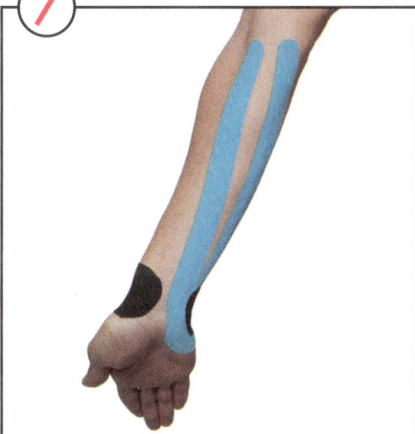

7. Have the patient move their wrist into extension and apply the ends of the Kinesio strip with no tension. When laying down the ends leave a space between them as this will minimize pressure applied directly over the carpal tunnel.

If appropriate, this technique may be applied to the palmar surface of the wrist for an injury due to wrist extension. If it is applied over the palmar surface, care must be taken to minimize any irritation of the carpal tunnel.

APPLICATION OF THE FUNCTIONAL CORRECTIVE TECHNIQUE TO LIMIT EITHER WRIST FLEXION OR WRIST EXTENSION, DEPENDING UPON INJURY.

9. Measure the length of the Kinesio I strip from approximately 6" proximal to the wrist and to the heads of the metacarpals. The practitioner may attach the anchor for the metacarpal heads by using a "button hole" technique as shown in Carpal Tunnel Syndrome.

   Apply the proximal anchor with no tension approximately 4" above the wrist. Apply moderate to severe, 50+% of available tension to the Kinesio I strip. Remember the combination of applied tension and tension created in the next step creates the total tension. Place the wrist in extension and apply the second anchor onto the heads of the metacarpals with no tension. Make sure the length of the distal anchor is sufficient enough to remain attached due to high tension within the middle section of the I strip.

10. Hold the anchors and have the patient move their wrist into flexion. While the patient is in flexion slide your hands to the middle to initiate adhesive prior to any further patient movement. Rub vigorously to initiate adhesive prior to any further patient movement.

    The practitioner will need to experiment with the correct degree of tension in the tape during application. For less restriction, less tension is required. For increased restriction, more tension is required.

11. Completed wrist sprain Kinesio Taping Technique application.

    If the injury is due to excess wrist extension then the functional correction and ligament correction can be placed on the palmar side of the wrist.

    If the injury is due to ulnar deviation place the functional correction and ligament correction on the radial side of the wrist.

    If the injury is due to radial deviation place the functional correction and ligament correction on the ulnar side of the wrist.

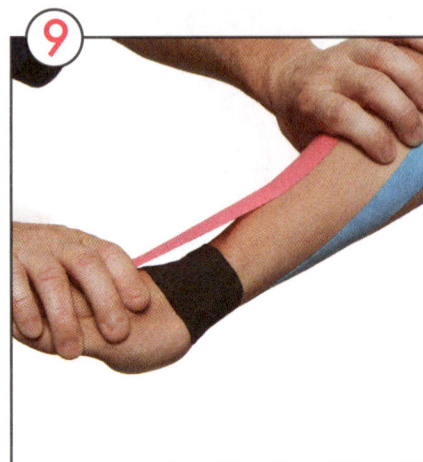

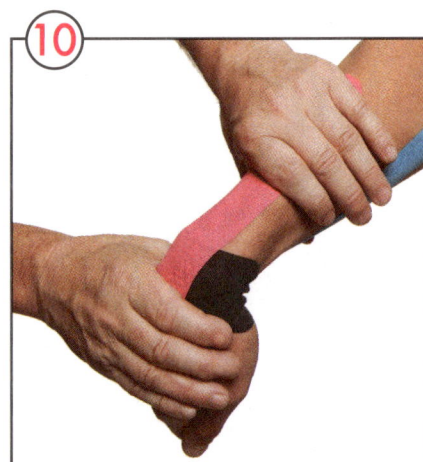

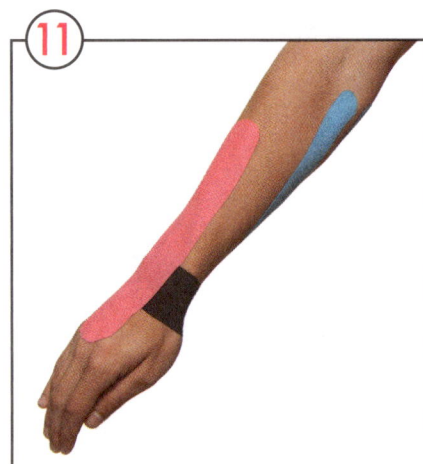

De Quervain's

De Quervain's is a tendonosus of the abductor pollicis longus and extensor pollicis brevis. It may be related to a narrowing in the tendon abductor sheath or from repetitive movements of the thumb.

The Kinesio Taping Method will assist in reducing edema, pain and will create more space with the application of a mechanical correction.

This technique can be applied using two 1″ Kinesio I strips or a 2″ Kinesio Y strip cut at the radial styloid process. The technique demonstrated will use two Kinesio 1″ I strips.

The practitioner may select to apply a space correction technique in place of the mechanical correction technique, or a fascia correction if deemed appropriate.

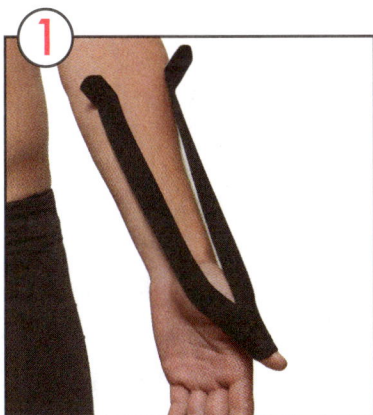

OPTIONAL: 2″ KINESIO Y STRIP WITH THE ANCHOR ON THE DISTAL TIP OF THE THUMB ON THE RADIAL SIDE.

1. Place the anchor of the Y cut from the middle of the proximal phalanx to the tip of the distal phalanx on the dorsal side with no tension. The anchor may wrap around the thumb to assist in adhesion.

   A button hole can be cut in the anchor and applied over the thumb. This will assist with adhesion of the anchor. The hand and fingers are difficult for adhesion due to heavy oils and heavy usage of the hand and fingers. This is demonstrated at the end of this clinical condition.

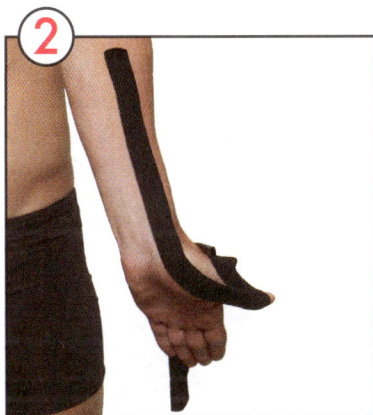

2. Have the patient move their wrist into extension with radial deviation, thumb flexion and elbow extension.

   Apply paper off to light, 15-25% of available tension to the tail along the adductor pollicis brevis (palmar side of thumb). Direct the tail from the radial styloid process towards the lateral epicondyle of the humerus. Rub to initiate adhesive prior to any further patient movement.

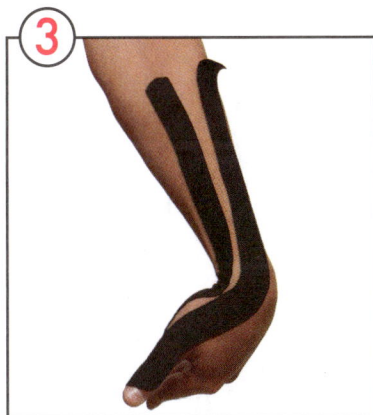

3. Have the patient move into wrist flexion with ulnar deviation, thumb flexion and extension at the elbow.

   Apply paper off to light, 15-25% of available tension to the tail along the extensor pollicis (dorsum side of the thumb). Leave a space in the anatomical snuff box region, or the region of pain between the two tails. Direct the tail from the ulnar styloid process towards the lateral epicondyle of the humerus. Rub to initiate adhesive prior to any further patient movement.

APPLICATION OF A MECHANICAL/SPACE CORRECTION COMBINATION TECHNIQUE WITH TENSION ON BASE

4. Prior to laying down the anchor, estimate its location, so when tension has been applied, the split in the Y cut will bisect with the previously applied tape in the anatomical snuff box region.

   Place the patients wrist in ulnar deviation and thumb extension. Place the anchor of an approximately 4-6" long Kinesio Y strip on the palmar aspect of the wrist with no tension. With one hand hold the anchor of the Kinesio Y strip to ensure no tension will be added.

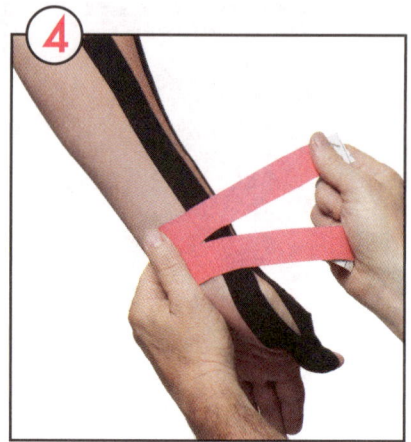

5. With the hand holding the anchor apply an inward pressure on the tissue and "lift" this tissue towards the anatomical snuff box. Apply 50-75% of available tension to the base of the Kinesio Y strip with downward/inward pressure. Be careful to not "over correct" and in initial application remember that "less is more".

   End the tension when the split in the Y bisects with the previously applied tape in the anatomical snuff box region. Move the hand on the anchor up the base to the point of end tension this will initiate adhesive.

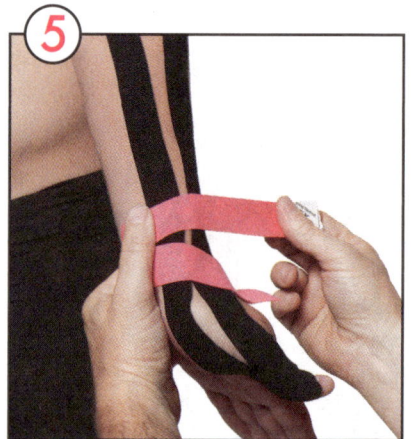

6. Continue to maintain one hand at the end point of tension from the mechanical correction. Have the patient move into wrist flexion with ulnar deviation and thumb flexion. Apply paper off to light tension, 15-25% of available tension to each tail. Apply each tail on either side of the area of pain or inflammation. As you pass the area of pain by approximately 1", decrease to no tension. Rub this area of tail application to initiate adhesion, then lay down the remainder of the tail of the Kinesio Tex Tape Y strip with no tension. Finally rub entire tape application to initiate adhesive prior to any further patient movement.

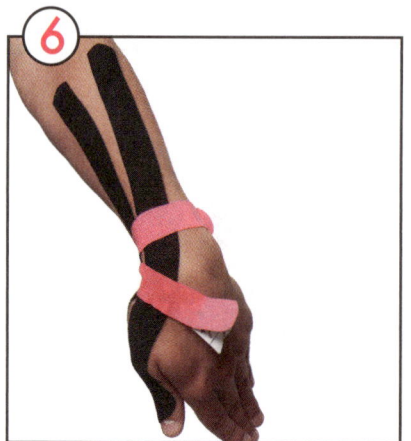

7. If applied correctly, a "square" should form between the two Kinesio Y strip applications, over the area of pain.

   Completed Kinesio Taping Technique for De Quervain's.

   The practitioner may select to apply a donut hole space correction technique in place of the mechanical/space correction combination technique, or a fascia correction if deemed appropriate.

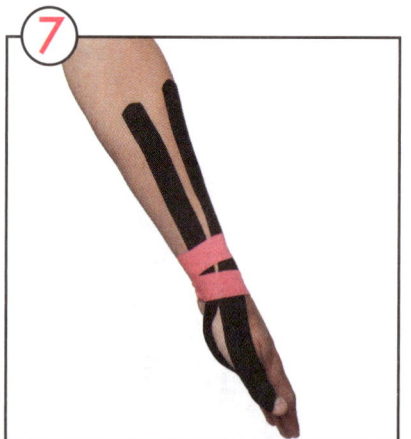

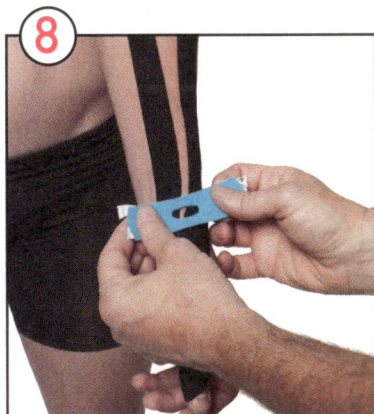

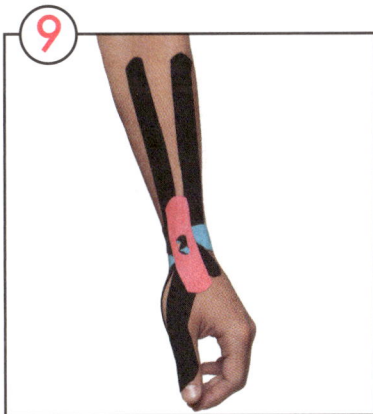

OPTIONAL DONUT HOLE TECHNIQUE APPLICATION

8-9. First select one of the Y techniques as described in this section. Cut a donut hole in the center of 1" Kinesio I or X strip, not to exceed ½ of tape width. Place the patient in wrist radial deviation and thumb flexion. Tear the center backing and apply 15-25% of available tension. Move the wrist into flexion and lay down the lateral end with no tension. Move the wrist into extension and lay down the medial end with no tension. Rub to initiate adhesive prior to any further patient movement. A series of 2-3 strips can be applied. With the 2nd and 3rd strips repeat the above steps. Make sure that when laying down ends the wrist is moved into flexion, extension or deviation as needed to limit tension on the ends.

OPTIONAL: USE A BUTTON HOLE TECHNIQUE Y STRIP: TO ASSIST WITH ADHESION

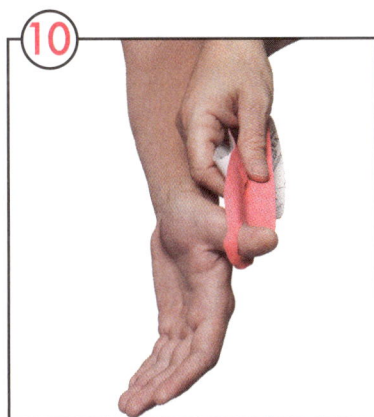

10. Cut the appropriate length of 2" Kinesio Tex Tape. In the center of one end, make a "button hole" approximately ½" from the end. Begin the Y cut at the MCP joint. Remove the paper backing from the "button hole" and apply slightly above the DIP on the dorsal side with no tension and rub to initiate adhesive prior to any further patient movement.

11. Have the patient move their wrist into flexion with radial deviation, thumb flexion and elbow extension.

Apply paper off to light, 15-25% of available tension to the tail along the adductor pollicis brevis (palmar side of thumb). Direct the tail from the radial styloid process towards the lateral epicondyle of the humerus. Rub to initiate adhesive prior to any further patient movement.

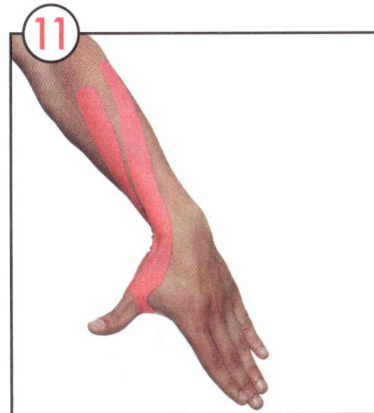

12. Have the patient move into wrist flexion with ulnar deviation, thumb flexion and extension at the elbow.

Apply paper off to light, 15-25% of available tension to the tail along the extensor pollicis (dorsum side of the thumb). Leave a space in the anatomical snuff box region, or the region of pain between the two tails. Direct the tail from the ulnar styloid process towards the lateral epicondyle of the humerus. Rub to initiate adhesive prior to any further patient movement.

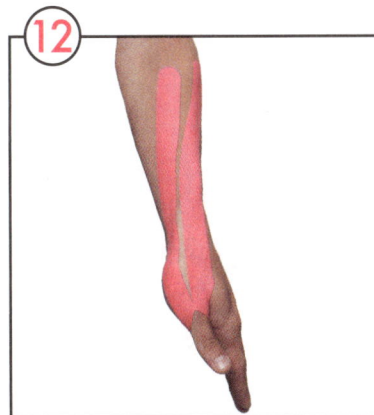

De Quervain's

Finger Sprain, Radial or Ulnar Collateral Ligament

A sprain to the proximal or distal interphalangeal joint is a common injury resulting from activity. It may result from an axial load on the fingertip, abduction, or adduction force on the joint. This condition is also commonly referred to as a, "jammed finger".

The Kinesio Taping Method will assist in reducing edema, pain and provide ligament stability.

Finger Sprain, Radial or Ulnar Collateral Ligament

1. An optional anchor may be placed in the middle of both the proximal and distal phalanx (above or below the joint you are attempting to stabilize).

   The anchor is not required. Kinesio Tex Tape adheres best when placed directly to the skin.

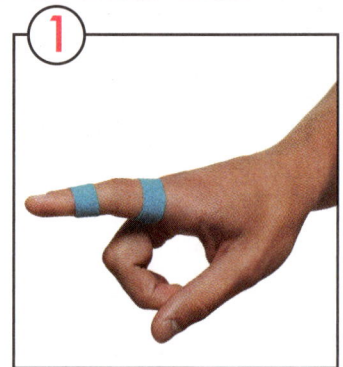

2. With the finger in as much extension as possible apply one anchor distally on the palmar side of the finger with no tension.

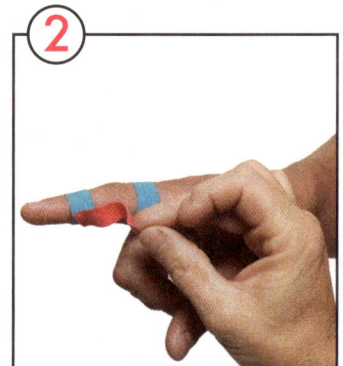

3. With one hand hold the distal anchor to ensure no tension will be added. Angle the Kinesio I strip at a 45 degree angle. Apply a ligament correction, severe to full, 75-100% of available tension, to the center of the Kinesio I strip. Lay down the center of the Kinesio I strip directly over the central area of the joint line in the area of laxity.

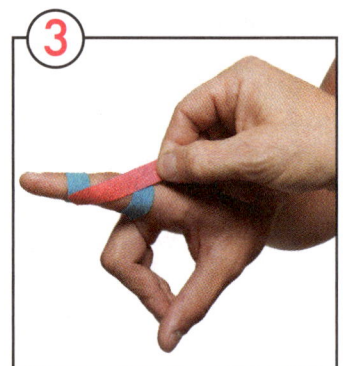

4. Lay down the end of the Kinesio I strip with no tension. Rub vigorously to initiate adhesive prior to any further patient movement.

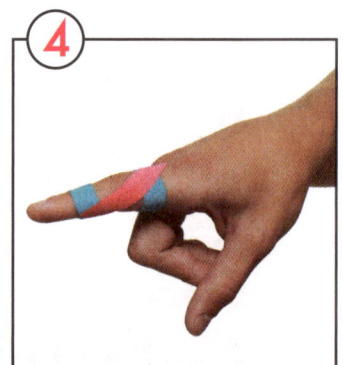

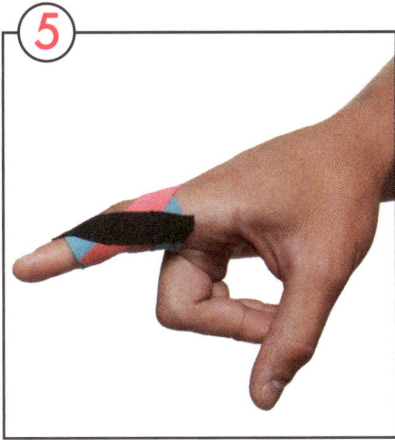

5. Apply a second ligament correction.

   With the finger in as much extension as possible apply one anchor distally on the dorsal aspect of the finger with no tension.

   With one hand hold the distal anchor to ensure no tension will be added. Angle the Kinesio I strip at a 45 degree angle. Apply a ligament correction, severe to full, 75-100% of available tension, to the center of the Kinesio I strip. Lay down the center of the Kinesio I strip directly over the central area of the joint line in the area of laxity.

   Lay down the end of the Kinesio I strip with no tension. Rub vigorously to initiate adhesive prior to any further patient movement.

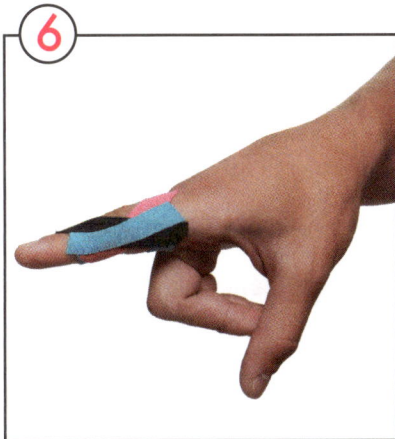

6. A third ligament correction parallel to the injury ligament can be applied. It will depend upon the size of the individual. A larger patient or athlete may need the third strip to provide adequate protection.

   With the finger in as much extension as possible apply one anchor distally on the dorsal aspect of the finger with no tension.

   With one hand hold the distal anchor to ensure no tension will be added. Direct the I strip horizontally along the joint line. Apply a ligament correction, severe to full, 75-100% of available tension, to the center of the Kinesio I strip. Lay down the center of the Kinesio I strip directly over the central area of the joint line in the area of laxity.

   Lay down the end of the Kinesio I strip with no tension. Rub vigorously to initiate adhesive prior to any further patient movement.

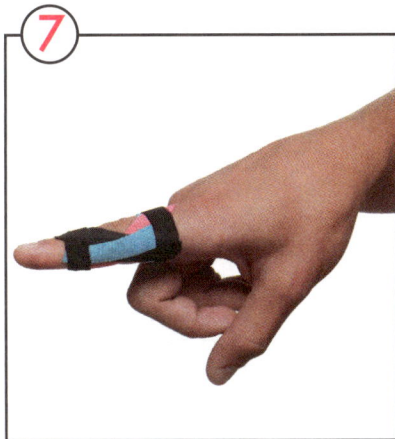

7. Apply a second set of anchors in the middle of both the proximal and distal phalanx (or above and below the joint you are attempting to stabilize).

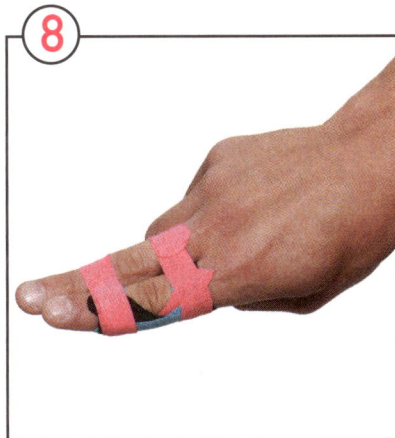

OPTIONAL: BUDDY TAPING

8. Application of a "buddy taping technique" to the injured finger with an adjacent finger or its "buddy". Apply an anchor strip below and above the injured joint. A spray adherent may be used to limit tape migration due to moisture which may develop during activity.

   A small pad may be placed between the fingers to minimize irritation to the skin.

Mallet Finger

A Mallet Finger is the result of the finger being in an extended position and forced into flexion by a direct trauma. The extensor digitorum tendon is avulsed from the base of the distal phalanx. The tension of the flexor tendon pulls the distal phalanx into flexion giving the appearance of the head of a mallet.

The Kinesio Taping Technique will assist by limiting the distal phalanx movement into flexion. If the patient has sustained a mallet finger, which has resulted in the extensor tendon being avulsed, this needs to be treated in a splint, or surgically repaired. If the patient has sustained a mild injury, recovering from treatment in a splint or surgery, the Kinesio Taping Method will be beneficial.

APPLICATION OF THE FUNCTIONAL CORRECTION TECHNIQUE TO LIMIT DISTAL PHALANX FLEXION.

1. Begin by measuring a Kinesio I strip from the palmar surface of the distal tip, over the fingernail and continuing past the metacarpal phalangeal (MCP) joint of the injured finger.

   Place distal anchor of the Kinesio I strip on the palmar surface of the injured joint with no tension and wrap around to the dorsal surface of the injured finger.

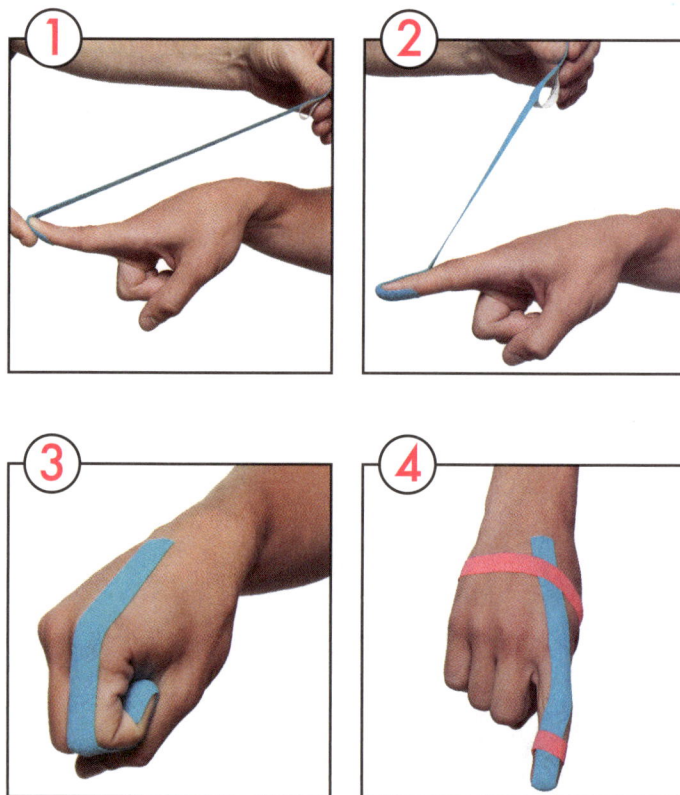

2. With one hand hold the distal anchor which has been applied to the distal phalanx, to ensure no tension will be added. Place the patient's finger into as much extension as pain or range of motion allows. Apply functional correction, 50+% of available tension to the Kinesio I strip. Apply the proximal anchor of the Kinesio I strip to the dorsum surface of the injured finger. Apply tension until the Kinesio I strip is minimum of 2" distal to the MCP joint. The longer the anchor, within reason, the effectiveness of adhesion will be maximized.

3. While holding both the distal and proximal anchors have the patient move into flexion. Rub to initiate adhesive prior to any patient movement. This is important when using higher tension levels. Vigorously rub to initiate adhesive prior to any further patient movement.

   A second functional correction strip may be applied depending upon the size of the individual and the degree of finger movement limitation desired.

4. Apply an anchor at both the tip of the injured finger and as close to the MCP joint as possible. This will assist in providing better support and limit the Kinesio Tex Tape from coming off the skin due to the high tension used during application.

   A splint may be worn directly over this technique.

Dislocation of the Phalanges of the Fingers

Dislocations of the phalanges occur at a higher rate when compared to dislocations in other areas of the body. Dislocations can occur at the metacarpal phalangeal joint (MCP), proximal interphalangeal joint (PIP) or distal interphalangeal joint (DIP). They can dislocate in both the palmar or dorsal direction.

The Kinesio Taping Technique will provide pain relief, reduce inflammation by use of a lymphatic correction, provide joint stability with a ligament correction, and use a functional correction to limit flexion or extension.

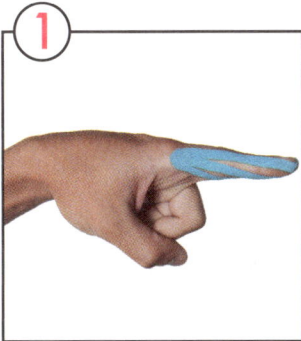

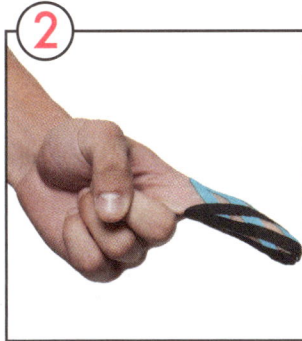

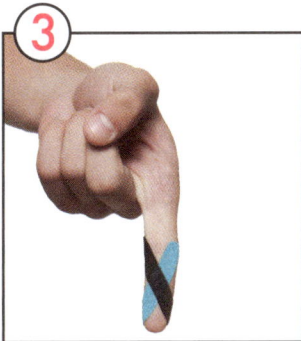

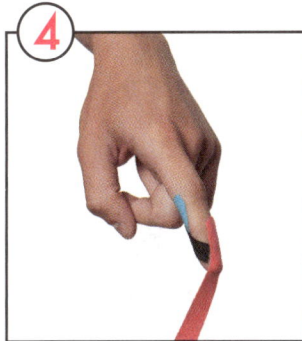

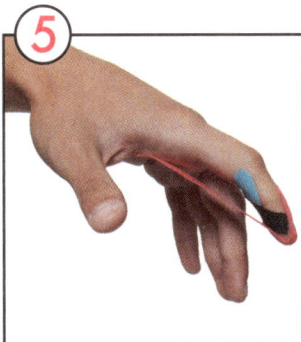

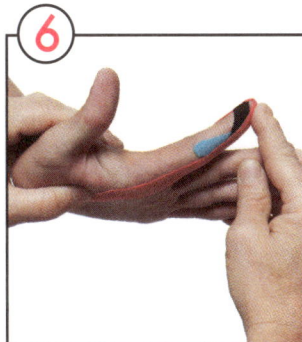

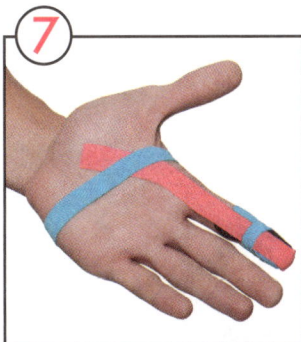

Apply a lymphatic correction technique to the dorsal surface, palmar surface or both.

1-2. Application shown is from the base of the first proximal phalanx to the distal phalanx, anchor on dorsum side, wrapping the Kinesio Tex Tape around the entire finger. Use 10-20% tension.

3. Apply a ligament correction technique to the region in which the dislocation or fractured region is located.

If the finger was a dorsal dislocation, apply the ligament correction on the dorsal aspect of the finger. If the dislocation caused laxity to either the medial, collateral, or lateral ligaments of the finger, apply the correction strip to these regions in a crisscross pattern. For review of this technique, see finger sprain.

4. Apply a functional correction technique that will limit the motion which caused the mechanism of the injury. Generally, dislocations occur in the dorsal direction. Limiting the joint range of motion in extension will assist with joint stability. Begin by placing the patient's finger in a flexed position. Apply the anchor over the dorsal side of the distal tip of the phalanx and over the fingernail.

5. Apply 50+% of available tension to the I strip. The palmar anchor is applied proximal to the head of the corresponding metacarpal head.

6. Hold both the dorsal and palmar anchors. Have the patient move into finger extension. The degree of joint limitations is determined by the degree of tension applied to the functional correction as applied by the practitioner.

7. Strips of Kinesio Tex Tape to hold the corrective technique in place.

Not Shown: an additional Kinesio Strip may be used to "buddy tape" the injured finger to the finger located next to it, its buddy. Please see finger sprain for description.

Gamekeepers or Skier's Thumb

Gamekeepers or Skier's Thumb is a sprain to the ulnar collateral ligament of the 1st metacarpal phalangeal joint (MCP). Generally the mechanism of the injury forces the thumb into abduction with extension. Without this ligament, it is difficult for the patient to grasp items between the thumb and index finger.

The Kinesio Taping Technique will assist with reducing edema, pain and provide ligament stability. For a grade two (increased laxity of ligament) and grade three (ligament rupture), the patient should be treated in a cast. Prior to and following cast treatment, the Kinesio Taping Method would be appropriate.

Gamekeeper's or Skier's Thumb

ACUTE PHASE: 24-72 HOURS:

Application of the lymphatic corrective technique to reduce edema resulting from a sprain to the MCP joint.

1. Strip One, apply anchor with no tension on the dorsum of the thumb between the base of the 1st and 2nd ray. Apply 0-20% of available tension and angle the fan strip over the MCP joint. Pat or rub to initiate adhesive prior to any further patient movement.

2. Strip Two, on the palmar side of the thumb near the base of the of 1st metacarpal and angle the fan strip over the MCP joint with 0-20% of available tension. Pat or rub to initiate adhesive prior to any further patient movement.

   The two strips should form a crisscross pattern over the area of pain or edema.

POST ACUTE PHASE: POST 72 HOURS

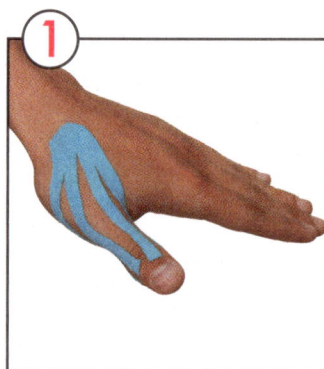
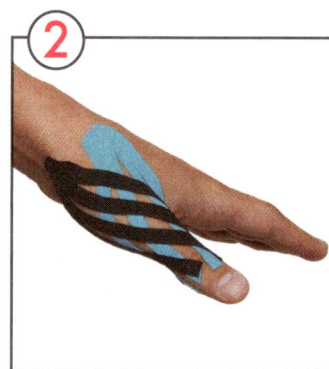
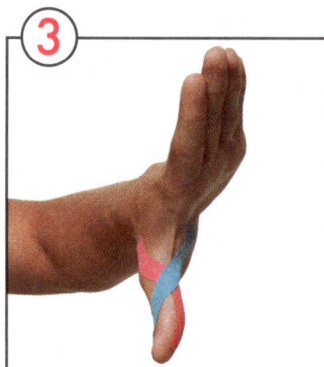
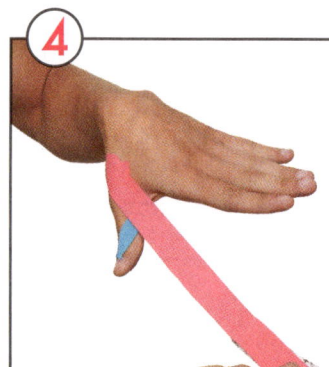

3. Apply a ligament correction technique to the ulnar side of the 1st MCP joint. Ligament correction should be applied forming an X over the UCL ligament of the MCP joint.

   Apply a ligament correction as described in sprained finger.

4. Figure of 8 I strip. Begin by applying the anchor of a figure of 8 strip of 1" Kinesio Tex Tape starting on the ulnar aspect of the proximal phalanx. Angle at approximately 45 degrees over the MCP joint. Apply 15-35%, light to moderate tension as you direct the tape around the proximal MCP joint.

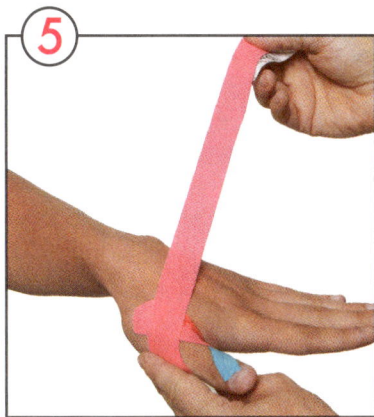

5. Continue the Kinesio I strip, applying 15-35%, light to moderate, tension around the dorsal surface of the thumb, apply slight downward tension as you cross over the dorsum of the hand, be careful not to pull the thumb into an abducted position. Continue the strip towards the base of the 5th metacarpal. As you cross over the palmar surface of the palm, angle the tape back towards the MCP joint. This strip is to provide adduction pressure to assist the joint capsule and to control abduction movement.

Be careful to not apply too much tension when using a figure of 8 to ensure that circulation is not compromised.

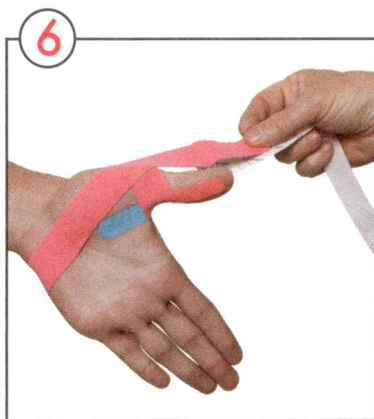

6. Continue the Kinesio I strip, applying light to moderate, 15-35% of available tension around the palmar surface of the thumb. As you again reach the 1st MCP joint apply slight downward tension but be careful not to pull the thumb into an abducted position. Continue the strip over the MCP joint, over the dorsum of the hand angled towards the base of the 5th metacarpal.

7. As you cross over the palmar surface of the palm, angle the tape back towards the MCP joint. This strip is to provide adduction pressure to assist the joint capsule and to control abduction movement.

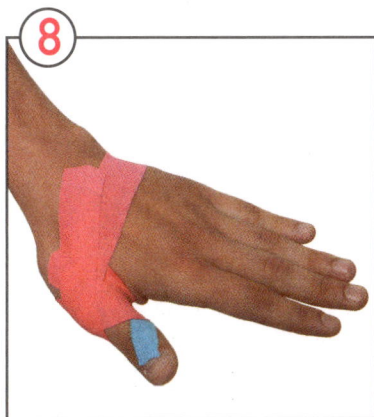

8. Lay down the end with no tension. Try to apply the end onto skin, as the Kinesio Tex Tape is designed to adhere to the skin not to itself. Be careful to not apply too much tension when using a figure of 8 to ensure that circulation is not compromised. Completed application.

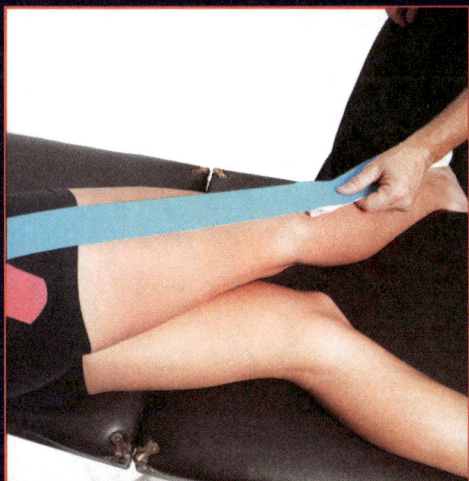

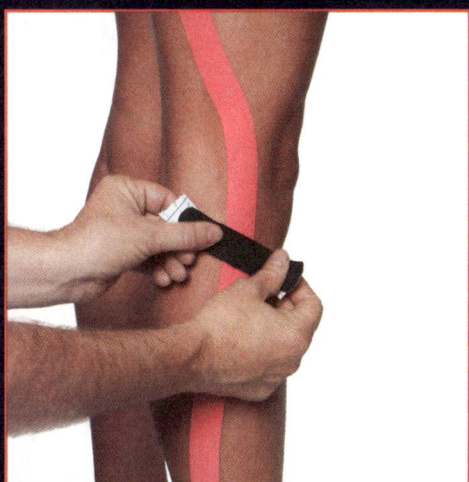

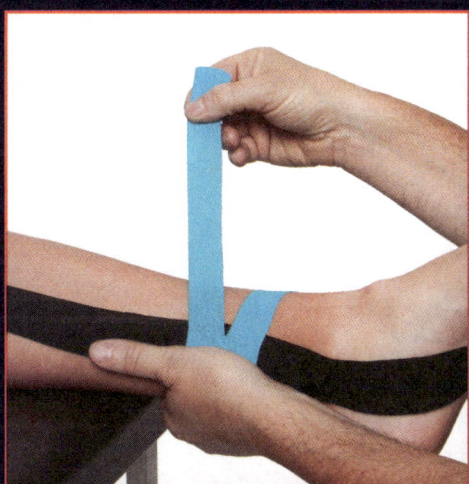

SECTION 7
Hip and Leg

Section 7

Osteoarthritis of the Hip

Osteoarthritis of the hip is degnerative destruction of the articular surfaces within the joint. It may be associated with normal degenertive changes from chronic impact loading caused by high levels of physical activity. The etiology of chronic hip effusion may be unknown, the resulting chronic joint effusion will cause continuing degenerative changes, and decreased muscle function.

The Kinesio Taping Method will assist by reducing effusion and joint pain.

Osteoarthritis of the Hip

Initial treatment for inflammation or edema is provided by applying two Kinesio lymphatic corrective strips.

1. Begin by placing the first anchor with no tension at approximately the anterior superior iliac spine. Apply 0-20% of available tension to the tails. Angle the fan tails at a 45 degrees in a posterior and inferior direction. Lay down the ends with no tension, rub to initiate adhesive prior to any further patient movement.

2. The second anchor is applied approximately at the posterior superior iliac spine. Apply 0-20% of available tension to the tails. Angle the fan tails at a 45 degrees in a posterior and inferior direction. Lay down the ends with no tension, rub to initiate adhesive prior to any further patient movement. The fan strips should form a crisscross pattern.

OPTION 1: INHIBITION FOR THE GLUTEUS MEDIUS MUSCLE USING A Y STRIP AND IT BAND FASCIA CORRECTION.

3. Apply anchor of Kinesio Y strip on the lateral surface of the greater trochanter with no tension.

   Patient is side lying, hip flexion and adduction direct the posterior tail to the lateral aspect of the posterior iliac spine, with paper off to light, 15-25% of available tension. Lay the final 1-2" down with no tension. Rub to initiate adhesive prior to any further patient movement.

   Then place the patient side lying and hip adduction direct the anterior tail towards the lateral aspect of the anterior iliac spine with paper off to light, 15-25% of available tension. Lay the final 1-2" down with no tension. Rub to initiate adhesive prior to any further patient movement.

4. The iliotibial band attaches to the tensor fascia lata muscle and generally is not involved due to weakness, but increased tension in the iliotibial band. The increased tension in the IT band can increase pressure over the hip joint. The TFL may need to be inhibited or the practitioner may find the TFL muscle may be weak and so a facilitation tension may be appropriate.

   The iliotibial band fascia application can begin at either the origin or insertion. For this application, the origin to insertion technique will be shown.

   Begin by measuring the length of Kinesio Tex required. Place the anchor of the Kinesio I strip superior to the iliac crest with no tension.

   Several other optional applications are shown in the iliotibial band friction syndrome section.

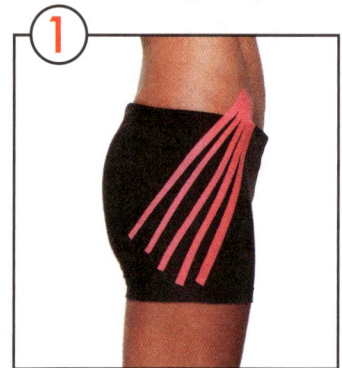

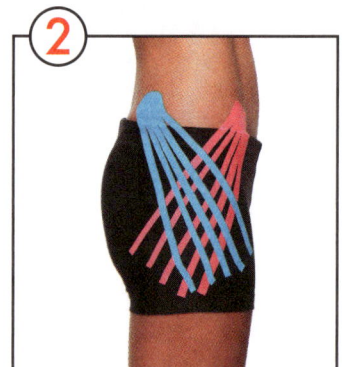

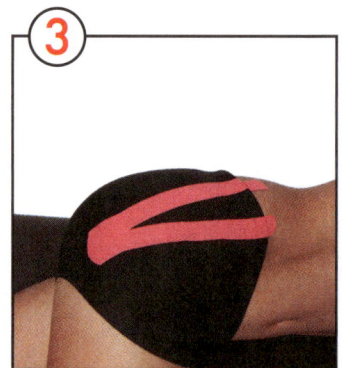

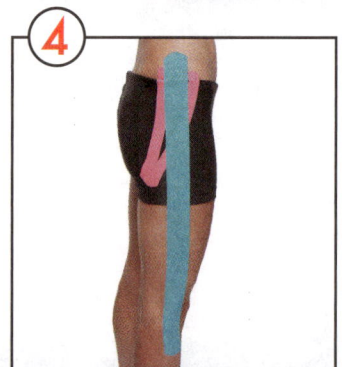

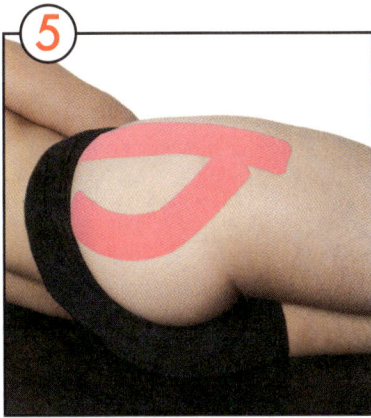

OPTION 2: FACILITATION FOR THE GLUTEUS MEDIUS MUSCLE USING A TWO I STRIP TECHNIQUE TO MAKE A Y STRIP.

5. Patient is side lying, hip adduction and extension place the anchor with no tension at the lip of Iliac Crest just lateral to the ASIS. Direct the posterior tail to the lateral aspect of the posterior iliac spine. Apply paper off to moderate, 15-35% of available tension and direct the I strip slightly distal to the greater trochanter. Lay down end with no tension and rub to initiate adhesive prior to any further patient movement.

Next place the patient in hip flexion and adduction and place the anchor with no tension at the lip of the Iliac Crest lateral to the PSIS. Apply paper off to moderate, 15-35% of available tension and direct the I strip towards the greater trochanter. Lay down end with no tension and rub to initiate adhesive prior to any further patient movement.

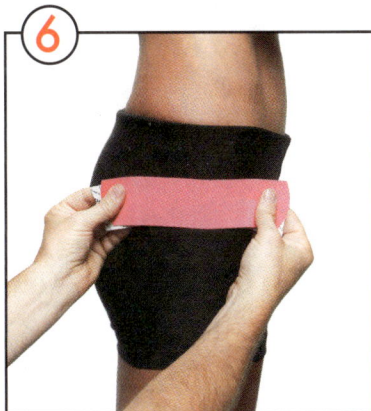

OPTION 3: APPLICATION SPACE CORRECTION, STAR TECHNIQUE TO REDUCE EDEMA OR INFLAMMATION DIRECTLY OVER THE AREA OF PAIN OR EDEMA.

6. Begin by measuring three to four, 6-8" Kinesio I strips. Tear the center backing and apply light to moderate, 10-35% of available tension to the exposed Kinesio Tex Tape. Apply the center of the I strip directly over the greater trochanter or area of pain. Lay down the ends with no tension. Rub to initiate adhesive prior to any further patient movement.

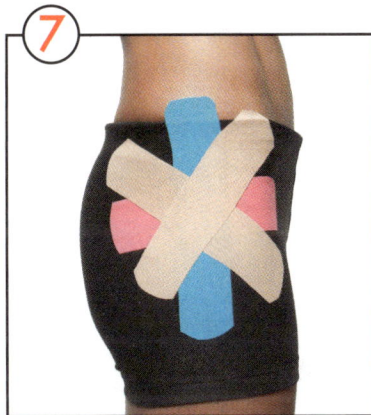

7. Repeat the above steps for each of the remaining I strips. For each of the remaining strips have the patient move into a stretched position prior to laying down the I strips and ends. Rub to initiate adhesive prior to any further patient movement.

OPTION 4: APPLICATION OF SPACE CORRECTION, WEB CUT

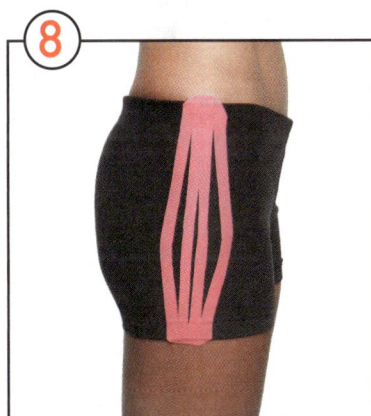

8. Measure an appropriate length of Kinesio Tex Tape and cut into a Web Cut of 4 to 5 strips. Application choice 1: Apply anchor at approximately the ischium with no tension. Peel back the paper backing and apply 10-20% of available tension to the strips and apply over the greater trochanter. Lay down the end with no tension. Application choice 2: Tear the center backing of the strips and apply 10-20% of available tension and apply the center of the strips over the greater trochanter. Lay down the ends with no tension and rub to activate adhesive prior to any further patient movement.

Trochanteric Bursitis

Trochanteric Bursitis is a common condition of the hip which results in inflammation of the trochanteric bursae located on the greater trochanter of the femur. It may also be associated with pain from the gluteus medius insertion or iliotibial band friction as it passes over the greater trochanter.

The Kinesio Taping Technique will assist in reducing edema and pain.

Initial treatment for inflammation or edema is provided by applying two Kinesio lymphatic corrective strips.

1. Begin by placing the first anchor with no tension at approximately the anterior superior iliac spine. Apply 0-20% of available tension to the tails. Angle the fan tails at 45 degrees in a posterior and inferior direction. Lay down the ends with no tension, rub to initiate adhesive prior to any further patient movement.

2. The second anchor is applied approximately at the posterior superior iliac spine. Apply 0-20% of available tension to the tails. Angle the fan tails at 45 degrees in a posterior and inferior direction. Lay down the ends with no tension, rub to initiate adhesive prior to any further patient movement.

The fan strips should form a crisscross pattern.

OPTION 1: INHIBITION FOR THE GLUTEUS MEDIUS MUSCLE USING A Y STRIP AND IT BAND FASCIA CORRECTION.

3. Apply anchor of Kinesio Y strip on the lateral surface of the greater trochanter with no tension.

Patient is side lying, hip flexion and adduction direct the posterior tail to the lateral aspect of the posterior iliac spine, with paper off to light, 15-25% of available tension. Lay the final 1-2" down with no tension. Rub to initiate adhesive prior to any further patient movement.

Then place the patient side lying and hip adduction direct the anterior tail towards the lateral aspect of the anterior iliac spine with paper off to light, 15-25% of available tension. Lay the final 1-2" down with no tension. Rub to initiate adhesive prior to any further patient movement.

4. The iliotibial band attaches to the tensor fascia lata muscle and generally is not involved due to weakness, but increased tension in the iliotibial band. The increased tension in the IT band can increase pressure over the hip joint. The TFL may need to be inhibited or the practitioner may find the TFL muscle may be weak and so a facilitation tension may be appropriate.

The iliotibial band fascia application can begin at either the origin or insertion. For this application, the origin to insertion technique will be shown. Several other optional applications are shown in the iliotibial band friction syndrome section.

Begin by measuring the length of Kinesio Tex required. Place the anchor of the Kinesio I strip superior to the iliac crest with no tension.

Place the patient in a stretched position for the iliotibial band. Apply paper off to moderate, 15-25% of available tension along the entire length of the iliotibial band. A side to side or long and short oscillation technique can be used. For longer wider fascia limitations the side to side technique may work better.

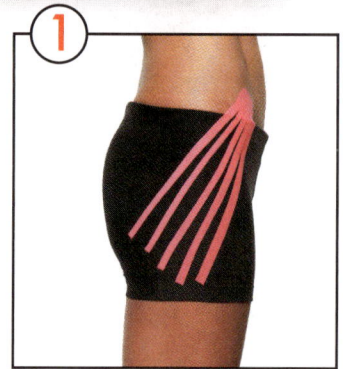
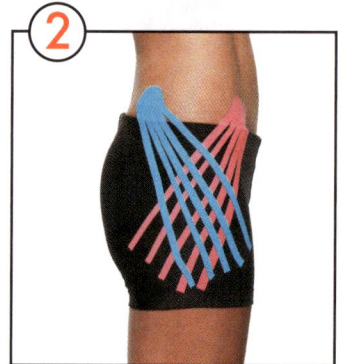
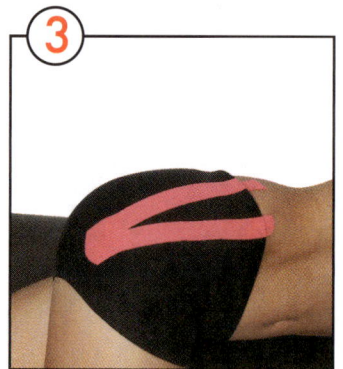
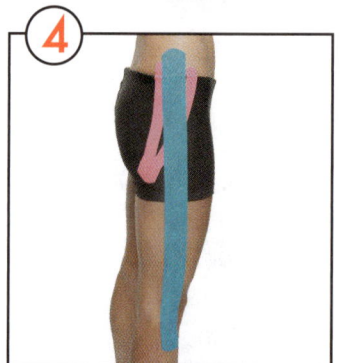

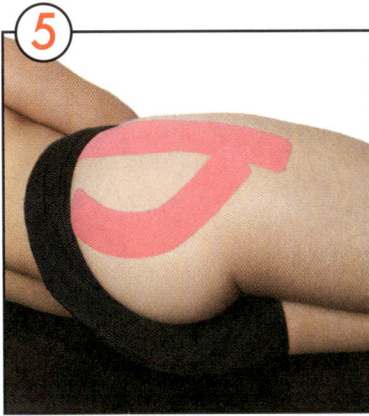

OPTION 2: FACILITATION FOR THE GLUTEUS MEDIUS MUSCLE USING A TWO I STRIP TECHNIQUE TO MAKE A Y STRIP.

5. Apply anchor of Kinesio Y strip on the lateral surface of the greater trochanter with no tension.

Patient is side lying, hip adduction and extension place the anchor with no tension at the lip of Iliac Crest just lateral to the ASIA. Direct the posterior tail to the lateral aspect of the posterior iliac spine. Apply paper off to moderate, 15-35% of available tension and direct the I strip slightly distal to the greater trochanter. Lay down end with no tension and rub to initiate adhesive prior to any further patient movement.

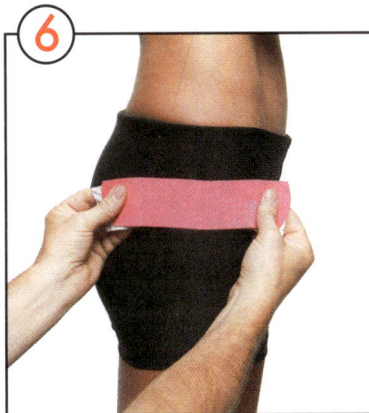

Next place the patient in hip flexion and adduction and place the anchor with no tension at the lip of the Iliac Crest lateral to the PSIS. Apply paper off to moderate, 15-35% of available tension and direct the I strip towards the greater trochanter. Lay down end with no tension and rub to initiate adhesive prior to any further patient movement.

OPTION 3: APPLICATION SPACE CORRECTION, STAR TECHNIQUE

6-7. For complete review, see star technique in herniated disk lesion. Apply a series of 3-4 space correction I strips tension in the center. Tear the center of a 6-8" Kinesio I strip and apply 15-35% of available tension directly over the area of pain or edema. Lay down the ends with no tension and rub to initiate adhesive prior to any further patient movement. Repeat the above description for each strip. With a series of 3-4 space corrections the technique may be more effective by reducing the degree of tension to each strip. The accumulative effect will create a "pocket" above the edema.

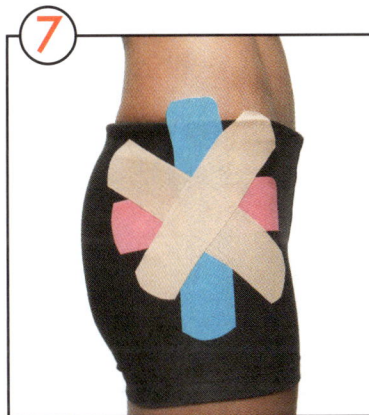

OPTION 4: APPLICATION OF SPACE CORRECTION, WEB CUT

8. Measure an appropriate length of Kinesio Tex Tape and cut into a Web Cut of 4 to 5 strips. Application choice 1: Apply anchor at approximately the ischium with no tension. Peel back the paper backing and apply 10-20% of available tension to the strips and apply over the greater trochanter. Lay down the end with no tension. Application choice 2: Tear the center backing of the strips and apply 10-20% of available tension and apply the center of the strips over the greater trochanter. Lay down the ends with no tension and rub to activate adhesive prior to any further patient movement.

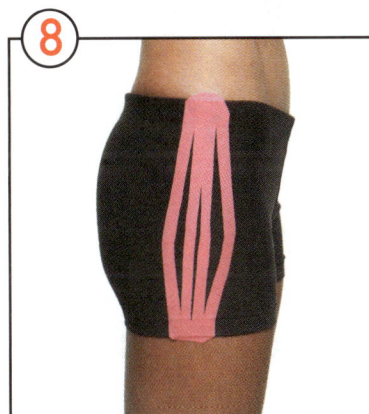

Hip Pointer – Iliac Crest Contusion

Hip Pointer is a contusion to the muscular attachments of the abdominal muscles as they insert on the iliac crest. The injury occurs from blunt trauma on an unprotected iliac crest. A hematoma may form causing a pinching action on the muscle attachments. It is generally vary painful and can significantly affect an individual's ability to be physically active.

The Kinesio Taping Technique will assist by reducing effusion, possible hematoma and pain.

ACUTE PHASE: 24-72 HOURS:

Initial treatment for inflammation or edema is provided by applying two Kinesio lymphatic corrective techniques.

1. Place the patient in lateral flexion to the opposite side and place the first lymphatic Kinesio fan anchor approximately 3-4" anterior and superior to the iliac crest with no tension. Apply 0-20% of available tension and angle the fan tails at 45 degrees in a posterior direction. Rub to initiate adhesive prior to any further movement.

2. The second anchor is approximately 3-4" posterior and superior to the iliac crest. Angle the fan tails at 45 degrees in an anterior direction. Applying 0-20% of available tension. Rub or pat to activate adhesive prior to any further patient movement.

   The fan strips should form a crisscross pattern.

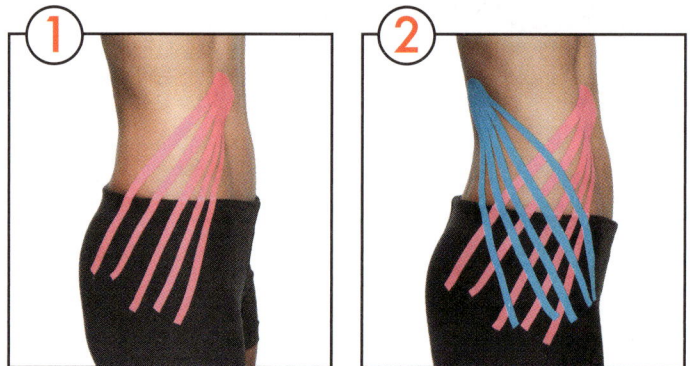

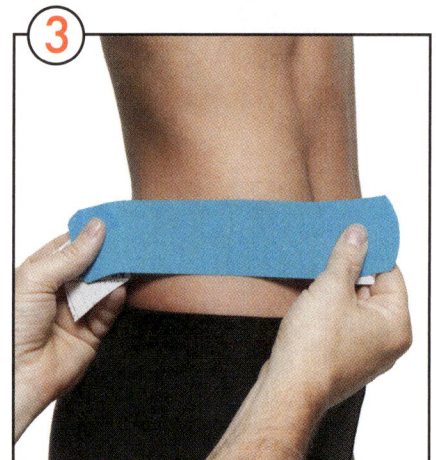

POST ACUTE PHASE: POST 72 HOURS

Application of a Space Correction Technique to assist in reducing edema.

3. Begin by tearing the center of the paper backing of a 6-8" Kinesio I strip. Apply light to moderate, 10-35% of available tension to the Kinesio I strip in the exposed section.

   Place the Kinesio I strip directly over the region of pain on the iliac crest. Lay down the ends of the Kinesio I strip with no tension, have the patient move through as much range of motion as possible when applying the ends of the Kinesio I strip.

4. In an acute iliac contusion, three to four space correction strips are recommended. As the patient improves, fewer strips may be required. As the strips are applied, have the patient move through as much range of motion as possible when applying the ends of the Kinesio I strip. This is to ensure that no tension will be added to the ends. In acute iliac crest contusions, the iliac crest may be very sensitive and tender, it is recommended to be careful not to add any downward pressure when applying the space correction technique.

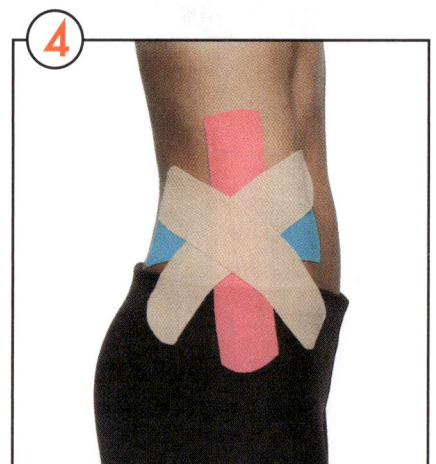

Quadriceps Contusion/ Strain

Contusion to the quadriceps muscle, the largest muscle group in the body, can result in the formation of a hematoma. The hematoma may limit the patient's ability to walk, or participate in physical activity. Mild hematomas may only affect the patient for a few days. Significant or severe hematomas may result in the formation of bone, myositis ossificans, within the muscle tissue.

The use of the Kinesio Taping Method will aid in the reduction of the hematoma, as well as, assist in the weakness which may have developed due to injury and inactivity.

The quadriceps muscle may be treated using the basic quadriceps technique to limit muscle weakness. A lymphatic and/or space correction technique may be applied over the basic muscle taping or prior to its application.

The basic Kinesio Taping Technique can also be used to assist with a strain to the quadriceps muscle resulting from over-extension or over-contraction.

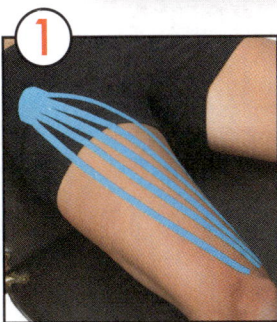

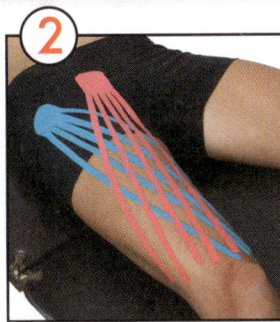

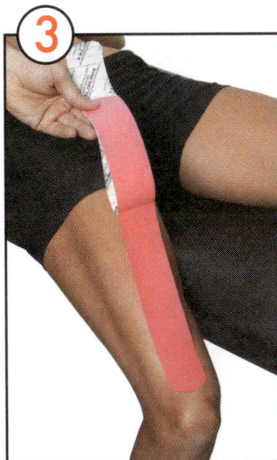

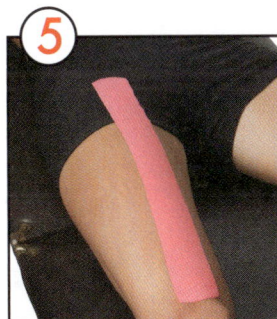

Application of lymphatic corrective technique to reduce hematoma resulting from bleeding.

1. Apply anchor of fan strip near the inguinal fold with no tension. Apply 0-20% of available tension and cross over the anterior aspect of the thigh or area of hematoma. Lay down ends with no tension and rub to initiate adhesive prior to any further patient movement.

2. The second anchor fan should start from as high up on the medial side of the thigh as patient comfort will allow. Apply 0-20% of available tension and cross over the anterior aspect of the thigh or area of hematoma. Lay down ends with no tension and pat or rub to initiate adhesive prior to any further patient movement.

   The fan strips should create a crisscross pattern over the anterior aspect of the thigh.

3. Inhibition application of a rectus femoris muscle using a Kinesio I strip. The Kinesio strip is placed directly over the area of pain.

   Begin by placing the anchor of the Kinesio I strip inferior to the area of the contusion or stain and generally superior to the patella. An optional anchor can be applied at the tibial tuberosity.

   If using the Kinesio Y strip technique, surround the area of injury with the tails of the Y. In post acute or rehabilitation stages facilitation application is appropriate.

4. Have the patient move into hip extension and knee flexion. Apply paper off to light, 15-25% of available tension until the Kinesio I strip reaches past the area of injury or to the upper rim of the anterior superior iliac spine.

5. Lay down the end with no tension. Rub to initiate adhesive prior to any further patient movement.

OPTIONAL APPLICATION OF A RECTUS FEMORIS INHIBITION TECHNIQUE - SLIT TECHNIQUE.

6. Begin by measuring an appropriate length Kinesio I strip from either the ASIS or approximately the superior 1/3 of the quadriceps muscle group.

7. Cut a slit in the distal end of the I strip. The slit should begin approximately 3" from the end. The slit should be cut to surround the medial and lateral border of the patella and reach the musculotendinous junction of the quadriceps.

8. Peel back the paper backing from the anchor only. Apply the anchor inferior to the tibial tuberosity with no tension.

9. Peel back the paper backing of the section with the slits. Gently separate the two 1" slits and apply paper off to light, 15-25% of available tension. Apply the medial slit along the medial border of the patella and the lateral slit along the lateral border. As the slits pass the patella angle them towards the musculotendonous junction. Rub to initiate adhesive prior to any further patient movement.

10. Move the patient into hip extension. Peel back the remaining paper backing and apply 15-25% of available tension either through the center of the quadriceps or along the involved individual muscle. Lay down the end with no tension. Rub to initiate adhesive prior to any further patient movement.

11. Finished application of optional inhibition for rectus femoris, slit technique.

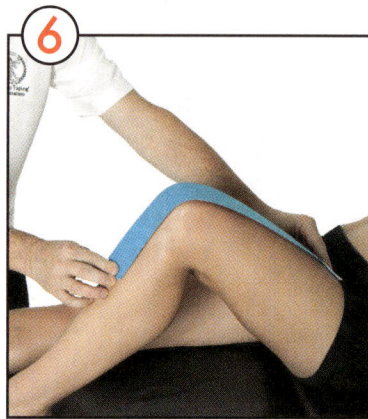

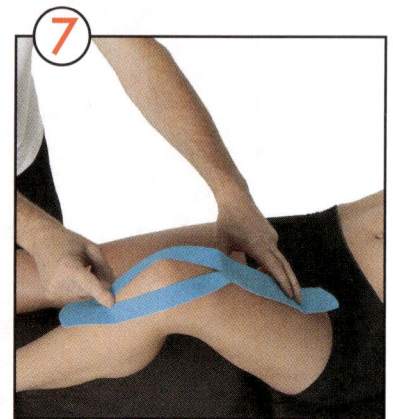

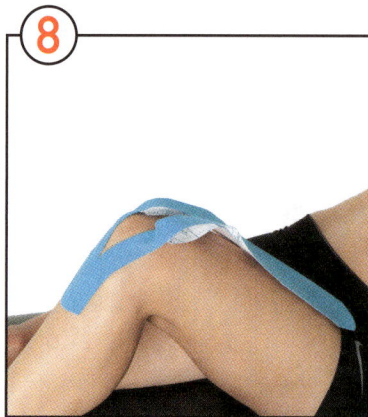

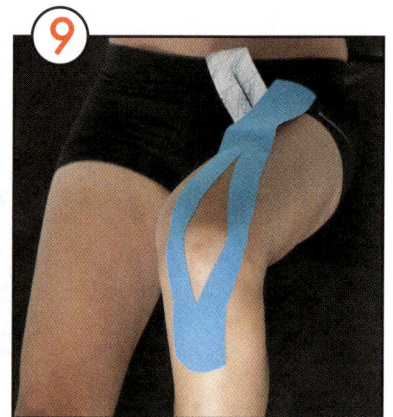

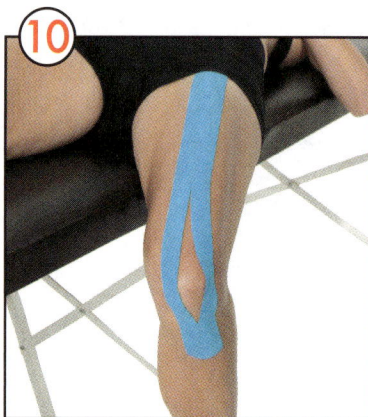

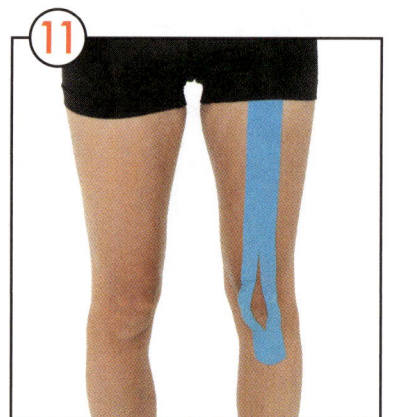

Quadriceps Contusion / Strain

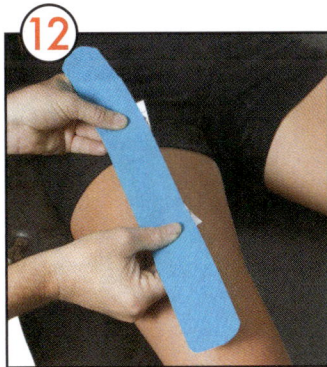

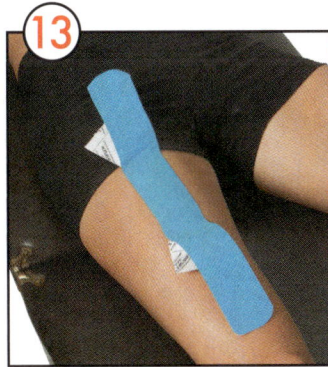

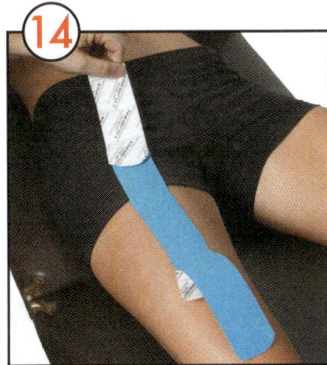

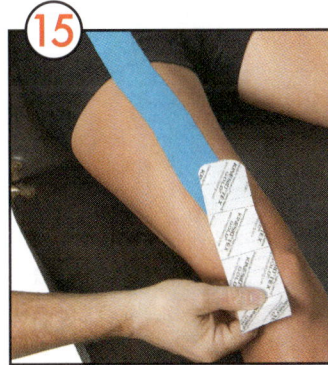

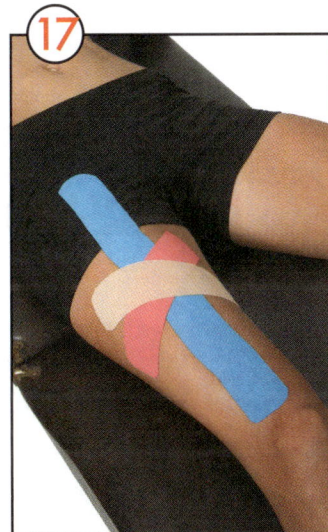

OPTION 1: APPLICATION OF A SPACE CORRECTION STRIP WITH "MODIFIED STAR TECHNIQUE"

The space correction I strip is placed directly over the injured area. This further assists the removal of an edema or hematoma formation.

12. Measure an I strip from the ASIS to the superior pole of the patella.

13. Begin by tearing the paper backing in the center of an I strip. Apply paper off to moderate, 15-35% of available tension to the exposed Kinesio I strip and apply directly over the treatment zone.

14. Lay down the superior portion of the I strip with paper off tension to the last 1-2". Lay down the end with no tension.

15. Lay down the inferior portion of the I strip with paper off tension to the last 1-2". Lay down the end with no tension.

    Rub to initiate adhesive prior to any further patient movement.

16. Apply a modified star technique by applying 2 space correction strips over the area of edema or hematoma. The first space correction I strip was just applied.

    Begin by tearing the paper backing in the center of a 6-8" Kinesio I strip. Apply 10-35% tension to the center of the I strip. Place the center of the tension zone at approximately a 45 degree angle over the area of pain. Lay down the ends with no tension.

17. Repeat the above steps for the second 6-8" Kinesio I strip. Rub to initiate adhesive prior to any further patient movement.

Quadriceps Contusion / Strain

OPTION 2: APPLICATION OF A MECHANICAL CORRECTION STRIP POST ACUTE OR DURING REHABILITATION, FACILITATION TECHNIQUE

18. Place the patient into hip extension and knee flexion. Apply anchor with no tension inferior to the ASIS. Apply 15-35% of available tension to the I strip.

    Lay the I strip down the center of the rectus femoris, or adjust the strip as indicated by practitioner evaluation.

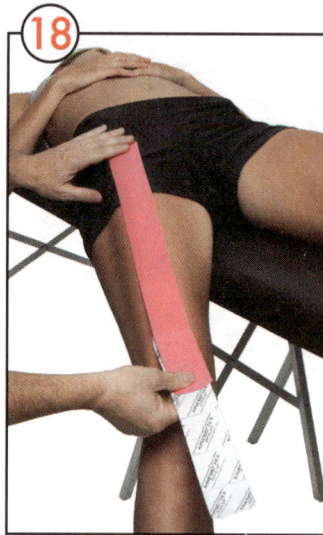

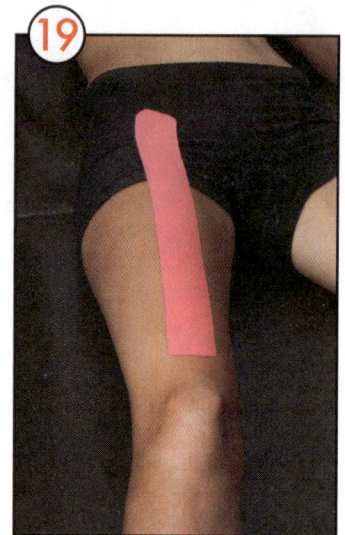

19. Lay down the end either superior to the patella or you may continue the application to the tibial tuberosity using a Y technique. Rub to initiate adhesive prior to any further patient movement.

20. Two mechanical correction I strips are placed directly over the injured area. This provides additional proprioceptive stimuli to the muscle for support, similar to wearing a neoprene sleeve. The patient should be in a neutral position or slight hip extension and knee flexion.

    Begin by tearing the center of the paper backing of an approximately 6-8" Kinesio I strip. Apply 50-75% of available tension and apply the strip with downward/inward pressure over the treatment zone.

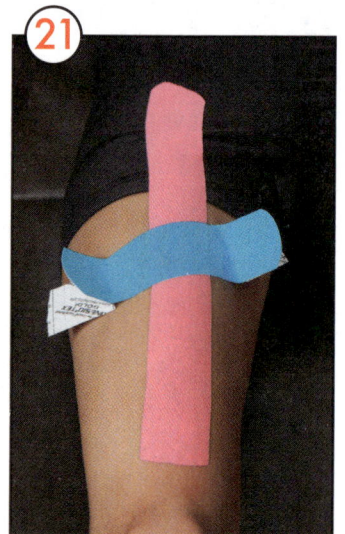

21. Lay down the ends of the Kinesio I strip with no tension. Rub to initiate adhesive prior to any further patient movement.

22. Repeat the above application of the mechanical correction at approximately a 45 degree angle.

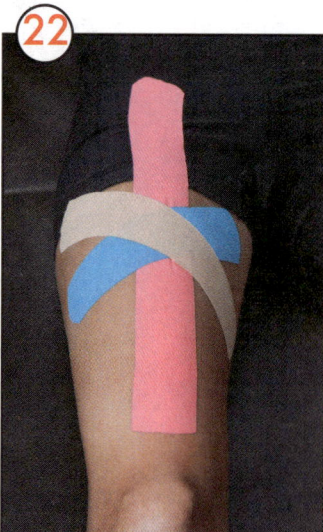

Adductor or Groin Strain

A strain to the adductor muscle group, commonly referred to as the groin, is the result of over-extension or acute overload of the muscle tissue. It may involve the iliopsoas, rectus femoris, gracilis, pectineus, adductor brevis, adductor longus, or adductor magnus. The practitioner will need to determine which muscle(s) are involved and apply the appropriate Basic Kinesio Taping Techniques.

The Kinesio Taping Method will assist in reducing edema, pain and provide ligament stability. For acute muscle strains, use the Kinesio I strip directly over the area of injury during the first 24-72 hours. Following this period, use the Kinesio Y strip, with the tails of the Y, surrounding the injured area.

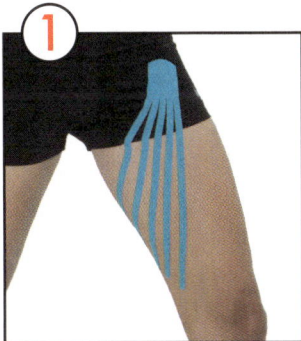

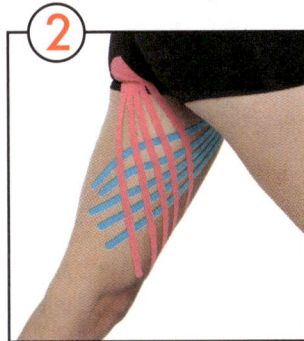

ACUTE INJURY: LYMPHATIC TECHNIQUE

1. Place the anchor of a fan strip with no tension in the inguinal fold with no tension. Apply 0-20% of available tension to the fan strips over the area of injury. Lay down ends with no tension and rub to initiate adhesive prior to any further patient movement.

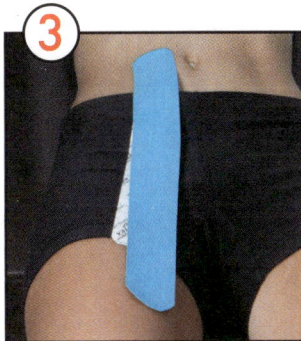

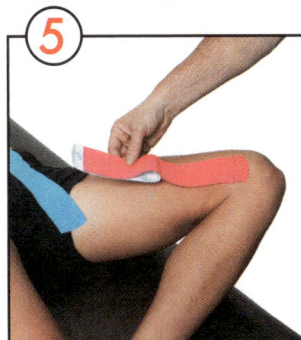

2. Place the anchor with no tension near the ischial tuberosity. Apply 0-20% of available tension over the area of injury at approximately 45 degrees to the first strip. Lay down the ends with no tension and rub or pat to initiate adhesive prior to any further patient movement.

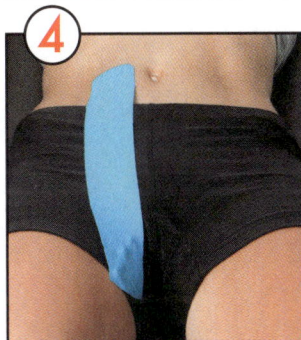

3. Basic Kinesio Taping Method inhibition application of an Iliopsoas (psoas major, psoas minor, and iliacus) using a Kinesio I strip. This is an optional inhibition technique.

   Begin by placing the anchor of the Kinesio I strip above the umbilicus at approximately T 12 with no tension.

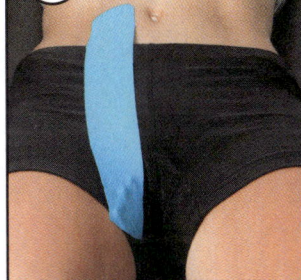

4. Have the patient move into hip extension. Apply paper off to light, 15-25% paper off tension to the Kinesio I strip.

   Direct the Kinesio I strip towards the lesser trochanter of the femur. Lay down the last 2-3" of the Kinesio I strip with no tension. Rub to initiate adhesive prior to any further patient movement.

5. Basic Kinesio Taping inhibition application of the common adductor muscle group. The Kinesio I strip is placed directly over the area of pain. Place the patient in hip abduction and the knee in some degree of extension.

   Begin by placing the anchor of the Kinesio I strip as close as possible to the supracondylar line of the femur with no tension. For an acute injury anchor inferior to the area of pain.

6. Have the patient move into hip abduction. Apply paper off to light, 15-25% of available tension to the Kinesio I strip. Photo has knee in flexion, it would be better if the knee was in extension.

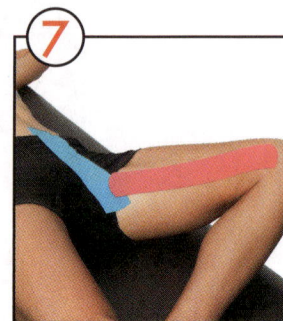

7. Direct the Kinesio I strip directly over the area of pain and applying the anchor as close to the body of pubis & inferior pubic ramus as body hair or professional practice allows. Lay down the end with no tension. Rub to initiate adhesive prior to any further movement.

OPTION 1: SPACE CORRECTION DIRECTLY OVER THE AREA OF PAIN

For an optional I strip "modification" to the space correction please see quad contusion.

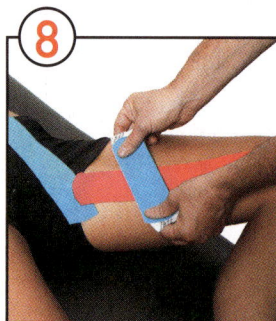

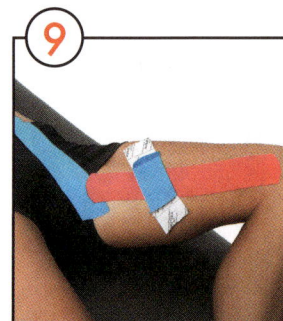

8. Begin by tearing the center of the paper backing of a 6-8" Kinesio Tex I strip. Apply 15-35% of available tension to tape center and place the center of the tension zone directly over the area of muscle strain.

9. Lay down the ends with no tension. Rub to initiate adhesive prior to any further patient movement.

10. Repeat the above steps angling the second strip at approximately 45 degrees.

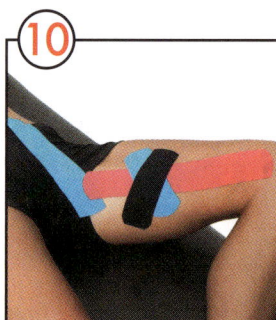

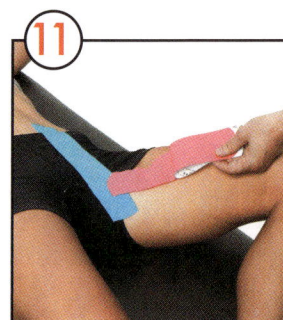

The space correction further assists in the removal of edema or hematoma formation from the injured area.

For complete review see Hamstring or Quad Strain.

OPTION 2: ADDUCTOR FACILITATION WITH MECHANICAL CORRECTION

The mechanical correction provides additional proprioceptive stimuli to the muscle for support, similar to wearing a neoprene sleeve and is applied directly to the area of pain.

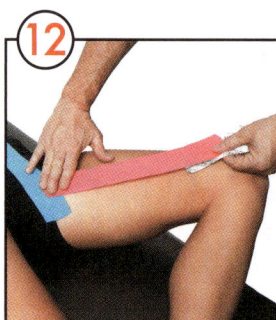

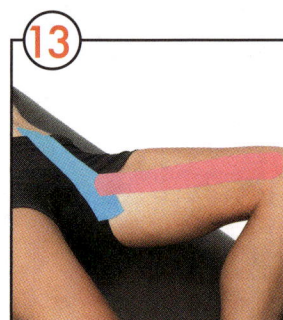

11. Apply a Kinesio I strip facilitation, or Kinesio Y strip.

The practitioner may determine that an inhibition technique may be more appropriate.

Begin by applying the anchor of an appropriate length Kinesio I strip with no tension as close to the body of pubis & inferior pubic ramus as body hair or professional practice allows.

12. Apply light to moderate, 15-35% of available tension to the Kinesio I strip and direct the end towards the supracondylar line of the femur.

13. Lay down the end with no tension. Rub to initiate adhesive prior to any further patient movement.

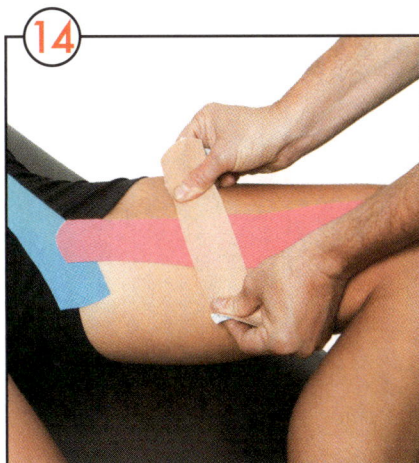

OPTION 3: APPLICATION OF A MECHANICAL CORRECTION STRIP

The mechanical correction I strip is placed directly over the injured area. The application of the mechanical correction is to provide a proprioceptive stimulation directly over the area of injury. Soft tissue injuries, and in particular muscle tissue "feels" better with pressure.

14. Begin by tearing the center of an approximately 6-8" Kinesio I strip and peel back the paper backing. Apply 50-75% of available tension to the exposed Kinesio strip. Lay down the I strip over the treatment zone with downward/inward pressure directly over the area of pain.

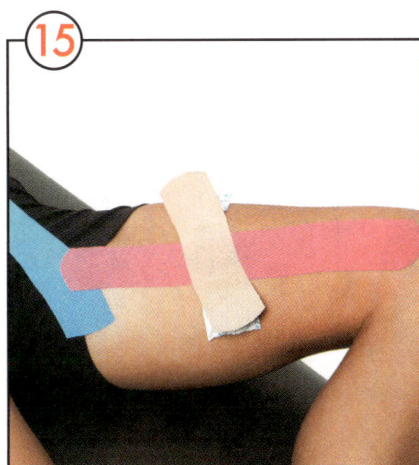

15. Lay down the ends of the Kinesio I strip with no tension. Rub to initiate adhesive activation prior to any further patient movement.

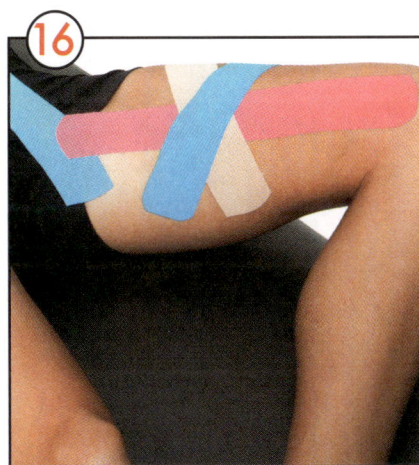

16. A second mechanical correction is applied at approximately a 45 degree angle.

Hamstring Strain

A strain to the hamstring muscle group (semimembranosus, semitendinous, or biceps femoris) is one of the most common muscle strains which results from physical activity. This muscle group may be overpowered by the larger quadriceps muscle group, be injured due to lack of flexibility or over contraction. Many hamstring strains can become chronic in nature.

Begin by applying the Basic Kinesio Taping Technique for the hamstring strain. During the evaluation of the injury the practitioner will need to determine which of the hamstring is involved. It has been found to be helpful to apply a space or mechanical correction strip directly over the area of injury.

For acute muscle strains use the Kinesio I strip directly over the area of injury during the first 24-72 hours. Following this period use the Kinesio Y strip, with the tails of the Y, surrounding the injured area.

Application of lymphatic corrective technique to reduce hematoma resulting from bleeding.

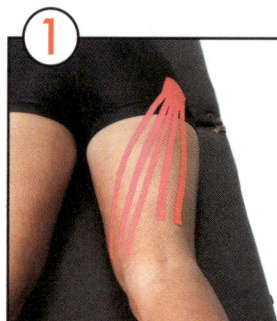

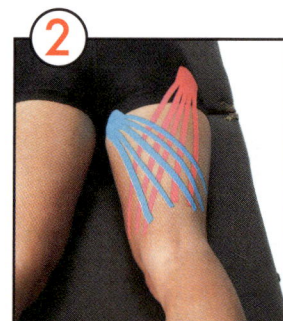

1. Place the first anchor with no tension on the lateral aspect of the ischial tuberosity. Apply 0-20% of available tension to the tails and cross over the medial aspect of the posterior thigh or area of possible hematoma. Lay down the ends with no tension and rub to initiate adhesive prior to any further patient movement.

2. Place the second anchor with no tension medial to the ischial tuberosity and apply 0-20% of available tension. Cross over the medial aspect of the thigh in the area of possible hematoma. Lay down the ends with no tension and rub to initiate adhesive prior to any further patient movement. The fan should create a crisscross pattern over the posterior aspect of the thigh.

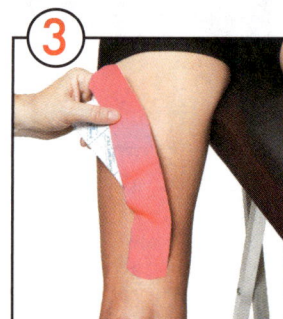

POST ACUTE: INHIBITION APPLICATION USING A KINESIO I STRIP.

If using the Kinesio Y strip technique lay down the medial anchor on the medial condyle of the tibia, lay down the lateral anchor on the lateral aspect of the fibula with no tension. The split in the Y should occur above the popliteal fossa. A Y strip or I strip can be applied to the biceps femoris alone, and the semi-membranosus and semi-tendinosus alone or both can be taped with individual strips.

3. Begin by placing the anchor of the Kinesio I strip superior to the popliteal fossa with no tension.

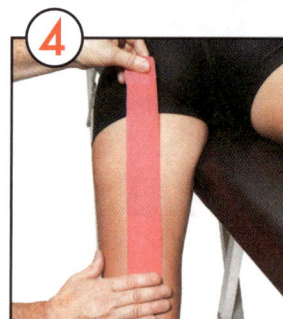

4. Have the patient move into hip flexion to place the hamstring on stretch. If the patient's range of motion is limited due to injury move them through as much ROM as possible. Apply paper off to light, 15-25% of available tension to the Kinesio I strip over the area of pain. Lay down the end over or close to the ischial tuberosity with no tension. Rub to initiate adhesive prior to any further patient movement.

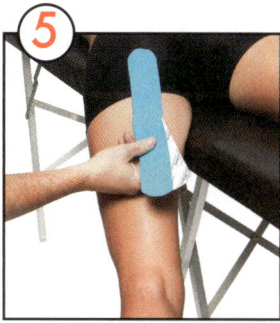
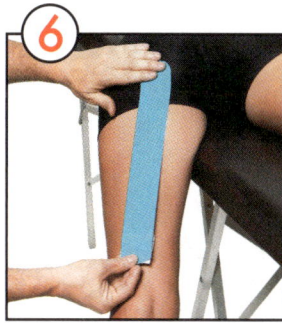

OPTION 1: APPLICATION OF A FACILITATION I STRIP AND SPACE CORRECTION

Basic facilitation muscle taping combined with space correction I strip is placed directly over the injured area. This further assists the removal of an edema or hematoma formation.

5. Place anchor near or over the ischial tuberosity with no tension and the patient in hip flexion. With the patient in hip flexion "lift" the skin to ensure there is no tension prior to anchor application.

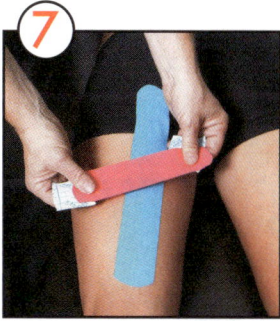
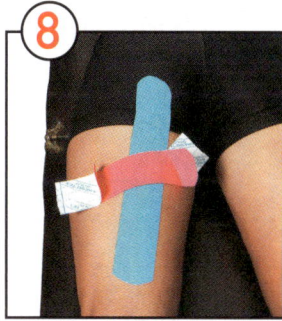

6. Apply 15-35% tension to the Kinesio I strip. End superior to the popliteal fossa with no tension. Rub to initiate adhesive prior to any further patient movement.

7. Begin by tearing the center of an approximately 6-8" Kinesio I strip. Apply light to moderate, 15-35% of available tension directly over the treatment zone.

8. Lay down the ends of the Kinesio I strip with no tension. Rub to initiate adhesive prior to any further patient movement.

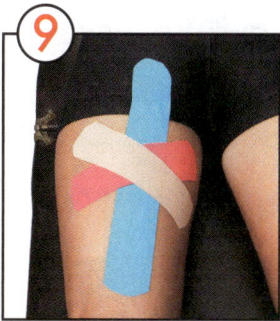

9. Repeat the above steps for the second space correction strip over the area of edema or hematoma.

OPTION 2: APPLICATION OF A FACILITATION I STRIP AND MECHANICAL CORRECTION STRIPS

First place a Kinesio I strip facilitation application, as described above, then apply a mechanical correction directly over the injured area. This provides additional proprioceptive stimuli to the muscle for support, similar to wearing a neoprene sleeve.

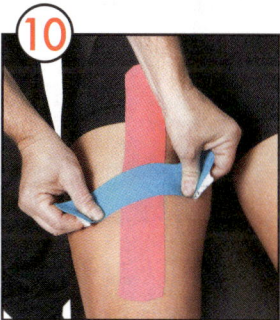
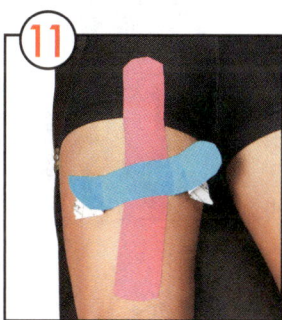

10. Begin by tearing the Kinesio I strip in the middle of the paper backing and apply the Kinesio I strip with 50-75% of available tension and downward/inward pressure directly over the injury site.

11. Lay down the ends with no tension. Rub to initiate adhesive prior to any patient movement.

12. Apply a second mechanical correction repeating the above steps.

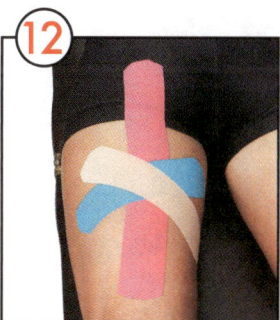

Completed application of Basic Kinesio Taping Method inhibition or facilitation for a hamstring muscle using the Kinesio I strip with mechanical correction strip.

Iliotibial Band Friction Syndrome

Iliotibial Band Friction syndrome is an inflammation of the Iliotibial band as it either crosses over the lateral femoral condyle or at its insertion on the tibia. The syndrome is generally caused by overuse and is most common in runners, cyclists, and soccer players. It has been associated with individuals who present with pronated feet and genu varum.

The Kinesio Taping Technique will assist in inflammation reduction and decreased tension in the iliotibial band by application of a muscle taping, fascia correction, space correction or mechanical correction.

The IT band has deep fascia tissue in the longitudinal direction and superficial fascia tissue in the horizontal direction. To effectively treat the IT band both layers may need to be treated.

Iliotibial Band Friction Syndrome

Fascia correction technique along the entire IT band length in the longitudinal fiber direction using a three tail technique. A two tail technique can also be applied, and later in the IT Band description an I strip is described.

The IT band taping application can begin at either the origin or insertion. For this application, insertion to origin technique will be shown.

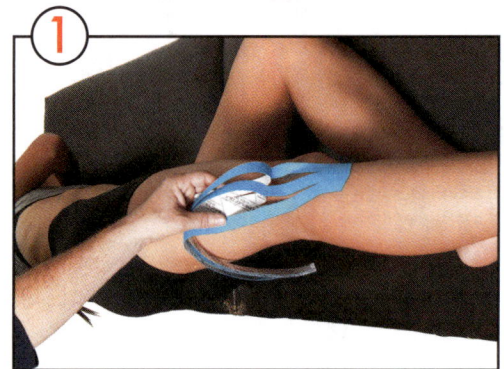

1. Begin by placing the anchor of the 3 tail Kinesio strip inferior to the insertion of the iliotibial band, gertie's tubercle with no tension.

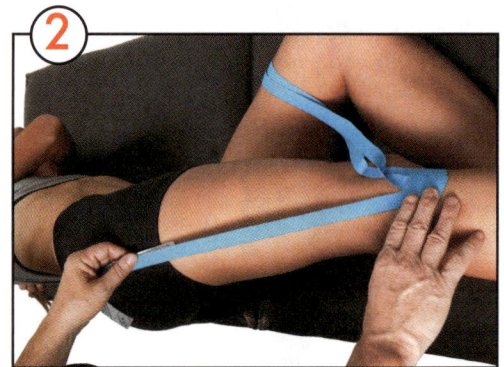

2-3. Place the IT band in a stretched position. Apply the fascia correction either using the long and short or side to side oscillation technique with 10-50% of available tension. With one hand hold the anchor while the other hand applies the fascia correction application. For the large wide IT band the side to side technique should be tried first. It has been found to be more effective on wider fascia tissue.

Apply the posterior tail (as shown in photo) along the lateral fibers of the IT band.

Apply the middle tail in the center of the IT band.

Apply the anterior tail along the anterior fibers.

Lay down the ends with no tension. Rub to initiate adhesive prior to any further patient movement.

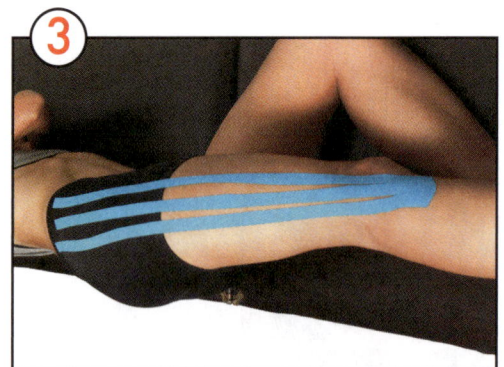

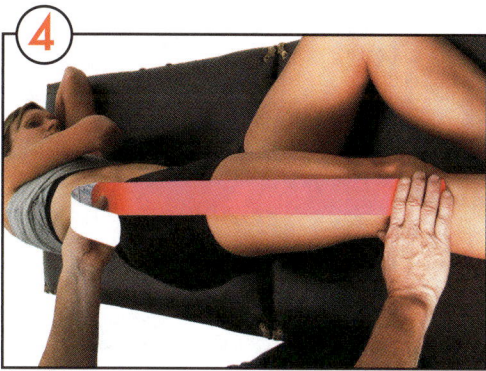

APPLICATION OF KINESIO I STRIP OVER THE LENGTH (LONGITUDINAL) OF THE ILIOTIBIAL BAND AND TENSOR FASCIA LATAE MUSCLE

The longitudinal strip can be modified for tension over the inflammation for space correction (15-35% of available tension), or increased tension over the tendon sheath for tendon correction (50-75% of available tension), or fascia correction (long and short, side to side - 10-50% of available tension). For fascia correction side to side may be more effective than long and short. Fascia Correction will be shown.

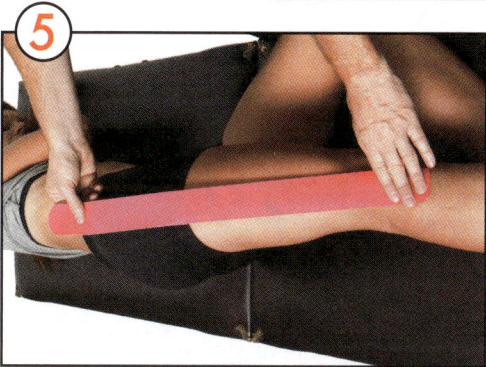

4. Begin by measuring the length of Kinesio Tex Tape required. Place the anchor of the Kinesio I strip inferior to the insertion of the iliotibial band (gertie's tubercle) with no tension.

5. Application of long and short: place the patient in a position which stretches the IT band. Apply 10-50% of available tension and apply the long and short technique along the entire length of the IT band.

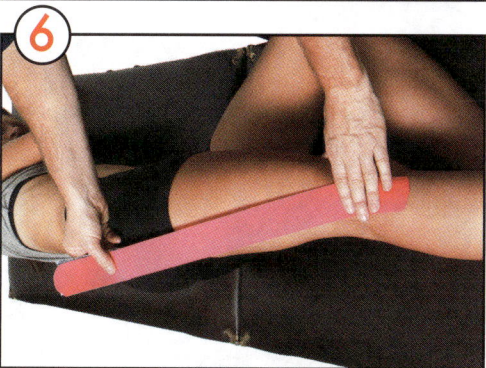

6. Application of side to side technique. Place the patient in a position which stretches the IT band. Apply 10-50% of available tension and apply side to side technique along the entire length of the IT band. Photo shows an exaggeration of the side to side technique.

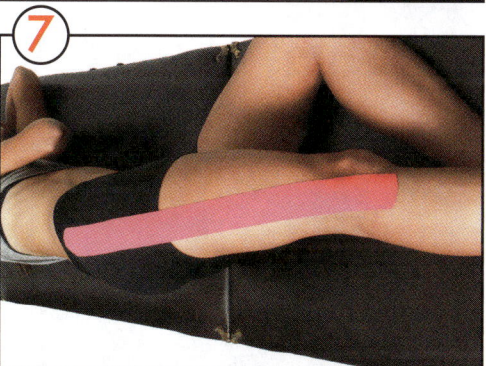

7. Lay down the end with no tension. Rub to initiate adhesive prior to any further patient movement.

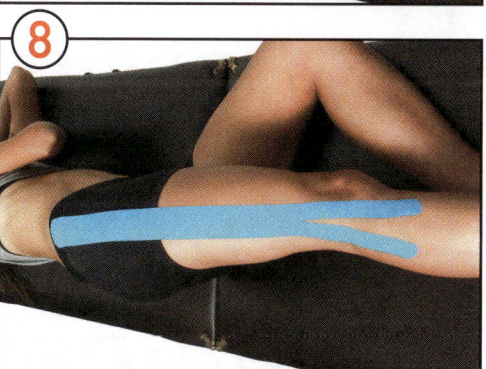

OPTIONAL APPLICATION OF A FASCIA CORRECTION USING THE Y TECHNIQUE.

8. Repeat above steps for application of the anchor. Apply side to side or long and short technique using 10-50% tension. The split in the Y should be made superior to the lateral condyle. The tails should be placed on either side of the area of inflammation or pain. Lay down the ends without tension and rub to initiate adhesive prior to any further patient movement.

The gluteus medius, or other muscles, may be long and weak or inhibited in function due to the tension of the IT Band. Muscles may be short and weak and may need to be facilitated. Your evaluation will assist you to choose which is best for the patient.

Iliotibial Band Friction Syndrome

OPTION 1: DONUT HOLE TECHNIQUE

9. Begin by cutting a donut hole, approximately the size of a dime, not to exceed 50% of tape width, in the center of a 4-6" Kinesio Tex tape strip. The width of the strip is determined by the size of the patient, a 1 ½" width is demonstrated. Apply 15-25% of available tension to the center of the strip and place the hole over the area of pain or inflammation.

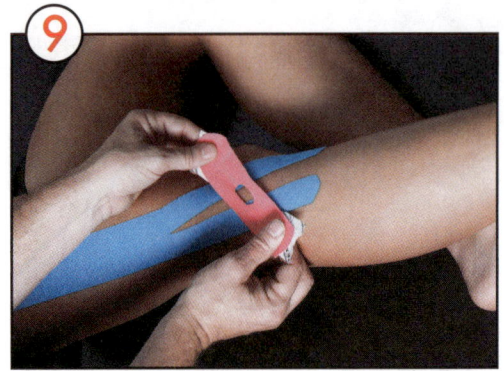

10. Lay down the ends without tension, and if appropriate have the patient move the knee into flexion or extension to ensure when the end is laid down it does not "pull" on the end during movement. The ends can be cut into tails and splayed out to dissipate tension.

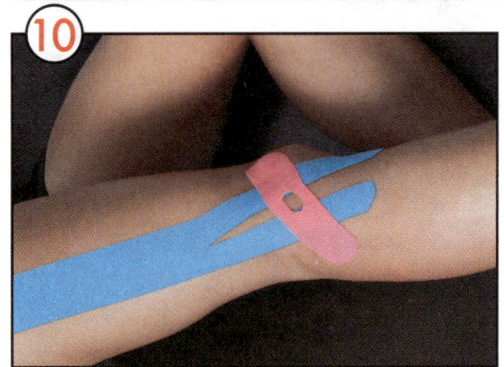

11. A second, or if space allows, a third donut hole can be applied. The strips should be angled so as to ensure tape on skin and not tape on tape for ends application.

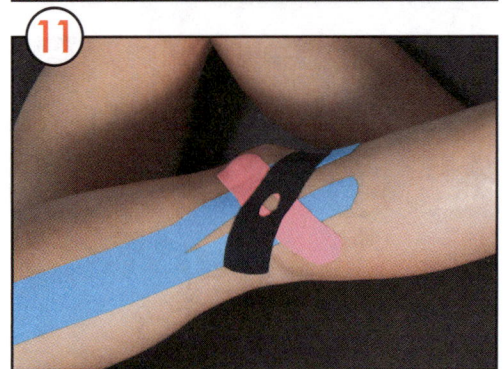

OPTION 2: MECHANICAL CORRECTION WITH TENSION ON THE TAILS

The Mechanical correction is chosen to limit movement of the iliotibial band over the lateral femoral condyle as it changes from an abductor of the hip to a knee flexor past 30-45 degrees of flexion of the knee. Tension in the base is appropriate for more aggressive treatment.

12. Begin by placing the anchor of the Kinesio Y strip inferior to the lateral femoral condyle with no tension. Have the split in the Y begin slightly below the point of pain. With one hand hold the anchor so no tension is added.

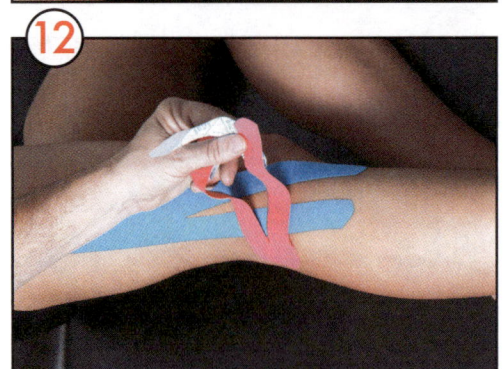

13. Start with the patient's knee in extension. Apply 50-75% of available tension and downward/inward pressure to the inferior tail of the Kinesio Y strip.

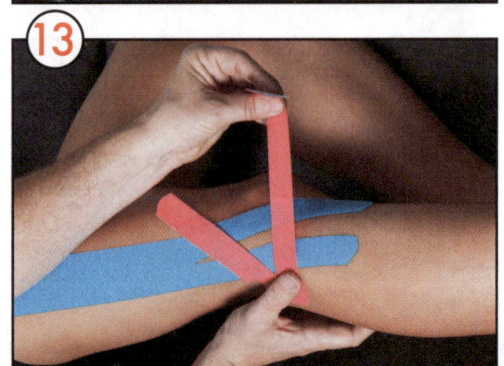

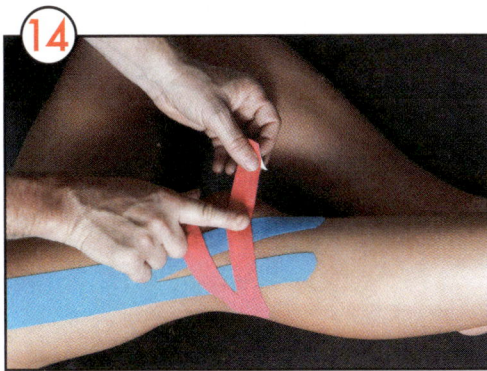

14. The mechanical correction ends when the tail crosses above the IT band. Slide the hand holding the anchor up the tail which initiates adhesive.

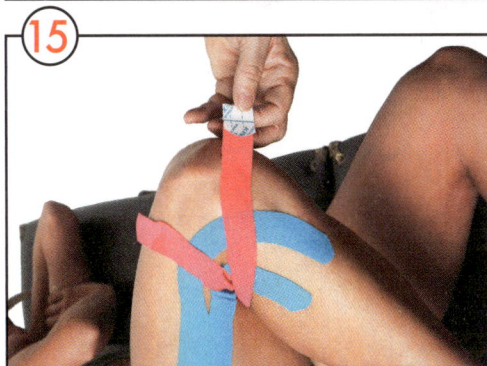

15. Have the patient move their knee into flexion. This will ensure that no tension will be applied to the end when it is laid down. If the knee is not moved prior to end application, when the patient moves into flexion it will cause tension on the end. This will cause a "pulling" on the end, possibly causing pain or at a minimum cause the end to "pull away" from the skin. Lay down the end with no tension. Further rub to initiate adhesive prior to any further patient movement.

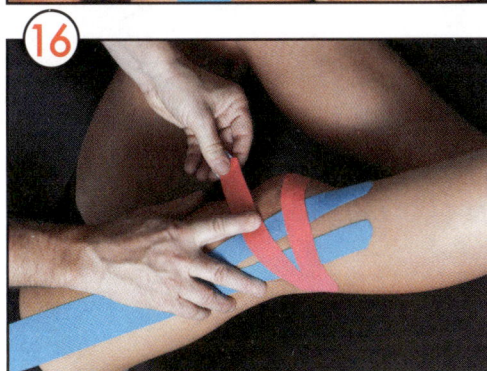

16. Repeat the above steps for the superior tail.

17. Prior to laying down the end, have the patient again move into flexion and lay down the last 1-2" with no tension.

    Rub to initiate adhesive prior to any further patient movement.

    The area of pain or inflammation should be located in the space between the mechanical correction and the IT band fascia correction that was applied first. This will reduce any compressive forces over the area of pain.

OPTIONAL: FACILITATION FOR THE GLUTEUS MEDIUS MUSCLE USING A TWO I STRIP TECHNIQUE TO MAKE A Y STRIP.

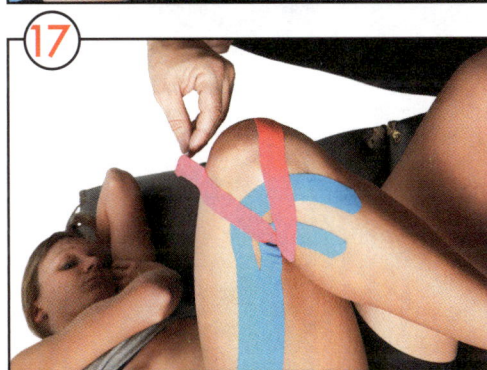

18. Apply anchor of Kinesio Y strip on the lateral surface of the greater trochanter with no tension.

    Patient is side lying, hip adduction and extension. Place the anchor with no tension at the lip of Iliac Crest just lateral to the ASIS. Direct the posterior tail to the lateral aspect of the posterior iliac spine. Apply paper off to moderate, 15-35% of available tension and direct the I strip slightly distal to the greater trochanter. Lay down end with no tension and rub to initiate adhesive prior to any further patient movement.

    Next place the patient in hip flexion and adduction and place the anchor with no tension at the lip of the Iliac Crest lateral to the PSIS. Apply paper off to moderate, 15-35% of available tension and direct the I strip towards the greater trochanter. Lay down end with no tension and rub to initiate adhesive prior to any further patient movement.

Shin Splint or Medial Tibial Stress Syndrome

The treatment for shin splints is as varied as the cause of the condition, which is not always known. Many practitioners have started to refer to shin splints as medial tibial stress syndrome. The general cause of pain is an excessive repetitive trauma in the lower leg located on the distal 1/3 of the medial tibial border. Associated with repetitive stress may be poor arches, muscle weakness, surface changes and improper footwear to name a few.

When selecting a Kinesio Taping Technique for treatment, the practitioner must first evaluate the cause of the pain and adapt a treatment protocol to treat the symptoms. The treatment protocol may include taping for muscles, arch, and space correction.

Several possible treatment protocols will be described. Basic Kinesio Taping Method application for the tibialis anterior, and two methods of space correction on the medial border of the tibial.

Shin Splint or Medial Tibial Stress Syndrome

APPLICATION OF MUSCLE INHIBITION FOR TIBIALIS POSTERIOR.

The tibialis posterior is generally associated with shin splints or medial tibial stress syndrome due to it attempting to limit overpronation (foot flattens out when weight is applied). If the medial longitudinal arch is not providing appropriate support to assist in dissipation of forces resulting from landing or take off, the anterior tibialis may become inflamed to compensate.

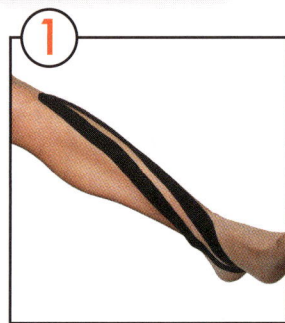

1. Begin by placing the anchor of a Kinesio Y strip, an I strip is also effective, at the navicular tuberosity with no tension. Place the patient in dorsiflexion and eversion, apply 15-25% of available tension and surround the muscle. End the tails near lateral portion of posterior proximal tibia with no tension. Rub to initiate adhesive prior to any further patient movement.

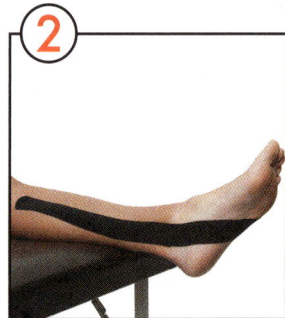

2. Tibialis anterior inhibition technique I strip. Begin by placing the anchor of an I strip, a Y strip is also effective, at the medial cuneiform and base of 1st ray with no tension. Place the foot in plantar flexion and eversion and apply the I strip towards the lateral condyle & superior 2/3 of anteriorlateral surface of tibia. Lay down the end with no tension. Rub to initiate adhesive prior to any further patient movement.

OPTION 1: MECHANICAL & SPACE CORRECTION TENSION IN BASE AND TAILS COMBINATION: TISSUE TOWARD.

This technique may be more effective with 3" instead of 2" Kinesio Tex Tape. A series of two or three mechanical corrections along the area of pain has also been shown to be very effective.

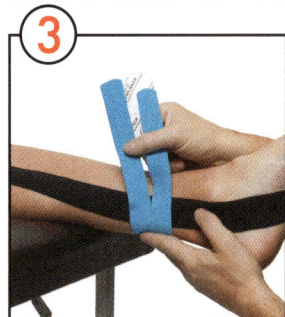

Application of mechanical correction on medial border of the tibia. This method lifts the skin and attempts to hold the soft tissue up and against the medial border of the tibia.

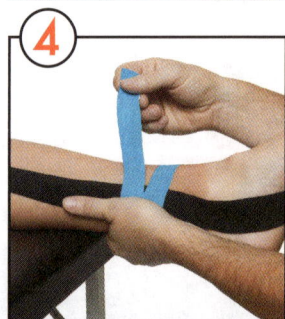

3. Cut a Kinesio Tex Y strip with about equal parts of base and tails. Apply the anchor inferior to the area of pain without tension.

4. With one hand hold the anchor to ensure no tension will be added.

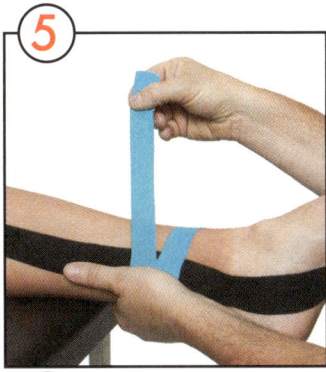

5. With the hand holding the anchor, compress and "roll" the tissue towards the medial border of the tibia. While holding the tissue, apply 50-75% of available tension and downward/inward pressure to the base of Y strip inferior to the point of pain. Slide the hand holding the anchor to the split in the Y, initiating adhesive activation.

The effect will be to hold the tissue against the medial border of the tibia, simulating other prophylactic taping techniques.

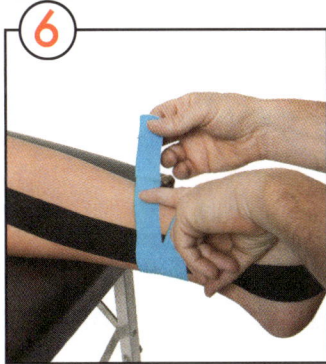

6. Apply paper off to light, 15-35% of available tension to the next section of the tail to the last 1-2". The recoil effect of the Kinesio Tex Tape will "pull" the skin back towards the medial border of the tibia creating space. Lay down the end with no tension. Rub to initiate adhesive prior to any further patient movement.

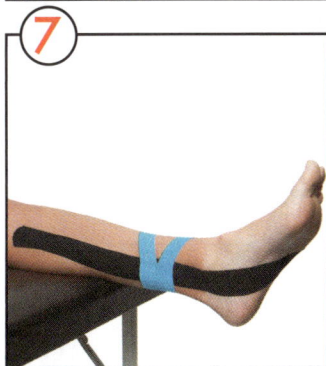

7. Completed Mechanical and Space Correction Combination. A series of two or three strips can be applied over the area of pain along the medial tibial border.

OPTION 2: MECHANICAL CORRECTION TENSION IN BASE.

This method pulls skin away from the medial border of the tibia. It can be applied in combination with the tibialis anterior or posterior techniques described earlier.

8. Begin by placing the anchor of a Kinesio Y strip just inferior to the area of pain with no tension.

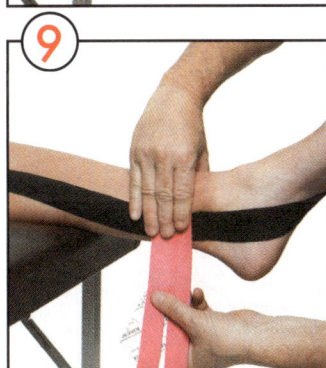

9. Hold the anchor with one hand to reduce unwanted tension on the skin. Apply 50-75%% of available tension and downward/inward pressure to the base and pull the skin away from the medial tibial border. Laying down the Kinesio strip as it continues to move more medially.

When tension is applied to the base slide the holding the anchor to the point where the tails begin. Have the patient dorsiflex their ankle.

10. Apply the tails of the Y in a splaying out pattern on the lateral aspect of the ankle with paper off to light, 15-25% of available tension. Lay down the ends with no tension and rub to initiate adhesive prior to any further patient.

   A series of two or three strips may be applied along the medial border of the tibia depending upon the length of painful area. Using a 3" Kinesio strip with tension in the base may be more effective than using a 2" strip.

OPTION 3: MECHANICAL CORRECTION TENSION IN TAILS.

This method pulls skin away from the medial border of the tibia. It can be applied in combination with the tibialis anterior or posterior techniques described earlier.

11. Begin by placing the anchor of a Kinesio Y strip just inferior to the area of pain with no tension.

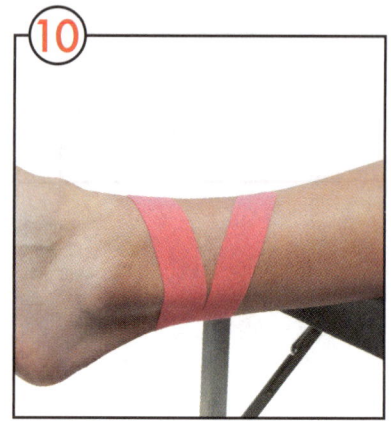

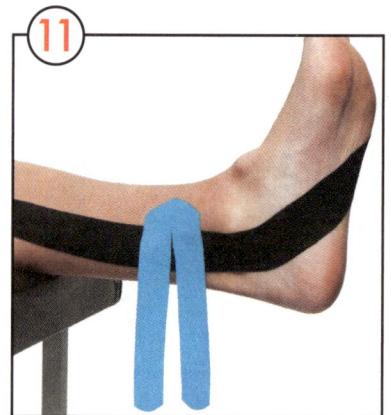

12. Hold the anchor with one hand to reduce unwanted tension on the skin. Apply 50-75% of available tension and downward/inward pressure to each tail and pull the skin away from the medial tibial border. Laying down the Kinesio strip as it continues to move more medially.

   When tension is applied to the point where the Kinesio tension in the tails reaches the Achilles tendon, end tension and slide the hand holding the anchor to this point to initiate adhesive. Have the patient dorsiflex their ankle.

   Continue to lay down the tail in a splaying out pattern on the lateral aspect of the ankle with paper off to light, 15-25% of available tension to the last 1-2". Lay down the end with no tension and rub to initiate adhesive prior to any further patient movement.

13. A series of two or three strips may be applied along the medial border of the tibia depending upon the length of painful area. Using a 3" Kinesio strip with tension in the base may be more effective than using a 2" strip.

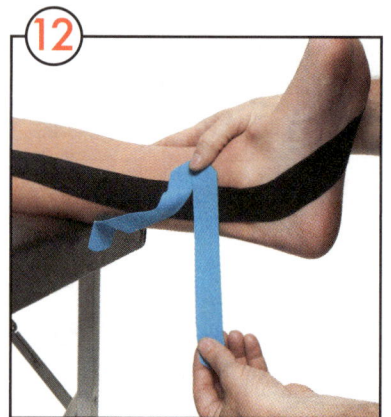

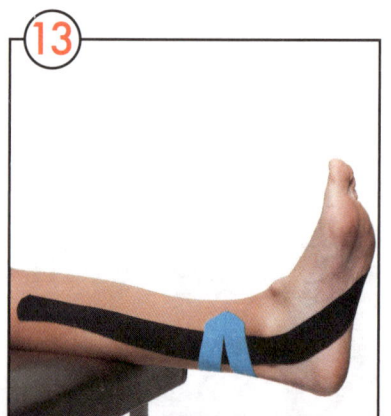

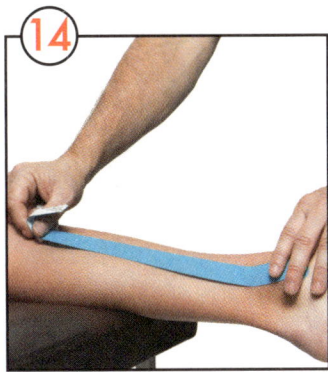

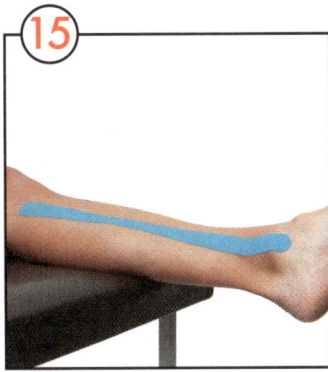

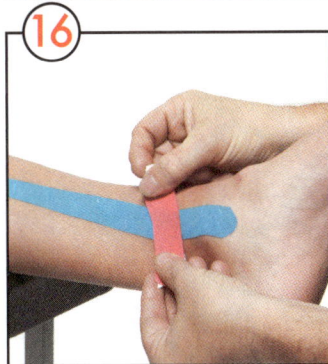

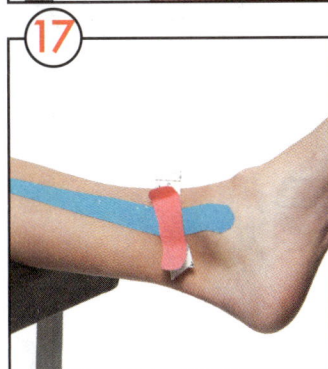

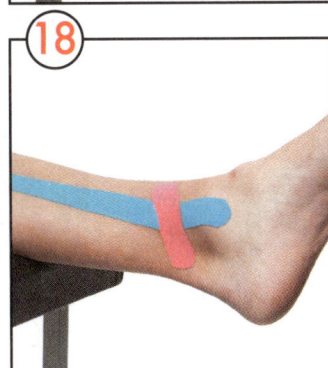

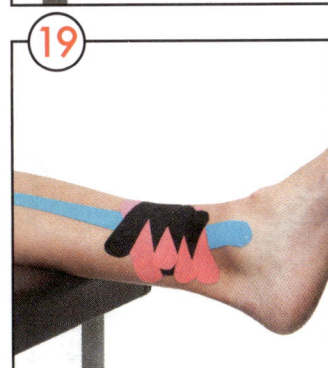

OPTION 4: SPACE CORRECTION

14. Begin by placing an appropriate length of a 1" Kinesio I strip, inferior to the area of pain along the medial border of the tibia with no tension. The anchor can be placed across the plantar surface on the lateral border of the 5th metacarpal to assist in adhesion. With one hand hold the anchor to ensure no tension will be added. Apply paper off to light, 15-25% of available tension to the Kinesio I strip. Lay the I strip along the medial border of the tibia or directly over the area of pain. End tension 2-3" above the area of pain. Lay down the end with no tension and rub to initiate adhesive prior to any further patient movement.

15. Completed Kinesio I strip applied along the area of pain.

    The practitioner may choose to use a Y technique and apply an inhibition application to the Tibialis anterior. If you choose this option the space between the tails should be the area of pain.

16. Application of a space correction tension in the center of an I strip. Tear the center of the paper backing of an approximately 4-6" long 1" wide Kinesio Tex Tape. Apply 25-35% of available tension to the exposed tape. Place the I strip 1-2" inferior to the area of pain at approximately 45 degrees to the space correction strip.

17. Leave approximately 1-2" on each end. Lay down the ends with no tension. Rub to initiate adhesive prior to any further patient movement.

18. Completed first crisscross space correction space in the center of an I strip.

19. A series of space correction I strips are applied over the area of pain. The I strips should begin 1-2" below the area of pain and end 1-2" above the area of pain. As much as possible try to have each end of the strip ending on skin to maximize adhesion.

Sciatica

Sciatica is an inflammation to the sciatic nerve which is generally associated with low back pain resulting from neurological symptoms. Sciatic nerve involvement may be the result of inflammation occurring directly to the nerve itself, lumbar disk herniation, or tightness of the piriformis.

The Kinesio Taping Method will assist by reducing effusion, inflammation, pain and paresthesia. A lymphatic correction will assist with edema reduction and then the length of the sciatic nerve involvement will be taped along its dermatome.

Two options that are not shown: 1) use of a star space correction technique to remove lymphatic fluid (see disk herniation), and 2) basic Kinesio Taping Technique for piriformis muscle (see myofascial low back pain).

OPTION 1: APPLICATION OF LYMPHATIC CORRECTION STRIP

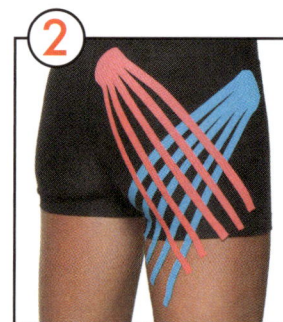

1. Begin the first Kinesio fan strip by placing the anchor near the PSIS with no tension. Have the patient move into hip flexion and adduction. Apply 0-20% of available tension across the region of pain or paresthia, ending in the mid posterior thigh region. Lay down the ends with no tension. Rub to initiate adhesive prior to any further patient movement.

2. Apply second anchor near the SI joint with no tension. Have the patient move into hip flexion and adduction. Apply the fan strips with 0-20% of available tension across the region of pain or paresthesia. Lay down the ends with no tension rub to initiate adhesive prior to any further patient movement.

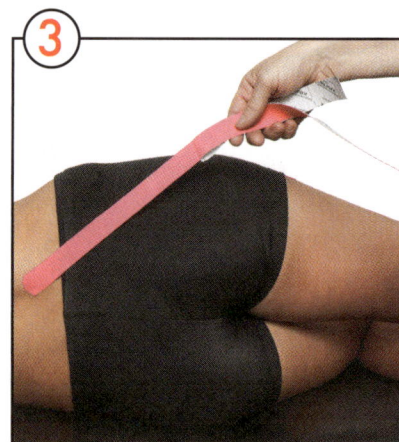

OPTION 2: 1" I STRIP APPLICATION
The sciatic nerve strip can be initiated from either the hip or foot. The importance is that with each segmental application of the sciatica strip the segment must be placed in a stretched position prior to tape application. Application shown is a 1" Kinesio I strip, a 1 ½ or 2" I strip may also be appropriate.

3. Begin by measuring the length of tape required from the PSIS, or above the paresthesia to the distal point of paresthesia. Measure the length of tape in a position of comfort for the patient.

4. Application from the hip to foot will be demonstrated. Apply the anchor of the Kinesio I strip, 1" width, at the PSIS with no tension. The width of the Kinesio I strip is determined by the size of the patient.

The sciatic strip only needs to be applied as far down the leg as the radiating pain is felt by the patient. As each segment is taped and before you move to the next section rub to initiate adhesive prior to any further patient movement.

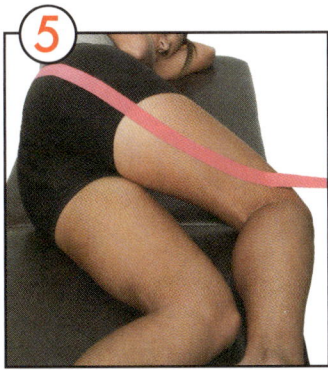

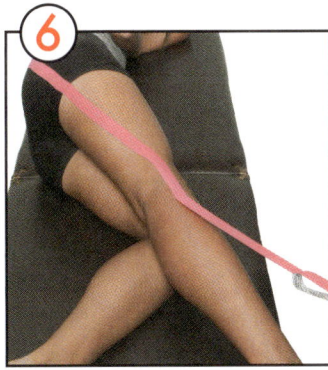

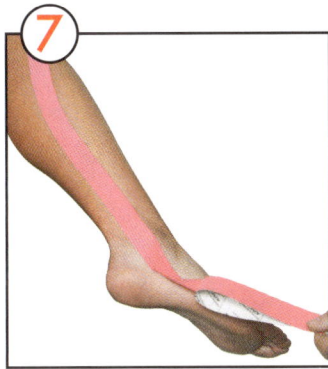

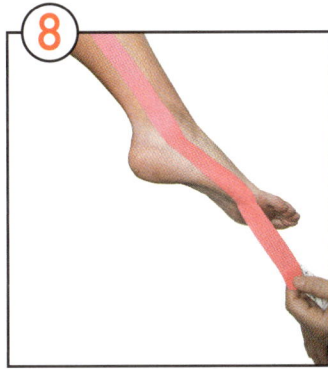

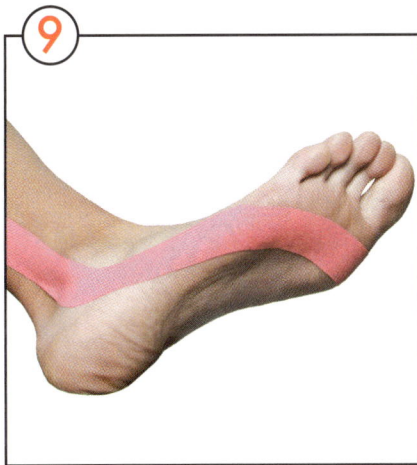

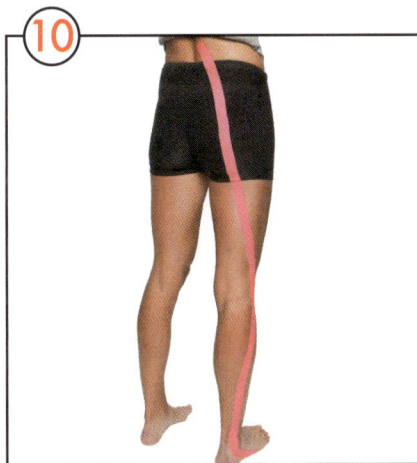

5. Place the patient in hip flexion and adduction.

   Apply the Kinesio I strip with paper off to light 15-25% of available tension along the radiating path of paresthesia. Generally this is the middle aspect of the posterior thigh.

6. With the hip remaining in a flexed position, have the patient move their knee into extension.

   Continue the Kinesio I strip with paper off to light, 15-25% of available tension along the radiating pathway.

7. While the hip remains in a flexed position, and the knee in extension have the patient move their ankle into dorsiflexion and inversion. Continue the I strip along the area of paresthesia over the lateral calf area.

8. Continue the Kinesio I strip with paper off to light, 15-25% of available tension along the radiating pathway over the lateral ankle to the mid-foot area and to the plantar surface of the foot.

9. Lay down the final 2-3" of the Kinesio I strip with no tension.

10. Completed Sciatic Nerve Taping

    The sciatic strip only needs to be applied as far down the leg as the radiating pain or paresthesia is felt by the patient.

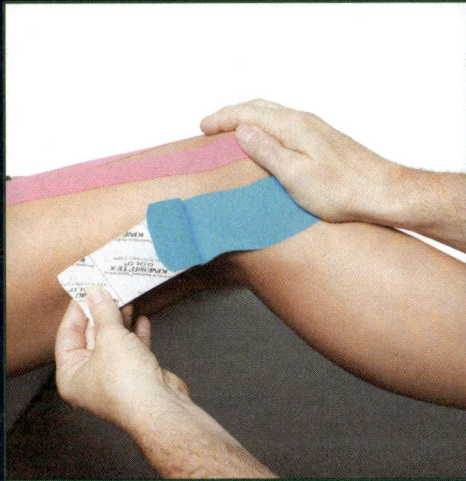

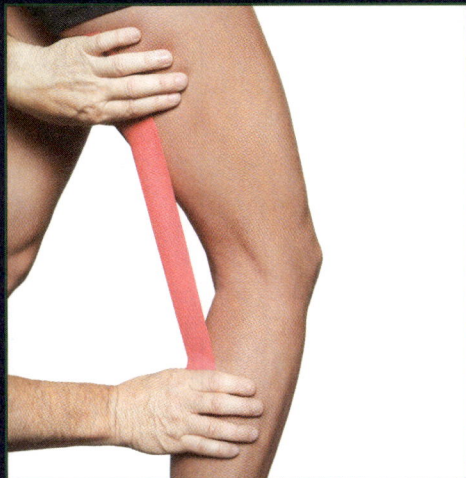

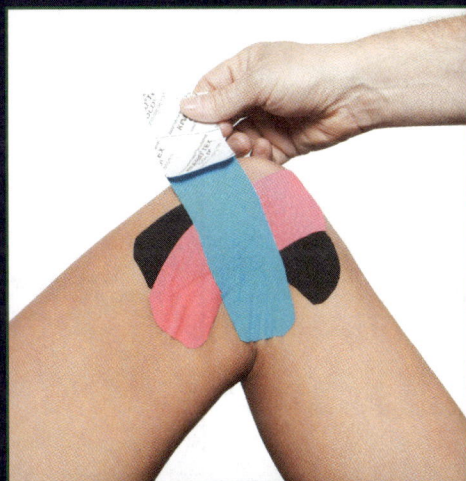

SECTION 8

Knee
and
Lower Leg

Section 8

Anterior Compartment Hematoma/Syndrome

An injury to the anterior compartment may result from direct trauma or from a loss of fascia expansion surrounding any one of the four compartments. Each of the four compartments of the lower leg: anterior, lateral, posterior superficial and posterior deep, are surrounded by a fascia which expands during exercise. Each compartment contains muscles, artery, vein and nervous tissue. When an acute trauma occurs a hemorrhage it may result in decreasing circulation and cause pressure on the nerve. A compartment may also be affected by a decrease in the elasticity of the fascia surrounding the compartment, resulting in increased pressure causing numbness.

Acute compartment hematomas are treated by reducing the hemorrhage. Chronic exertional compartment syndromes are treated by reducing the increased pressures within the compartment.

OPTION 1: ACUTE
For both the acute and exertional compartment syndrome, a lymphatic correction can be used to reduce pressure within the compartment.

1. Begin the first lymphatic fan by placing the anchor with no tension at the medial aspect of the calf just superior to the joint line. Apply 0-20% of available tension to the fan strips as they are angled over the area of edema. Lay down the ends with no tension and rub to initiate adhesive prior to any further patient movement.

2. Begin the second lymphatic fan by applying the anchor with no tension at the lateral aspect of the calf just superior to the joint line. Apply 0-20% of available tension to the fan strips as they are angled over the area of edema. Lay down the ends with no tension and rub to initiate adhesive prior to any further patient movement.

OPTION 2: POST-ACUTE

3. Post 72 hours or with an acute hemorrhage resulting in a hematoma, a space correction technique may be used. This space correction I strip(s) should provide additional space directly above the hemorrhage allowing for the edema to be removed.

   Tear the center of the paper backing of a 6-8" Kinesio I strip. Apply paper off to moderate, 15-35% of available tension to the center of the strip. Apply this central area directly over the hematoma or tightness in anterior compartment. If appropriate have the patient move into a stretched position, lay down ends with no tension. Rub to initiate adhesive prior to any further patient movement.

4. A series of two or three space corrections with tension in the center of an I strip can be applied. Another option is the use of the donut hole technique over the area of acute injury may be effective. For either the space correction I strip or donut hole technique when using multiple strips tension level for each strip should be lower, in the 15-25% range.

   The application of a basic Kinesio Taping inhibition for the tibialis anterior may also be appropriate. For an explanation please see medial tibial stress syndrome. A fascia correction application maybe appropriate for chronic compartment syndrome.

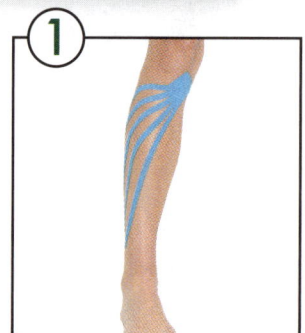

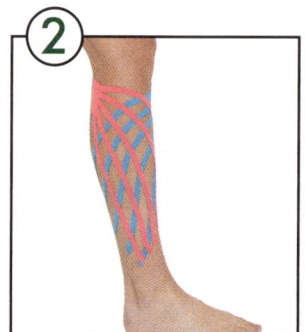

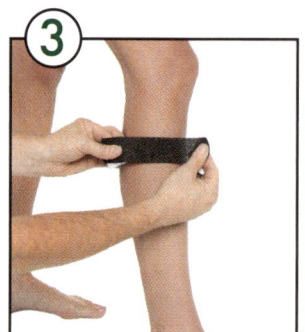

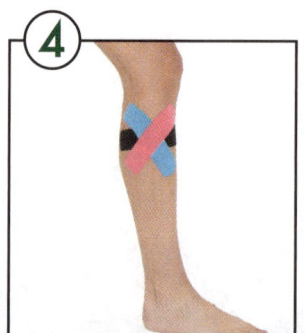

Lymphedema of Lower Leg

Lymphedema of the lower extremity is the result of edema that forms in the lower extremity from acute or chronic dysfunction. In an acute injury, the degree of edema may be too significant for the lymph system to remove in a short period of time. In a chronic condition, the lymph system is not able to channel the fluid in the normal pathways and edema has formed in the dependent extremity.

The Kinesio Taping Method will assist in reducing edema by application of the lymphatic corrective technique. The practitioner will need to determine where the lymphatic system has diminished function and by application of the lymphatic corrective technique channel the fluid to another part of the system which is functioning normally.

Precautions for Kinesio Taping on Lymphedema applications may include: Diabetes, Kidney Disease/Dynamic forms of Lymphedema, Congestive Heart Failure, Thyroid Disease, and possibly pregnancy with associated medical conditions.

Lymphatic drainage will be demonstrated from the proximal to the distal lymph vessel. Direct the tails over the area of edema.

1. Have the patient place the knee in extension and the foot in dorsiflexion. Place the anchor of the Kinesio Fan strip on the posterior medial aspect of the knee, with no tension. Be careful of placing strips in the popliteal fossa, as this may cause irritation. Angle the fan strips in an inferior direction using 0-20% of available tension. Lay down the ends with no tension and rub or pat to initiate adhesive prior to and further patient movement.

2. A second Kinesio Fan strip is applied from the posterior lateral aspect of the knee. Have the patient place the knee in extension and the foot in dorsiflexion. Angle the fan strips in an inferior direction using 0-20% of available tension forming a crisscross pattern over the area of edema. Lay down the ends with no tension and rub or pat to initiate adhesive prior to any further patient movement.

Try to apply the ends of each tail onto the patients skin. Ending the fan tails on each other will limit the length of time the Kinesio Tex tape will adhere.

OPTIONAL: Gastrocnemius muscle inhibition in an acute edema. For a chronic edema or lymphedema apply a facilitation application to enhance deep lymphatic function.

3. Place the anchor of the Kinesio Y strip on the plantar surface near the anterior calcaneous region with no tension. Place the patient in knee extension and foot dorsiflexion. Apply paper off to light, 15-25% of available tension to the medial and lateral tails as they surround the heads of the gastrocnemius. Lay down the ends with no tension and rub to initiate adhesive prior to any further patient movement.

For a facilitation technique apply paper off to moderate, 15-35% of available tension and anchor at the origin and end tails at the insertion.

Patella Tendonitis: Superior and Inferior Pole

Patella Tendonitis at either the superior pole or inferior pole (jumpers knee) develops from an overuse of the quadriceps muscle group. The patella acts like a mechanical lever to magnify the forces created by the quadriceps muscle. From repetitive activity, an inflammation may develop.

There will be several examples of methods of taping for patella tendonitis. Examples presented will be for regions of the superior pole, and inferior pole. Each of the techniques have been used successfully on different patients. The practitioner will need to evaluate the patient and determine which technique may be best. If one technique is not showing the desired results, then change to another application technique.

PATELLA TENDONITIS: SUPERIOR Y TECHNIQUE

The tape is applied for facilitation. A inhibition technique may be also be applied depending upon the evaluation. The split of the Y application begins at the superior pole of the patella instead of the junction of the musculotendonous junction.

1. Anchor the Kinesio Y strip on the proximal 1/3 of the rectus femoris with no tension. Position the hip in extension and the knee in flexion.

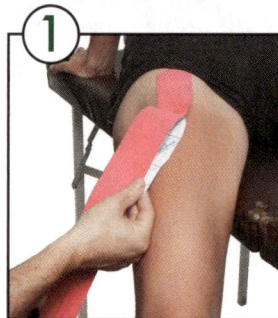

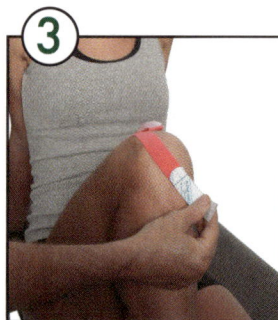

2. Apply light to moderate, 15-35% of available tension until the split of the Y in the Kinesio strip is slightly above the superior pole of the patella. Rub to initiate adhesive prior to any further patient movement.

3. Position the patient in hip and knee flexion. Apply paper off to light, 15-25% of available tension to the tails of the Kinesio Y strip around the medial and lateral borders of the patella.

4. Lay down the ends with no tension overlapping each other onto skin on or near the tibial tuberosity. Rub to initiate adhesive prior to any further patient movement.

   Completed quadriceps facilitation with modification. The split in the Y occurs at the superior aspect of patella instead of the musculotendonous junction.

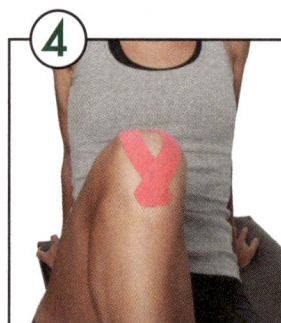
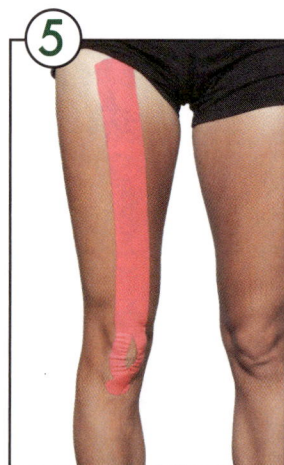

5. Completed Patella Tendonitis Superior Y Technique.

   The practitioner may select to modify the Superior Y technique by shortening the I strip. The I strip can be anchored in the distal 1/3 junction of the rectus femoris if facilitation of the quadriceps muscles is not a therapeutic goal.

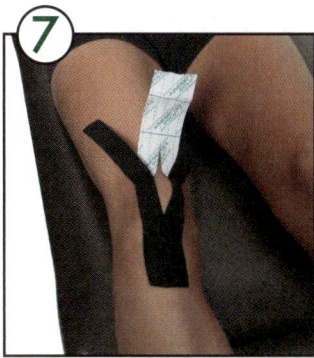

PATELLA TENDONITIS: INFERIOR Y TECHNIQUE

Measure a Kinesio Y strip from 2-3" below the tibial tuberosity to 4-5" above the superior pole of the patella. Cut the Y strip with 2-3" for an anchor to be placed below the tibial tuberosity and the anchor long enough to reach the inferior pole of the patella.

OPTION 1:

7. Apply the anchor 2-3" below the tibial tuberosity with no tension.

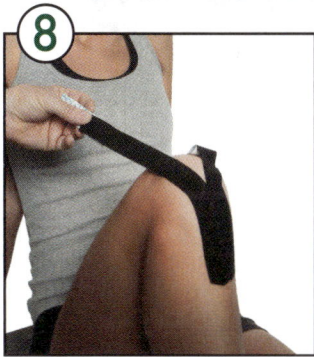

8. Have the patient place the hip and knee in flexion. Apply paper off to light, 15-25% of available tension to the longer than normal anchor to the inferior pole of the patella. Then apply paper off to light, 15-25% of available tension to the medial and lateral tail along the edge of the patella. Tails can be splayed (as shown) or applied to surround the patella. Lay down the ends with no tension and rub to initiate adhesive prior to any further patient movement.

9. Completed inferior Y technique option one.

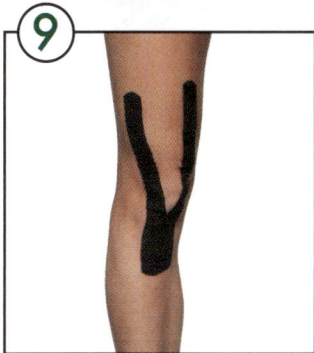

OPTION 2: Cut strip as described above. An example can be seen in Modified Mechanical Correction later in this section.

10. Place one hand on the anchor to limit tension being added during application. Have the patient in a position of function, 20-30 degrees of flexion. While holding the anchor and exposing the Kinesio Tex Tape from the anchor to the split in the Y, apply a mechanical technique, 50-75% of available tension and downward/inward pressure to the tape. Apply this section of the Kinesio Y strip to the inferior pole of the patella. The split in the Y technique should be applied so the split begins at the inferior pole of the patella.

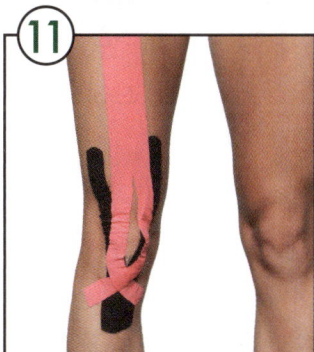

Slide the hand holding the anchor to the inferior pole of the patella.

The tails should be applied with light, 15-25% of available tension. The medial tail should end near or on the vastus medialis muscle. While the lateral tail should end on or near the vastus lateralis muscle. Lay down the ends with no tension. Rub to activate adhesive prior to further patient movement.

This technique applies "pressure" over the area of pain, in cases of patella tendonitis this area likes "pressure" over the area of inflammation.

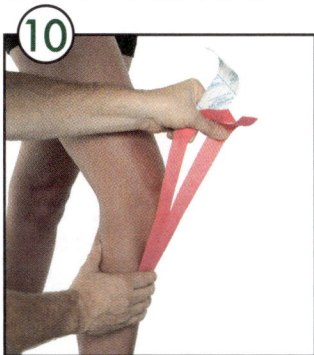

11. Completed Patella Tendonitis Inferior Y and Superior Y Technique as an option during acute or particularly painful periods.

Patella Tendonitis: Superior and Inferior Pole

Patella Tendonitis – I Strip

This technique for treating patella tendonitis uses an I strip placed from the tibial tuberosity over the patella. It is important during application that little or no tension or downward pressure is applied to the patella to create increased compression force between the patella and intercondylar notch.

Several examples will be given. The practitioner will need to evaluate each patient and apply what is in their opinion the best course of treatment. If one method is selected and the results are not as effective as desired, try another method.

MODIFIED SPACE CORRECTION: It is a "modified" space correction since the tension will NOT be added to the center of the I strip as is the normal application.

1. Start with the patient in knee extension. Apply the anchor 2-3" below the tibial tuberosity with no tension. Rub to initiate adhesive prior to any further patient movement.

2. **OPTION 1:** Have the patient move into knee flexion. Apply paper off to light, 15-25% of available tension to the Kinesio I strip and apply to the skin over the patella to the superior aspect of the patella.

2. **OPTION 2:** Have the patient move into flexion slowly as the practitioner peels the paper backing off and applies it directly to the patients skin (paper off tension 15%).

3. Lay down the end with no tension. Rub to initiate adhesive prior to any further patient movement.

4. Completed Modified Space Correction, note convolutions.

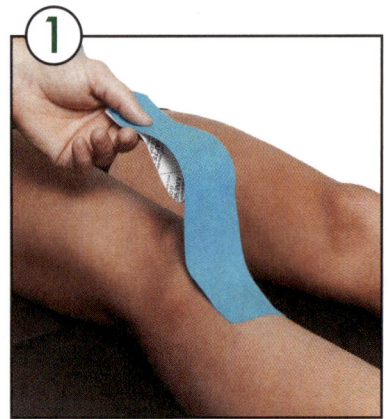

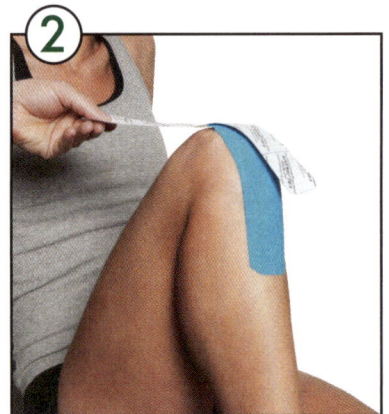

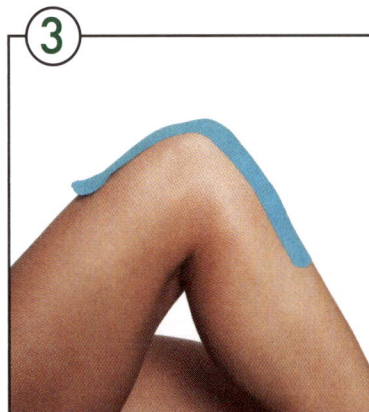

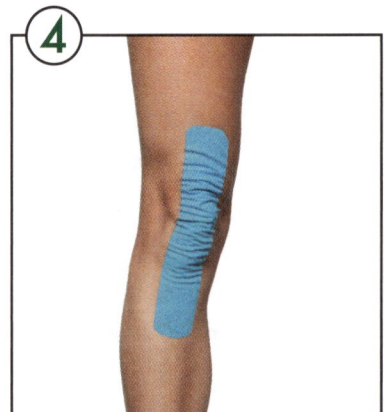

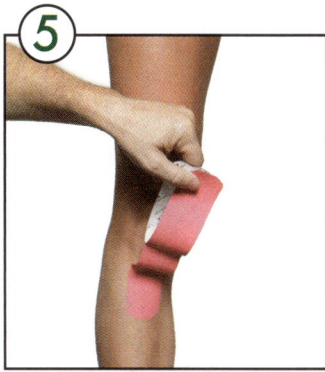

MODIFIED MECHANICAL CORRECTION:

Two methods of application: 1) patient sitting on table (follow basic directions below); 2) patient weight bearing - demonstration described below.

5. Cut a length of Kinesio I strip from 2-3" below the tibial tuberosity to the mid-thigh area. With the patient weight bearing begin by placing the anchor of the Kinesio I strip 2-3" below the tibial tuberosity with no tension.

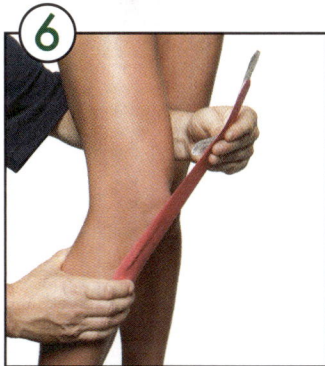

6. Have the patient move into approximately 20-30 degrees of flexion. With one hand, hold the anchor, specifically directly over the tibiala tuberosity, to ensure no tension will be added. Apply 50-75% of available tension from the tibial tuberosity to the inferior pole of the patella.

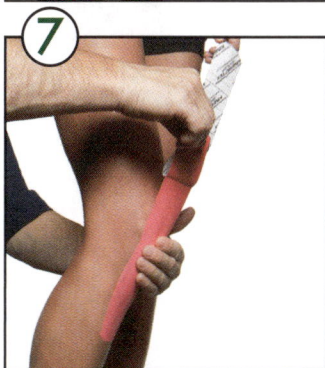

7. Slide the hand from the tibial tuberosity to the inferior pole of the patella. This will initiate adhesive.

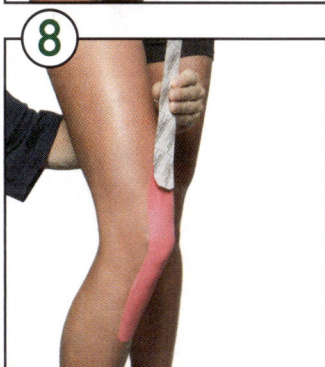

8. Apply paper off to light, 15-25% of available tension from the inferior pole of the patella to the last 2" of the Kinesio I strip.

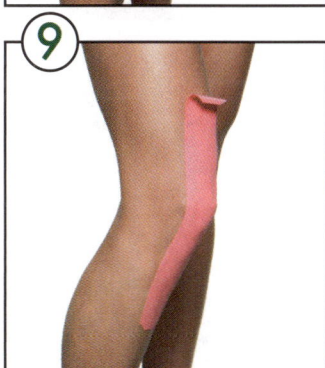

9. Lay down the end with no tension. Rub to initiate adhesive prior to any further patient movement.

When the patient extends their knee, the tape should create visible convolutions above the inferior pole of the patella but none below the inferior pole. If there are limited number of convolutions above the inferior pole of the patella, it would be an indicator of too much tension being applied to the Kinesio Tex tape.

This technique can be applied by itself, or in combination with the following U strip.

Patella Tendonitis – U Strip

This technique for treating patella tendonitis uses a U-shaped application of the Kinesio strip under and around the patella. The function of the U strip is to apply downward pressure on the inferior pole of the patella to create a "tilting" effect. This "tilting" effect is thought to decrease pressure on the inferior pole of the patella and reduce inflammation and pain. The practitioner should exercise judgment as to the amount of downward pressure starting with less pressure with initial applications.

This can be used for Inferior Pole Tendonitis (Jumper's Knee), or Tendonitis on Tibial Tuberosity. It may also be effective for Osgood-Schlatter syndrome or Larsen-Johannson syndrome.

Patella Tendonitis – U Strip

Measure an I strip of Kinesio Tex Tape from the inferior pole of the patella to 4-5" above the patella, bilaterally.

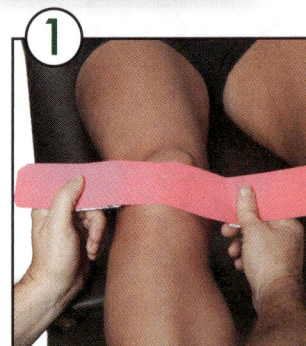

1. You can either place the patients knee in extension, or in 20-30 degrees of flexion to begin application. Begin by tearing the paper backing in the center of the Kinesio I strip and place the center portion of the I strip with 1/3 to ½ width of the Kinesio strip over the inferior pole of the patella.

2. Instruct the patient to move their knee slowly into flexion. As the patient moves their knee into flexion a mechanical correction technique is applied using 50-75% of available tension and downward/inward pressure. Pushing the inferior pole of the patella in a downward and inferior motion is an attempt to "tilt" the patella.

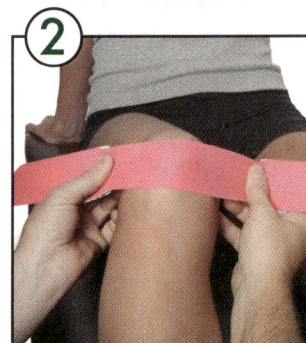

> **ℹ** With this application the therapeutic zone is directly inferior to the patella and around the medial and lateral inferior border. When the above tension is applied to the inferior pole of the patella the tension is beyond this zone. "Peel" back off of the skin any tension area outside of the therapeutic zone.

3. With one hand hold the tension over the inferior pole of the patella, so tension is maintained over the target tissue. "Peeling" back the tension outside of the therapeutic zone on the medial border of the patella.

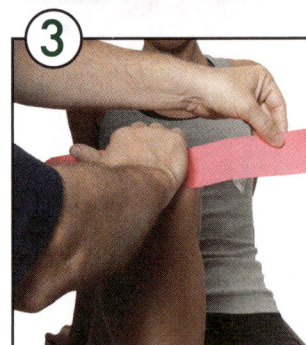

4. You may need to switch hands over the inferior pole of the patella. "Peeling" back the tension outside of the therapeutic zone on the lateral border of the patella. Rub to initiate adhesive prior to any further patient movement.

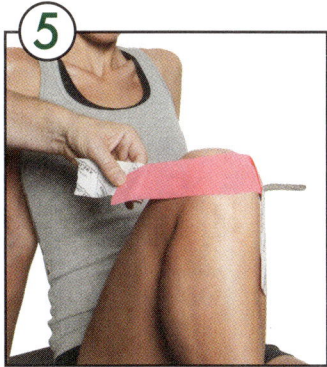

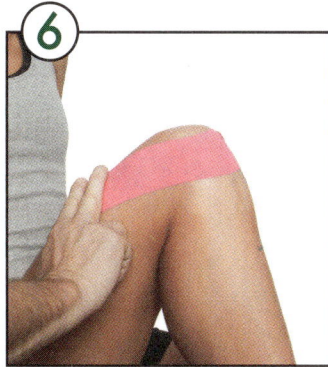

5. Apply the Kinesio strip around the patella and over the vastus lateralis with paper off to light, 15-25% of available tension.

6. Lay down the ends with no tension. Rub to activate adhesive prior to any further patient movement.

7. Repeat the above two steps for the vastus medialis.

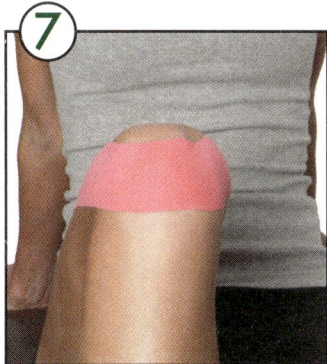

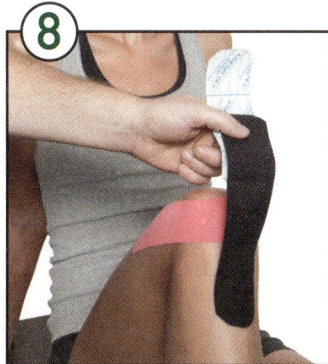

"PITCHFORK" OR "U OF I" TECHNIQUE: U TECHNIQUE COMBINES WITH MODIFIED SPACE CORRECTION: It is a "modified" space correction since the tension will NOT be added to the center of the I strip as is the normal application.

8. Have the patient in knee flexion. Apply the anchor 2-3" below the tibial tuberosity with no tension. Rub to initiate adhesive prior to any further patient movement.

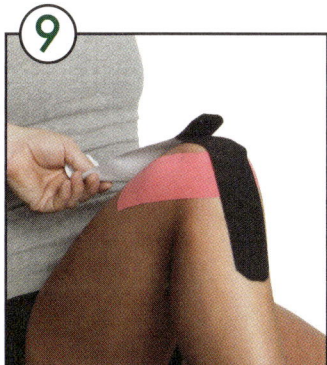

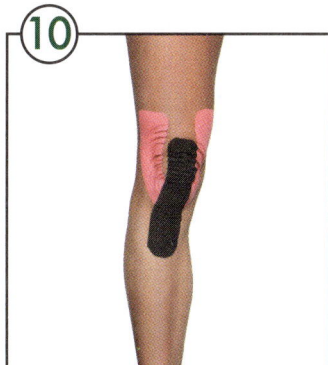

9. Apply paper off to light, 15-25% of available tension to the Kinesio I strip and apply to the skin over the patella to 4-5" above the superior pole of the patella.

10. Lay down the end with no tension. Rub to initiate adhesive prior to any further patient movement.

It is more effective, and the technique wear time is longer if the U technique is applied first because the U technique is the higher tension technique. If the modified space correction is applied first, the U technique mechanical correction over the top, will "pull off" the space correction limiting effectiveness and wear time.

Patella Tendonitis – U Strip

Patella Tracking Syndrome

Patella Tracking Syndrome is generally thought of as one of the most common conditions of the knee. It may be caused by many factors: patella malalignment, genu varum, genu valgum, genu recurvatum, patella alta, patella balta and weak vastus medialis to name a few. It is a chronic or degenerative condition in which the symptoms of pain and inflammation become more pronounced with increased activity.

Proper evaluation of the underlying cause of patella tracking syndrome is critical to the success of the taping technique applied.

The Kinesio Taping Technique assists in reduction of edema and pain by providing a proprioceptive stimuli through the skin requiring the surrounding tissues to normalize skin tension. This is accomplished primarily through the use of mechanical correction techniques.

FACILITATION OF VASTUS MEDIALIS OBLIQUE.

Following evaluation the practitioner may determine muscle weakness as a causative factor in the patella tracking syndrome. A vastus medialis oblique facilitation will be demonstrated.

1. Have the patient contract the quadriceps muscle group to determine the location of the origin, which begins on the front and middle side (anteriomedially) on the intertrochanteric line of the femur. Place the anchor and split in the Y superior to the origin with no tension.

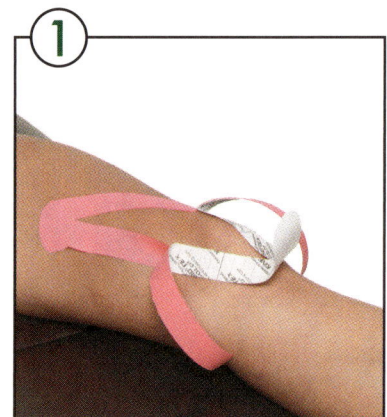

2. Have the patient move into knee flexion. Apply light to moderate, 15-35% of available tension to the tails and surround the inferior edges of the muscle, aiming for the medial part of the quadriceps femoris tendon and the medial border of the patella. Repeat for superior fibers of the vastus medialis oblique.

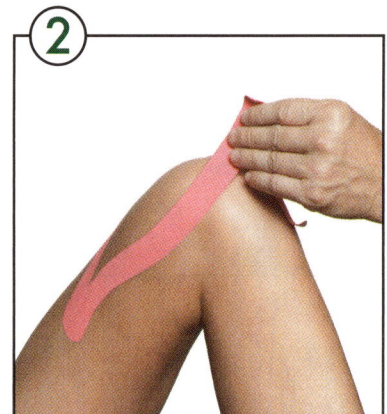

3. Lay down the ends with no tension. Rub to initiate prior to any further patient movement.

    The practitioner may also apply a quadriceps facilitation as well as or in place of the vastus medialis oblique. Tensor fascia lata, gluteus medialis are also examples of muscle tissue that can either be facilitated or inhibited.

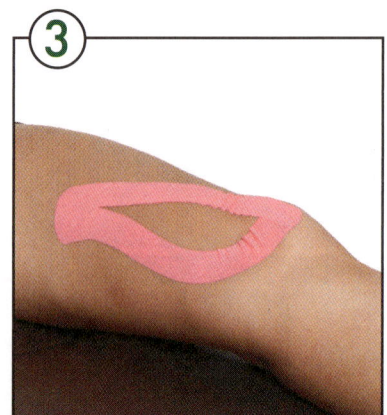

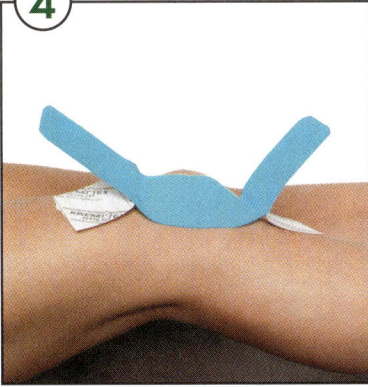

OPTION 1: PATELLA TRACKING LATERALLY - MECHANICAL CORRECTION TENSION IN THE MIDDLE OF AN I STRIP

Application of a mechanical correction I strip. As a result of the evaluation of the knee, the practitioner determines where the mechanical corrective strip should be applied: lateral border directly, or could be a slightly inferior or superior angle.

4. Begin by placing the patients knee in 20-30 degrees of flexion. Alternatively this technique can be applied with the knee in extension. Tear the paper backing in the center of a 6-8" long Kinesio I strip.

   Holding both ends, apply 50-75% of available tension, to the middle of the Kinesio I strip. Place the I strip so 1/3 to ½ of the I strip is on the lateral border of the patella.

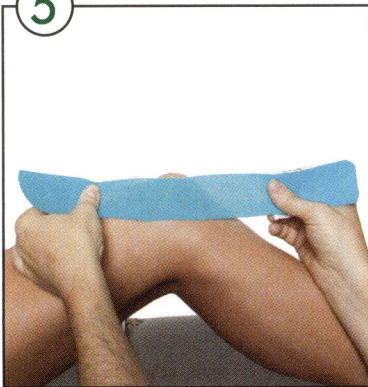

5. Have the patient slowly move into further knee flexion and continue applying downward/inward pressure as the 50-75% of available tension to the I strip is maintained, the mechanical correction is applied until end range of motion.

   Apply the mechanical correction tension around the lateral border of the patella, tension ends as the Kinesio Tex Tape passes the superior and inferior poles of the patella.

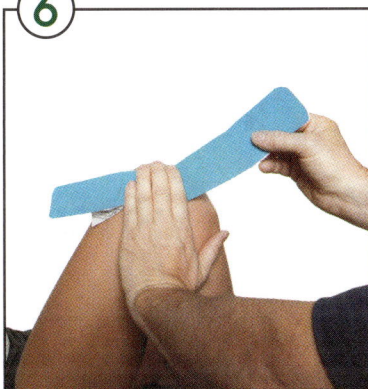

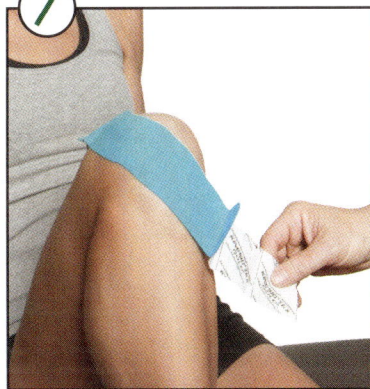

6. Place one hand on the Kinesio I strip covering the lateral border of the patella. This will initiate adhesion. If there is any Kinesio Tex Tape past the superior and inferior poles of the patella, gently pull the tape back to that point. Ensuring tension only on the target tissue.

7. Apply paper off to light, 15-25% of available tension to the Kinesio I strip forming a C to the mid thigh region for upper portion of the strip and past the tibial tuberosity for the lower portion.

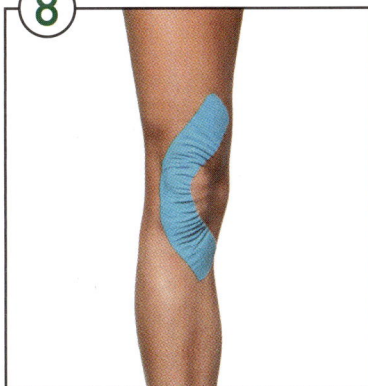

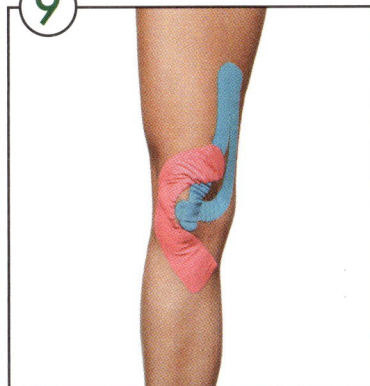

8. The last approximately 2" is applied with no tension. Rub to initiate adhesive prior to any further patient movement.

9. Completed Patella Tracking Laterally -Mechanical Correction and Facilitation of vastus medialis

OPTION 2: PATELLA TRACKING LATERALLY - MECHANICAL CORRECTION TENSION IN THE BASE:

10. Measure a Kinesio Y strip so there is an approximately 2" anchor, and the base of the Y strip will end with the split in the Y located just superior to the lateral border of the patella. Lay down the approximately 2" anchor with no tension. The knee can be in extension or 20-30 degrees of flexion.

11. With one hand, hold the anchor to ensure no tension will be added. Apply 50-75% of available tension to the base. As you apply the base to the skin also apply downward/inward pressure to or just above the lateral border of the patella. As the base is applied move the hand holding the anchor up the Kinesio strip to the split in the Y.

12. While holding the base, have the patient move their knee into flexion. Apply paper off to light, 15-25% of available tension to the tails.

    Apply the superior tail along the superior border of the patella. Apply the inferior tail along the inferior border of the patella. Lay down the remaining ends with no tension.

    Rub to initiate adhesive prior to any further patient movement.

13. Completed Kinesio Taping mechanical correction tension in the base for patella tracking syndrome.

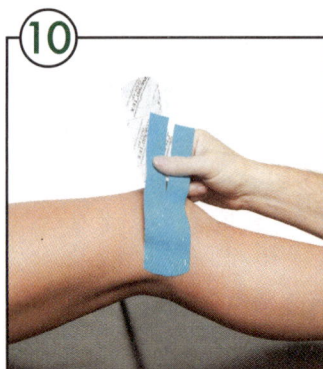
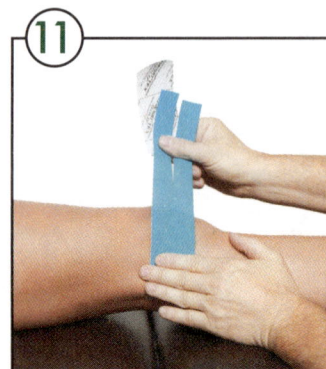
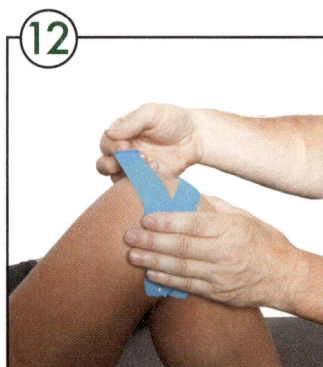
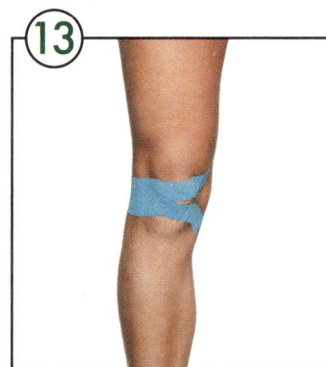
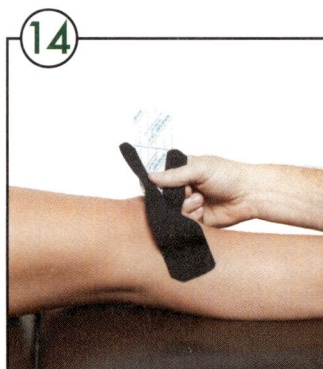

OPTION 3: PATELLA TRACKING LATERALLY - TENSION ON BASE: Inferior to superior angle. Based upon the evaluation the practitioner may determine that the mechanical correction should be applied with some degree of angle to affect patella.

14. Measure a Kinesio Y strip so there is an approximately 2" anchor, and the base of the Y strip will end with the split in the Y located inferior to the border of the patella. Apply the anchor inferior and at the appropriate angle based upon evaluation. The knee can be in extension or 20-30 degrees of flexion.

15. Hold the anchor to ensure no tension will be added.

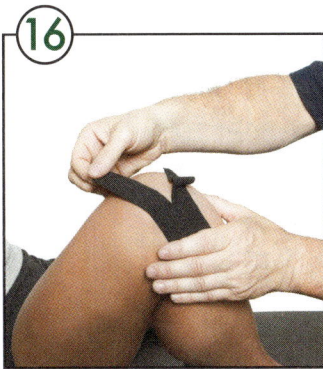

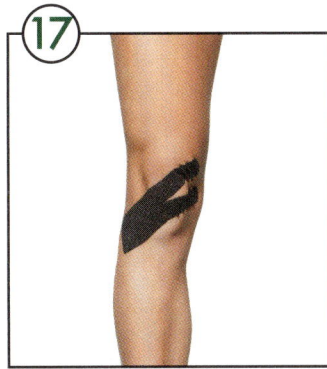

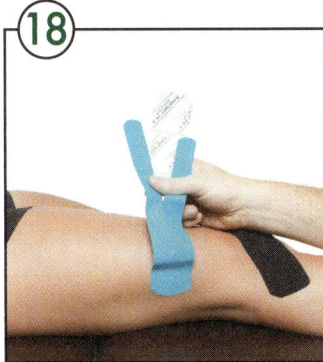

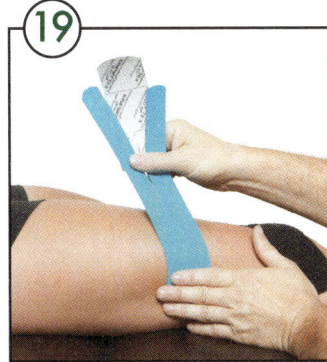

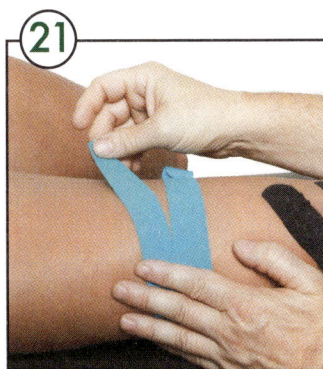

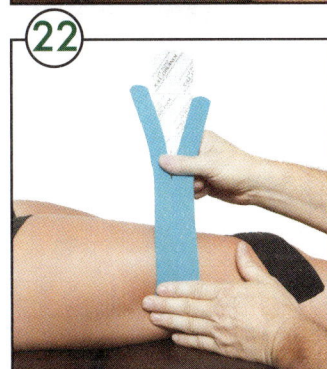

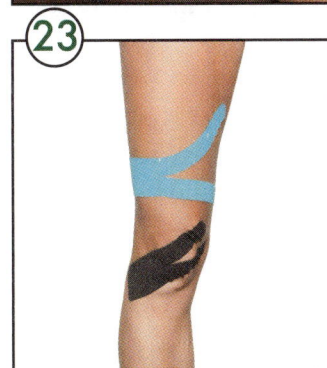

16. With one hand, hold the anchor to ensure no tension will be added. Have the patient move into flexion. Apply 50-75% of available tension to the base. As you apply the base to the skin also apply downward/inward pressure to or just above the lateral border of the patella. As the base is applied move the hand holding the anchor up the Kinesio strip to the split in the Y. Apply paper off to light, 15-25% of available tension to the tails.

Apply the tails so they surround the patella. Lay down the ends with no tension. Rub to initiate adhesive prior to any further patient movement.

17. Completed mechanical correction tension in the base at an angle.

OPTIONAL APPLICATION OF FASCIA CORRECTION: SIDE TO SIDE OR LONG AND SHORT TENSION IN THE BASE. Based
upon the evaluation a fascia correction may be applied: example is to IT Band.

18. Apply anchor ½" to 1" from treatment zone with no tension.

19-20. With one hand hold the anchor and apply 10-50% tension in a side to side technique. Side to side motion is exaggerated.

21. Lay down tails with no tension, rub to initiate adhesive prior to any further patient movement.

22. Apply anchor as explained above. Application of long and short fascia correction, 10-50% tension. Lay down tails with no tension, rub to initiate adhesive prior to any further patient movement.

23. Completed application of mechanical correction at an angle and fascia correction on the IT Band.

Patella Tracking Syndrome

Chondromalacia Patella

Chondromalacia patella is a softening and degeneration of the under surface of the patella. The exact cause is unknown, generally it is related to patella tracking abnormalities, increased quadriceps angle, abnormal patella alignment, and muscle weakness, just to name a few. Patients with the possible list of causes sometimes do not develop chondromalacia, some without any known factors develop chondromalacia. The condition is generally associated with inflammation surrounding the patella, medial patella retinaculum pain, and increased symptoms with increased activity levels.

The Kinesio Taping Method will assist by reducing pain, inflammation, and if indicated provide proprioceptive stimuli to alter patella tracking.

For additional reference of Kinesio Taping Technique options, see patella tracking syndrome.

Following evaluation the practitioner may determine muscle weakness as a causative factor in the chondromalacia patella. A vastus medialis oblique facilitation will be demonstrated. See Lateral Tracking Syndrome for complete description.

1. Have the patient contract the quadriceps muscle group to determine the location of the origin. Place the anchor and split in the Y superior to the origin with no tension. Apply light to moderate, 15-35% of available tension and surround the superior and inferior edges of the muscle. Angling towards the superior medial aspect of the patella.

   Lay down the ends with no tension. Rub to initiate adhesive prior to any patient movement.

2. The primary therapeutic goal of Kinesio Taping for chondromalacia patella is to reduce inflammation as a result of the effusion caused by the hyaline cartilage degeneration. Measure two Kinesio I strips. One, approximately 10-12" and the second 12-14".

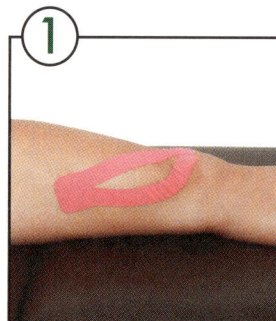
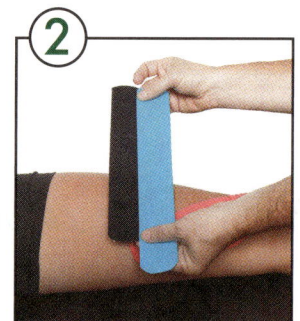
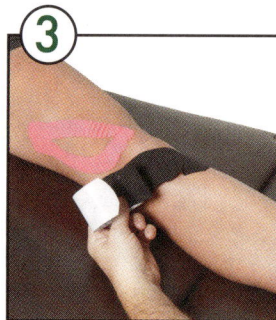
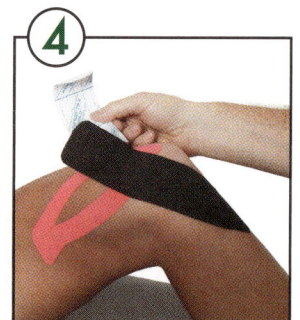
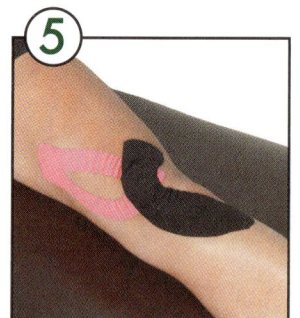

MODIFIED SPACE CORRECTION:

3. A modified space correction technique will be applied. Place the anchor of a Kinesio I strip lateral to the tibial tuberosity angling the Kinesio strip so 1/3 will be on the lateral border of the patella and the remaining over the area of edema with no tension and with the knee in extension.

4. Instruct the patient to move their knee slowly into flexion and apply paper off to light, 15-25% of available tension. For this technique less tension is usually better. As the tension is applied to the Kinesio strip, apply the Kinesio I strip around the patella and over the anterior aspect of the thigh forming a C shape around the patella. Lay down the last approximately 2" of the Kinesio strip down with no tension. Keeping the knee in extension rub to initiate adhesive prior to any further patient movement.

5. Completed Medial Strip.

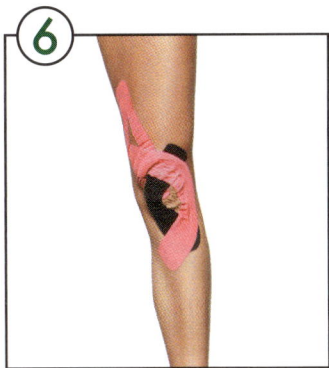

6. Repeat the above steps on the lateral border of the patella. When the patient moves their knee into extension following the application technique, convolutions should be visible surrounding the patella. If convolutions are not evident, the Kinesio strip was applied with too much tension. The technique works best if the middle third or more of the patella is visible between the two modified space correction I strips.

The Kinesio Tex Tape will adhere best if all tape anchors are placed upon the skin.

OPTION 1: MECHANICAL CORRECTION TENSION IN THE MIDDLE OF AN I STRIP

Apply the previously described vastus medialis oblique technique if appropriate. The practitioner may determine that patella alignment correction may be beneficial. In addition a modified space correction to the medial border of the patella will be added to reduce edema.

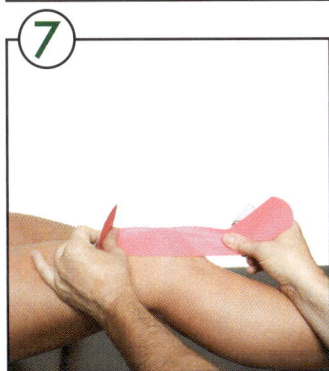

7. The use of the mechanical correction technique for patella tracking may be appropriate. Technique application depicted in photo is for lateral tracking using an I strip. See Lateral Tracking for full description.

8. Application of modified space correction on the medial border of the patella. For complete description see Modified Space Correction on previous page.

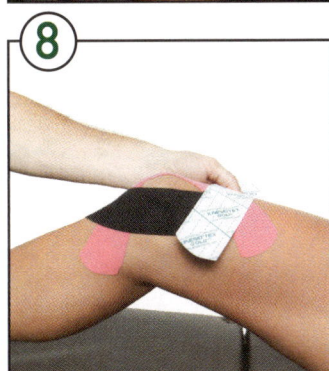

Other patella alignment abnormalities may be present, this is only given as an example of one potential problem. An angled application of the tension in the middle of the I strip could be chosen. Also other muscles or possibly a fascia correction maybe appropriate.

9. Application of mechanical correction with modified space correction techniques.

OPTION 2: MECHANICAL CORRECTION TENSION ON BASE

Once the described vastus medialis oblique technique is applied, the practitioner may determine that patella alignment correction may be beneficial.

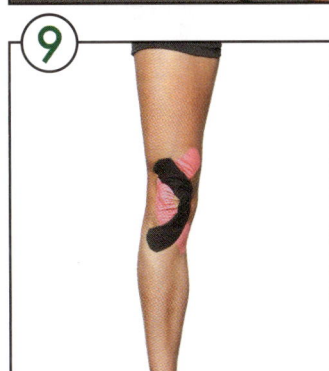

10. The use of the mechanical correction technique tension in the base for patella tracking may be appropriate. Technique application depicted in this photo is for lateral tracking using tension on the base.

Apply the anchor so the Y will be located on the lateral border of the patella if not slightly higher. Hold the anchor to ensure no tension will be added. Apply 50-75% of available tension from the anchor to the lateral border of the patella. Slide the hand holding the anchor to the end point of tension to initiate adhesive. Have the patient flex the knee. Lay down the tails with paper off tension to surround the inferior and superior pole. Lay down ends with no tension and rub to initiate adhesive prior to any further patient movement.

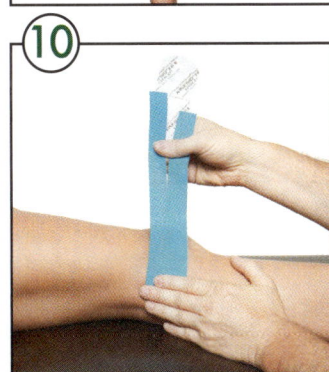

Chondromalacia Patella

Plica of the Knee

A Plica of the Knee is the result of non-absorption of the synovial walls that make up the three knee cavities during the initial months of development. Resulting in a thickening of synovial capsule causing folds that are referred to as plica. This condition of plica development occurs in approximately 20 percent of the population. The plica becomes inflamed and causes joint effusion located near the infrapatellar fat pad.

The Kinesio Taping Method will assist by reducing edema, pain and limiting patella movement which may increase pressure on the plicae.

APPLICATION OF LYMPHATIC CORRECTIVE TECHNIQUE

Lymphatic drainage should be directed to anterior aspect of thigh and posterior medial aspect of the knee.

1. Strip one, place anchor on the superior medial aspect of the thigh no tension. Apply 0-20% of available tension to the fan strips over the medial plica ending below the edema. Rub to initiate adhesive.

2. Strip two, place anchor superior and over the mid-belly of quadriceps with no tension. Apply 0-20% of available tension and direct fan tails over the medial plica ending below the edema. Lay down ends with no tension and rub to initiate adhesive prior to any further patient movement. The fans should form a crisscross pattern.

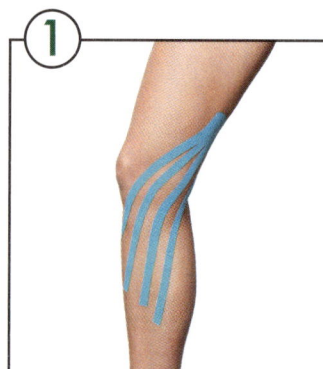
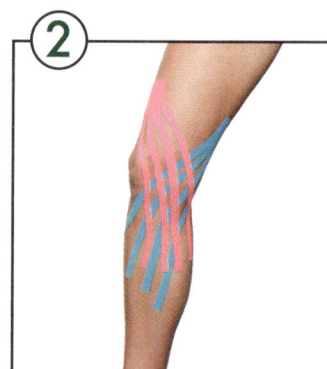
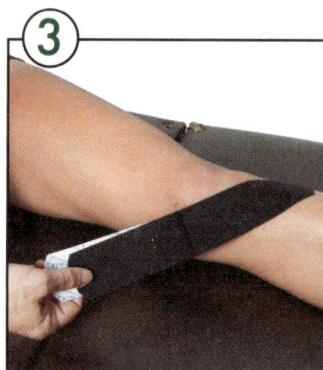
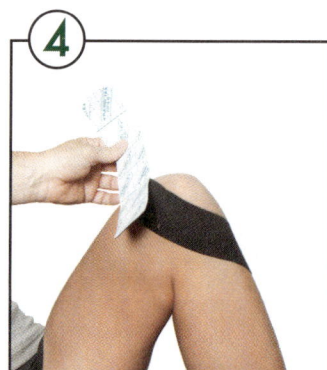

OPTION 1: MODIFIED SPACE CORRECTION

3. A modified space correction technique will be applied. Place the anchor of a Kinesio I strip on or laterally to the tibial tuberosity with no tension and with the knee in extension. Angle the Kinesio strip over the area of edema.

4. Instruct the patient to move their knee slowly into flexion and apply paper off to light, 15-25% of available tension during patient movement, for this technique less is usually better. Apply the Kinesio I strip over the area of edema then angle over the anterior aspect of the thigh forming a C shape around the patella. Lay down the end with no tension. Rub to initiate adhesive prior to any further patient movement.

5. Completed modified space correction technique. A second strip may be applied to the medial aspect of the knee depending upon the amount of pain and/or edema.

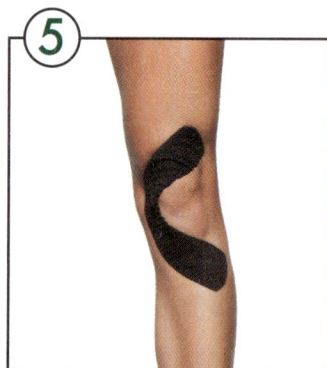

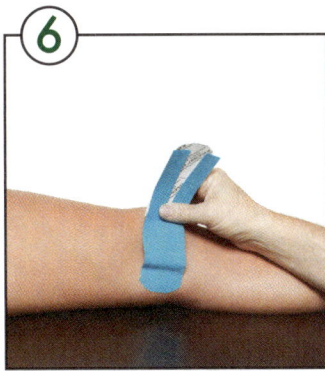

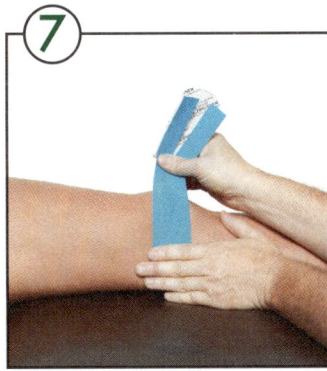

OPTION 2: MECHANICAL CORRECTION TENSION IN BASE

Application of Mechanical correction with tension on the base will be shown. The Mechanical correction is chosen to limit movement of the pes anserinus tendon bands over the lateral femoral condyle.

6. Begin mechanical correction by placing the anchor of the Kinesio Y strip below the anteromedial surface of the tibia with no tension.

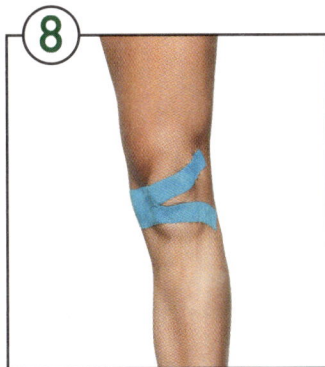

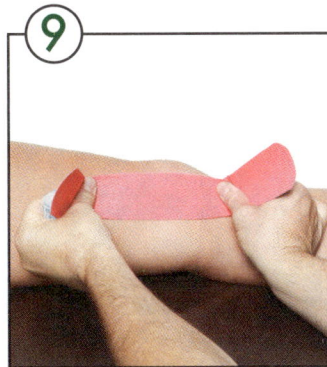

7. Start with the patient's knee in extension, with one hand hold the anchor of the Y to ensure no tension is added. Apply moderate to severe, 50-75% of available tension and downward/inward pressure to the base of the Kinesio Y strip to the superior aspect of the lateral border. The effect of the mechanical correction will provide restriction to the inferior movement of the plica and/or iliotibial band during knee flexion as it crosses over the lateral femoral condyle. Lay down the tails with paper off tension, lay down the end with no tension and rub to initiate adhesive prior to any further patient movement.

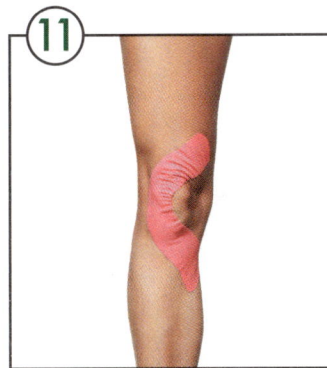

8. Mechanical Correction tension in base completed.

OPTION 3: MECHANICAL CORRECTION TENSION IN CENTER OF I STRIP

For complete description see lateral tracking syndrome.

9. Tear the center backing of a 10-12" Kinesio I strip and apply to the lateral border of the patella with the knee in extension or 20-30 degrees of flexion.

10. As you apply 50-75% of available tension with downward/inward pressure to the lateral border of the patella have the patient slowly move into flexion. Only have tension along the lateral border of the patella, if there is tension outside of this target zone remove strip and reapply. Apply the next section of tape with paper off to light, 15-25% of available tension forming a C around the patella. Lay down the ends with no tension and rub to initiate adhesive prior to any further patient movement.

11. Completed mechanical correction tension in the center of an I strip.

Other options may be to apply a Donut Hole technique (see lateral epicondylitis) or space correction star technique (see low back section) over the area of pain or edema.

Osgood-Schlatter and Larsen-Johannson Syndrome

Osgood-Schlatter syndrome is an apophysitis of the patella ligament from its insertion onto the tibial tuberosity in an adolescent patient. Larsen-Johannson syndrome is an apophysitis to the patella ligament from its origin on the inferior pole of the patella. Both are characterized by localized swelling, pain, and point tenderness of either the insertion or origin of the patella ligament.

There are several Kinesio Taping techniques which may provide reduced inflammation and pain, the practitioner will need to determine which techniques is best for their patient. If one technique does not provide significant results, another technique may.

OPTION 1: MECHANICAL CORRECTION

For acute pain relief, a mechanical correction strip may be applied in an attempt to "hold down" the apophysitis of the tibial tuberosity or inferior pole of the patella. If using this technique for Larsen-Johannson, do not apply too much pressure as to alter patella tracking. A Space Correction may also decrease pain by creating space over area of pain.

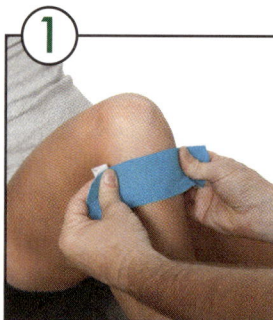
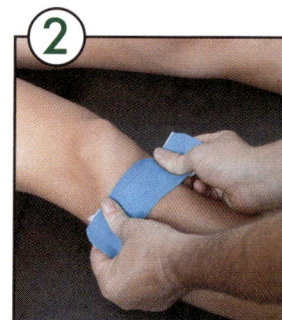

1. Osgood-Schlatter: Place the patient's knee in 20-30 degrees of flexion. Begin by tearing the center of the paper backing in a 4-6" long Kinesio I strip. Holding both ends, apply moderate to severe, 50-75% of available tension with downward/inward pressure to the center of the Kinesio strip. Place over the tibial tuberosity or inferior pole of the patella Larsen-Johannson's.

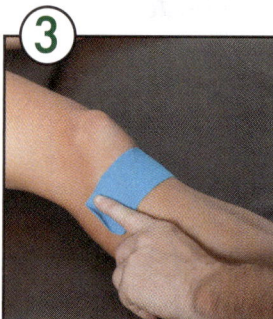
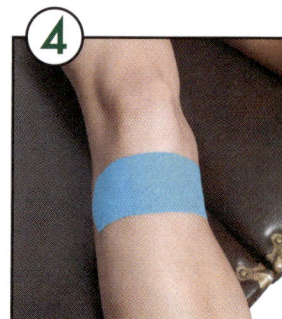

2. Prior to laying down the Kinesio strip ends, have the patient move their knee into full extension.

3. Lay down the ends with no tension. Rub to initiate adhesive prior to any further application.

4. Completed application.

OPTION 2: SPACE CORRECTION

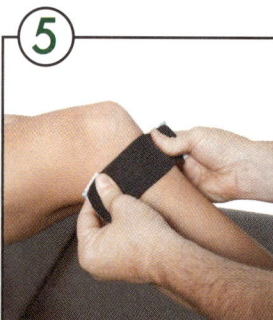
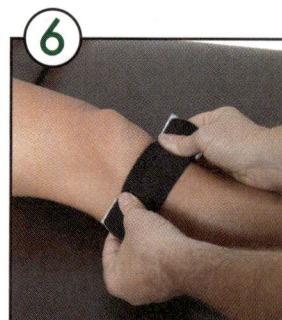

5. Place the patient's knee in 20-30 degrees flexion. Begin by tearing the center of the paper backing in a 4 - 6" long Kinesio I strip. Holding both ends, light to moderate, 15-35% of available tension to the center of the Kinesio strip. Place over the tibial tuberosity or inferior pole of the patella.

6. Prior to laying down the Kinesio strip ends, have the patient move their knee into full extension.

7. Lay down the ends with no tension. Rub to initiate adhesive prior to any further application.

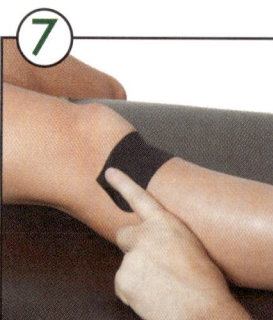
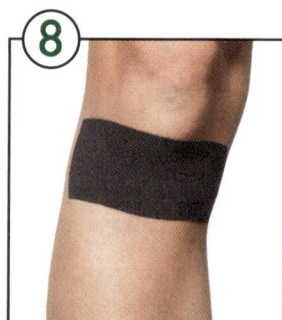

8. Completed application. Several I strips can be used to create a Star Technique. If a star technique is used the I strips should be narrower, 1 ½" or maybe 1".

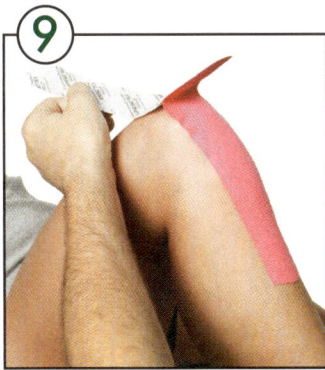

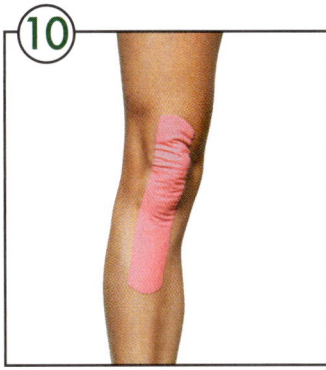

OPTIONAL TAPING OR COMBINATION TAPING

Techniques with higher tension levels should be applied first and then a second Kinesio Taping Technique may be applied over the top. The patient may find the greatest decrease in pain during acute pain phases from a combination of taping techniques. Then as the patient's pain is reduced, only one technique may be indicated.

OPTION 1: Modified space correction I strip. For complete review see patella tendonitis.

9. Begin by placing the anchor 2-3" below the tibial tuberosity with no tension. Have the patient slowly move the knee into flexion and at the same time apply paper off to moderate, 15-35% of available tension over the patella. End tension 2-3" from the end. Lay down the end with no tension, rub to initiate adhesive prior to any further patient movement.

10. Completed modified space correction, convolutions should be evident, if they are not then too much tension was applied.

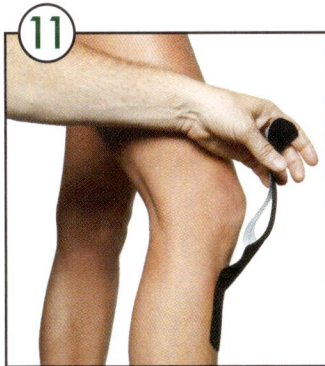

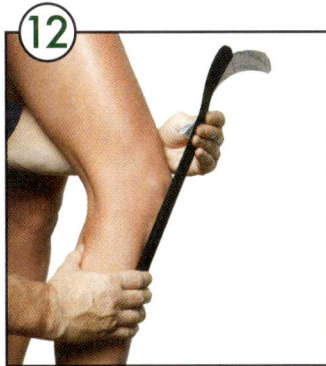

OPTION 2: Modified Mechanical Correction. For complete description see patella tendonitis.

11. Begin by placing the anchor 2-3" below the tibial tuberosity with no tension. The patient should be weight bearing and the knee in 20-30 degrees of flexion.

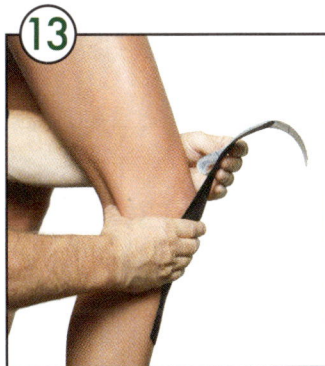

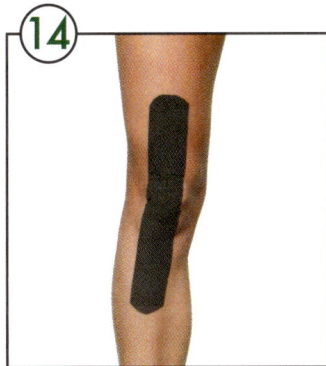

12. With one hand hold the anchor over the tibial tuberosity. Apply 50-75% of available tension from the tibial tuberosity to the inferior pole of the patella.

13. Slide the hand from the anchor to the inferior pole of the patella, this will initiate adhesive. Next apply paper off to light, 15-25% of available tension from the superior pole of the patella to the last 2-3" of the I strip. Lay down the end with no tension and rub to initiate adhesive prior to any further patient movement.

14. Completed Modified Mechanical Correction. Note: there are no convolutions over the tibial tuberosity to the inferior pole of the patella due to high tension level.

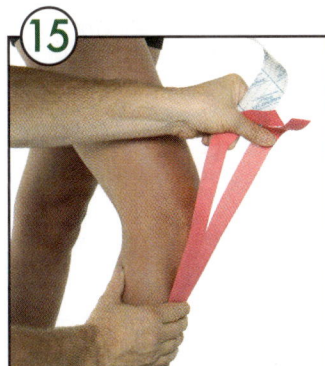

15. Optional application of Modified Mechanical Correction using a Y technique. Please see Patella Tendonitis for complete description.

OPTION 3:
16. Apply a patella tendonitis superior Y technique. For review, see patella tendonitis.

OPTION 4:
17. Apply a patella tendonitis inferior Y technique. For review, see patella tendonitis.

OPTION 5:
18. Combination of Superior Y and Inferior Y technique. For complete review see patella tendonitis.

OPTION 6: U Technique, for complete review see patella tendonitis. This technique can be combined with modified space correction as shown earlier in this section. For Osgood-Schlatter have the base of the U on the tibial tuberosity. For Larsen-Johannson have the base of the U on the inferior pole of the patella.

19. Cut an I strip from mid-thigh to either inferior pole of patella or tibial tuberosity and back to the mid-thigh area. Tear the center of the I strip and paper backing and apply to either the tibial tuberosity or inferior pole of patella with very light to severe tension, 15-75% of available tension as the patient is instructed to flex the knee. Tension level is determined by practitioner.

20. With one hand hold the anchor and pull back any tension that is on the medial or lateral border of the patella that is not wanted. Apply paper off to light, 15-25% of available tension to the lateral strip around the lateral border of the patella.

21-22. Lay down the end with no tension, rub to initiate adhesive prior to any further patient movement.

23. Repeat the above two steps for the medial portion of the U strip. Finished U Technique.

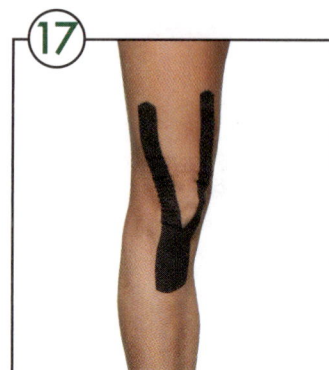

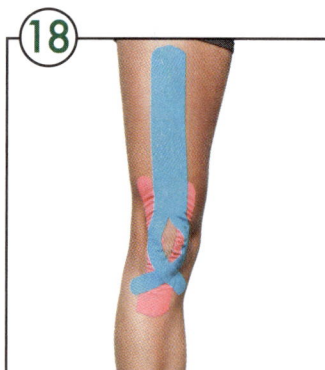

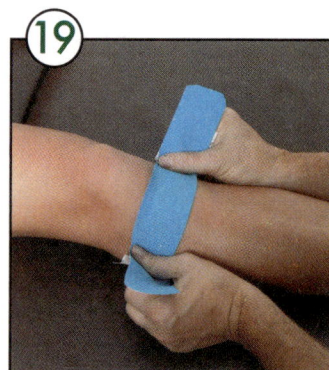

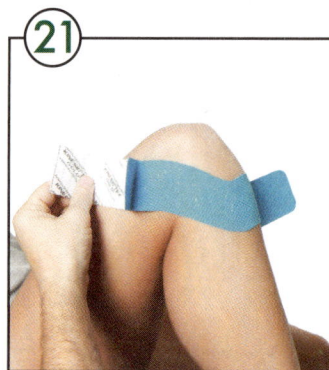

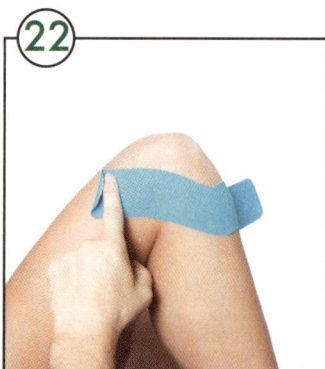

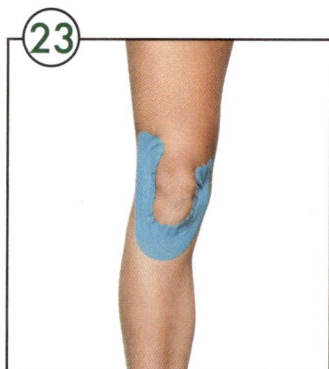

Osgood-Schlatter and Larsen-Johannson Syndrome

Medial Collateral Ligament Correction

Following a grade 1 to grade 3 MCL/LCL ligament sprain, use the ligament correction strip across the length of the ligament applying the tape from distal to proximal. The practitioner may choose to apply a lymphatic correction to assist with edema reduction from the knee region to the thigh or inguinal lymph nodes.

The tension of the Kinesio Strip should be greatest over the length of the ligament to create tension over the ligament length to provide sensory stimuli to the proprioceptive receptors. The tension transfer to the receptors will provide the perception of a more stable joint. The Kinesio strip should be applied as soon as possible following the injury. After the tape is applied, continue with treatment protocol with application of ice, elevation, compression, and hinged brace support. The Kinesio strip can be worn during all phases of rehabilitation and can be placed under any additional taping the practitioner feels would be appropriate.

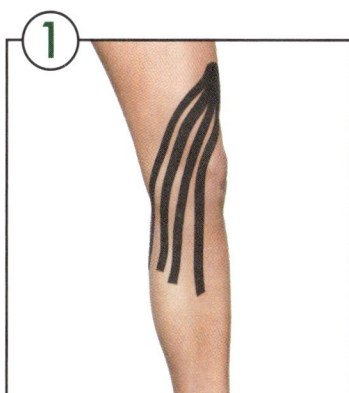

① ACUTE PHASE : FIRST 24-72 HOURS

Application of Lymphatic Corrective Technique. Lymphatic drainage should be directed to anterior aspect of thigh and ingunial region.

1. Place anchor of lymphatic fan tail on the superior aspect of the medial aspect of the thigh. Apply 0-20% of available tension and direct the fan strips over the medial collateral ligament ending below the edema. Lay down the ends with no tension, rub or pat to initiate adhesive prior to any further patient movement.

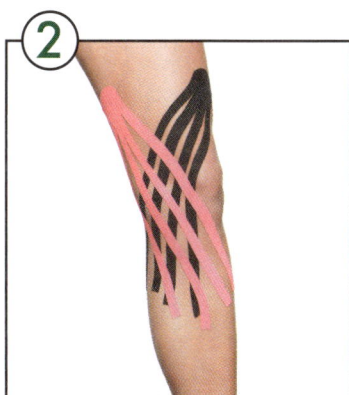

②

2. Place anchor superior and over the mid-belly of adductor muscle group with no tension. Apply 0-20% of available tension and direct the fan strips over the medial collateral ligament ending below the edema. Lay down the ends with no tension, rub or pat to initiate adhesive prior to any further patient movement.

   The fans should form a crisscross pattern over the MCL.

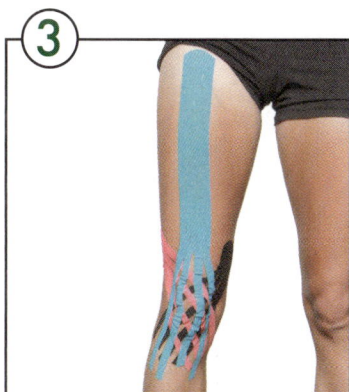

③ APPLICATION OF QUADRICEPS FACILITATION WITH LYMPHATIC FAN STRIP TECHNIQUE See ACL for complete description.

3. First apply quadriceps facilitation as described in patella tendonitis. From the traditional split in the Y the musculotendonous junction, cut the strip into a fan technique and apply over the patella with 0-20% of available tension.

   One or two additional Fan Strips may be applied as described above.

LIGAMENT CORRECTION FOR

MCL: Application of the Ligament Correction can be applied in the acute phase or wait until post 72 hours.

4. The knee is placed in 20-30 degrees of flexion, the position of function. Place anchor of ligament correction Kinesio I strip slightly below and medial to the tibial tuberosity at approximately 45 degree angle with no tension.

5. Place one hand on the anchor of the correction strip. Begin with paper off to light, 15-25% of available tension angling the I strip to slightly inferiorly to the MCL. It is important to have a low tension level to the point where the Ligament Correction I strip has been turned, forming the bottom of a J. If there is a high degree of tension in the bottom of the J, the Kinesio Tex Tape will pull away from the skin.

6. Slide the hand that was holding the anchor to the bottom of the J, where the tape has been turned, this will initiate adhesive. Next apply severe to full, 75-100% of available tension directly over the length of the ligament.

7. When the Kinesio strip has passed the femoral condyle, the superior border of the ligament slide the hand holding the anchor to this point. This will initiate adhesive.

8. Lay down the next section of Kinesio I strip down with paper off to light, 15-25% of available tension up the center of the adductor muscle group. Lay down the end with no tension and rub to initiate adhesive prior to any further patient movement. If you do not intiate adhesive the high tension level will cause the Kinesio Tex Tape to "pull" away from the skin, or decrease wear time.

9. Completed application of ligament technique for the medial collateral and lateral collateral ligament; during acute phase of MCL/LCL injury.

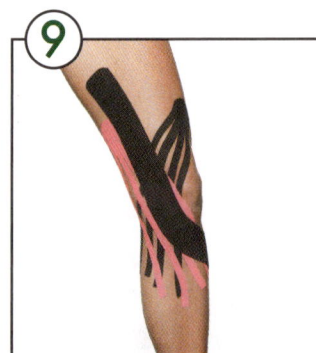

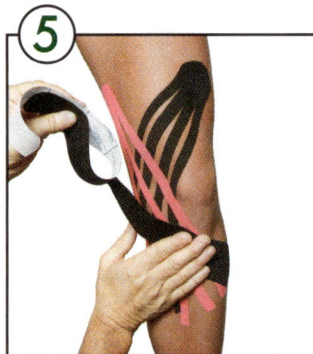

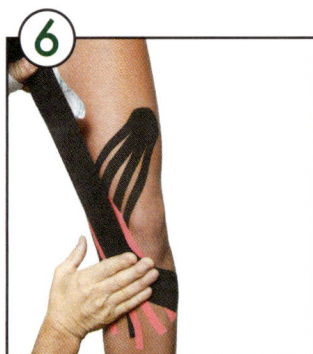

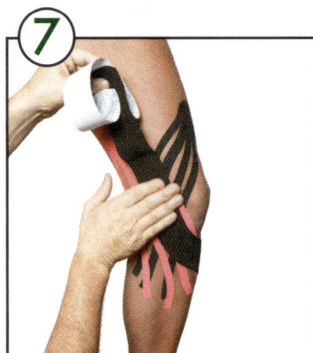

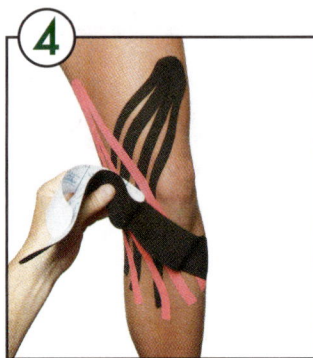

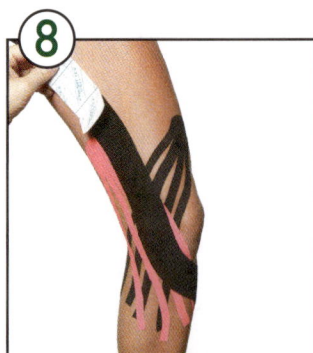

Medial Collateral Ligament Correction

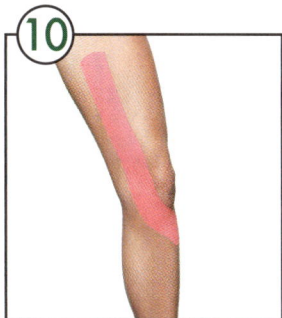

POST-ACUTE: AFTER 72 HOURS
OPTION 1:

10. Completed application of ligament correction technique as described above for acute phase treatment. This application should be worn during all rehabilitation activities. This technique is not intended and should not be used in replacement of a brace. It can be worn in conjunction with a brace or sleeve.

OPTION 2: Application of quadriceps facilitation. To assist facilitation with quadriceps muscle contraction. See Patella Tendonitis for complete description.

11. Place the patient in hip extension, apply anchor from the proximal 1/3 of quadriceps to the ASIS with no tension. Apply paper off to moderate, 15-35% of available tension to the Kinesio I strip to the musculotendinous junction.

    Have the patient move into hip and knee flexion. Direct the tails around the medial and lateral border of the patella with paper off to light, 15-25% of available tension.

    Lay down ends with no tension. Rub to activate adhesive prior to any patient movement.

OPTION 3: Application of hamstring inhibition technique. The technique can be applied to the group or an individual muscle. For complete review see Hamstring Strain. Photo shows individual muscles taped with an I technique. A Y technique is effective as well.

12. Place patient in hip flexion and knee extension. Anchor inferior to the popliteal fossa with no tension. Apply paper off to light, 15-25% of available tension over the mid-line of the hamstring, medial or lateral group angled towards the ischial tuberosity. Lay down the end with no tension. Rub to activate adhesive prior to any patient movement.

OPTION 4: Application of a mechanical correction technique tension in tails, using three tails instead of two.

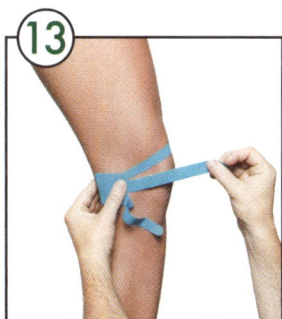
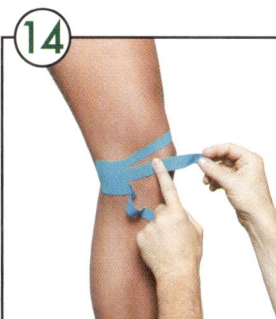

13. Start the patient in knee extension, place the base of the Kinesio strip posterior to the posterior fibers of the medial collateral ligament with no tension. Next have the patient move into 20-30 degrees of flexion. Hold the anchor with one hand; with the other hand, apply moderate to severe 50-75% of available tension, with downward pressure over the MCL.

14. When the Kinesio strip has passed over the ligament, have the patient move into knee flexion. Lay down the remaining tail with no tension, the tails are splayed out to minimize tension.

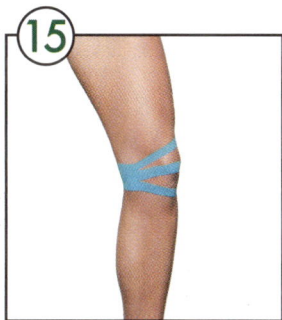
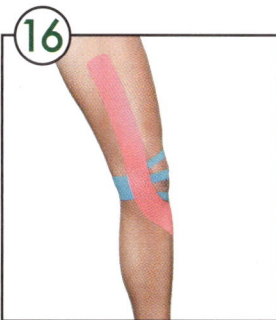

15. Competed mechanical correction over MCL.

16. Completed application of ligament correction technique as described in acute technique for the MCL ligament acute phase, over the mechanical correction technique as described above.

Anterior Cruciate Ligament Kinesio Technique

The Anterior Cruciate Ligament (ACL) of the knee is most commonly injured as the result of extension and rotation forces. The ACL may be injured by itself or in combination with the medial collateral ligament, medial meniscus, or lateral meniscus. When the ACL is sprained, there is generally an associated joint effusion which occurs. The joint effusion causes a loss in range of motion and delays the rehabilitation of the injured knee joint.

The injured ACL will be treated acutely by reducing the joint effusion by application of a lymphatic correction. Following an acute injury a ligament correction technique may be used to provide proprioceptive stimuli to reduce anterior translation of the tibia on the femur.

Anterior Cruciate Ligament

DURING THE FIRST 24 - 72 HOURS: Apply a lymphatic corrective technique to the anterior aspect of the knee. Two, three, or four fan strips should be applied.

1. Begin by placing the anchor with no tension 5-6" above the patella on the medial aspect of the thigh. Place the knee in as much flexion as possible. Apply 0-20% of available tension and angle the tails over the area of edema. Lay down the ends with no tension and rub or pat to initiate adhesive prior to any further patient movement.

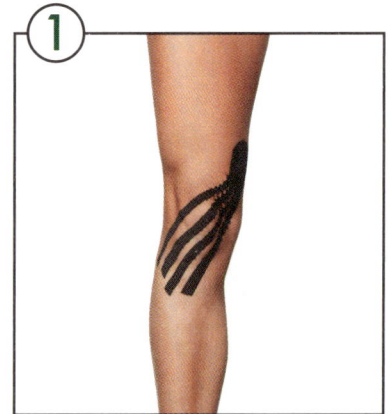

2. Begin by placing the anchor with no tension 5-6" above the patella on the lateral aspect of the thigh. Place the knee in as much flexion as possible. Apply 0-20% of available tension and angle the tails over the area of edema. Lay down the ends with no tension and rub or pat to initiate adhesive prior to any further patient movement.

   A third lymphatic fan can be placed down the center of the knee. A quadriceps facilitation and lymphatic correction can be combined, for complete description see next page.

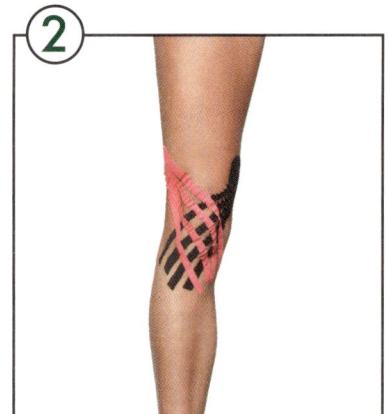

OPTIONAL POPLITEAL AREA LYMPHATIC:

3. With an ACL there may be edema in the posterior region. Place the anchor without tension 5-6" above popliteal region. Place the knee in extension. Apply 0-20% of available tension and angle the tails over the area of edema. Lay down the ends with no tension and rub or pat to initiate adhesive prior to any further patient movement.

   This lymphatic application will not last 3-4 days, most likely only 2-3 days due to the tails "rolling" due to movement.

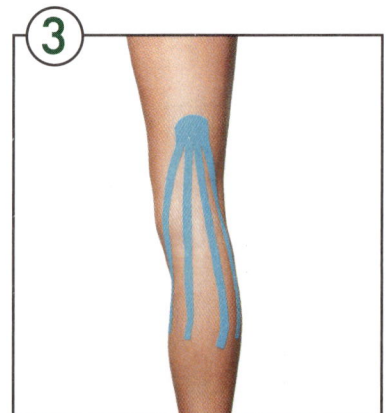

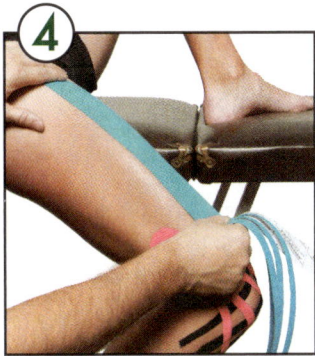

OPTIONAL QUADRICEPS FACILITATION:

Either during acute phase or post-acute phase the practitioner may apply a quadriceps muscle facilitation technique from origin to insertion to facilitate muscle contraction and enhance deep lymphatic fluid flow.

4. Place the anchor at or near the ASIS with no tension. Place the hip in extension. Apply light to moderate, 15-50% of available tension to the musculotendonous junction.

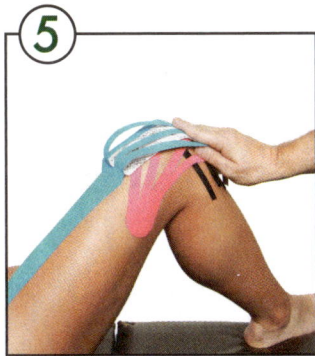

5. Then cut the remaining Kinesio Tex Tape into 4 or 5 fan strips. Place the patient in knee and hip flexion. Apply 0-20% of available tension and angle the tails over the area of edema. Lay down the ends with no tension and rub or pat to initiate adhesive prior to any further patient movement.

6. Completed Quadriceps Facilitation with combination of Lymphatic Correction. With increased quadriceps contraction deeper lymphatic drainage may be improved. This application can be applied first or following the medial and lateral strips as described above.

POST ACUTE: Application of Quadriceps Facilitation. For complete review see Patella Tendonitis.

7. Place anchor near upper 1/3 of quadriceps with no tension. Place the hip in extension. Apply 15-35% of available tension to the muscultendonous junction. Rub to initiate adhesive prior to any further patient movement. Flex the knee and apply the tails around the patella with paper off to light, 15-25% of available tension. End on or over the tibial tuberosity with no tension. Rub to initiate adhesive prior to any further patient movement.

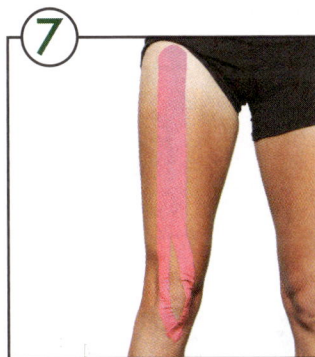

8. Modification of the U technique as described in Patella Tendonitis. U strip will be trying to limit anterior translation of the tibia on the femur. Place the patient in 20-30 degrees of flexion. Tear the center of the paper backing of an I strip and apply over the anterior tibial plateau. Apply 50-75% of available tension with downward pressure.

9. With one hand placed upon the tibial tuberosity push in a downward pressure in an attempt to cause posterior translation of the tibia on the femur. Apply 50-75% of available tension to the next 4-5" of the I strip along the lateral aspect of the knee.

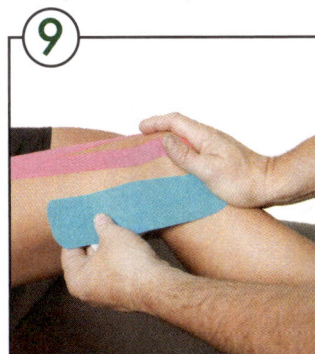

10. While holding the tibial tuberosity change the tension in the I strip to paper off to light, 15-25% of available tension.

11. Lay down the end with no tension. Rub to initiate adhesive prior to any further patient movement. This is important since with such a high degree of tension the Kinesio Tex Tape will "pull away" from the skin if the patient moves prior to adhesive activation.

Repeat the above steps for the medial, or opposite side of the knee.

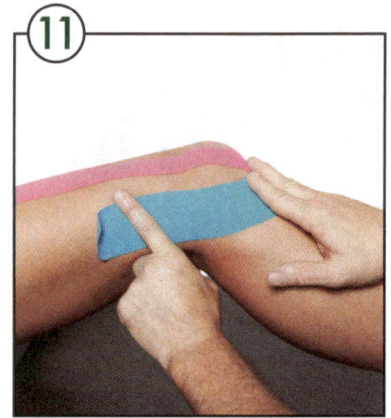

12. Completed application of Quadriceps Facilitation and modified U technique.

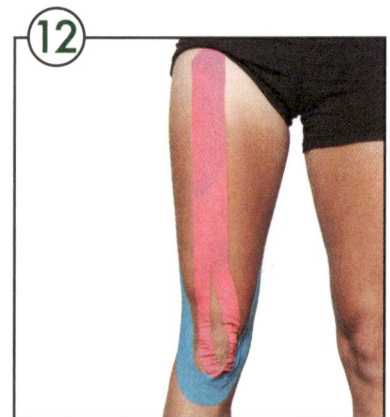

13. A second modified U technique may be applied to provide additional support to "limit" anterior translation of the tibia on the femur.

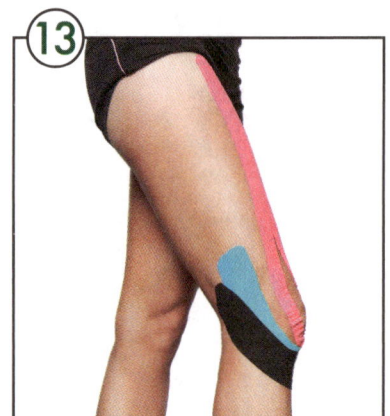

14. The practitioner may choose to apply a hamstring facilitation to further assist in limiting tibial translation. The hamstrings may provide a "pulling back" on the tibia providing a proprioceptive sensation of a stable joint.

Place the patient in hip flexion. Begin by placing the anchor of an I strip superior to the ischial tuberosity with no tension. Apply light to moderate, 15-35% of available tension to the I strip and direct over the semi-membranosus-semi-tendonosus, or biceps femoris or two strips with one over each of the muscle groups. Lay down the end with no tension and rub to initiate adhesive prior to any further patient movement.

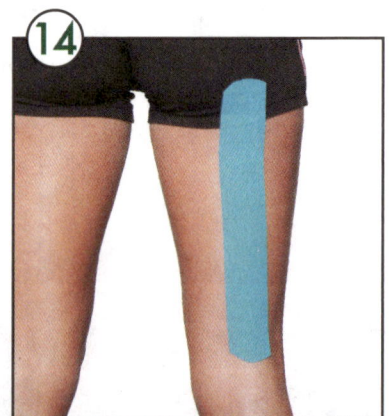

Knee Hyperextension

A hyperextension injury to the knee is a common injury resulting from the knee being forced past 0 degrees of extension (for females normal extension position may be up to +3 degrees). Generally, the knee has marked edema with pain occurring in knee extension.

The Kinesio Taping Technique will include a lymphatic corrective taping to reduce acute edema, basic hamstring muscle taping, and functional correction to limit knee extension during the acute phase.

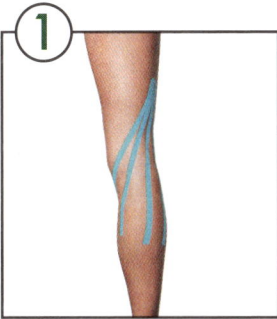
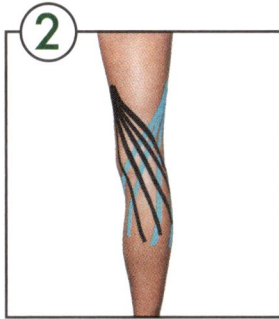
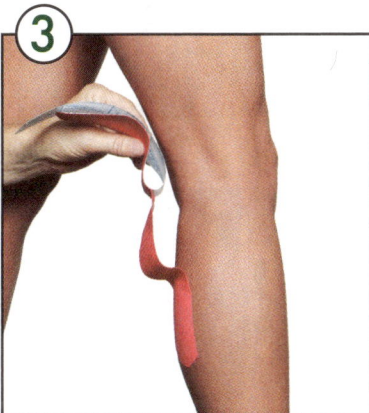
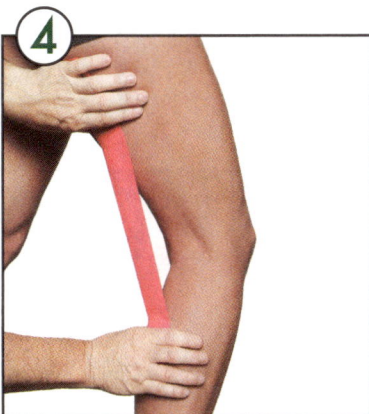

APPLICATION OF THE LYMPHATIC CORRECTIVE TECHNIQUE TO THE POPLITEAL FOSSA

1. Place the patient in as much extension as possible. Apply anchor with no tension 4-5" superior to the lateral condyle of the femur. Apply 0-20% of available tension crossing over the popliteal space, ending below the region of swelling. Lay down the ends with no tension, rub or pat to initiate adhesive.

2. Apply anchor 4-5" superior to the medial condyle of the femur. Apply 0-20% of available tension crossing over the popliteal space, ending below the region of swelling. Lay down the ends with no tension, rub or pat to initiate adhesive prior to any further patient movement.

The two lymphatic corrective strips should form a crisscross pattern over the popliteal space.

An option may be to apply two or three web cut space corrections. The web cut may last longer than the lymphatic fan technique.

POST ACUTE: Application of the functional corrective technique to limit knee extension. During evaluation the practitioner determines the degree of knee extension to limit. The desired result would be limitation of knee extension just short of a painful position by the patient.

3. Have the patient place their knee in a flexed position, ending prior to the point of pain. Place the distal anchor with no tension 6-8" below the knee.

4. With one hand hold the distal anchor. Apply 50+% of available tension to the Kinesio I strip. Place the proximal anchor 6-8" above the knee with no tension. This creates the "bridge or tent" in the functional correction.

5. Hold both the anchors and have the patient move into extension. Vigorously rub to initiate adhesive prior to any further patient movement.

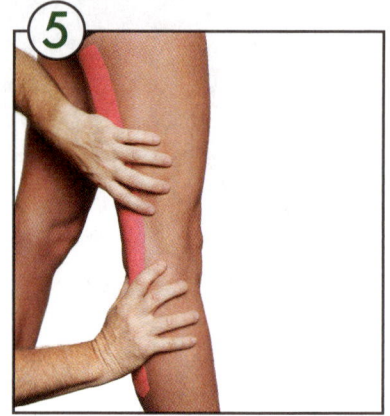

6. Application of the hamstring muscle inhibition Kinesio Taping Technique. The desired result will be decreased muscle spasm in the hamstring muscle from over extension during forced knee hyperextension.

   I Strip: Place anchor 3-4" inferior to popliteal fossa with no tension. Place the patient in knee extension and hip flexion. Apply paper off to light tension, 15-25% of available tension directly over the area of pain or tightness. Lay down end with no tension on or above the ischial tuberosity, rub to initiate adhesive prior to any further patient movement.

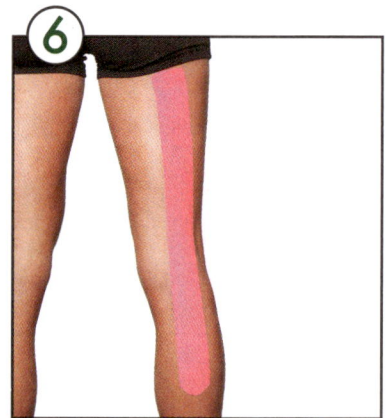

7. Y Strip: Place anchor 3-4" inferior to popliteal fossa with no tension. Place the patient in knee extension and hip flexion. The split in the Y should be below or above the popliteal fossa. Apply paper off to light tension, 15-25% of available tension to each tail. Medial tail along the semi-membranosous/tendonosous ending on or above the ischial tuberosity. Lateral tail along the biceps femoris ending on or near the ischial tuberosity. Lay down end with no tension, rub to initiate adhesive prior to any further patient movement.

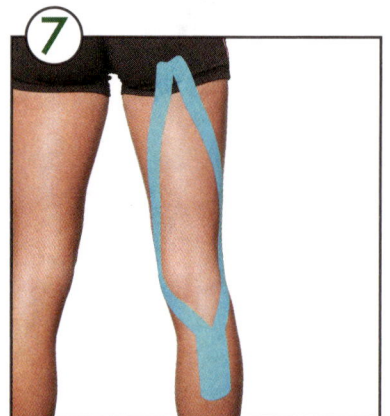

8. I Strip application to both of the hamstring groups. Medial strip for the semi-membranosous and the lateral strip for the biceps femoris. This technique in the acute and sub-acute phase will be an inhibition. In the rehabilitation stages a facilitation technique may be chosen to activate the hamstrings.

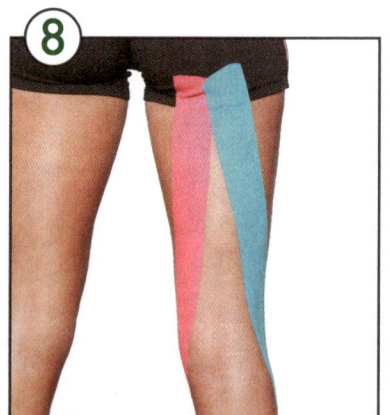

Meniscus of the Knee

An injury to the meniscus of the knee generally presents itself with pain during movements of extension and rotation. There will be joint line pain and in chronic meniscus lesions a meniscal cyst. An increased incidence of meniscus lesions occur to the medial meniscus due to its attachment to the medial capsule. Lateral Meniscus is usually associated with ACL injury or rotation while loaded.

The Kinesio Taping Method will assist by reducing joint effusion and pain. Optional treatments may include basic Kinesio muscle techniques for muscle weakness.

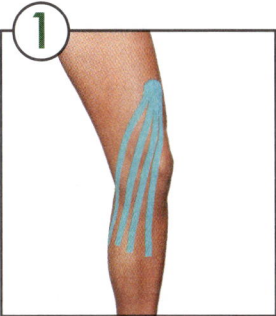

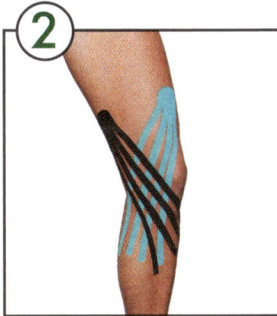

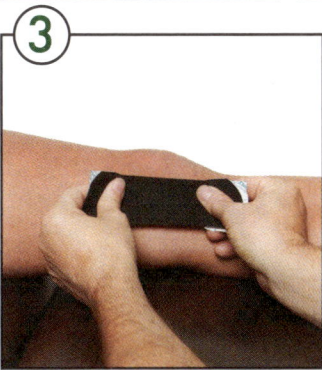

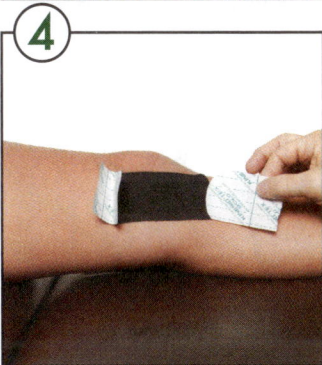

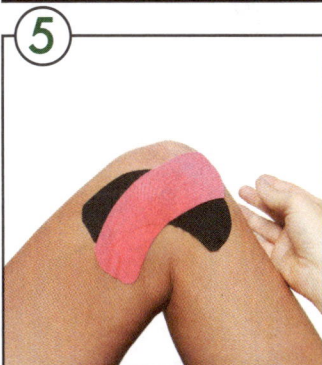

ACUTE TREATMENT: Application of Lymphatic Corrective Technique. Lymphatic drainage should be directed to anterior aspect of thigh and inguinal region.

1. Place anchor 4-5" above the superior aspect of the medial anterior aspect of the thigh with no tension. Direct the fan strips over the medial meniscus with 0-20% of available tension, ending below the edema. Lay down the ends with no tension and rub or pat to initiate adhesive.

2. Place anchor 4-5" above the superior and over the mid-belly of adductor muscle group with no tension. Direct the fan strips over the medial meniscus with 0-20% of available tension, ending below the edema. Lay down the ends with no tension and rub or pat to initiate adhesive prior to any further patient movement.

   The fans should form a crisscross pattern of the medial meniscus or lateral meniscus if treating it.

POST ACUTE: SPACE CORRECTION Apply a space correction technique to either the lateral or medial aspect of the knee depending upon the patient's symptoms.

3. Begin by placing the patient's knee in full extension. Tear the paper backing in the center of a 4-6" Kinesio I strip. Apply paper off to moderate, 15-35% of available tension to the Kinesio strip and apply directly over the area of pain.

4. Lay down the two ends of the Kinesio I strip without tension. Rub to initiate adhesive prior to any further patient movement.

5. A series of two to three strips may be applied. The series of strips should be applied creating a star, for complete review see star technique low back. Begin with knee in extension and repeat application of I strip as described above at approximately a 45 degree angle. As the end(s) are being laid down have the patient move the knee into flexion.

6. A third space correction is added. Again the knee is placed in flexed position when applying the end.

   If skin surrounding the knee is not stretched the ends will "pull off". This will diminish the effectiveness of the technique and length of wear time.

   An optimal technique may be application of the donut hole technique.

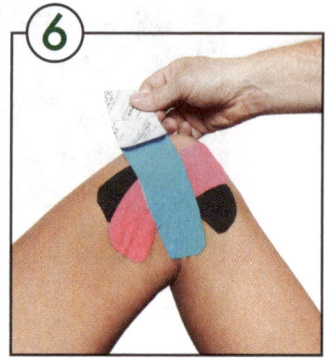

7. Completed space correction star technique for medial, or lateral meniscus.

   Optional Donut hole technique: Apply a donut hole technique in a star technique as described above. The "hole" in the donut hole technique should be placed directly over the area of pain or edema. See bursitis of the knee

   Optional Web Cut: A Web cut technique can also be applied over the medial or lateral meniscus. The web technique may be selected as it has fewer ends to catch or come off. This may lengthen the longevity of the application.

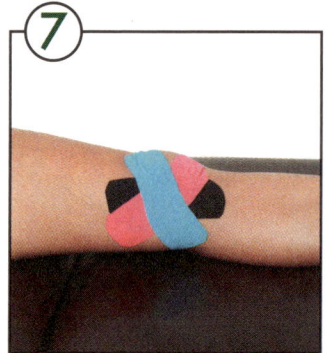

OPTION 1: FACILITATION OF THE VASTUS MEDIALIS OBLIQUE

8. Application of Kinesio Y strip technique for vastus medialis facilitation. This is to assist a weakened vastus medialis resulting from effusion or pain. For complete description see lateral tracking.

OPTION 2: RECTUS FEMORIS FACILITATION

9. Application of Kinesio Y strip technique for rectus femoris, facilitation technique. For complete review, see patella tendonitis.

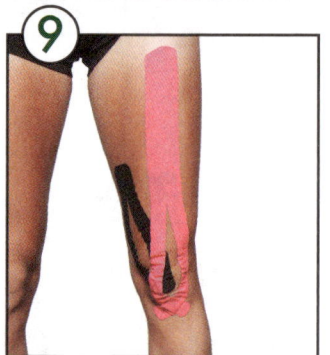

OPTION 3: PROPRIOCEPTIVE STIMULI OR STABILITY

10. Application of the Kinesio patella tendonitis U strip. For complete review, see patella tendonitis.

    For additional options see: Osteochondrosis of the Knee, Patella Tracking Syndrome, Subluxating Patella, or Chondromalacia Patella.

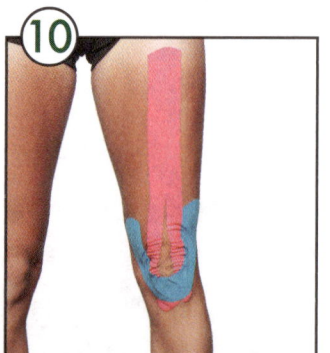

Osteoarthritis or Chronic Effusion of the Knee

Osteoarthritis is a degeneration of the articular surfaces within a joint. In the knee, it may be associated with normal degenerative changes from chronic impact loading caused by high levels of physical activity. Chronic knee effusion is a primary sign and its cause may be unknown. The resulting chronic joint effusion will cause continuing degenerative changes, and decreased muscle function.

The Kinesio Taping method will assist by reducing effusion and joint pain. For additional options, see Patella Tracking Syndrome, Subluxating Patella, or Chondromalacia.

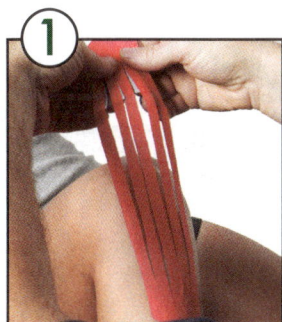

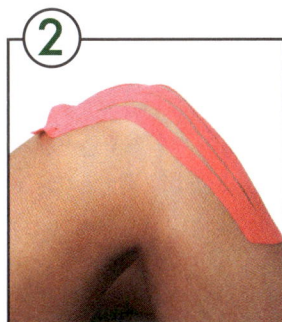

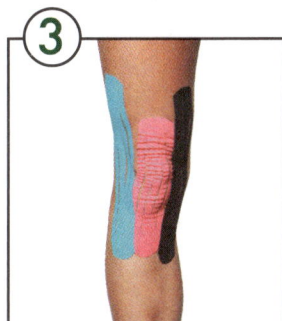

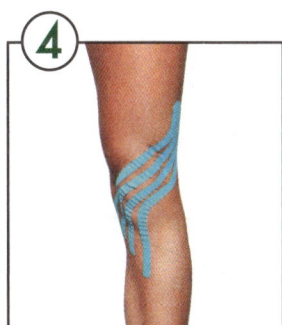

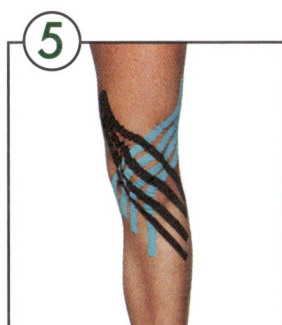

OPTION 1: WEB SPACE CORRECTION

1-2. Fold an appropriate length I strip over and cut 4-5 fan strip cuts making sure to leave approximately 1" uncut on each end.

Technique 1: Apply the distal anchor with no tension. Peel the paper backing away and apply 10-20% of available tension. Gently spread the web cuts and apply over the treatment zone. Lay down end with no tension. Pat and gently rub to initiate adhesive prior to any further patient movement.

Technique 2: Tear the Kinesio web cut strips in the center and and peel away the paper backing to the ends. While holding each end apply 10-20% of availabe tension to the web cuts and gently separate the fans. Apply the center of the web cuts to the center of the treatment zone. Lay down the ends without any tension. Pat and gently rub to initiate adhesive prior to any further patient movement.

3. A series of two or three web cut strips can be applied and have been found to be effective.

OPTION 2: LYMPHATIC CORRECTION
The lymphatic strips position should be modified so the crisscross effect is directly over the area of chronic edema.

4. Begin lateral fan anchor approximately 4-5" superior to the lateral joint line. Place the knee in a flexed position. Apply the tails with 0-20% of available tension over the area of edema. Lay down the ends with no tension and pat or lightly rub to initiate adhesive prior to patient movement.

5. Begin lateral fan anchor approximately 4-5" superior to the medial joint line. Place the knee in a flexed position. Apply the tails with 0-20% of available tension over the area of edema. Lay down the ends with no tension and pat or lightly rub to initiate adhesive prior to patient movement.

Osteoarthritis or Chronic Effusion of the Knee

OPTION 1: HAMSTRING

5. Example shown is a Y strip, the practitioner may select to use an I strip. Place anchor inferior to the popliteal fossa with no tension. Place the patient in hip flexion with the knee in extension. Apply paper off to light, 15-25% of available tension to both the medial and lateral tail. End on or above the ischial tuberosity and lay down ends with no tension. Rub to initiate adhesive prior to any further patient movement. The Kinesio I strip can be placed over the central belly region or directed over individual muscles involved.

OPTION 2: QUADRICEPS FACILITATION WITH PATELLA TENDONITIS U STRIP TECHNIQUE

Either during acute, post-acute, or chronic phase the practitioner may apply a quadriceps muscle facilitation technique from origin to insertion to enhance deep lymphatic fluid flow.

6. **Slit Technique:** For complete description see Quad Contusion Slit Inhibition. Place anchor below ASIS or proximal 1/3 of quad with no tension. Place the patient in hip extension and apply 15-35% of available tension to the base to the musculotendonous junction. Rub to initiate adhesive. Place the patients knee in flexion and apply the slit towards the medial and lateral borders of the patella with paper off to light, 15-25% of available tension to the inferior pole of the patella. Lay down the end with no tension and rub to initiate adhesive prior to any further patient movement.

    For I and Y Technique: Place the anchor at or near the ASIS with no tension. Place the patient in hip extension. Apply light to moderate, 15-35% of available tension to the musculotendonous junction. Rub to initiate adhesive. Place the patient into hip and knee flexion.

7. **I Technique:** Apply 15-25% of available tension to the remaining I strip from the musculotendonous junction over the patella to the tibial tuberosity. Lay down the end with no tension and rub to initiate adhesive prior to any further patient movement.

8. **Y Technique (Red Y Strip):** Apply 15-25% of available tension; for the medial tail apply along the medial border of the patella, for the lateral border apply along the lateral border of the patella. Direct each tail over the tibial tuberosity and lay down the ends with no tension. Rub to initiate adhesive prior to any further patient movement.

    U-Strip (Black I Strip): can be applied alone or in combination as shown, or with any other combination.

This technique can be modified so the strip is shorter than going all the way up onto the vastus medialis and lateralis muscles. The Kinesio I Strip application can end approximately 2" above the superior pole of the patella.

See Patella Tendonitis or ACL for complete description of U Strip application.

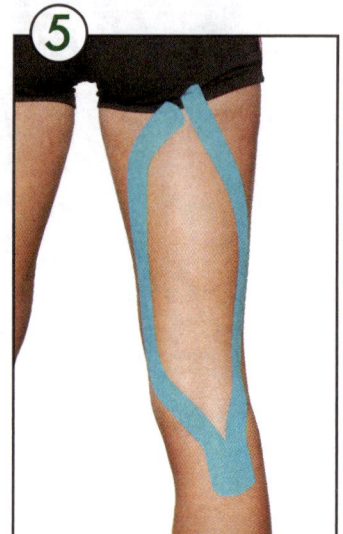

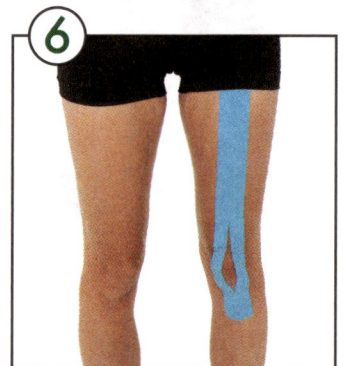

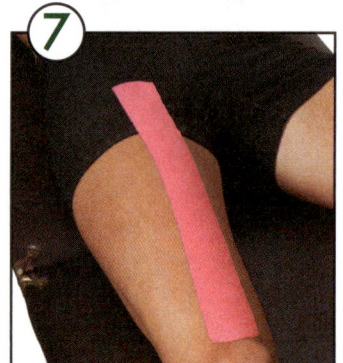

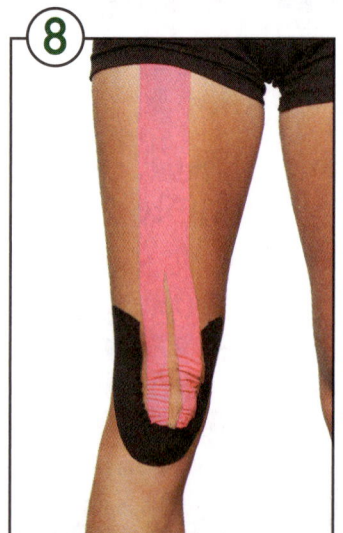

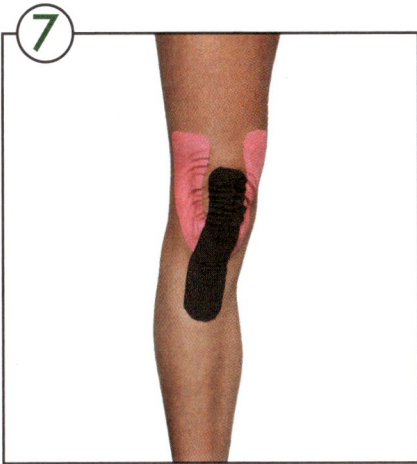

OPTION 3: MODIFIED SPACE CORRECTION I STRIP WITH U STRIP TECHNIQUE: For complete
description see Patella Tendonitis. The U-Strip is applied first, since it is applied with higher tension. If the modified space correction I strip is applied first the U Strip will "pull off" the initial I strip.

7. Apply a U Strip to the inferior pole of the patella. The length of the U Strip can be modified: higher or lower depending upon what the practitioner feels is best for their patient.

   Apply a modified space correction I strip from the tibial tuberosity, over the patella and to approximately 4-5" above the patella.

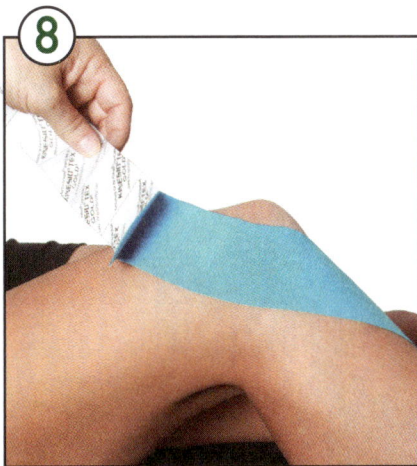

OPTION 4: BILATERAL MODIFIED SPACE CORRECTION KINESIO I STRIPS

Two modified space correction strips will be used to lift the skin surrounding the patella.

8. With the patient in knee extension, place one anchor on or slightly past the tibial tuberosity at approximately a 45 degree angle to the patella. Have the patient very slowly move into flexion, at the same time apply paper off tension to light, 15-25% of available tension over the lateral border of the patella. The Kinesio I strip should be placed with 1/2 to 1/3 of the strip onto the border of the patella and continuing to the mid thigh, forming a C shape. For the last 1-2" lay down with no tension. Rub to initiate adhesive prior to any further patient movement.

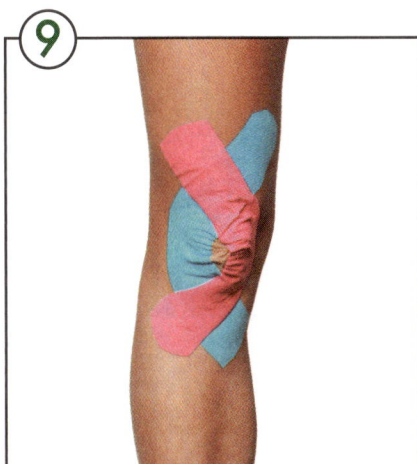

9. Repeat the above steps for the medial aspect of the patella. The photo shown has a space in the central patella region. This technique works best when there is exposed skin over the central region of the patella. The medial or lateral modified space correction I strip can be moved depending upon the area of edema. If the edema is located more lateral than the lateral border of the patella, then move the space correction strip so the center of the I strip is over the area of edema.

   Normally one strip is one square, 2" longer to allow for each anchor/end to end on skin. For most patients one I strip is 12" and one strip 14". The length can be modified depending upon the patients size.

Bursitis of the Knee

Bursitis of the knee can result from acute trauma or chronic overuse resulting in inflammation of either the prepatellar or infrapatellar bursa.

Inflammation to the prepatellar bursa generally results from acute trauma. Evaluation of this bursa is generally indicated by edema above the knee (superior to the patella).

The Kinesio Taping Technique will assist in reduction of edema and pain. During the first 24 to 72 hours of an acute trauma to a bursa of the knee, the primary goal is to limit inflammation; the prepatellar bursa will be demonstrated in this section.

ACUTE PHASE - 24 TO 72 HOURS LYMPHATIC CORRECTION:

1. Place anchor 4-5" superior to the area of pain or edema in bursa with no tension. Direct the fan strips over the involved bursa with 0-20% of available tension, ending below the edema. Lay down the ends with no tension and rub or pat to initiate adhesive.

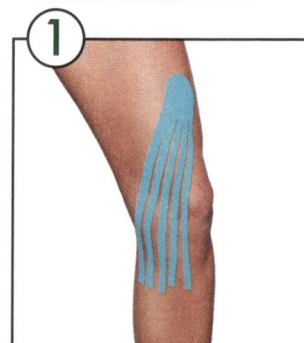

2. Place anchor 4-5" superior to area of pain or edema in bursa with no tension. Direct the fan strips over the bursa with 0-20% of available tension, ending below the edema. Lay down the ends with no tension and rub or pat to initiate adhesive prior to any further patient movement.

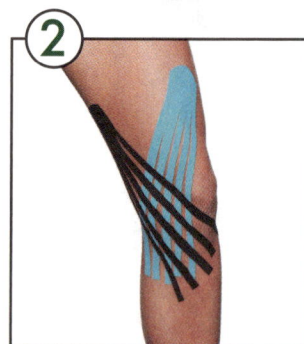

ACUTE PHASE - 24 TO 72 HOURS WEB CORRECTION:

3. Apply anchor superior or inferior to the bursa with no tension. Apply 10-20% of available tension to the web strips, gently spread the web cut strips and apply over area of pain or edema. Lay down end with no tension. Rub to initiate adhesive prior to any further patient movement. A series of two or three strips may be used, laying the strips down along side of each other.

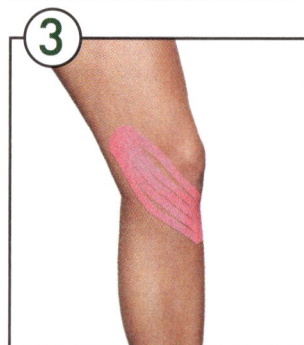

POST ACUTE: SPACE CORRECTION DONUT HOLE TECHNIQUE

4. Begin by cutting a hole approximately the size of a dime in the center of the approximately 4-6" I strip. Tear the center of the Kinesio I strip through the paper backing and apply 15-25% of available tension to the Kinesio Tex Tape and align directly over the area of pain or inflammation.

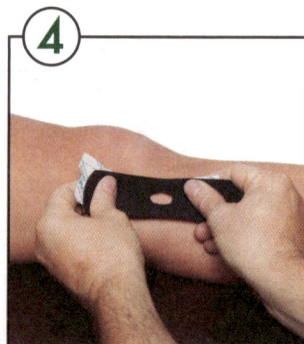

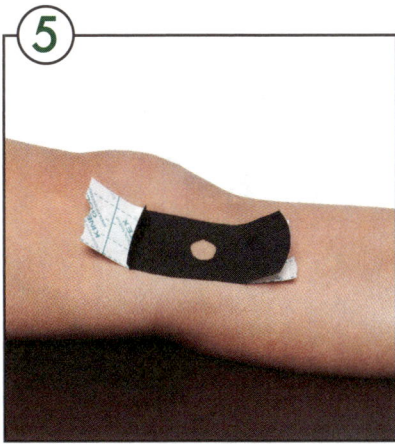

5. Place the donut hole over the area of pain or inflammation having the central third of the Kinesio Donut Hole strip onto the skin. Lay down the ends with no tension. Rub or pat to initiate adhesive prior to any further patient movements.

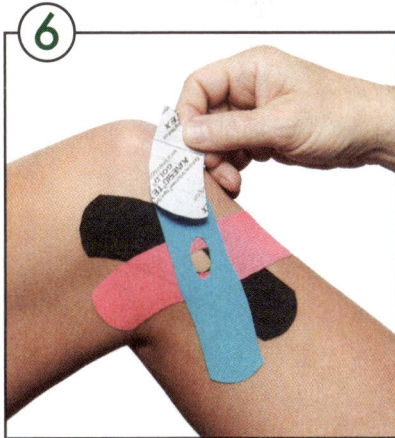

6. A series of two or three donut hole strips can be applied. It is important to apply each donut hole strip with the knee in extension. As the ends are laid down the patient should be placed in a stretched position: it could be flexion, extension or some degree of rotation. If the ends are laid down without the skin in a stretched position it will cause the ends to pull on the skin and decrease the ability of the Kinesio Tex Tape to adhere to the skin.

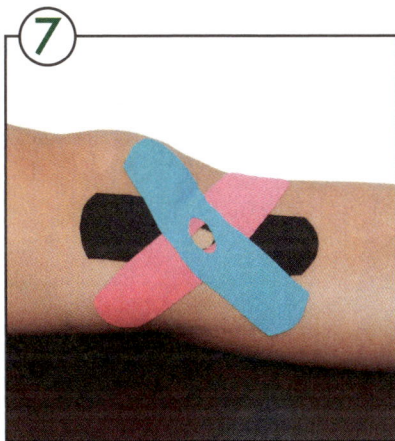

7. Completed multiple strip application of the Donut Hole Technique.

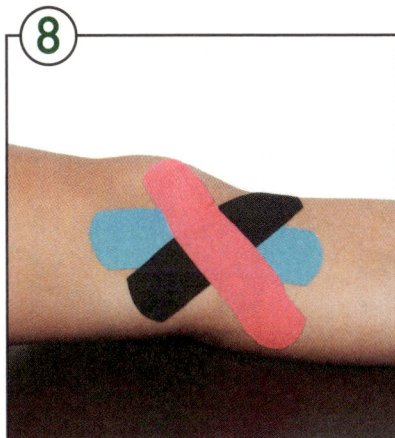

POST ACUTE: SPACE CORRECTION STAR TECHNIQUE

8. Using the Donut Hole Technique application description you can use a Tension in the Center of an I strip Space Correction Application. This may be more effective in a chronic condition. If applied during the acute phase it may cause irritation directly over the bursa.

Pes Anserine Bursitis or Tendonitis

Pes Anserine Bursitis or Tendonitis is an inflammation to the common insertion onto the tibia of the semitendinous, gracilis, and sartorious muscles. The inflammation is generally caused by overuse and is most commonly caused by running on slopes. It has been associated with individuals who present with genu valgum and weakness of the medial muscles of the knee.

The Kinesio Taping Technique will assist with pain and inflammation reduction. The three muscles which make up the pes anserine will be taped with an additional space correction or mechanical correction technique.

Due to the amount of tape which will be applied for this technique, it is important to initially apply the correction technique first. The deepest layer of Kinesio Tex Tape applied is the most effective.

ACUTE PHASE: LYMPHATIC CORRECTION

1. Place anchor 4-5" superior to the area of pain or inflammation on the anterior medial aspect of the thigh. Direct the fan strips over the per anserine bursa with 0-20% of available tension, ending below the edema. Lay down the ends with no tension and rub or pat to initiate adhesive.

2. Place anchor 4-5" superior to the mid-belly of adductor muscle group with no tension. Direct the fan strips over the pes anserine bursa with 0-20% of available tension, ending below the edema. Lay down the ends with no tension and rub or pat to initiate adhesive prior to any further patient movement.

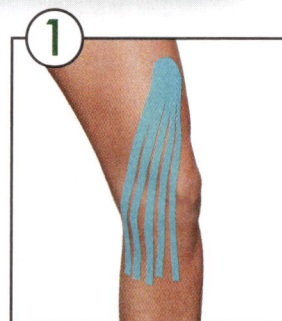

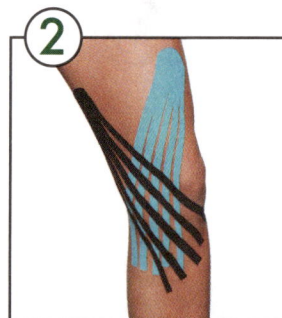

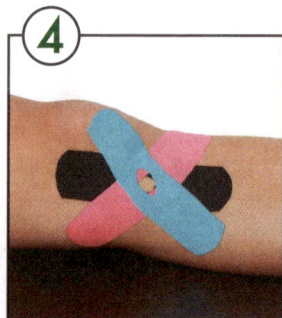

ACUTE PHASE: WEB CORRECTION

3. Apply anchor superior and either anterior or posterior aspect of the thigh with no tension. Apply 10-20% of available tension to the web strips, spreading them apart gently and apply over area of pain or edema. Lay down end with no tension. Rub to initiate adhesive prior to any further patient movement. A series of two or three strips may be used, laying them down next to each other or in a crisscross pattern increasing coverage of the tissue.

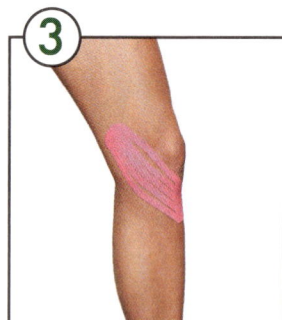

POST ACUTE: DONUT HOLE SPACE CORRECTION

4. Apply a Donut Hole space correction technique over the pes anserine bursa. Please see Knee Bursitis for complete description. Tear the center of an approximately 6" donut hole strip and apply a series of 2-3 donut hole strips with 10-25% of available tension over the area of pain or inflammation. Lay down the ends with no tension and rub to initiate adhesive prior to patient movement.

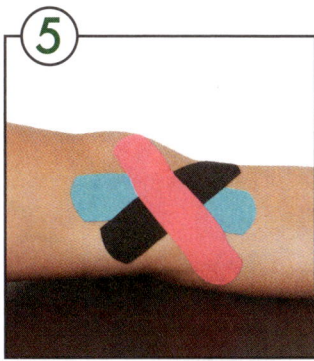

POST ACUTE: SPACE CORRECTION STAR TECHNIQUE

5. Using the Donut Hole Technique application described in bursitis of the knee you can use a Tension in the Center of an I strip Space Correction Application. This may be more effective in a chronic condition. If applied during the acute phase it may cause irritation directly over pes anserine bursa.

INHIBITION TECHNIQUE FOR PES ANSERINE BURSA MUSCLE GROUP

This technique as shown is using a 2″ wide Kinesio Tex Tape cut into 3 tails. For larger patients using a 3″ wide Kinesio Tex Tape can be used or possibly three 1½″ wide Kinesio Tex can be used.

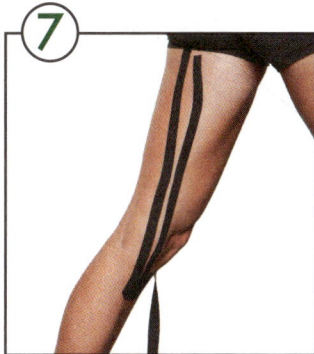

6. Semitendinosus muscle application inhibition technique. Begin by placing the anchor with no tension inferior to the tibial insertion of the medial collateral ligament (MCL) of the knee with the knee in extension and hip in extension. Apply paper off to light, 15-25% of available tension and direct the tail towards the ischial tuberosity. Lay down the end with no tension and rub to initiate adhesive prior to any further patient movement.

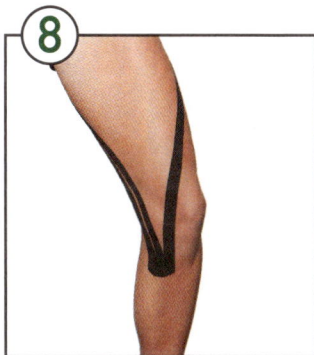

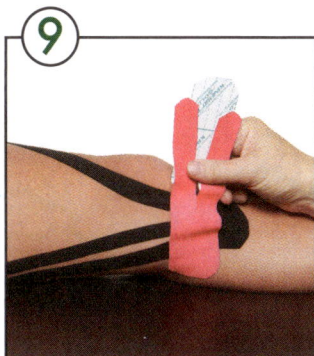

7. Gracilis inhibition application. With the knee remaining in extension and the hip in extension apply paper off to light, 15-25% of available tension and direct the tail towards the lower half of the symphysis pubis and the upper half of the pubic arch. Lay down the end with no tension and rub to initiate adhesive prior to any further patient movement.

8. Sartorius inhibition application. With the knee in slight flexion move the hip into extension apply paper off to light, 15-25% of available tension and direct the tail towards the iliac spine (anterior superior). Lay down the end with no tension and rub to initiate adhesive prior to any further patient movement.

An optional application technique would be to use three 1½″ or 2″ I strips, depending upon the size of the patient for Pes Anserine Bursitis.

MECHANICAL CORRECTION WITH TENSION IN THE TAILS

9. The Mechanical correction is chosen to limit movement of the pes anserine tendon bands over the lateral femoral condyle. Begin by placing the anchor of the Kinesio Y strip with no tension inferior to the tibial insertion of the medial collateral ligament (MCL) of the knee. Have the split in the Y begin slightly below the point of pain. Try to apply the anchor on exposed skin and not the previously applied three tail Y technique. Rub to activate adhesive.

Pes Anserinus Bursitis or Tendonitis

10. Start with the patient's knee in extension, with one hand hold the anchor of the Y to ensure no tension is added. Apply moderate to severe, 50-75% of available tension and downward/inward pressure to the inferior tail of the Kinesio Y strip. The inferior tail is applied from below the point of pain to just superior to the point of pain. Move the hand holding the anchor to this end tension position to initiate adhesive. Then decrease tension to paper off to light, 15-25% of available tension until the last 1-2" and lay down the end with no tension.

Rub to initiate adhesive prior to any further patient movement.

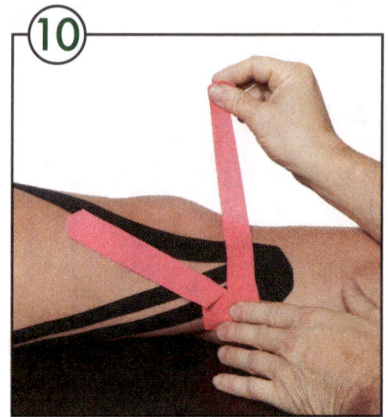

11. Repeat the above step for the superior tail. When applying the paper off to light, or the ends the knee will need to be moved into flexion to allow for full range of motion movement and proper end application. If the knee is not moved into extension it may cause the Kinesio Tex Tape to "pull" off the skin and decrease adhesive quality of the tape.

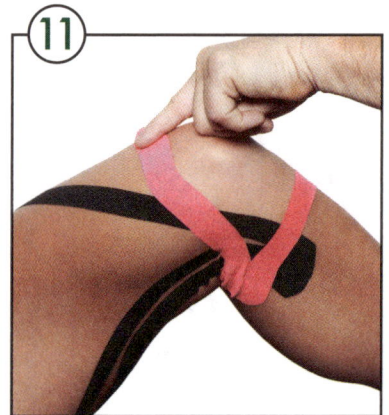

12. Completed application of the pes anserine bursitis or tendonitis using a mechanical correction. The effect of the mechanical correction will provide restriction to the inferior movement of the per anserine common insertion during knee movement as it crosses over the lateral femoral condyle and attaches to the tibia.

The practitioner may select a fascia correction using an I strip or tension in tails. Using the demonstrated three tail Y technique applying a fascia correction with long and short or short and long has also been effective.

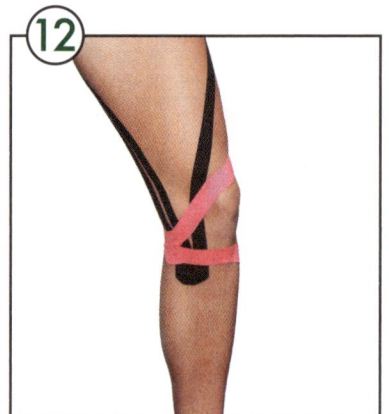

Runner's or Cyclist's Knee

Runner's or Cyclist's Knee is a general term used to describe several conditions of the knee resulting from overuse and overtraining. Examples of related conditions that are commonly referred to as runner's knee are: pes anserinus tendonitis, iliotibial band friction syndrome, and patella tracking syndrome. The practitioner during their evaluation will need to determine the tissues involved and devise an appropriate treatment protocol.

The Kinesio Taping Technique will assist by reducing effusion, pain, muscle imbalance, and possible patella tracking malalignment.

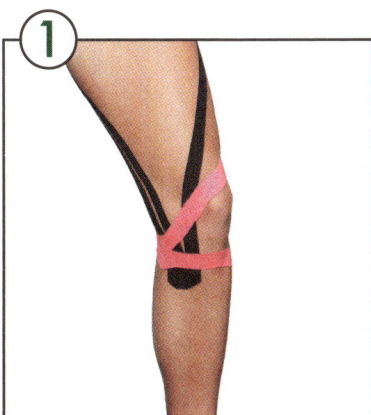

OPTION 1:

Completed Kinesio Taping application for Pes Anserine Bursitis or Tendonitis.

For complete description, see pes anserine bursitis or tendonitis.

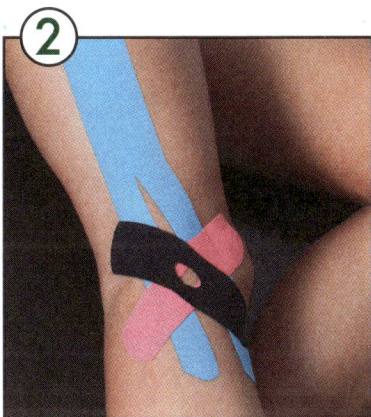

OPTION 2:

Completed Kinesio Taping application for Iliotibial Band Friction syndrome. Fascia Correction with Donut Hole Technique.

For complete description, see iliotibial band friction syndrome.

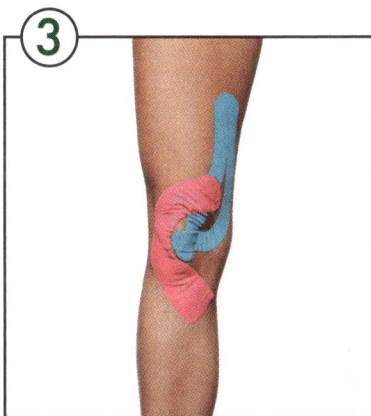

OPTION 3:

Completed Kinesio Taping application of Patella Tracking Syndrome. Vastus Medialis Oblique and Mechanical Correction tension in the center of an I strip technique.

For complete description, see patella tracking syndrome.

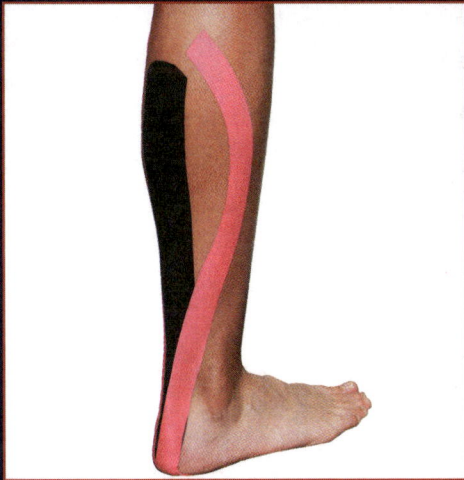

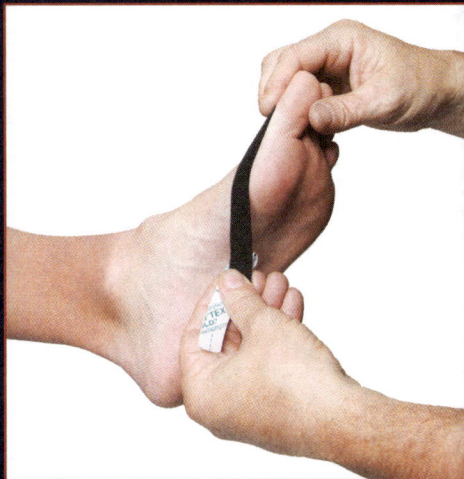

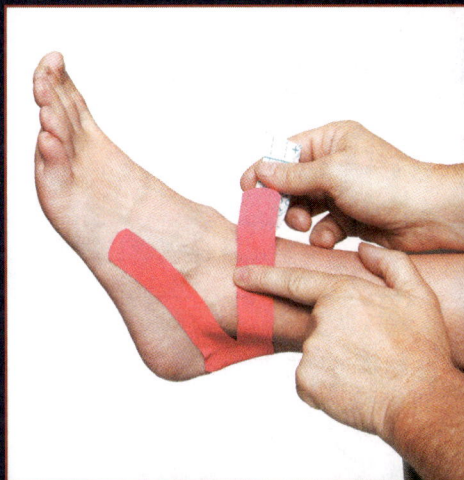

SECTION 9

Ankle and Foot

Section 9

Plantar Fasciitis

Plantar Fasciitis is an inflammation of the plantar aponeurosis. Pain and inflammation are generally felt at its origin on the epicondyle of the calcaneous (anterior aspect of calcaneous).

On the plantar surface full tension can be applied with little or no irritation to the skin due to skin thickness. It is highly recommended that both strips be used. The effectiveness of the technique is compromised with the use of only one strip.

This technique can be applied multiple times. During acute inflammation the technique should include the Achilles tendon and plantar aponeurosis for maximum effect.

STANDARD APPLICATION Effective for patients of average height and weight. Application of the Tendon Correction technique is optional.

1. Begin by measuring from the metatarsal heads to approximately 2" above the musculotendinous junction of the gastrocnemius and Achilles.

2. On one end cut a 4 strip fan technique from the metatarsal heads to the calcaneal tubercle. When first utilizing this technique, remember that full tension will be added to the Kinesio Tex, so cut your strip a little shorter than measured. The Kinesio strip paper backing is torn just superior to the fan. Tear the paper backing just superior to the fan strip and apply the exposed Kinesio Tex Tape on the heel with the foot in dorsi flexion.

3. While holding the tape which has been applied to the heel, to ensure no tension will be added, and keeping the foot in dorsiflexion begin by applying severe to full, 75-100% of available tension on one of the four strips which have been cut. Place this strip from the calcaneous to the space between the first and second ray (toe) on the metatarsal head, laying down the end with no tension.

4. Make sure you activate the adhesive before additional strips are placed. Repeat this step for the remaining three cuts.

5. With the ankle remaining in dorsiflexion apply a tendon correction technique 50-75% of available tension over the Achilles' to the musculotendonous junction with the remaining I strip.

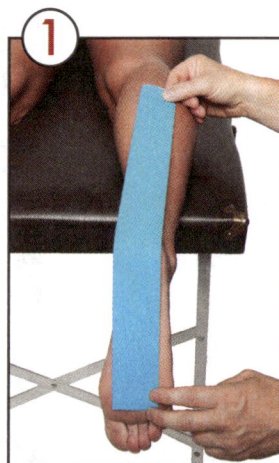

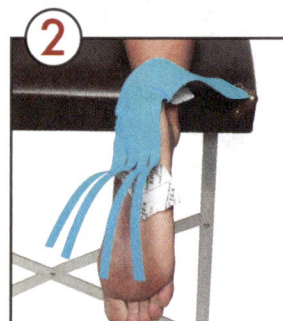

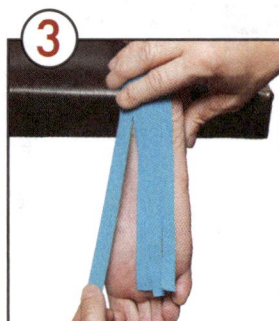

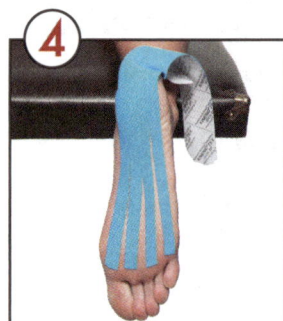

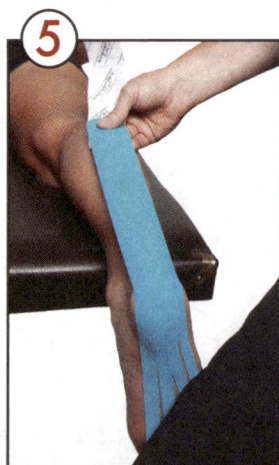

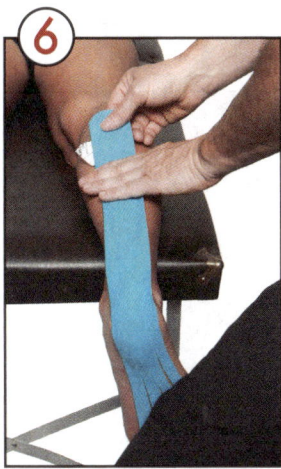

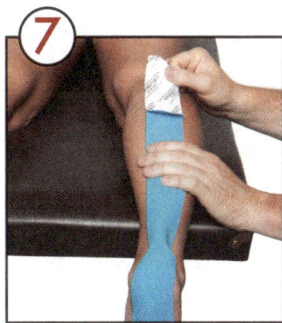

6-7. Decrease tension to paper off to light, 15-25% of available tension when past the musculotendonous junction until the end which is laid down with no tension.

8. It is important to initiate adhesive prior to any further movement due to the convex shape of the Achilles region.

METATARSAL ARCH MECHANICAL CORRECTION

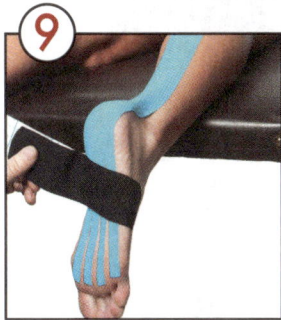

9. Begin with the foot in a dorsiflexed position. Place the anchor distal to the base of the 5th metatarsal.

10. Have the patient relax their foot. Apply tension to the I strip: the amount of tension applied is determined by the practitioner and the size of the patient. You are looking for wrinkles to appear on the plantar surface of the foot. Tension may be 15-50+%.

11. As the Kinesio Tex Tape reaches the tarsal navicular joint have the patient move back into a neutral or dorsiflexed position. Lay down the remaining tape with no tension.

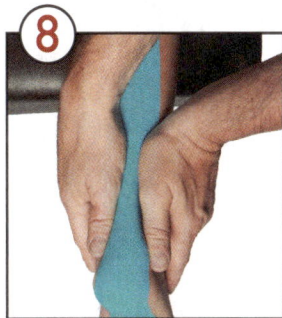

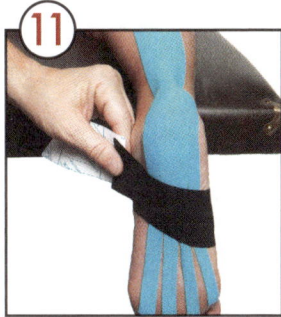

12. Rub to activate adhesive prior to any further patient movement.

When applied correctly, the patient's foot should show signs of "crinkles" in the metatarsal arch region when the foot is in a relaxed position.

Completed Standard Plantar Fasciitis Kinesio Technique.

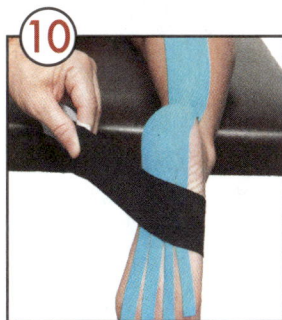

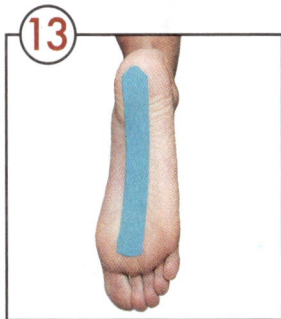

OPTIONAL PLANTAR FASCIITIS APPLICATION:

13. Begin by placing a 1" I strip from the calcaneous to space between the 2nd and 3rd metatarsal heads with 75-100% tension.

14. Apply a Y strip over the I strip in photo 13. For the lateral tail apply 75-100% of available tension from the calcaneous to the 5th metatarsal. For the medial tail apply 75-100% of available tension from the calcaneous to the 1st metatarsal. Rub to initiate adhesive prior to any further patient movement.

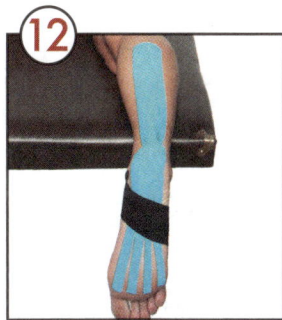

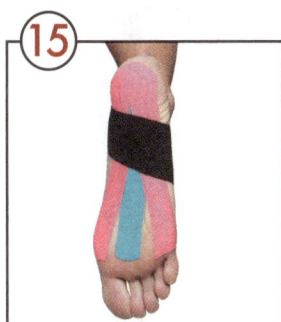

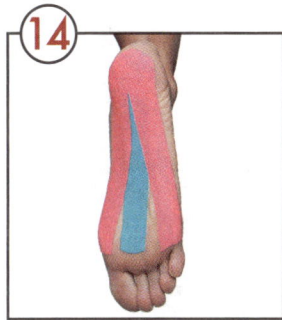

If the patient is larger or heavier you can apply two Y strips to have four 1" strips applied instead of the approximately ½" strips in the standard application method.

15. Apply a metatarsal arch mechanical correction as described above, images 9-12.

Achilles Tendonitis or Tenosynovitis

Achilles' Tendonitis is an inflammation to the Achilles' tendon which is formed from the combination of the gastrocnemius and soleus muscles. The tendonitis is generally located within the distal 1/3 of the Achilles' tendon close to its insertion into the calcaneous. The inflammation generally occurs from overuse activity.

Achilles' Tendonitis will be treated with three Kinesio strips. The first strip will be a tendon correction placed upon the Achilles' tendon. If the tendonitis is in acute phase, the practitioner may want to combine the tendon correction strip with the plantar fascia strip. Since the Achilles' tendon and the plantar fascia is a continual layer of connective tissue both may need to be treated to be most effective. The second strip will be a Y strip for the gastrocnemius muscle. The optional third strip is placed upon the plantar surface of the foot to anchor the two previous strips and aid in increased tape application length.

Achilles' Tendonitis or Tenosynovitis

For the Achilles Tendon the practitioner can choose to apply a plantar fasciitis fan strip or end the Tendon Correction I strip on the anterior aspect of the calcaneous.

1. Begin by measuring a strip of Kinesio Tex Tape approximately 2" past the musculotendinous junction of the soleus and Achilles' tendon to the metatarsal heads on the plantar surface of the foot. Cut one end of the Kinesio strip with a fan technique for placement on the plantar aponeurosis.

2. Tear the paper backing just past the end of the fan cut and place this on the heel of the patient with no tension. While holding the tape which has been applied to the heel, to ensure no tension will be added, and keeping the foot in dorsiflexion begin by applying severe to full, 75-100% of available tension on one of the four strips which have been cut. Place this strip from the calcaneous to the space between the first and second ray (toe) on the metatarsal head, laying down the end with no tension. Make sure you activate the adhesive before additional strips are placed. Repeat this step for the remaining three tails.

3. With the ankle remaining in dorsiflexion apply a tendon correction technique 50-75% of available tension over the Achilles tendon to the musculotendonous junction with the remaining I strip. Rub this area to initiate adhesive prior to any further Kinesio Tex Tape application.

4. Decrease tension to paper off to light, 15-25% of available tension past the musculotendonous junction.

5. The end is laid down with no tension.

6. It is important to initiate adhesive prior to any further movement due to the convex shape of the Achilles region. Rub entire tendon correction to initiate adhesive prior to any further patient movement.

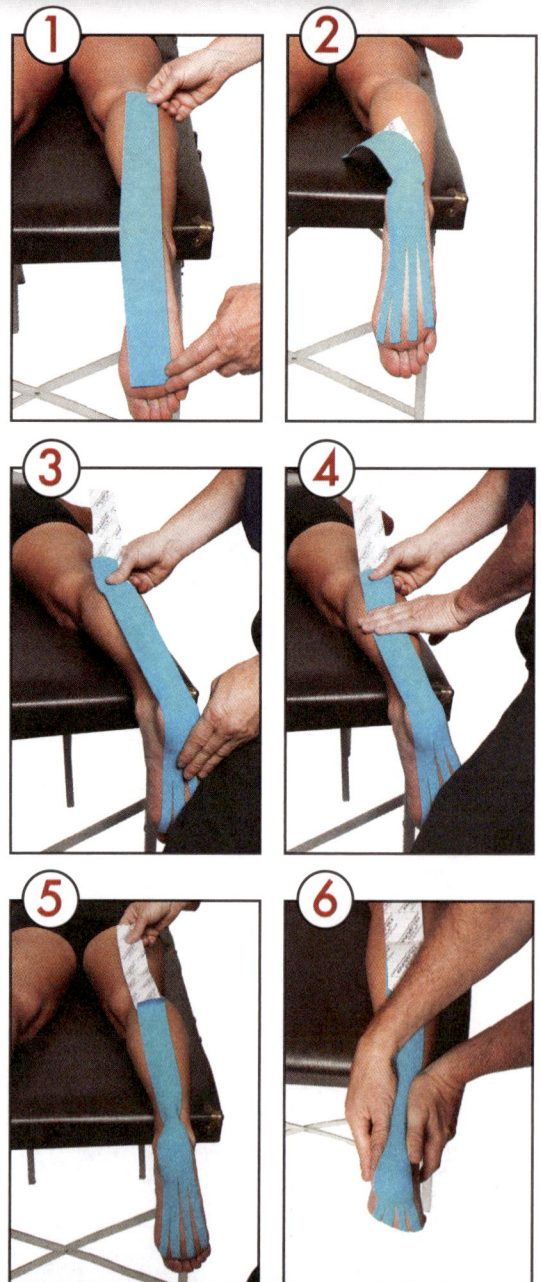

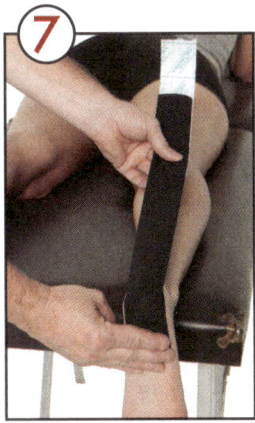

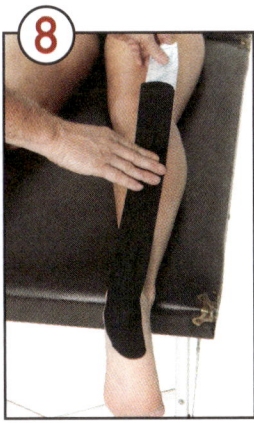

7. Tendon Correction Application without plantar fascia strips. Apply anchor with no tension on the anterior aspect of the calcaneous. Place the ankle in neutral or dorsiflexion and apply 50-75% of available tension over the Achilles tendon to the musculotendonous junction. Rub to initiate adhesive.

8. Apply paper off to light, 15-25% of available tension to the next section of I strip. Lay down end with no tension and vigorously rub to initiate adhesive prior to any further patient movement.

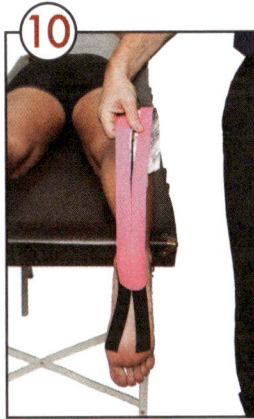

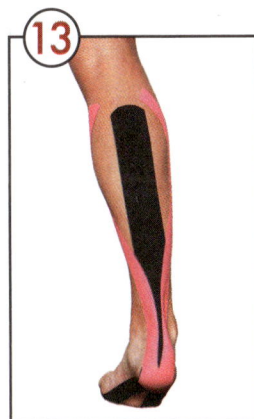

OPTIONAL:

9. Application of two strips for the plantar fascia. An additional central strip all 1" in width can be applied, see plantar fasciitis for complete description. For smaller patients cutting the 2" Kinesio Tex strip into three tails can be effective. For larger patients, or to provide more support first apply a single 1" I strip then apply a Y cut over the top. Application of the plantar fascia fan strips are optional for the Achilles tendonitis technique. For complete description see Plantar Fasciitis.

INHIBITION APPLICATION FOR THE GASTROCNEMIUS/SOLEUS COMPLEX

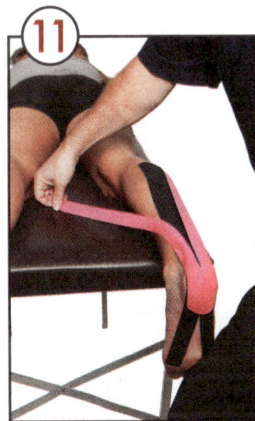

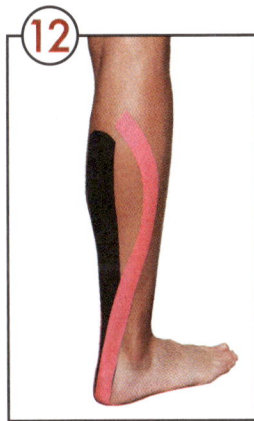

10. Begin by placing the ankle in a neutral position. Apply an anchor over the calcaneous to the anterior aspect of the calcaneous with no tension.

11. Have the patient move into dorsiflexion, or press the ankle and foot into a dorsiflexed position. Apply paper off to light, 15-25% of available tension to the medial strip of the Kinesio Y strip around the medial head of the gastrocnemius. Lay down the end with no tension and rub to initiate adhesive prior to any further patient movement.

12. Apply the lateral strip of the Kinesio Y strip around the lateral head of the gastrocnemius using paper of to light tension. Lay down the end with no tension and rub to initiate adhesive prior to any further patient movement.

13. If during the evaluation of the Achilles' Tendonitis, the practitioner determines there is muscle weakness, an origin to insertion application would be appropriate.

The third strip is placed upon the plantar surface of the foot to assist in the adhesion of the gastrocnemius Kinesio strip application.

14. Anchor: this strip is optional as it does not add to the effectiveness of the technique. It does, however, assist in holding the gastrocnemius strip in place which may increase the length of time the technique can be worn.

Tear the paper backing in the center of a 4-6" long Kinesio I strip. Peel back the paper backing and apply the center of the I strip with no tension over the anchor of the gastrocnemius inhibition muscle taping technique. Lay down ends with no tension.

Rub to initiate adhesive prior to any further patient movement.

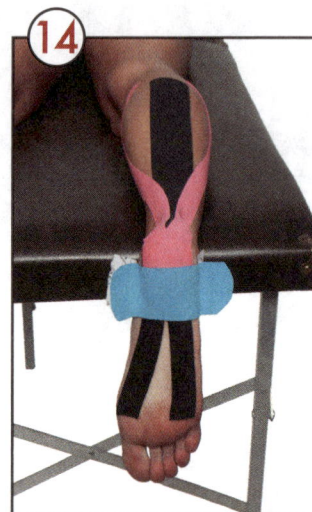

OPTIONAL: APPLICATION OF A MECHANICAL CORRECTION ALONG THE INFERIOR SURFACE OF THE CALCANEOUS.

15. Place the patient's ankle in a neutral position. Tear the center of the paper backing of an approximately 6-8" Kinesio I strip.

Apply moderate to severe, 50-75% of available tension, with downward/inward pressure to the center of the Kinesio I strip and apply over the center of the calcaneous on the plantar surface. The purpose of the mechanical strip is to elevate and compress the calcaneous in the ankle mortise and shortening the Achilles tendon.

Have the patient move the ankle into dorsiflexion and lay down the two ends of the Kinesio I strip down with no tension.

Rub to initiate adhesive prior to any further patient movement.

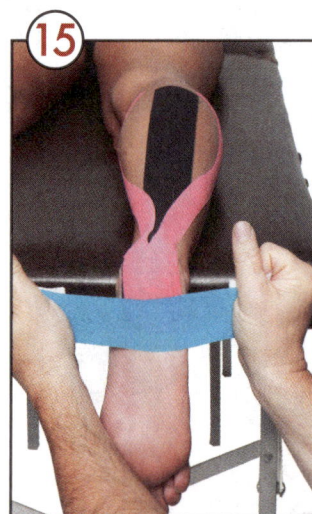

16. Completed Achilles' Tendonitis Kinesio Taping application.

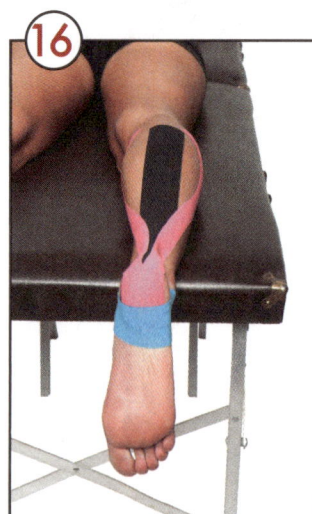

Retrocalcaneal Bursitis

Retrocalcaneal Bursitis is an inflammation to the retrocalcaneal bursae located behind the insertion of the Achilles' tendon and the calcaneous. It may also be referred to as a "pump bump". Pressure from footwear may cause the pressure which initiates the inflammation.

The Kinesio Taping Technique assists in reducing edema and pain.

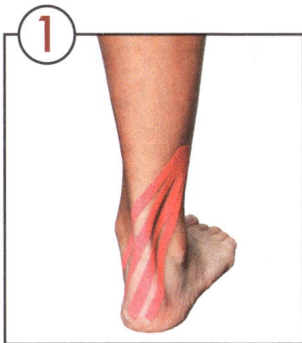

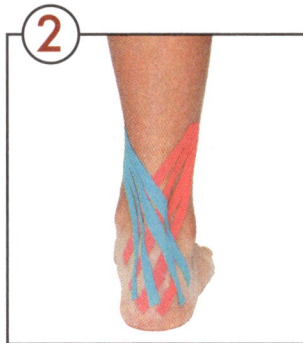

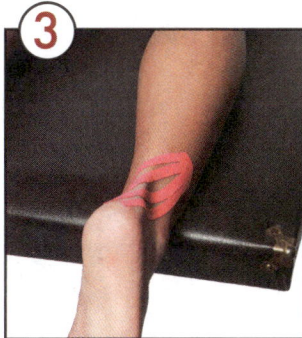

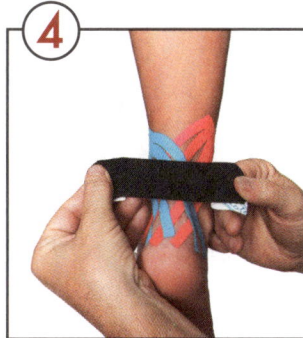

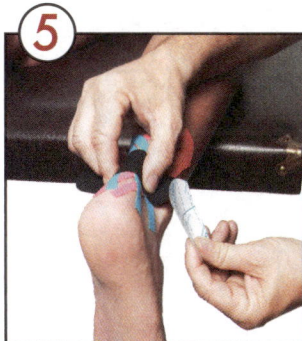

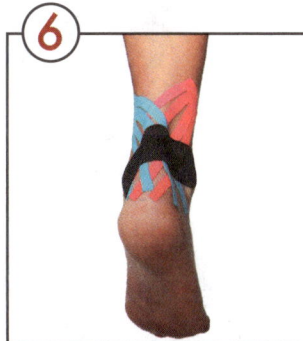

ACUTE INJURY: LYMPHATIC CORRECTION

Initial treatment for inflammation or edema is provided by applying two Kinesio lymphatic corrective technique fans.

1. Begin by placing the anchor approximately 3-4" superior and lateral to the retrocalcaneal bursae. Apply 0-20% of available tension to each fan tail. Angle the fan tails at 45 degrees in an inferior and medial direction. Lay down the ends with no tension and rub to initiate adhesive.

2. Apply second anchor approximately 3-4" superior and medial to the retrocalcaneal bursa. Apply 0-20% of available tension to each fan tail. Angle the fan tails at 45 degrees in an inferior and lateral direction. Rub or pat to initiate adhesive prior to any further patient movement.

   The fan strips should form a crisscross pattern.

ACUTE INJURY: WEB CORRECTION

3. Apply one or two web space correction strips. Apply 15-25% of available tension to each web cut. For one web cut strip apply anchor directly superior to bursae. For two strips apply anchors as described above.

APPLICATION FOR CHRONIC INJURY:

Application of a space correction technique tension in the center of the I strip to assist in reducing edema.

4. Begin by tearing the center of the paper backing of a 4-6" Kinesio I strip. Apply 25-35% of available tension and place the Kinesio strip with applied tension directly over the retrocalcaneal bursae.

5-6. Lay down the ends of the Kinesio I strip with no tension.

   This technique can be applied either horizontal or vertical to the retrocalcaneal bursae. A series of two or three space corrections with tension in center can be used to form a "star".

   An additional option is to apply a donut hole technique instead of a space correction tension in the center of an I strip forming a "star". For an example see lateral epicondylitis.

Sever's Syndrome or Apophysitis of the Calcaneous

Sever's syndrome is an inflammation of the insertion of the Achilles' tendon onto the calcaneous. This insertion point is a traction epiphysis, it may result in a partial avulsion of the epiphysis or cause degeneration from a decreased circulation.

The Kinesio Taping Method will assist in reducing edema and pain.

There are two Kinesio Taping Techniques which may provide reduced inflammation and pain, the practitioner will need to determine which technique is best for their patient. If one technique does not provide significant results, another technique may.

An option which is not shown is to apply the Achilles' tendon Kinesio Taping Technique.

ACUTE INJURY: LYMPHATIC CORRECTION

1. Begin by placing the anchor approximately 3-4" superior and lateral to the insertion of the Achilles'. Apply 0-20% of available tension to each fan tail. Angle the fan tails at 45 degrees in an inferior and medial direction. Rub to initiate adhesive.

2. Apply second anchor approximately 3-4" superior and medial to the insertion of the Achilles'. Apply 0-20% of available tension to each fan tail. Angle the fan tails at 45 degrees in an inferior and lateral direction. Rub or pat to initiate adhesive prior to any further patient movement.

   The fan strips should form a crisscross pattern.

CHRONIC INJURY: MECHANICAL CORRECTION
Application of a mechanical technique tension in the center of the I strip to assist in reducing pain by applying pressure.

3-4. Begin by tearing the center of the paper backing of a 4-6" Kinesio I strip. Apply 50-75% of available tension with downward/inward pressure and place the Kinesio strip with applied tension directly over the area of pain.

5. Lay down the ends of the Kinesio I strip with no tension.

6. Completed application for Sever's Syndrome

   Optional taping is to apply a donut hole, or web cut technique instead of a space correction tension in the center of an I strip forming a "star". For an example see lateral epicondylitis.

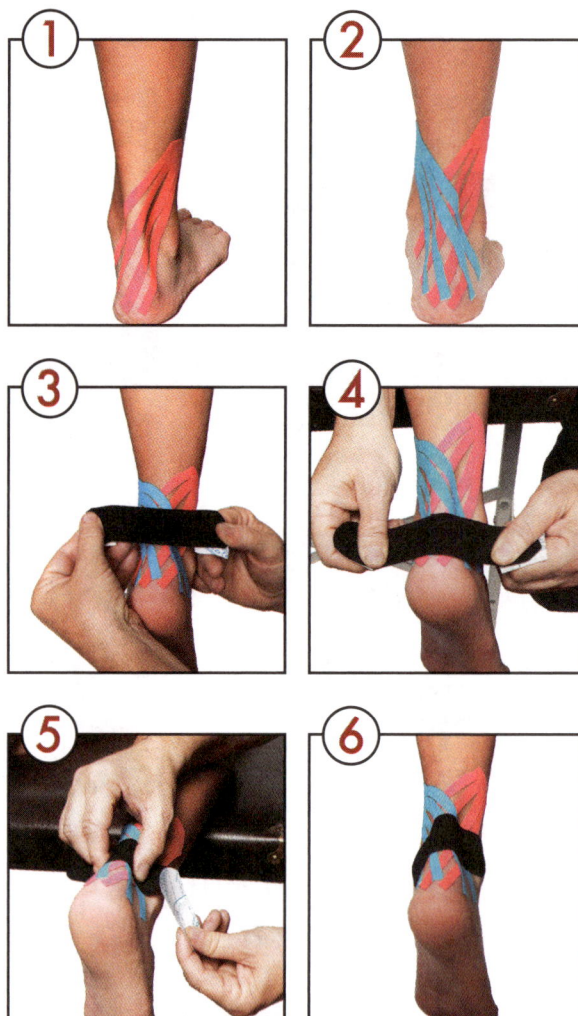

Lateral Ankle Sprain

A sprain to the lateral ligaments of the ankle (anterior talofibular, calcaneofibular and posterior talofibular) is the most common location for a sprained ankle. Lateral ankle sprains are generally considered to account for approximately 90% of all ankle sprain injuries. The most commonly injured ligament in the ankle is the anterior talofibular.

Treatment of a lateral ankle sprain consists of edema reduction due to acute injury, maintenance of muscle strength, proprioceptive stimuli, and prophylactic taping to reduce reoccurrence. The treatment of an acute ankle sprain should be thought of as occurring in stages. Acute, 24-72 hours, minimize edema. Post-acute, when acute post traumatic symptoms subside, to return patient to pre-injury level of activity.

The following is derived from an article, "A New Approach to the Management of Ankle Sprains", by Jayson Goo, MA, ATC, Head Athletic Trainer at the University of Hawaii. If your profession does not allow you to use electrical modalities, eliminate those steps from your treatment protocol.

ACUTE 0-24 HOURS

RICE: (Rest, Ice, Compression, and Elevation)

CRUTCHES: Proper fitting and instructions

ELECTRIC STIMULATION: First 24 hours: Microcurrent .3Hz. 10 min. followed by 1.0 Hz for 10-20 min.

CORRECTIVE KINESIO TAPING: Anterior, Posterior, Medial and Lateral Lymphatic drainage strips. If the patient wears footwear which may affect the application of the Kinesio strips, modify the lymphatic correction appropriately.

HOME CARE INSTRUCTIONS: Patient should be sent home with crutches, appropriate compression (elastic bandage or compression dressing), and if indicated or allowed, pain medication. When at home, the patient should keep the ankle elevated and apply ice 20 minutes once per hour. If it is not possible to ice the ankle, it is recommended that the patient keep the ankle elevated and continual compression. If compression and/or elevation become painful, have the patient cycle periods of compression and elevation. Instruct the patient to gently plantar and dorsiflex their ankle in a pain free range of motion. If the patient is able to, have them spell the alphabet with their toes. The patient should sleep with a compressive dressing, single thickness from below the knees and extending over the toes (TUBIGRIP®, or TetraGrip)

ACUTE 24-72 HOURS

ELECTRIC STIMULATION:
24 HOURS TO POST-ACUTE: Interferential or Pre-mod at 80-150 Hz.

LOWER LEG LYMPHEDEMA MASSAGE: 10 minutes anteriorly, 5 to 10 posteriorly, 5 to 10 minutes anteriorly

RANGE OF MOTION (ROM): Active to active resistive as tolerated, 3 X 12 plantar flexion, dorsiflexion. For inversion sprain, eversion while inversion if it is an eversion sprain.

WHIRLPOOL: Cold Whirlpool while wearing compression, 10 to 20 minutes

Repeat the above treatment protocol several times per day if possible. Continue RICE.

ACUTE (0-72 HOURS) TREATMENT OF LATERAL ANKLE SPRAIN - LYMPHATIC CORRECTION TECHNIQUE

Medial view of lymphatic corrective technique.

1. Begin by placing the anchor of the lymphatic strip superior to the lymphatic node, deep to the attachment of the Achilles tendon. Place the patients ankle in plantar flexion and eversion as pain or edema will allow.

   Direct fan tails over the area of edema over the medial malleolus with 0-20% of available tension. As the fan strip passes over the first ray have the patient move into as much plantar flexion and inversion as pain or edema allows. Lay down the ends with no tension.

   Pat or rub the fan strips to initiate adhesive prior to any further patient movement.

2. Lateral view of lymphatic corrective technique.

   Begin by placing the anchor of a lymphatic strip superior and medial to the lymphatic node located deep to the attachment of the Achilles tendon. Place the patients ankle in as much plantar flexion and inversion as pain or edema will allow.

   Direct the fan tails over the lateral malleolus and dorsum area with 0-20% of available tension. Lay down the ends with no tension.

   Rub or pat the fan strips to initiate adhesive prior to any further patient movement.

   A lymphatic fan technique may also be applied to the calf region to assist in edema reduction.

3. Use of appropriate compression over the lymphatic corrective technique. A "horseshoe" has been applied over the lateral malleolus. Made of ½" orthopedic felt in a U shape. Covered by a light compressive dressing: TUBIGRIP®, TetraGrip, or elastic wrap.

4. The compressive wrapping is used to apply constant downward and inward pressure to create higher pressure outside of the injured tissue to limit the cellular fluid from leaving the cells.

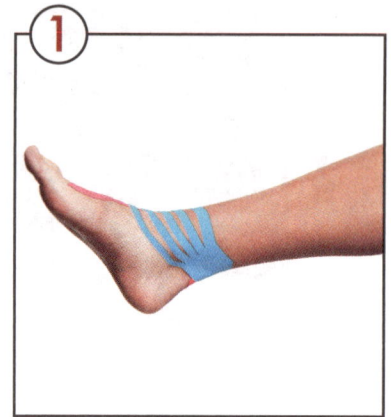

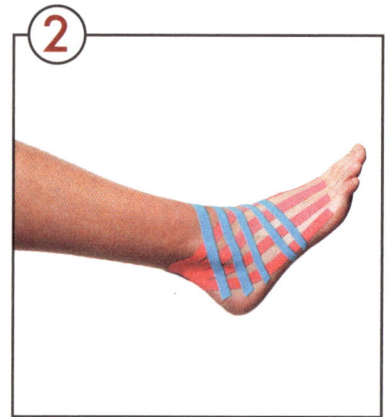

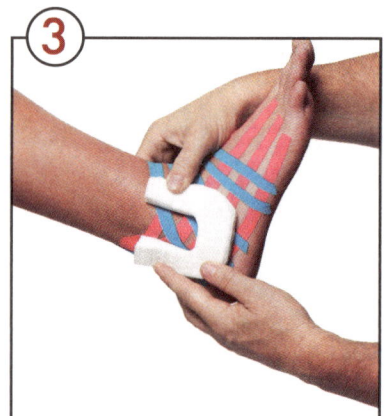

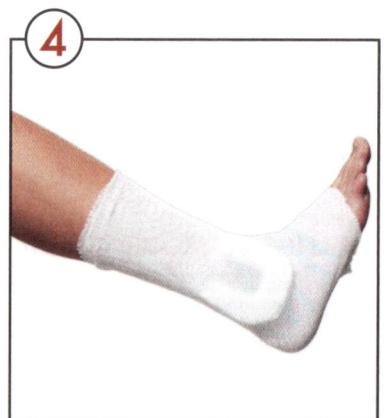

Lateral Ankle Sprain

POST ACUTE (WHEN TRAUMATIC SYMPTOMS SUBSIDE)

ELECTRIC MODALITIES: As indicated prior to treatment

LOWER LEG LYMPHEDEMA MASSAGE: 5 to 10 minutes posteriorly, 5 to 10 minutes anteriorly

CORRECTIVE KINESIO TAPING APPLICATION: Once the edema/swelling has been reduced, may only use anterior lymphatic drainage strip.

CONTRAST WHIRLPOOL: Contrast treatment initially from cold to warm whirlpool. May start patient in cold whirlpool for 4 minutes and hot for 1 minute, repeat cycle 5 times and end in cold whirlpool. As edema is reduced, use 3 cold - 2 hot, next 2 1/5 cold - 2 1/5 hot, next 3 hot and 2 cold, next 4 hot and 1 cold. Each treatment pattern is used for 1 to 2 days and, as edema is reduced, can initiate more hot than cold whirlpool treatments.

RANGE OF MOTION (ROM): Active movements as listed in acute treatment.
BAPS (balance) board: Clockwise rotations, counterclockwise rotations, dorsi/plantarflexion, inversion and eversion.

PROGRESSIVE RESISTANCE EXERCISES (PRE): Graduating resistance as tolerated by patient
3 x 20 dorsiflexion
3 x 20 dorsiflexion/external rotation
3 x 20 dorsiflexion/internal rotation (eversion sprains only)
3 x 20 plantarflexion
3 x 20 plantarflexion with femur internally rotated
3 x 20 plantarflexion with femur externally rotated

SLANTBOARD: 3 minutes, use of a board with increasing angle of inclination to stretch posterior compartment muscles (gastrocnemius, soleus), which becomes shortened due to lack of movement.

STABILIZATION: Stand on toes of the injured foot for a total of 3 minutes with the longest repetition being no longer than 1 minute.

CARDIOVASCULAR TRAINING: Minimum of 30 minutes daily.

OPEN KINETIC CHAIN EXERCISES: When able to walk with normal gait may begin straight line jogging and sport specific exercises as indicated by patient tolerance.

ELECTRIC MODALITIES: As indicated following treatment.

KINESIO TAPING METHOD APPLICATION: Basic Kinesio Taping for muscles as indicated by mechanism of injury, or weakness. Application of Correction Techniques to assist limitation of injury.

ACUTE AND POST ACUTE:

1. Basic Kinesio Technique inhibition for gastrocnemius muscle to improve dorsiflexion range of motion due to possible spasm. For complete application description see Achilles Tendonitis.

   As the patient improves or during rehabilitation a facilitation technique should be used. This will assist in gastrocnemius strength development and deep lymphatic fluid flow from improved muscle contractions.

   As the patient progresses, a tendon correction may be applied over the Achilles' tendon to assist with movement. See Achilles Tendon for complete description.

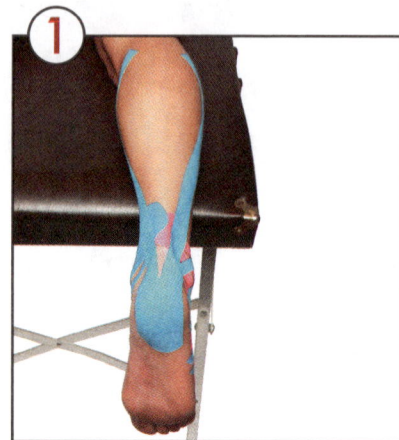

POST - ACUTE BASIC AND CORRECTIVE TECHNIQUE APPLICATION

2. Basic Kinesio Technique facilitation application for tibialis anterior muscle to assist in dorsiflexion and limit muscle weakness.

   As the patient improves or during rehabilitation a facilitation technique should be used. This will assist in gastrocnemius strength development and deep lymphatic fluid flow from improved muscle contractions.

   Begin by applying the anchor of an appropriate length I strip at the superior 2/3 of the anteriolateral surface of tibia with no tension.

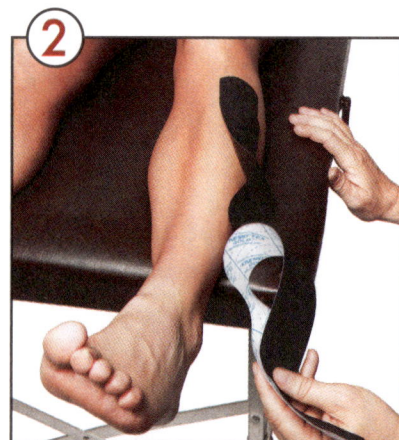

3. Have the patient move into as much plantarflexion and inversion as pain and edema allows. Apply light to moderate 15-35% of available tension to the I strip and direct the I strip along the lateral aspect of the tibia to the lateral malleolous. Rub to initiate adhesive prior to any further patient movement.

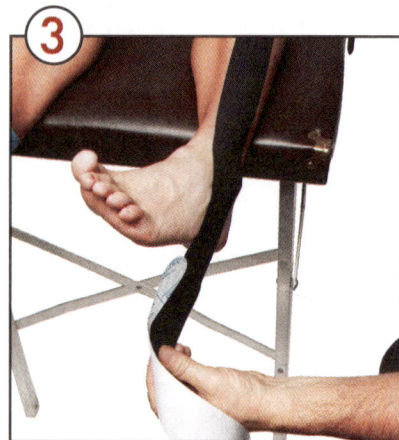

4. As the Kinesio I strip passes the lateral aspect of the ankle, have the patient move into eversion and dorsiflexion. Direct the tail towards the medial cuneiform and first metatarsal bones of the foot. It is helpful to "wrap" the end around towards the medial malleolus to assist in adhesion. Rub to initiate adhesive prior to any further patient movement.

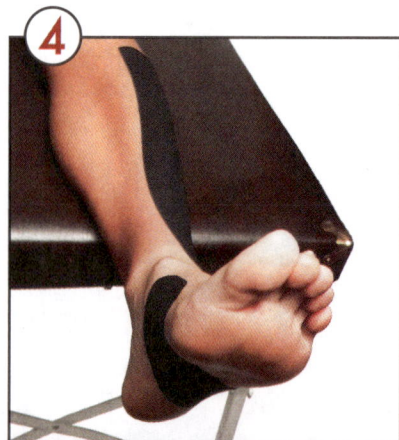

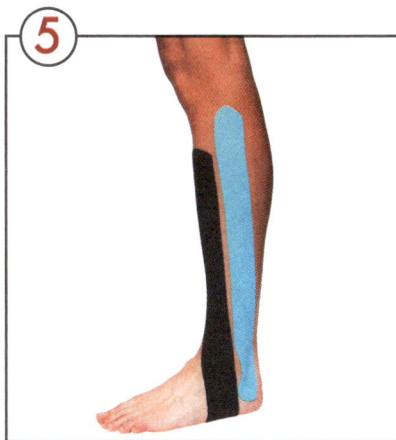

5. Basic Kinesio Technique facilitation application for peroneus longus and/or brevis muscle during rehabilitation. This will assist in gastrocnemius strength development and deep lymphatic fluid flow from improved muscle contraction

Begin by placing the anchor with no tension at the fibular head and lateral 1/2 to 2/3 lateral side of fibula. Place the patient in plantar flexion and inversion and apply 15-35% of available tension and aim the I strip slightly posterior to the lateral malleolus. For the image shown, lay down anchor without tension. Rub to initiate adhesive prior to any further patient movement. In this example the anchor is applied inferior to the lateral malleolous to assist in adhesion. For anatomical placement of the anchor end on the first cuneiform and first metatarsal.

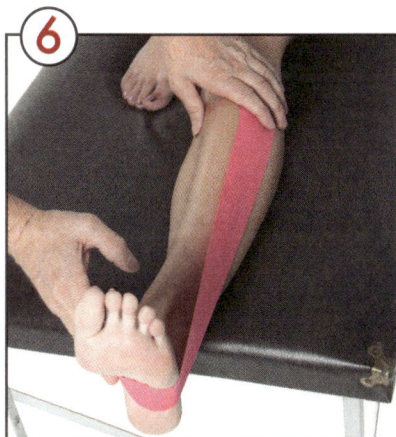

6. Functional Correction to assist in dorsiflexion and eversion to limit re-injury.

Begin by placing the anchor with no tension on the medial aspect of the arch above the base of the 1st metatarsal. Place the patients ankle in dorsiflexion and eversion and bring the I strip over the plantar surface with no tension. Then apply 50+% of available tension to the I strip and apply the anchor in the mid to proximal 1/3 lateral aspect of the tibia with no tension. The anchor should be a minimum of 3-4".

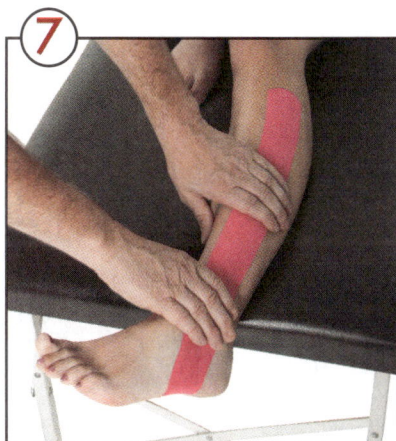

7. While holding both anchors have the patient move into inversion and plantarflexion. Bring both hands together to initiate adhesive. Vigorously rub to initiate adhesive prior to any further patient movement.

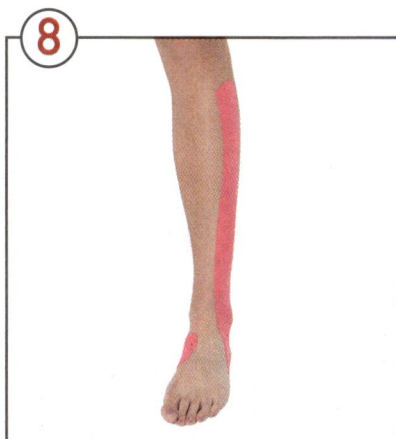

8. Completed Functional Correction to assist dorsiflexion and eversion and limit plantarflexion and inversion, the most common mechanism of injury for a lateral ankle sprain.

OPTIONAL:

9. Application of ligament correction for anterior talofibular ligament, using a figure of 8 pattern and one lateral heel-lock around the ankle. Begin the Kinesio Strip on the medial aspect of the ankle approximately at the tarsal navicular joint. Apply light 15-25% of available tension across the plantar surface of the foot at approximately 45%. Aim the Kinesio strip for the anterior aspect of the lateral malleolus.

10. As the Kinesio Strip rounds the lateral aspect of the ankle, hold the tape onto the skin with one hand.

11. Apply 75-100% of available tension over the anterior talofibular ligament. Move the hand which was holding the tension on the lateral aspect of the foot to the superior aspect of the lateral malleolus.

12. Again apply light 15-25% of available tension to the Kinesio Strip as the strip is applied around the upper anterior aspect of the ankle.

13. Continue the corrective Kinesio strip onto the medial aspect of the ankle with an angle which crosses back over the initial starting point of the strip. The strip continues back onto the plantar surface of the ankle and angles towards the lateral aspect of the heel.

14. As the corrective Kinesio strip angles from the plantar surface onto the lateral aspect of the heel, again increase tension to 75-100% of available tension over the posterior talofibular ligament.

15. After passing over the posterior talofibular ligament decrease tension to paper off - light, 15-25% of available tension.

16. End the Kinesio Strip by finishing on the medial aspect of the ankle near the superior aspect of the medial malleolus. Forming a figure of 8 pattern.

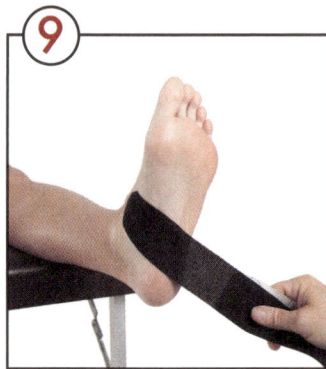

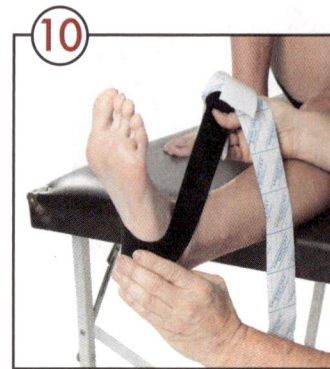

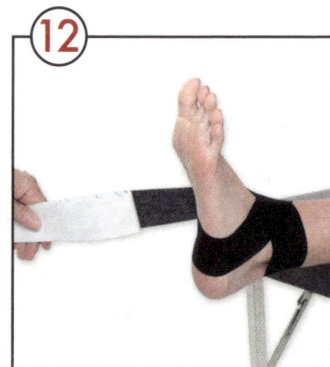

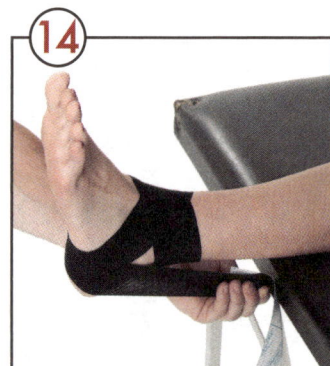

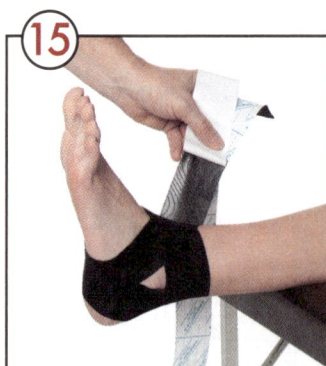

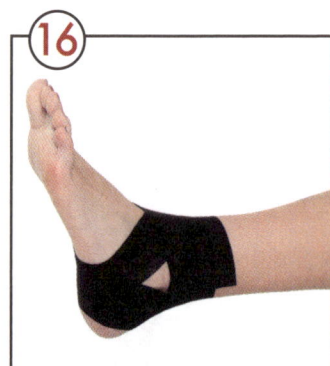

Lateral Ankle Sprain

MEDIAL ANKLE SPRAIN

A sprain to the medial ligaments of the ankle (deltoid) occurs as the result of ankle eversion. This is the result of the large thick deltoid ligament located on the medial aspect of the ankle and the stability of the ankle mortise during eversion motion.

Treatment of medial sprains consists of edema reduction due to acute injury, maintenance of muscle strength, proprioceptive stimuli, and prophylactic taping to reduce reoccurrence. For a complete treatment protocol, refer to lateral ankle sprains.

A common occurrence with medial ankle sprains is the loss of the medial longitudinal arch resulting from injury.

A prophylactic traditional athletic taping can be applied to limit re-injury. For complete description, see lateral ankle sprain combination technique.

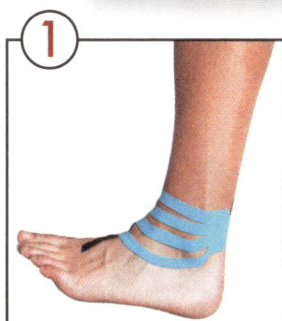

1. Begin by placing the anchor superior to the Achilles tendon. Place the patients ankle in as much plantarflexion and inversion as pain or edema will allow. Direct fan tails over the area of edema over the lateral malleolus with 0-20% of available tension. As the fan strip passes over the first ray have the patient move into as much plantarflexion and eversion as pain or edema allows. Lay down the ends with no tension. Pat or rub the fan strips to initiate adhesive prior to any further patient movement.

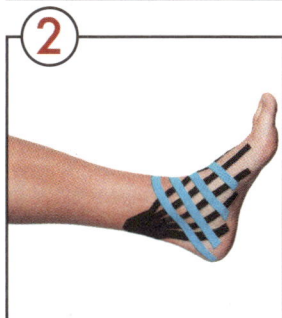

2. Begin by placing the anchor superior to the Achilles tendon. Place the patients ankle in as much dorsiflexion and eversion as pain or edema will allow. Direct the fan tails over the medial malleolus and dorsum area with 0-20% of available tension. Lay down the ends with no tension. Rub or pat the fan strips to initiate adhesive prior to any further patient movement.

   A lymphatic fan technique may also be applied to the calf region to assist in edema reduction.

APPLICATION OF MUSCLE INHIBITION FOR TIBIALIS POSTERIOR OR TIBIALIS ANTERIOR.

The tibialis posterior is generally associated with medial ankle sprains due to it attempting to limit overpronation (foot flattens out when weight is applied). If the medial longitudinal arch is not providing appropriate support to assist in dissipation of forces resulting from landing or take off, the anterior tibialis may become inflamed to compensate.

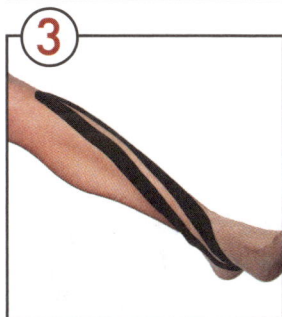

3. Begin by placing the anchor of a Kinesio Y strip, an I strip is also effective, at the navicular tuberosity with no tension. Place the patient in dorsiflexion and eversion, apply 15-25% of available tension and surround the muscle. End the tails near lateral portion of posterior proximal tibia with no tension. Rub to initiate adhesive prior to any further patient movement.

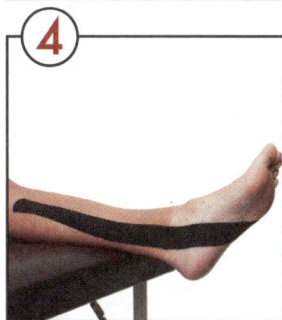

4. Tibialis anterior inhibition technique I strip. Begin by placing the anchor of an I strip, a Y strip is also effective, at the medial cuneiform and base of 1st ray with no tension. Place the foot in plantarflexion and eversion and apply the I strip towards the lateral condyle & superior 2/3 of anterolateral surface of tibia. Lay down the end with no tension. Rub to initiate adhesive prior to any further patient movement.

5. Gastrocnemius muscle taping: Initial application is inhibition to limit spasm, then facilitation to assist in deep lymphatic function and muscle function. Inhibition will be shown. Begin the anchor of a Y technique with no tension at the anterior aspect of the calcaneous. Have the split in Y occur just inferior to the musculotendonous junction. Apply paper off to light, 15-25% of available tension to the tails. The medial tail follows the medial aspect of the medial head and the lateral tail follows the lateral head. Lay down the ends with no tension and rub to initiate adhesive prior to any further patient movement.

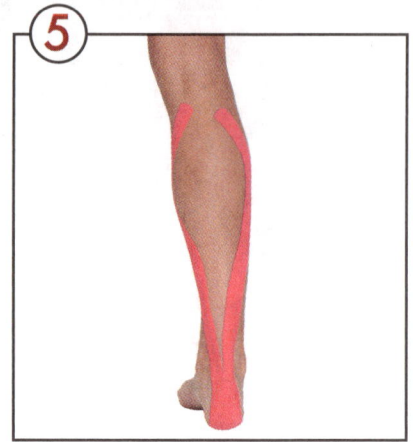

POST ACUTE: APPLICATION OF MUSCLE FACILITATION FOR TIBIALIS POSTERIOR

During post-acute and rehabilitation phases apply a facilitation application to assist in inversion range of motion and limit muscle weakness.

6. Place the anchor with no tension on the lateral portion of posterior proximal tibia.

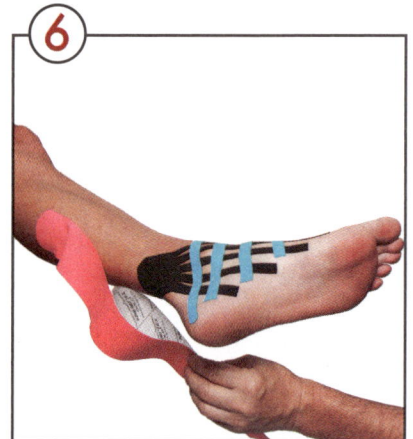

7. Have the patient move into dorsiflexion and eversion. Apply light to moderate, 15-35% of available tension and direct the I strip towards the posterior aspect of the medial malleolus. Then direct the I strip towards the navicular tuberosity. Lay down the end with no tension. Rub to initiate adhesive prior to any further patient movement.

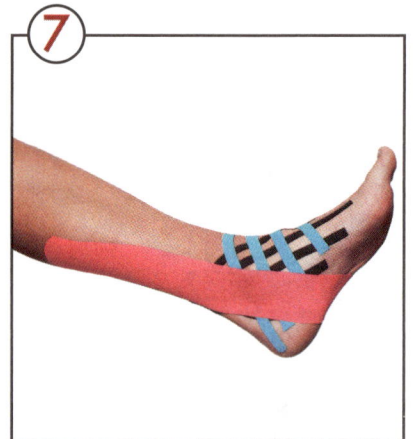

8. The image is a lateral view of the ankle. The anchor can be applied over the lateral border of the 5th metatarsal to assist in the adhesion of the technique.

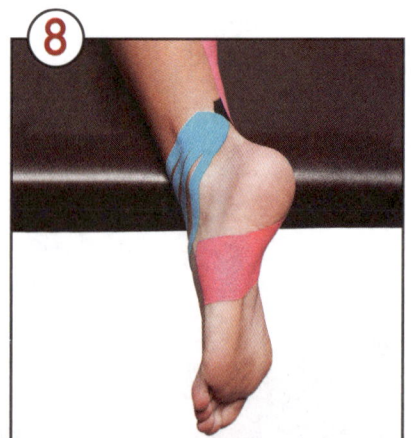

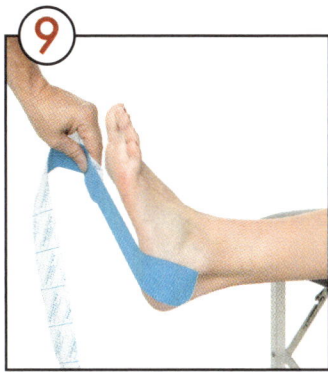

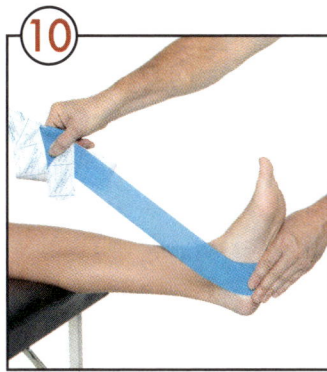

APPLICATION OF A FIGURE OF 8 FOR DELTOID LIGAMENT SUPPORT.

9. Begin the Kinesio Strip on the lateral aspect of the ankle distal to the base of the 5th metatarsal with no tension. Apply light 15-25% of available tension across the plantar surface of the foot at approximately 45%. Aim the Kinesio strip toward the anterior aspect of the calcaneous.

10. As the Kinesio Strip rounds the medial aspect of the ankle, hold the tape onto the skin with one hand. Over calcaneofibular ligament, apply a ligament correction technique 75-100% of available tension over the ligament. Move the hand which was holding the tension on the medial aspect of the foot to the superior aspect of the medial malleolus.

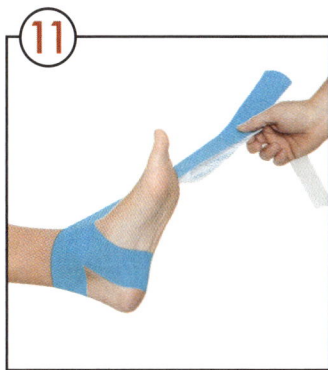

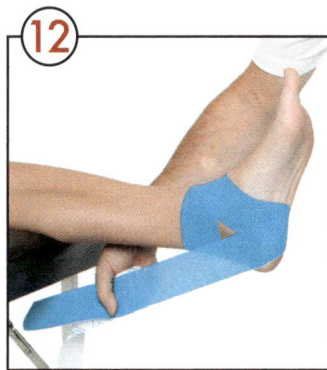

11. Again apply paper off to light, 15-25% of available tension to the Kinesio Strip as the strip is applied around the upper anterior aspect of the ankle.

12. Continue the corrective Kinesio strip onto the lateral aspect of the ankle. As the corrective Kinesio strip angles from lateral aspect of the heel and crosses over the plantar surface again increase tension to ligament correction, 75-100% of available tension over the calcaneotibial ligament.

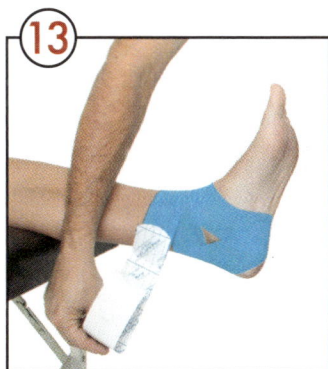

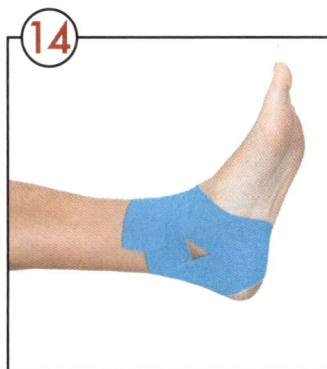

13. Decrease tension to paper off to light, 15-25% of available tension angling the I strip towards the lateral aspect of the ankle.

14. Lay down the end with no tension and rub to initiate adhesive prior to any further patient movement. Completed figure of 8 for Deltoid Ligament Support.

With medial ankle sprains it is common for the medial arch to begin to experience weakness. To assist with this tendency the following is a suggestion.

MECHANICAL CORRECTION WITH POSTERIOR TIBIALIS FACILITATION

15. Begin with the foot in a dorsiflexed position. Place the anchor on the 5th metatarsal distal to the base with no tension.

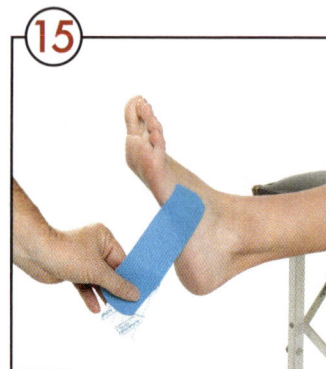

16. Have the patient relax their foot. Apply tension to the I strip: the amount of tension applied is determined by the practitioner and the size of the patient. You are looking for wrinkles to appear on the plantar surface of the foot. Tension may be 15-50+%.

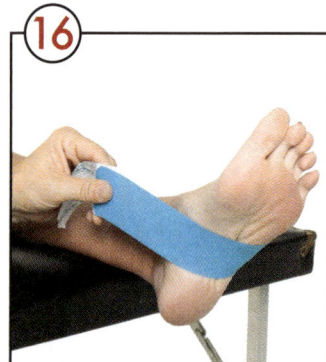

17. As the Kinesio Tex Tape reaches the tarsal navicular joint have the patient move back into a neutral or dorsiflexed position. Lay down the remaining tape with no tension.

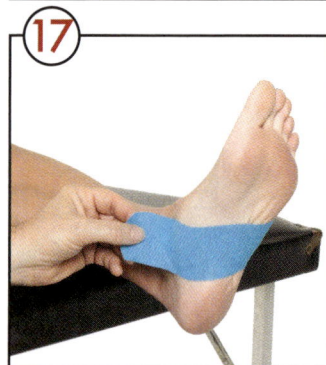

18. Rub to activate adhesive prior to any further patient movement.

    When applied correctly, the patient's foot should show signs of "crinkles" in the metatarsal arch region when the foot is in a relaxed position.

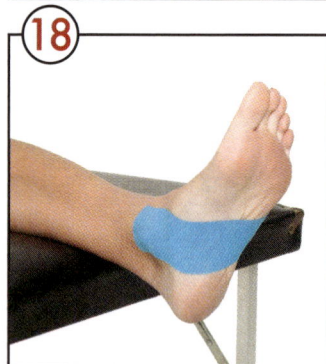

19. Place the anchor with no tension on the lateral portion of posterior proximal tibia.

    Have the patient move into dorsiflexion and eversion. Apply light to moderate, 15-35% of available tension and direct the I strip towards the posterior aspect of the medial malleolus. Then direct the I strip towards the navicular tuberosity. Lay down the end with no tension. Rub to initiate adhesive prior to any further patient movement.

    The image is a lateral view of the ankle. The anchor can be applied over the lateral border of the 5th metatarsal to assist in the adhesion of the technique.

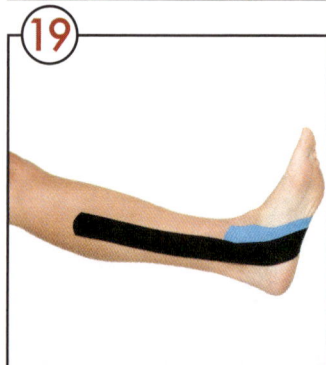

Peroneal Tendon Subluxation

A subluxation of the peroneus longus and brevis tendons can result following an inversion injury to the ankle. These two tendons pass through a common groove located on the posterior lateral aspect of the fibula. They are held in the groove by the peroneal retinaculum. During forced inversion this retinaculum may rupture as the result of significant peroneal tendon contraction to limited forced inversion.

The Kinesio Taping Technique will use a mechanical correction to apply resistance to the subluxation of the peroneal tendons from their common groove.

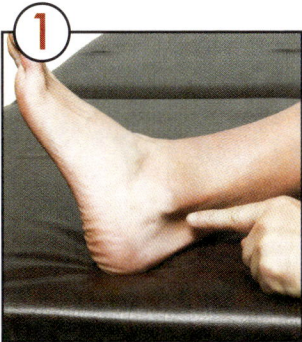

1. To determine the area of peroneal tendon subluxation, begin by placing the patient in ankle dorsiflexion and eversion. Instruct the patient to hold their ankle in this position. Place one hand on the posterior aspect of the lateral malleolus in the region of the peroneal aponeurosis. Apply a plantar flexion and inversion force feeling for a subluxation of the peroneal tendon with the hand on the lateral malleolus.

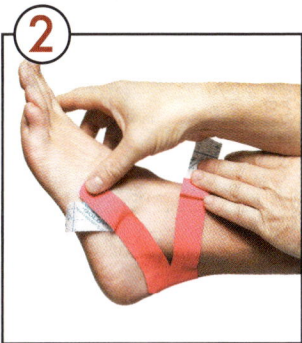

MECHANICAL CORRECTION FOR LIMITING PERONEAL TENDON MIGRATION

2. Begin by placing the Kinesio Y strip on the posterior aspect of the lateral malleolus with no tension, posterior to the location of the subluxing peroneal tendon. The split in the Y should be approximately 1" below the area to be treated. Have the patient move into dorsiflexion and eversion.

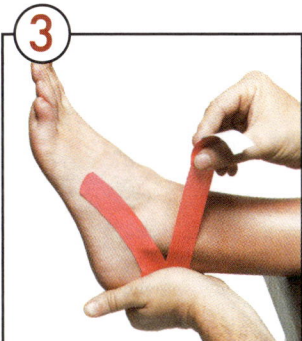

3. With one hand hold the anchor to ensure no tension will be added. Then apply 50-75% of available tension with downward and inward pressure to the superior tail placing it slightly above the peroneal subluxation.

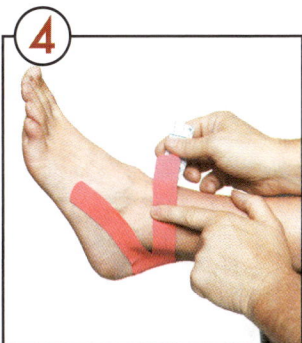

4. As you pass the area of the peroneal tendon, slide the hand holding the anchor over the correction tension area, to initiate adhesive. Then decrease tension applying paper off to light, 15-25% of available tension to the last approximately 1" of the tail. Lay down the end with no tension and rub to initiate adhesive prior to any further patient movement.

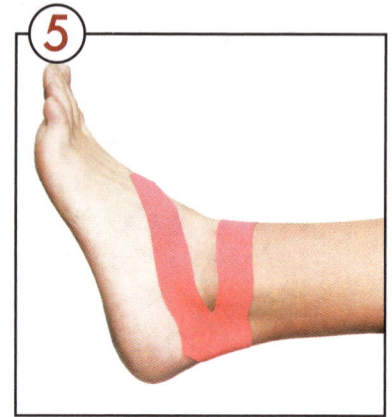

5. The inferior tail of the mechanical correction strip is placed slightly below the peroneal subluxation with the application technique as described above.

Completed Mechanical Correction Technique.

OPTIONAL: Application of the peroneal tendon subluxation technique using a donut hole space correction combined with inhibition of peroneals for edema during acute or chronic phase.

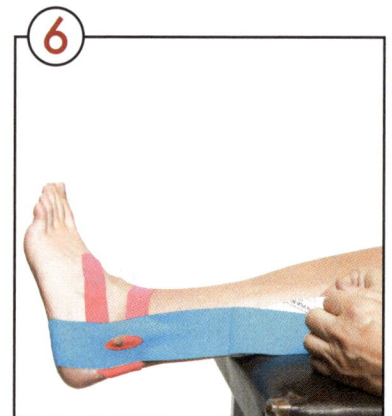

6. Measure a length of Kinesio Tex Tape for the peroneals starting on the plantar surface of the foot. Cut a hole of approximately the size of a dime in the area of tape over the area of pain. Have the patient move into inversion and plantarflexion. Tear the center of the paper backing in the donut hole area and apply 25-35% of available tension over the area of pain and apply to the patient. For the distal end lay down without tension towards the base of the first ray. For the proximal end apply paper off to light, 15-25% of available tension towards the head of the fibula. Rub to initiate adhesive prior to any further patient movement.

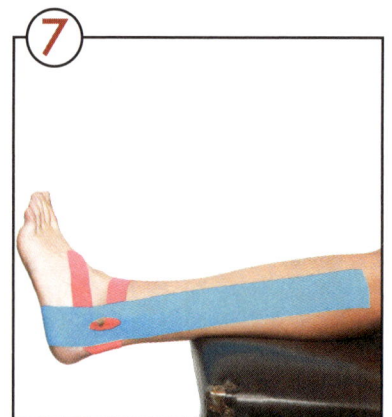

7. Completed donut hole technique in combination with inhibition of the peroneals.

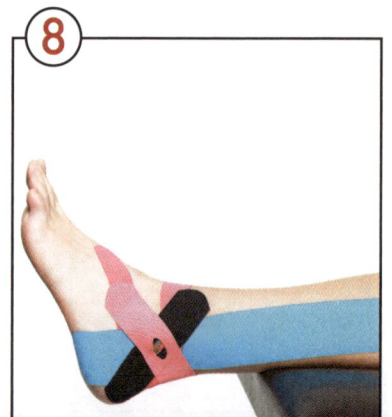

8. Series of three donut hole techniques can be applied. When applying series of donut hole space corrections use less tension with each strip application. For each additional donut hole strip begin with the patient plantarflexion and inversion. Apply 15-25% of available tension during application. If appropriate the patient may need to be repositioned when applying ends to ensure no tension will be caused during patient movement.

Hallux Valgus

Hallux Valgus is associated with forefoot varus which is evident from the 1st ray splaying in a Varus direction. The cause of hallux valgus is generally associated with footwear which is too narrow, too short, or has high heels. This condition is also recognized as hereditary and is more common in women than men.

The elastic qualities of the Kinesio Tex will be used to pull the great toe into a varus position and provide for pain relief from edema reduction.

Best results will be seen with the patient wearing the technique continually for several weeks to months.

Two options will be shown, the practitioner should try each technique on their patient to determine which applications is most effective.

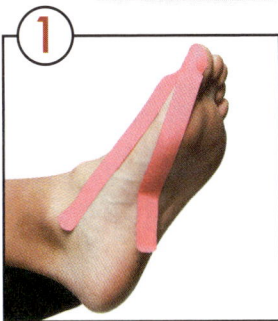

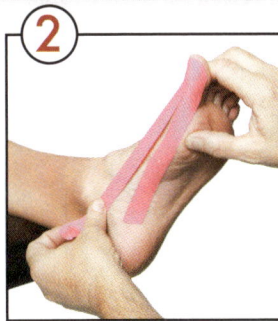

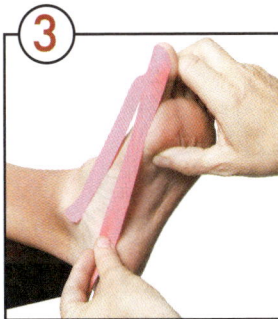

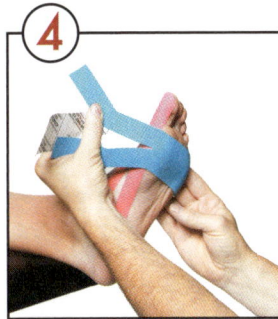

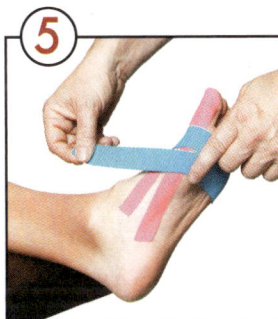

OPTION 1:

1. Begin by placing the anchor of a Y strip on the distal phalanx of the great toe, with the split in the Y cut on the medial aspect with no tension. This may be modified by cutting a button hole in the anchor and placing over the big toe to assist in adhesion.

2. Apply light to severe tension 25-75% of available tension to the upper strip in a varus direction, with the tail running slightly superior the 1st ray. The practitioner can assist this position by also applying a varus force on the big toe.

3. The second strip is applied slightly below the 1st ray with similar tension. The ends are laid down with no tension. Rub to initiate adhesive prior to any further patient movement.

   For the first application use less tension and then in future tapings increase tension to more aggressively "pull" the big toe into a varus position.

MECHANICAL CORRECTION APPLICATION:

4. Begin by placing the anchor of a second Y strip on the lateral surface of the 5th ray with no tension. This is to assist in the strip staying on longer. With one hand hold the anchor to ensure no tension will be added.

   Apply 15-25% of available tension from the 5th ray to the 2nd ray on the plantar surface. Then Apply 50-75% of available tension from 2nd to the media aspect of the 1st MCP joint. The split in the Y should begin just inferior to the area of pain. This tension is moving the 1st ray into supination. The practitioner may determine that placement in a pronated position may be more appropriate.

5. One tail is superior and one tail is inferior to the MCP joint. The mechanical correction, 50-75% of available tension should be maintained to the superior aspect of the 1st MCP joint.

6. As the mechanical tension passes the superior aspect of the 1st ray rub to initiate adhesive. Then with one finger remaining at the superior aspect of the 1st MCP lower tension level to 15-25% of available tension. Lay down this section of the tail to the last 1". Then lay down end with no tension. Repeat this step for both tails. Rub to initiate adhesive prior to any further patient movement.

Allow a space between the tails. This area between the tails should also be the area of pain the patient presented with.

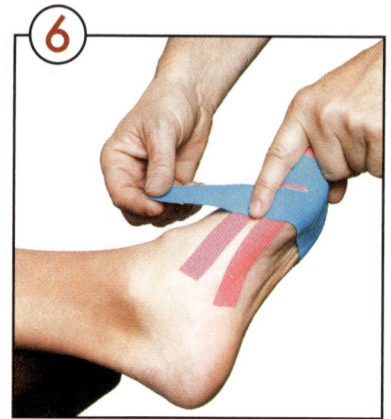

7. Completed Hallux Valgus Technique. The intention is to lift the 1st metacarpal phalangeal joint into a varus position. The degree of tension will need to be determined by the practitioner. In initial applications less tension may be applied then in later applications a higher tension may be used as determined by patient pain.

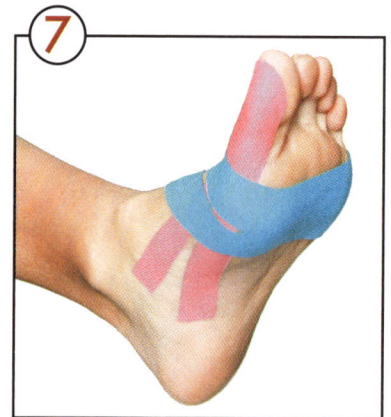

OPTION 2:

8. Begin by placing a Kinesio Y strip anchor near the tarso-navicular joint with no tension. With the medial/superior tail, apply a mechanical correction 50-75% of available tension, surrounding the metatarsal phalangeal "pulling" the joint into a varus position. With the lateral/inferior tail, apply similar mechanical tension with the desire to pull the metatarsal phalangeal joint into a varus position. The practitioner can assist this position by also applying a varus force on the big toe.

Lay down the ends with no tension and rub to initiate adhesive prior to any further patient movement.

Y strip shown has ½" wide tails, for larger patients use 1" or even as wide as 1.5" tails.

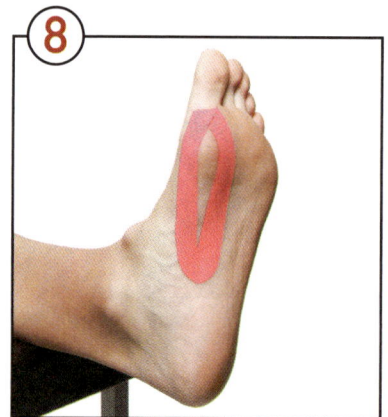

9. Begin by placing the anchor of a second Y strip on the lateral surface of the 5th ray with no tension. This is to assist in the strip staying on longer. With one hand hold the anchor to ensure no tension will be added. Apply 15-25% of available tension from the 5th ray to the 2nd ray on the plantar surface. Then Apply 50-75% of available tension from 2nd to the media aspect of the 1st MCP joint. The split in the Y should begin just inferior to the area of pain. The superior tail and inferior tail should "surround" the area of pain.

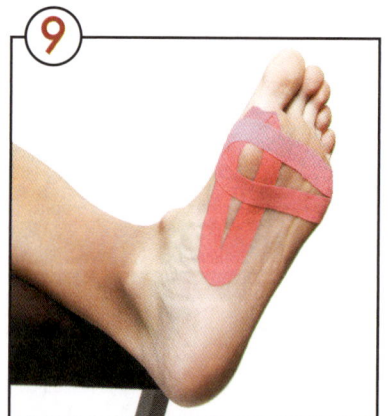

Hallux Valgus

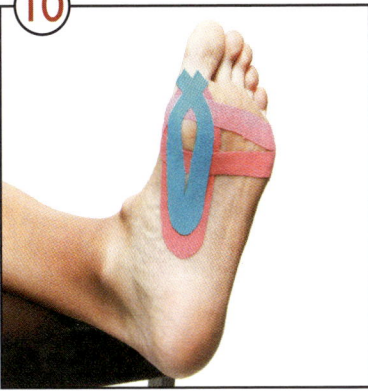

10. A second, but slightly smaller Y strip as described in Photo 8 can be applied to further assist in valgus position of the MCP joint. This strip can be applied either before or after the Y strip applied in Photo 9.

11. The next strip applied is a Kinesio strip with a "donut hole" cut-out, and two to three tails cut into the last 1 ½" of the strip. This strip is trying to affect the rotational component of Hallux Valgus. With the donut hole reducing any pressure directly over the area of pain. As demonstrated, the 1st ray is being "pulled" into a pronated position. The practitioner may determine a supination correction may be more appropriate.

The anchor of the donut hole strip is placed superior to the 1st MCP joint with no tension. The donut hole is placed over the MCP joint.

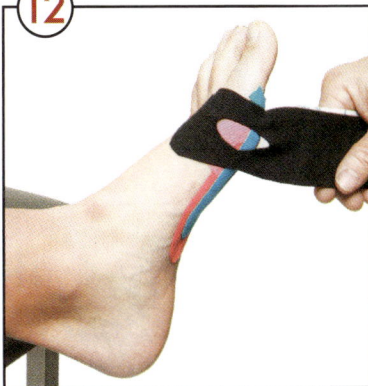

12. With one hand hold the anchor so no tension is added. Apply a mechanical correction, 50-75% of available tension in a plantarflexion and pronated direction. The mechanical correction should be maintained to the head of the second ray.

The practitioner may select to assist this movement by applying plantarflexion and abduction force to the 1st ray manually with their hand.

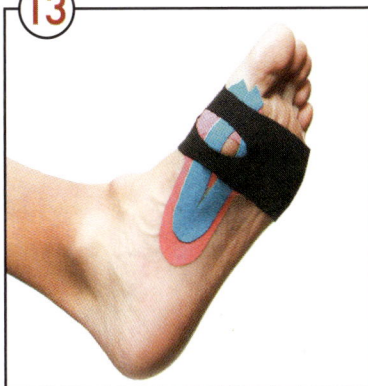

13. From the 2nd ray to the plantar surface of the 5th ray apply 15-25% of available tension. Lay down the end with no tension and rub to initiate adhesive prior to any further patient movement.

Hammer Toe

Hammer toe can be a congenital abnormality or it can be caused by improper fitting footwear. The most common location for a hammer toe is the second or third toe; if more than one toe is involved it is generally referred to as clawed toes. It manifests itself as overly tightened flexor tendon and over-stretched extensor tendons.

The Kinesio Taping Technique will assist by reducing edema, pain and limit flexion of the phalanx.

APPLICATION OF THE FUNCTIONAL CORRECTION TECHNIQUE TO LIMIT DISTAL PHALANX FLEXION

Measure a Kinesio I strip from the plantar surface of the distal tip, over the toe nail and continuing to the metatarsal phalangeal (MTP) joint of the hammer toe.

1. Begin by placing the anchor of the Kinesio I strip on the plantar surface of the injured joint and wrap around to the tip of the dorsal surface of the hammer toe, with no tension.

2. With one hand, hold the anchor which has been applied to the distal phalanx tip, to ensure no tension will be added.

3. Place the patient's toe into as much extension as possible. Apply moderate to severe, 50+% of available tension (with this I strip being narrow be careful as to not add too much tension to the I strips you might "overload" the elastic fibers of the tape) to the Kinesio I Strip, laying down the Kinesio I Strip on the dorsum surface of the hammer toe. Apply tension until the Kinesio I strip is approximately 1" below the MTP joint. This will create a "tent or bridge".

   Lay down the remaining approximately 2-3" with no tension.

4. Hold both anchors and have the patient move their hammer toe into as much flexion as possible. Bring both hands holding the anchors together to initiate adhesive prior to any further patient movement.

   A second functional correction strip may be applied depending upon the size of the individual and the amount of toe movement limitation desired.

5. Apply an additional "anchor" around the distal and proximal anchors from the Kinesio I strip to assist in the ends adhesion and length of wear.

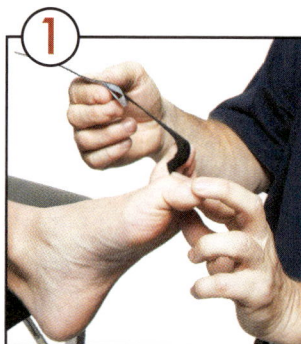

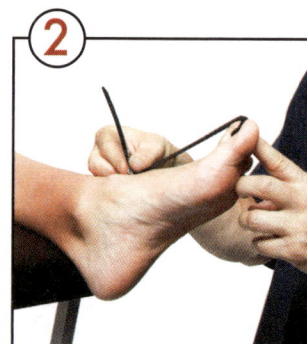

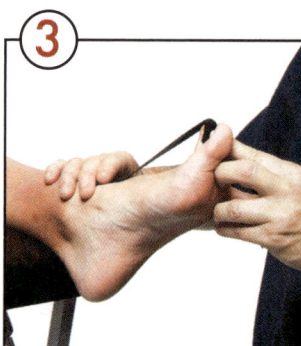

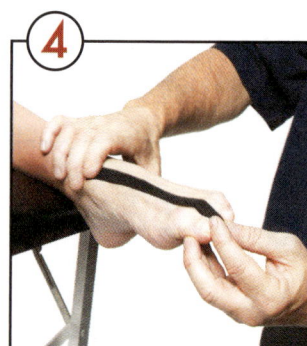

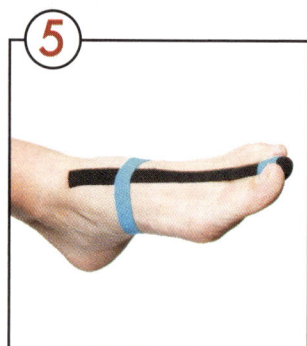

Dislocation of the Toe

Dislocated phalanges are a common injury to physically active patients. Although they are not common in comparison to overall injures which result from being physically active, they are generally very painful and few treatment options currently exist.

Anytime a dislocation occurs, it is important to refer the patient to a physician to evaluate the injury. The Kinesio Taping Technique will provide pain relief, reduce inflammation by use of lymphatic correction, provide joint stability with ligament correction, and use a functional correction to limit flexion or extension.

The practitioner may aid in their patient's comfort by recommending a stiff-soled shoe or boot to minimize forefoot movement.

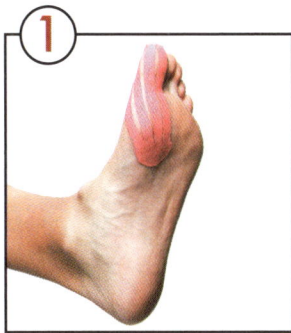

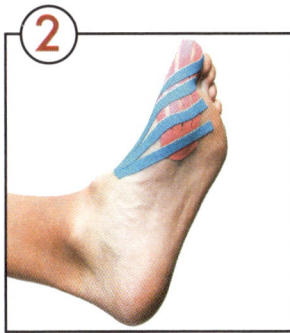

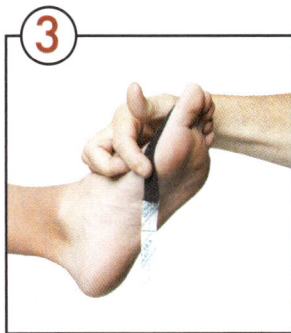

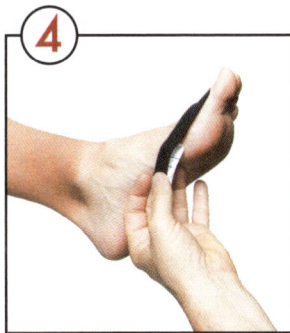

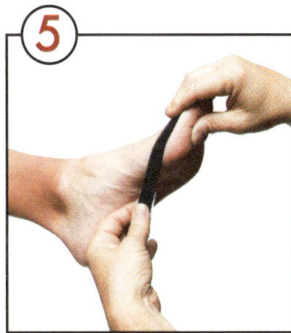

Apply a lymphatic correction technique to the dorsal surface, plantar surface, or both. The lymphatic correction should form a crisscross pattern over the area of specific patient pain or area of greatest joint effusion.

1. Begin the inferior anchor distal to the MCP joint with no tension. Direct the fan strips with 0-20% of available tension surrounding the MCP joint, proximal and distal phalanx. Lay down the ends with no tension and rub or pat to initiate adhesive prior to any further patient movement.

2. Begin the second strip anchor on the dorsal surface with no tension. Direct the fan strips with 0-20% of available tension surrounding the MCP joint, proximal and distal phalanx. Lay down the ends with no tension and rub or pat to initiate adhesive prior to any further patient movement.

LIGAMENT CORRECTION

Apply a ligament correction technique to the region in which the dislocation or fractured region is located. The ligament correction can be applied during all stages of the injury. A dorsal dislocation is the most common.

3. Begin the anchor of an approximately ½" I strip in the dorsal space between the first and second MCP joint with no tension.

4. With one hand hold the anchor to ensure no tension will be added. Apply 75-100% of available tension to the I strip and angle across the injured joint at approximately a 45 degree angle.

5. When the I strip passes inferior the injured joint end tension. Move the hand that was holding the anchor along the I strip initiating adhesive. Lay down the end with no tension and further rub the I strip to initiate adhesive prior to any further patient movement.

6. A second ligament correction is applied with the anchor starting on the dorsum of the distal phalanx with no tension. With one hand hold the anchor to ensure no tension will be added. Apply 75-100% of available tension to the I strip and angle across the injured joint at approximately a 45 degree angle. End tension when the I strip passes inferior to the injured joint. Move the hand that was holding the anchor along the I strip initiating adhesive. Lay down the end with no tension and further rub the I strip to initiate adhesive prior to any further patient movement.

A third ligament correction strip can be applied running parallel to the 1st ray.

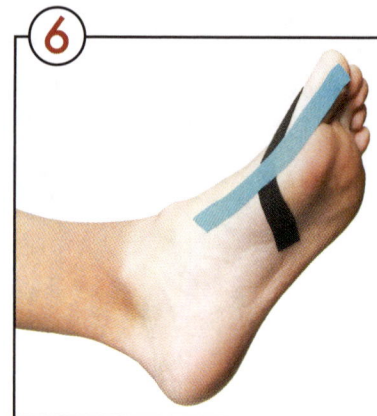

7. Apply a circular anchor over the initial anchors to assist in adhesion of the ligament correction I strips.

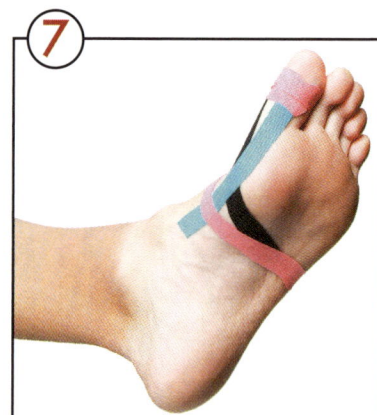

FUNCTIONAL CORRECTION: To limit toe flexion.

8. Begin by placing the anchor of the Kinesio I strip on the plantar surface of the injured joint and wrap around to the tip of the dorsal surface of the hammer toe, with no tension.

Place the patient's toe into as much extension as possible. Apply moderate to severe, 50-75% of available tension (with this I strip being narrow be careful as to not add too much tension to the I strip as you might "overload" the elastic fibers of the tape) to the Kinesio I Strip, laying down the Kinesio I strip on the dorsum surface of the hammer toe. Apply tension until the Kinesio I strip is approximately 1" below the MTP joint. This will create a "tent or bridge".

Lay down the remaining approximately 2-3" with no tension.

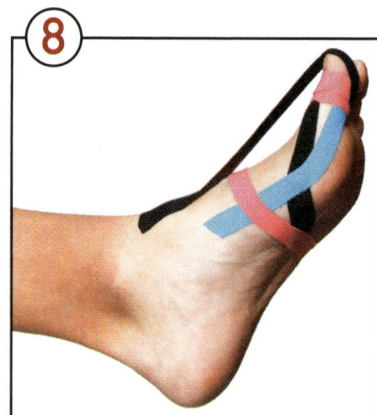

9. Hold both anchors and have the patient move their hammer toe into as much flexion as possible. Bring both hands holding the anchors together to initiate adhesive prior to any further patient movement.

A second functional correction strip may be applied depending upon the size of the individual and the amount of toe movement limitation desired.

Apply an additional "anchor" around the distal and proximal anchors from the Kinesio I strip to assist in the ends adhesion and length of wear.

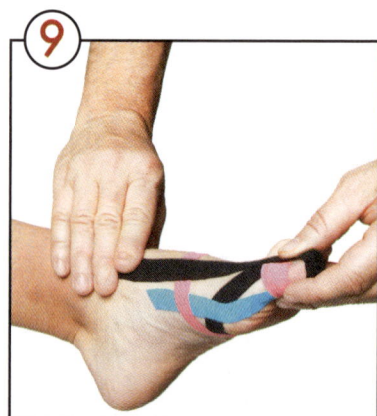

Turf Toe – Hyperextension of Great Toe

Turf Toe is the hyperextension of the metatarsophalangeal joint (MTP). It is generally caused by the great toe being hyperextended or forced into an extended position. This may result from pushing off during activity, or having the shoe "stick" to the surface as may occur with artificial turf (astroturf).

The patient will present with pain on toe extension, swelling, and possible discoloration of the MTP joint. They will have pain in weight bearing and toe push off. The desired outcome of the Kinesio Taping Technique is to limit toe extension and provide support of the MTP joint. Pain in the joint will also be reduced by reduction in edema, and joint motion will be reduced by application of a functional correction.

Begin by either having the patient or yourself move the great toe into extension to determine the position where the joint becomes painful. Prior to tape placement, the practitioner should place the joint in a non painful position and through the elasticity of the tape minimize joint motion past the painful point.

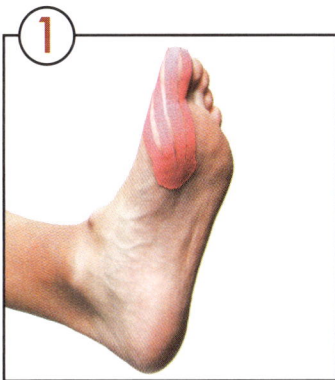

ACUTE: LYMPHATIC CORRECTION

Apply a lymphatic correction technique to the dorsal surface, plantar surface, or both. The lymphatic correction should form a crisscross pattern over the area of specific patient pain or area of greatest joint effusion.

1. Begin the inferior anchor distal to the MCP joint with no tension. Direct the fan strips with 0-20% of available tension surrounding the MCP joint, proximal and distal phalanx. Lay down the ends with no tension and rub or pat to initiate adhesive prior to any further patient movement.

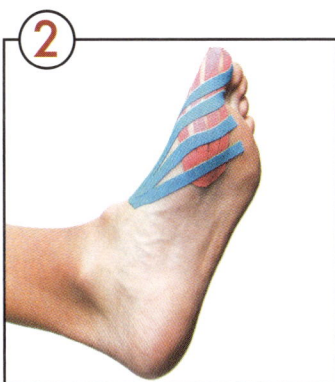

2. Begin the second strip anchor on the dorsum surface with no tension. Direct the fan strips with 0-20% of available tension surrounding the MCP joint, proximal and distal phalanx. Lay down the ends with no tension and rub or pat to initiate adhesive prior to any further patient movement.

   Prior to application it is important to make sure the surface is clean and dry. An adherent may also assist in the Kinesio Tex Tape adhering.

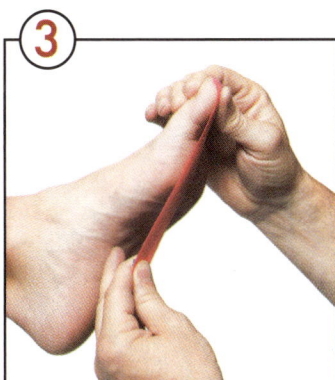

POST-ACUTE: MECHANICAL CORRECTION

3. Place the anchor of the first Kinesio I strip, 1" in width, on the toe nail and wrap over the distal tip of the great toe with no tension.

4. Manually move the toe into slight flexion. Hold the anchor and apply 50-75% tension to the Kinesio strip from the tip of the great toe, past the MTP joint, and down to mid plantar surface. Rub to initiate adhesive prior to any further patient movement.

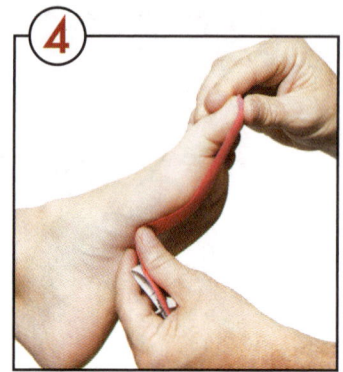

5. Manually move the great toe into extension and apply the end with no tension. Again rub to initiate adhesive prior to any further patient movement.

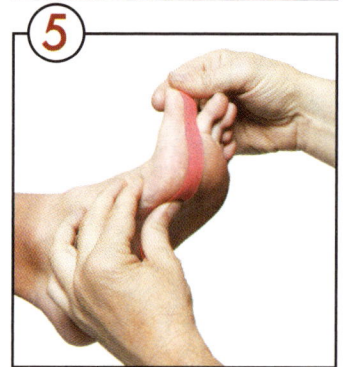

6. Repeat the above steps as described in photos 3-5. The second strip should be applied along the 1st ray.

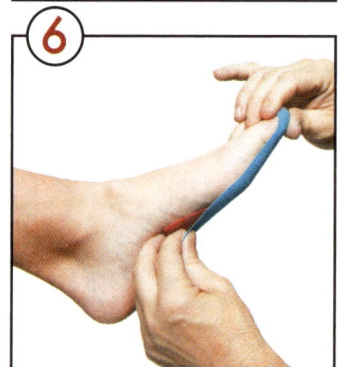

7. Two to three strips will be required, with each successive strip moving in an overlapping pattern more to the medial and towards the dorsal aspect of the MTP joint.

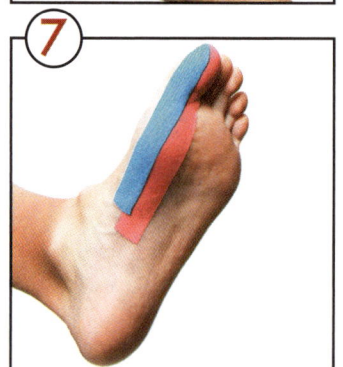

8. Apply a figure 8 strip using 1" Kinesio Tex Tape starting with the anchor on the medial aspect of the 1st MCP joint, between the 1st and 2nd distal phalanx with no tension. With paper off to light, 15-25% of available tension, pull the I strip in a medial direction aiming to cross the center of the 1st MCP joint. When the I strip reaches the medial aspect of the great toe, increase tension to 50% of available tension to place the MCP and toe in more pronation and flexion.

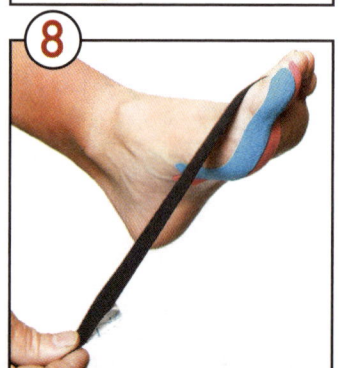

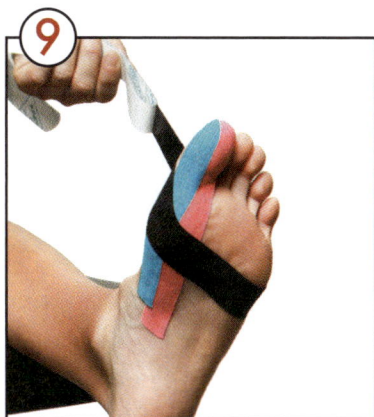

9. As the Kinesio I strip passes the dorsal aspect of the MCP decrease tension to 15-25% across the dorsum of the foot. Continue around the 5th ray and angle the I strip to the superior dorsal aspect of the 1st MCL.

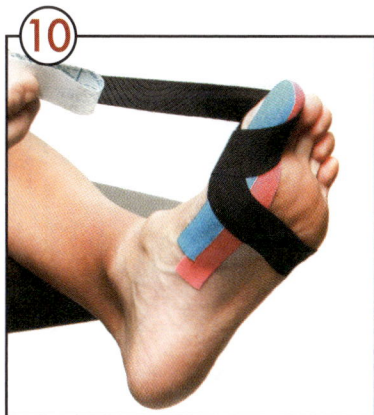

10. Maintaining 15-25% of available tension wrap around the medial aspect of the DIP joint of the toe. As the I strip reaches the lateral aspect, side between 1st and 2nd toe and then crosses to the dorsal aspect of the great toe, increase tension to 50% of available tension. Be careful to not apply any pressure that would cause the big toe to be pulled into extension (mechanism of injury).

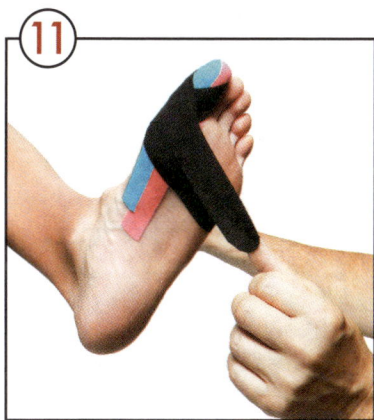

11. As the I strip reaches the medial aspect of the 1st ray begin to place the MCP and toe in more pronation and flexion. As the Kinesio I strip passes the dorsal aspect of the MCP decrease tension to 15-25% to the 1-2" and end tension. Lay down the end with no tension and rub to initiate adhesive prior to any further patient movement.

OPTIONAL: FUNCTIONAL CORRECTION

12. Apply a functional correction application to limit toe movement into extension. This strip can be used to "replace" one of the initial I strips.

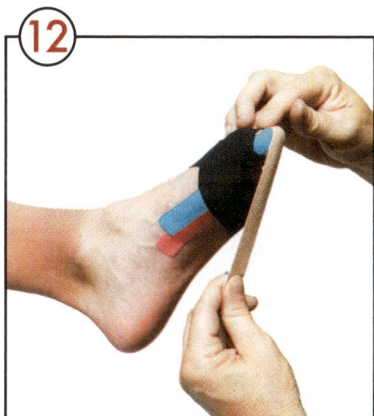

Apply distal anchor starting on the toe nail and crossing over to the dorsal surface of the great toe. With one hand hold the anchor, so no tension will be added, and place the great toe into flexion. Apply 25-50+% of available tension to the I strip and place the second anchor of 2-3" in length near the anterior aspect of the calcaneous, forming a "tent or bridge". The tension level is determined by the degree the practitioner desires to limit toe extension.

As you hold both anchors move the great toe into extension. Vigorously rub to initiate adhesion prior to any further patient movement.

Anchors can be applied surrounding the distal phalanx, and mid foot region to help with tape adhesion.

Metatarsal Arch

The metatarsal arch is located at the heads of the metatarsal bones which forms an arch to assist in force dissipation as the result of movement. The size of this arch can be reduced either through acute injury or chronic overuse. When this arch is not providing sufficient support, the metatarsal heads will absorb more force during activity than they are accustomed to. Calluses may form, and stress fractures may develop.

Using a mechanical correction technique, an I strip will be placed across the mid-arch to assist with metatarsal arch support.

MEDIAL AND LATERAL LONGITUDINAL ARCH: LIGAMENT CORRECTION

1. Begin by placing the anchor with the split in the Y superior to the insertion of the plantar fascia at the anterior aspect of the calcaneous with no tension.

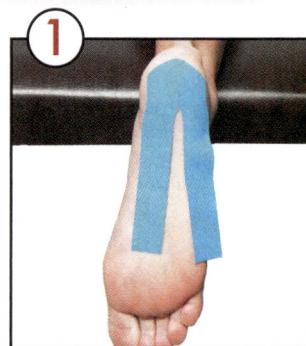

2. With one hand, hold the anchor to ensure no tension is added. Place the patient in dorsiflexion and apply 50-75% (a maximum of 100% tension can be used) of available tension to the medial tail and apply along the first metatarsal to the MCP joint, the last approximately 1".

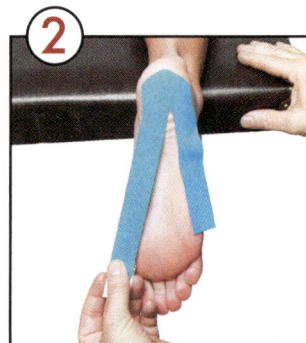

3. Lay down the end with no tension and rub to initiate adhesive prior to any further patient movement. The second tail follows the 5th metatarsal with end placement on the MCP joint. Rub to initiate adhesive prior to any further patient movement.

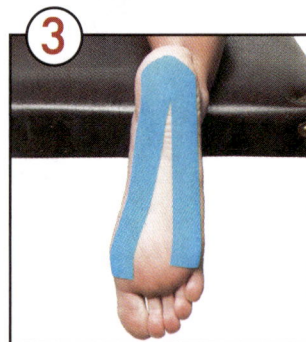

METATARSAL ARCH

4. Begin with the foot in dorsiflexion. Place the anchor on the 5th metatarsal proximal to the base. The strip is angled at approximately 45 degrees.

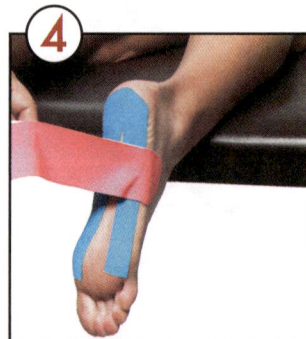

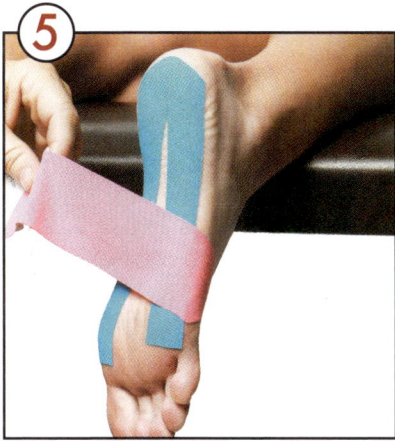

5. Have the patient relax their foot. Apply light to moderate, 25-50+% of available tension from the anchor to the tarsal navicular joint region. The amount of tension is determined by the practitioner and the size of the patient.

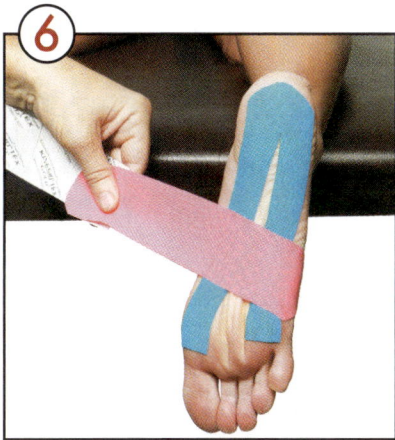

6. You are looking for wrinkles to appear on the plantar surface of the foot, as seen in this image. As the Kinesio Tex Tape reaches the tarsal navicular joint have the patient move back into neutral or dorsiflexion. Lay down the remaining tape with no tension.

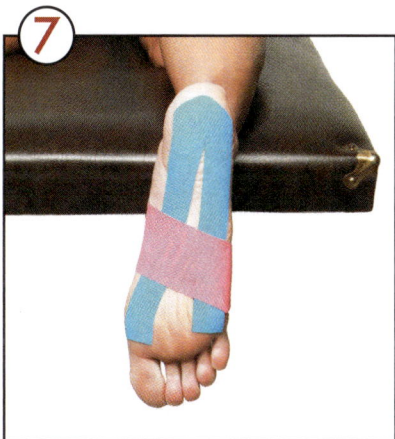

7. Rub to activate adhesive prior to any further patient movement.

Completed Metatarsal Kinesio Technique.

Interdigital (Morton's) Neuroma

Morton's neuroma is an enlargement of the myelin sheath which surrounds an inter-digital nerve located between the heads of the metatarsals. The myelin sheath becomes enlarged and entraps the nerve causing intermittent numbness. The most common location for this condition is the 3rd interdigital nerve, which is located between the third and fourth toes.

Treatment usually consists of widening the space between the metatarsal heads thus reducing pressure on the interdigital nerve. This can be done by having the patient wear loose fitting shoes, elevating the metatarsal heads directly under the neuroma, and reduction of inflammation.

The Kinesio Taping Technique assists in reduction of inflammation or edema.

OPTION 1: LYMPHATIC CORRECTION

1. Begin by placing the anchor with no tension with the fan cut near the anterior aspect of the calcaneous.

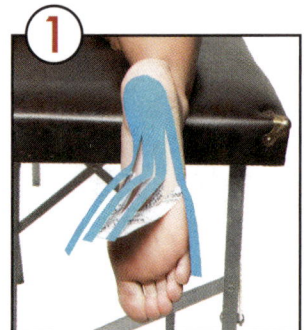

2. Apply 0-20% of available tension as you direct the fan tails between each metatarsal head. Lay down each end with no tension and rub to initiate adhesive prior to any further patient movement.

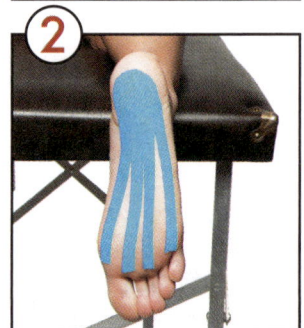

3. Apply an additional fan strip on the dorsum of the foot. Begin the anchor with no tension at the tarsal, metatarsal joint. Apply 0-20% of available tension as you direct the fan tails between each metatarsal head. Lay down each end with no tension and rub to initiate adhesive prior to any further patient movement.

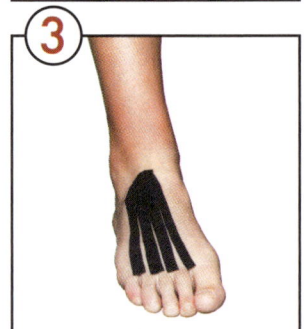

OPTION 2: BUTTON HOLE TECHNIQUE

4. Measure a length of Kinesio I strip from the mid dorsum of the foot to the mid plantar surface. Cut a series of two to three "button holes" in the center of the I strip, depending upon the size of the patient and width of Kinesio I strip used. Image shows a 2" wide Kinesio I strip, for a smaller patient a 1 ½" wide strip may be use, for a larger patient a 3" wide strip may be used.

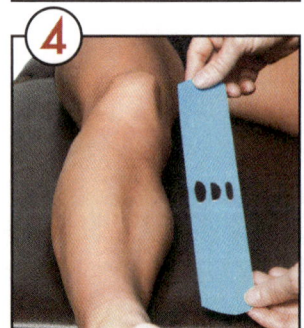

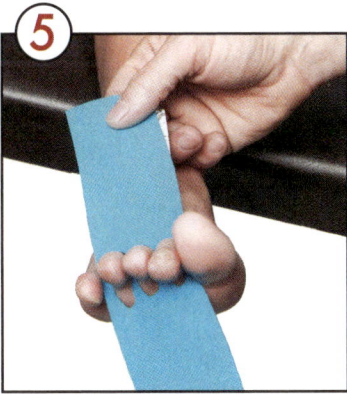

5. Tear the center of the paper backing and apply the button holes with the central hole being over the region of pain, usually the middle toe.

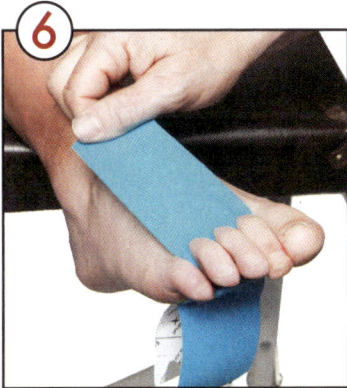

6. Apply light to moderate, 15-35% of available tension to the Kinesio Strip.

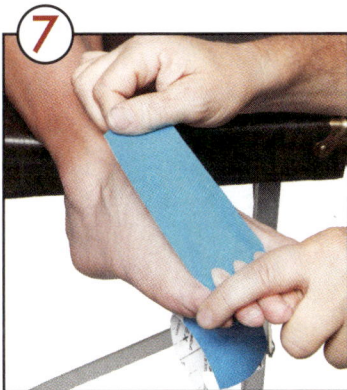

7. Move the toes into flexion and foot into plantarflexion and apply the Kinesio button hole strip over the area of the metatarsal heads to the mid shaft region on the dorsum of the foot. Rub to initiate adhesive. Now decrease tension to paper off to light, 15-25% of available tension to the last 1". Lay down the end with no tension and rub to initiate adhesive prior to any further patient movement.

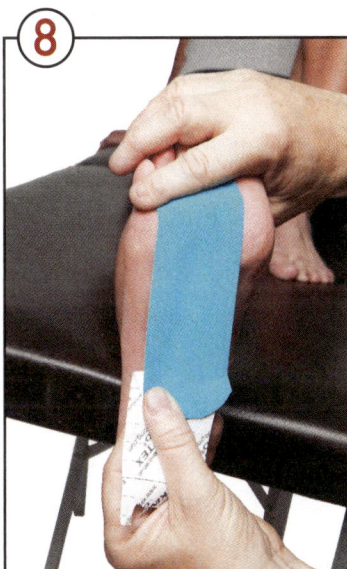

8. Place the patient in dorsiflexion with toe extension and apply 15-35% of available tension to the Kinesio Strip. Apply the button hole strip from the metatarsal heads to the mid shaft region on the plantar surface of the foot. Now decrease tension to paper off to light, 15-25% of available tension to the last 1". Lay down the end with no tension and rub to initiate adhesive prior to any further patient movement.

An anchor can be placed around the mid foot region to assist with adhesion.

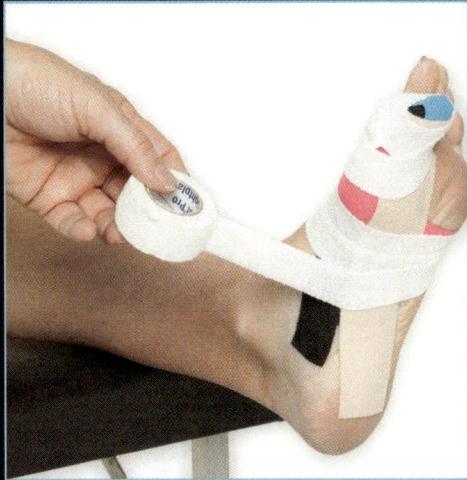

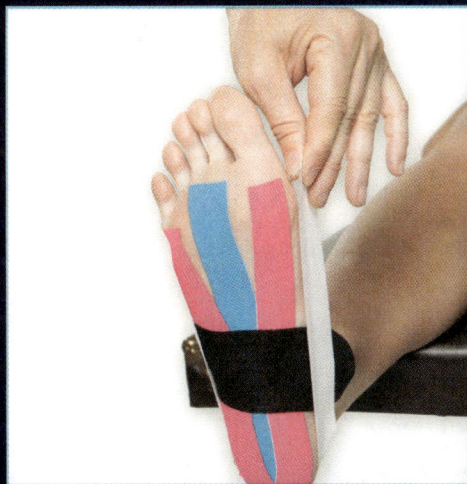

SECTION 10

Combination Tapings

Section 10

Achilles Tendonitis Combination Technique

The Achilles' Tendonitis Kinesio Taping Method will be combined with the traditional Achilles' tendon taping technique. The traditional Achilles' tendon technique is designed to both limit foot dorsiflexion and assist in foot plantarflexion. This is accomplished by using an elastic tape such as elastoplast or Elastikon®. The application will need to be anchored and filled in using a thinner elastic tape, Lightplast® or sheerlight.

It will be useful to have the patient wear the Kinesio technique at all times and apply the traditional Achilles' tendon technique during activity. After several days, only the Kinesio Technique may be necessary.

1. Completed application of the Kinesio Achilles' tendonitis technique. For review, see Achilles' tendonitis technique.

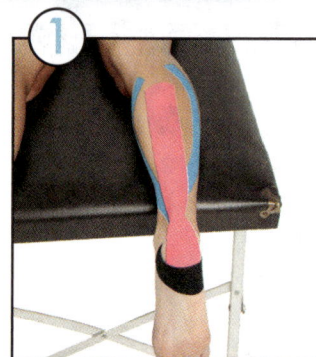

2. Place a lubricating pad over the heel and lace region of the ankle to minimize friction. Apply prewrap (underwrap) over the pads and Kinesio technique from the mid-foot area to just inferior to the musculotendonous junction of the Achilles.

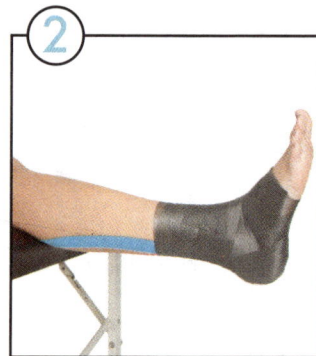

3. Place anchors on both the plantar surface and slightly above the musculotendinous junction of the Achilles and gastrocnemius. It is preferable that the anchors be a thin elastic tape to allow for expansion of the muscles during exercise. If non-elastic white tape is used, only use strips which go ½ way around the muscle then complete the anchor by a second strip going around the muscle.

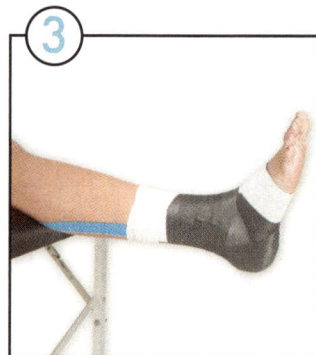

4. Begin by placing the foot in a neutral position. Move the foot into a dorsiflexed position until the patient indicates where the pain begins. The practitioner will want to tape the foot in a slightly more plantarflexed position to limit the patient's ability to move into a painful position. Using a 2" elastic tape (elastoplast or Elastikon®) begin by placing the base of the tape on the anchor on the plantar surface of the foot. Have the patient relax their foot. Apply tension to the elastic tape pulling the foot into plantarflexion. The amount of tension to add is the amount needed to allow for enough dorsiflexion to be physically active but not too much as to allow for movement into a painful position. Attach the elastic strip of tape onto the anchor located slightly above the musculotendinous junction.

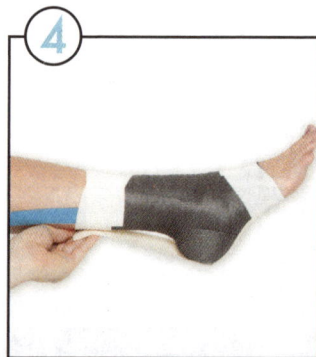

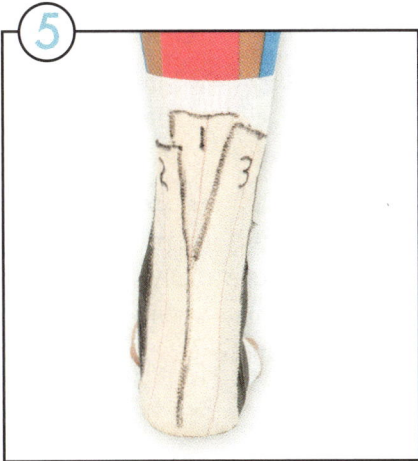

5. Repeat the above step two to three times depending upon the size of the patient.

The practitioner can also use a 3″ wide elastic tape if the patient is larger. The 3″ elastic tape may also be cut into a Y technique. With the split in the Y slightly inferior to the insertion of the Achilles tendon and using the tails of the Y to limit plantarflexion. A series of two or three strips may be appropriate.

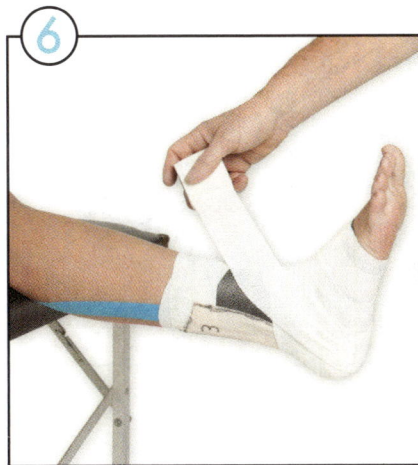

6. Have the patient move their foot into a neutral position (90 degrees). Use a thin elastic tape, such as Lightplast® or sheerlight, to cover in the area and anchor the already applied strips. Be careful not to apply too much tension with the elastic tape as to constrict normal tissue expansion during exercise.

A non-elastic white tape can also be used to cover up or fill in. Only use ½ strips around the joint to limit constriction of the muscle complex during activity.

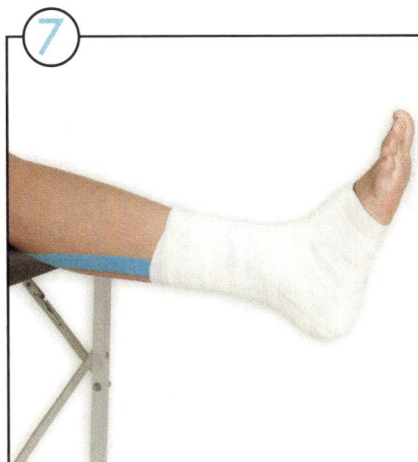

7. Completed combination of Kinesio Achilles' Tendonitis Technique and traditional Achilles' tendonitis taping technique.

Acromioclavicular Joint Combination

This technique will combine the Kinesio Taping AC joint technique with external protection. Following the application of the Kinesio Taping technique for the AC joint, and appropriate rest and rehabilitation the practitioner may determine that additional protection is required for the patient for return to activity.

The external protection may be in the form of a commercially produced AC pad which usually includes a cut-out or raised area (donut) directly over the AC joint. A second option is the fabrication of a pad out of a thermoplastic heat sensitive material, in which a pad or donut is placed directly over the AC. Following the application of the protective pad, additional tape is applied to restrict movement of the pad during activity. The practitioner may select to use additional Kinesio Tex Tape, or a thicker elastic tape such as Elastikon® or Elastoplast to hold the pad in place.

1. Completed application of the Kinesio AC joint technique with ligament correction. For complete review, see Kinesio AC joint application.

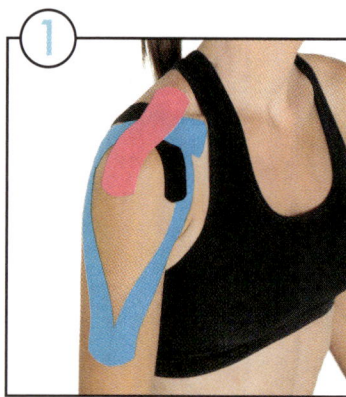

2. Application of a commercially available AC protective pad. This particular pad is available with straps to hold the protective padding in place.

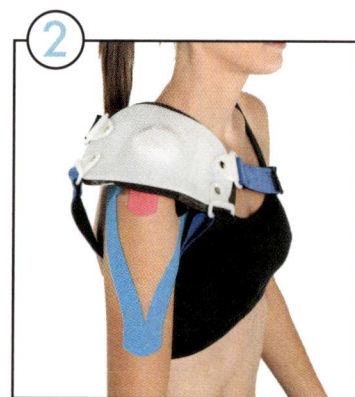

3. To fabricate a thermoplastic heat sensitive protective pad (Orthoplast®), begin by cutting a piece of material which is larger than the area to be treated. According to the product directions, apply appropriate heat source to soften material.

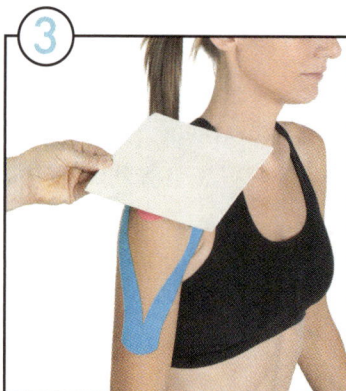

4. Place a small foam pad directly over the AC joint and hold in place with tape. The foam should be approximately ½" thick.

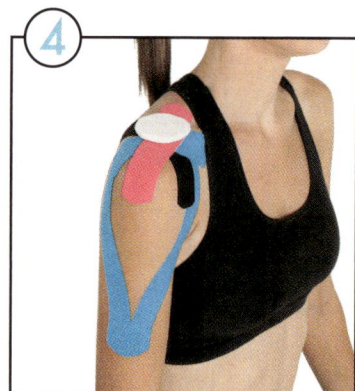

5. Heat the thermoplastic material in an appropriate heat source causing the rigid material to soften. Place the center of the thermoplastic material directly over the pad located over the AC joint. Apply pressure to the thermoplastic material to the contour of the skin.

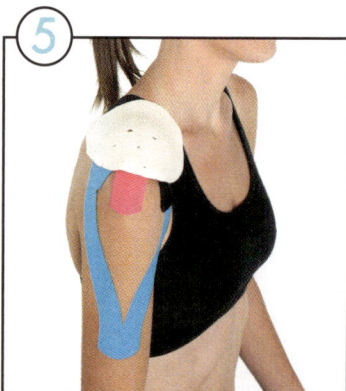

Do not press too hard as to cause pain or further injury to the AC joint.

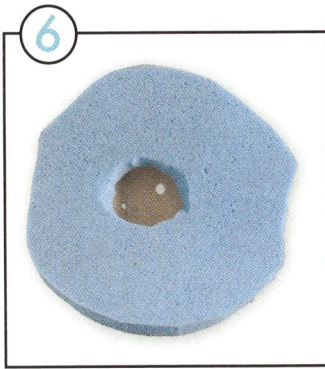

6. Apply a closed cell foam on the under surface of the thermoplastic material. Make sure to leave a "donut" or space directly over the raised area which was formed by the foam applied over the AC joint earlier. The foam material should extend about ½" over the edge of the thermoplastic material.

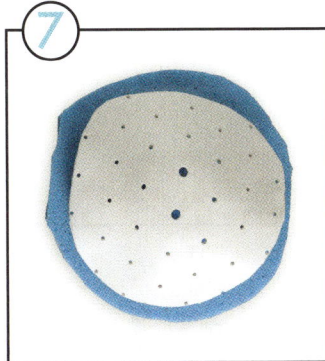

7. View from top, thermoplastic material on top of closed cell foam.

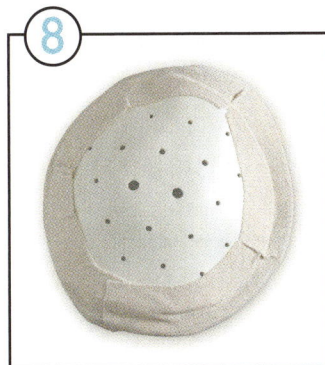

8. Apply a compound cement to the thermoplastic material and attach the closed cell foam. Around the edges of the thermoplastic material and the closed cell foam, apply an elastic tape to help maintain contact between the foam and plastic material.

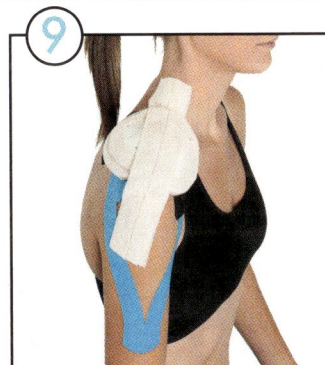

9. Apply several strips of tape over the fabricated thermoplastic pad making sure to have enough adhesion to the surrounding skin. The additional tape is required to minimize pad migration during activity and/or contact.

Strips of Kinesio Tex Tape or another elastic tape may be used. Examples of other tapes, may be Elastoplast or Elastikon®.

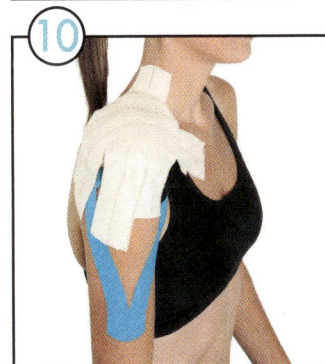

10. Completed combination taping using Kinesio AC Joint Taping and external protection.

Adductor Strain Combination Technique

Combination of the Kinesio Taping Technique and use of a neoprene sleeve or elastic wrap may be found to be helpful in both the acute and chronic adductor strain.

A strain to the adductor muscle group may result from over-extension or over-contraction. If the muscle is acutely inflamed or weakened use the inhibition technique. If the muscle is chronically weakened use the facilitation technique.

The use of the neoprene sleeve or elastic wrap may assist in limiting pain due to pressure created by elastic qualities of the products. Pressure around an injury limits pain possibly due to the initiation of the gate control theory of pain.

The length of tape application will be directly related to the patient's care during application and removal of the neoprene sleeve or elastic wrap.

1. Completed application of the Basic Kinesio Taping Method inhibition application of an adductor strain. The Blue Kinesio I strip is for the adductor muscle group and the Red I strip is an optional application of the Iliopsoas.

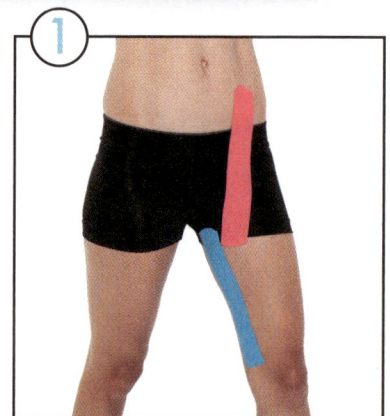

2. Application of neoprene sleeve wrap over the Kinesio Taping Method application.

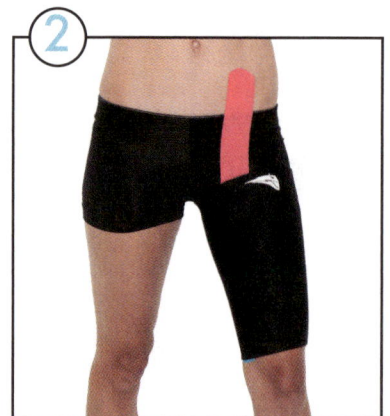

3. Application of elastic wrap over the Kinesio Taping Method application. Use a 6″ double length (10 yd.) elastic bandage. Apply a spray adherent to reduce elastic wrap migration. Start application from the farthest point from the heart of the area to be covered. Do not apply with too much tension as to result in compromised circulation.

   If the patient is smaller the practitioner may determine to use a 4″ elastic wrap 10 yd. length.

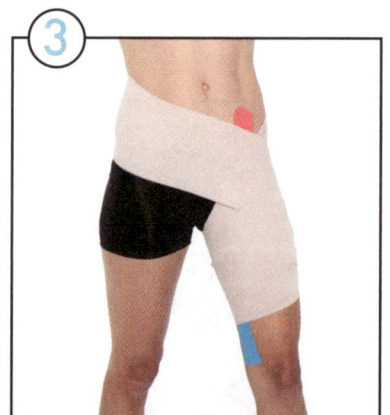

Elbow Hyperextension Combination Technique

Elbow Hyperextension combination taping will combine the Kinesio elbow hyperextension technique with traditional non-elastic white or if desired elastic tape (Elastikon® or Elastoplast). The use of an elastic tape is not intended to replace an injured ligament or appropriate rehabilitation; it is intended to provide proprioceptive stimuli and psychological assurance.

The non-elastic white tape or traditional elastic tape is intended to limit elbow extension past the point of the patient's pain. This is accomplished through the use of a fan or check-rein applied over the antecubital fossa. Care must be taken to not restrict the biceps or forearm muscles from expansion during physical activity. If expansion is limited, cramping may result.

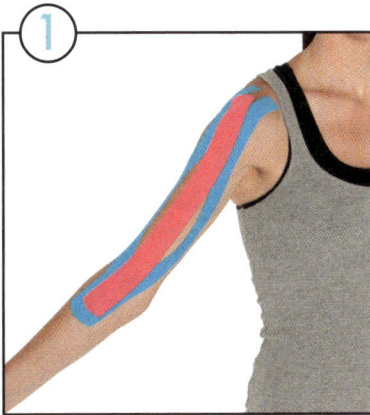

1. Completed application of the Kinesio hyperextension technique. For complete application review, see elbow hyperextension technique.

2. The elbow should be clean shaven and cleansed of any oils or lotions, placed in a position in which any further extension will cause pain. Lubrication would be appropriate in the antecubital space. Spray adherent should be applied to assist in limited migration of the tape. An underwrap (prewrap) may be applied, however it is highly recommended that the anchors be directly applied to the skin. Apply anchors approximately mid-biceps and mid-forearm using a thin elastic tape (Sheerlight or Lightplast®). If white tape is used be careful to allow for expansion of muscle tissue during activity.

3. Have the patent place their elbow in flexion prior to the point of pain. Begin placement of check-rein strips starting from the lateral aspect of mid-forearm to the medial aspect of mid-biceps, pulling in an upward direction. The strips should be placed in a series which when completed will form a fan or check-rein.

Non-elastic white tape may be preferable for fan use, since it does not allow for any increased motion following application.

4. Begin placement of second check-rein strip from the medial aspect of mid-forearm to the lateral aspect of mid-biceps, pulling in an upward direction.

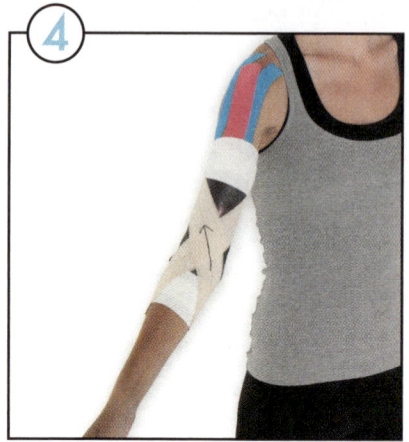

5. The third strip is started from below the ante-cubital fossa in the mid-forearm to the mid anterior aspect of the biceps. The strips should be placed in a series, which when completed will form a check-rein.

Generally a minimum of two check-reins are applied. For a larger patient, a third may be required.

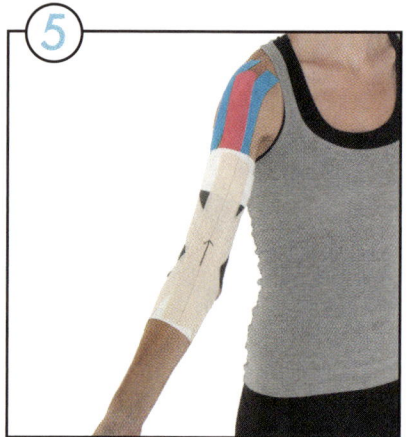

6. Anchor the check-rein application by using thin elastic tape (Lightplast® or Sheerlight) starting from the mid-forearm and ending at the mid-biceps. Enclose all open and exposed areas with the light elastic tape.

Remember that when the light elastic tape is used to "fill in" the exposed areas, do not apply too much tension. This may compromise circulation.

Completed combination of Kinesio elbow hyperextension technique with traditional non-elastic or elastic tape.

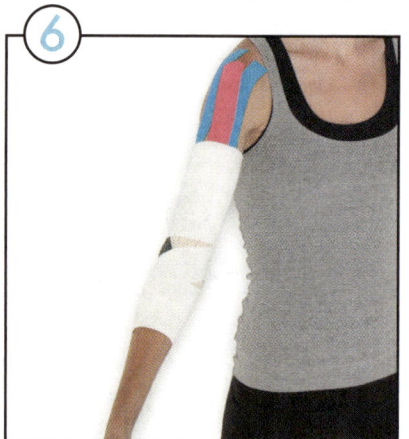

OPTIONAL:

7. Application of a neoprene sleeve or elbow brace that can be adjusted to limit range of motion to assist in limitation of elbow extension.

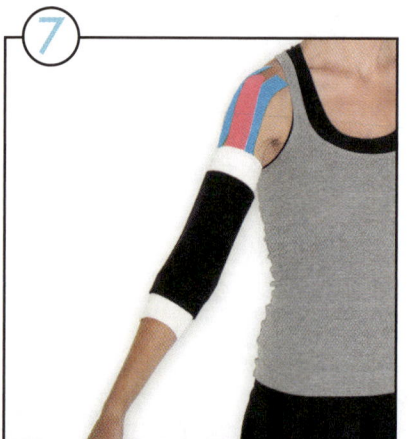

Hamstring Strain Combination

Combination of the Kinesio Taping Technique and use of neoprene sleeve or elastic wrap may be helpful for both acute and chronic hamstring strain.

Begin by applying the Basic Kinesio Taping Technique for the hamstring strain. During the evaluation of the injury, the practitioner will need to determine which of the hamstring group is involved (semimembranosus, semitendinosus, or biceps femoris). It has been found to be helpful to apply a space or mechanical correction strip directly over the area of injury.

The use of the neoprene sleeve or elastic wrap may assist in limiting pain due to pressure created by elastic qualities of the products. Pressure around an injury limits pain possibly due to the initiation of the gate control theory of pain.

The length of tape application will be directly related to the patient's care during application and removal of the neoprene sleeve or elastic wrap.

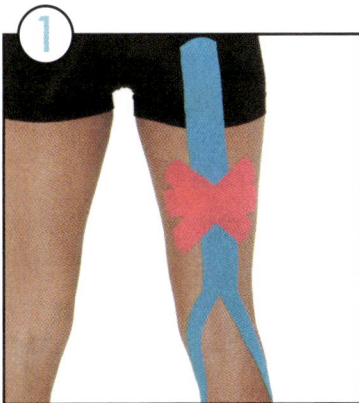

1. Completed Application of Basic Kinesio Taping Application of a Hamstring muscle with additional Space or Mechanical Correction strip.

   See Hamstring Strain Application for complete review.

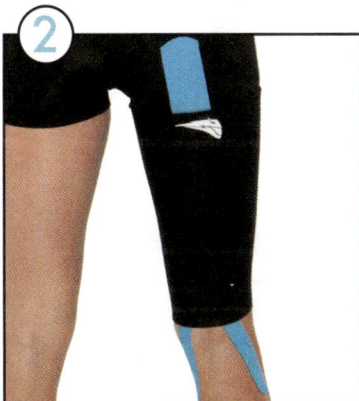

2. Application of neoprene sleeve over the Kinesio Taping Application.

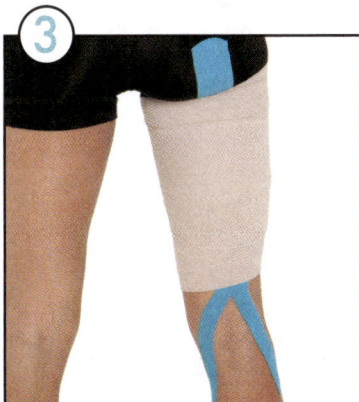

3. Application of an elastic wrap over the Kinesio Taping Application.

Hip Pointer or Iliac Crest Contusion Combination

This technique will combine the Kinesio Taping Technique for Hip Pointer or Iliac Crest contusion with external protection. Following the application of the Kinesio Taping Technique for hip pointer or iliac crest and appropriate rest and rehabilitation, the practitioner may determine that additional protection is required for the patient.

The external protection may be in the form of a commercially produced hip pointer pad or Acromioclavicular pad which usually includes a cut out or raised area (donut) directly over the iliac crest. A second option is the fabrication of a pad, out of a thermoplastic heat sensitive material, in which a pad or donut is placed directly over the iliac crest. Following the application of the protective pad, additional tape is applied to restrict movement of the pad during activity. The practitioner may select to use additional Kinesio Tex Tape, or a thicker elastic tape such as Elastikon® or Elastoplast.

1. Completed Application of the Kinesio Taping Technique for Hip Pointer or Iliac Crest.

   For complete review, see Hip Pointer Application.

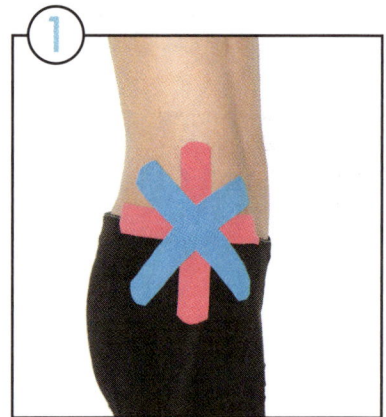

2. Application of a commercially available AC protective pad. This particular pad is available with straps to hold the protective padding in place.

   The pad is used directly over the iliac crest and may require the use of an elastic tape to maintain its position.

3. To fabricate a thermoplastic heat sensitive protective pad (Orthoplast®), begin by cutting a piece of material which is larger than the area to be treated.

   According to the product direction, apply appropriate heat source to soften the material.

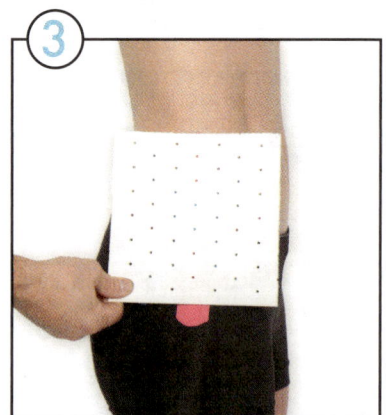

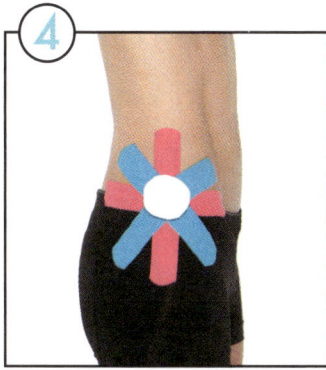

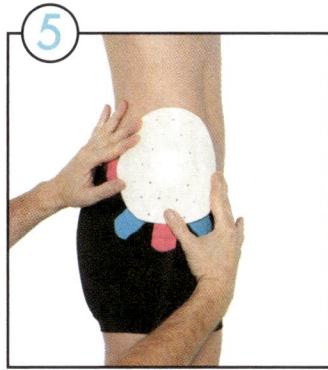

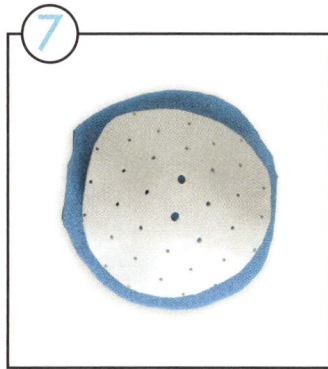

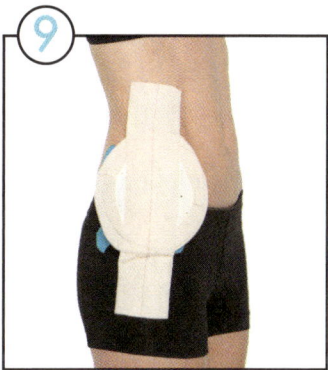

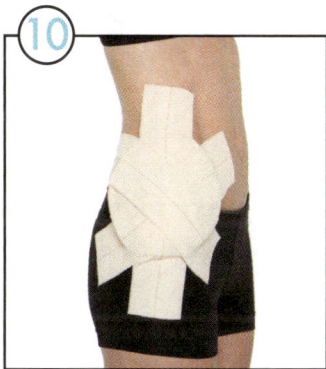

4. Place a felt or foam donut over the contusion on the ilium. Pad should be slightly larger than the area of pain.

5. Use the appropriate heat source as directed by manufacture of the thermoplastic material. Place the center of the thermoplastic material directly over the pad which has already been placed over the iliac crest. Apply pressure to the thermoplastic material to form the plastic material to the contour of the skin.

   Do not press too hard as to cause pain or further injury to the iliac crest.

6. View of the closed cell foam on top of the thermoplastic material. Leaving a "hole" over the raised area directly over the injured tissue. The foam should extend a minimum of ¼" over the edge of the plastic material.

7. View of thermoplastic material on top of the closed cell foam.

8. Apply a contact cement onto the thermoplastic material and attach closed cell foam. Around the edge of the closed cell foam and the plastic material place a 2" strip of tape. This is to limit the separation of the foam from the plastic material.

9. Apply several strips of tape over the fabricated thermoplastic pad making sure to have enough adhesion to the surrounding skin. The additional tape is required to minimize pad migration during activity and/or contact.

   Strips of Kinesio Tex Tape or another elastic tape may be used. Examples of other tape may be Elastoplast or Elastikon®.

10. Completed combination taping using Kinesio Hip Pointer or Iliac Crest Contusion Taping and external protection.

Knee Hyperextension Combination

Knee Hyperextension Combination Technique will combine the Kinesio Knee Hyperextension technique with traditional non-elastic white or if desired elastic tape (Elastikon® or Elastoplast). The use of an elastic tape is not intended to replace an injured ligament or appropriate rehabilitation; it is intended to provide proprioceptive stimuli and psychological assurance.

The non-elastic white tape or traditional elastic tape is intended to limit knee extension past the point of the patient's pain. This is accomplished through the use of a fan or check-rein applied over the popliteal fossa. Care must be taken to not restrict the hamstring or gastrocnemius muscles from expansion during physical activity. If expansion is limited, cramping may result.

1. Completed application of the Kinesio Hyperextension Technique.

   For complete review, see knee hyperextension technique.

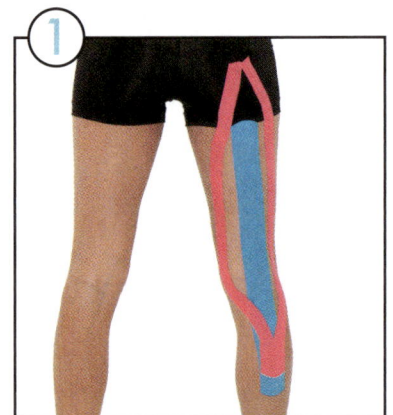

2. The knee should be clean, shaved and cleansed of any oils or lotions and placed in a position in which any further extension will cause pain. Lubrication would be appropriate in the popliteal space. Spray adherent should be applied to assist in limited migration of the tape. An underwrap (prewrap) may be applied; however, it is highly recommended that the anchors be directly applied to the skin.

   Apply anchors approximately mid-thigh and mid-calf using a thin elastic tape (Sheerlight, Lightplast®). If white tape is used, only apply ½ strips to allow for expansion of muscle tissue during activity.

3. Begin placement of strips starting from the mid-calf to the mid-thigh, pulling in an upward direction. The strips should be placed in a series, which when completed will form a fan or check-rein.

   If a traditional elastic tape (Elastikon® or Elastoplast) is used, make sure all tension is removed prior to tape application

   Non-elastic white tape may be preferable for use of the fan, since it does not allow for any increased motion following application.

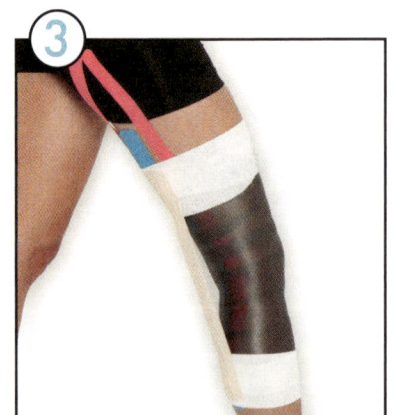

4. Begin the second strip on the inferior posterior medial aspect of the calf below the knee. The strip should be angled across the popliteal space and end on the posterior lateral aspect of the thigh.

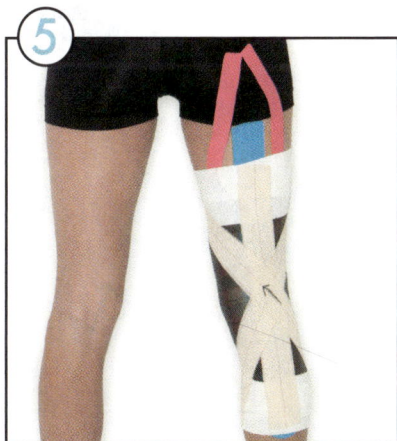

5. Begin the third step on the inferior posterior lateral aspect of the calf below the knee. The strip should be angled across the popliteal space and end on the posterior medial aspect of the thigh.

Normally, a series of 2-3 strips are used for each of the 3 strips. The number depends upon the size of the athlete and the degree of knee extension limitation desired.

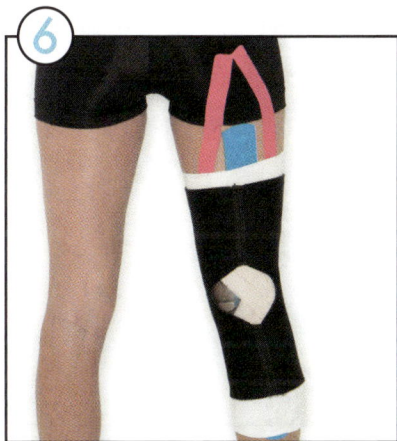

TWO OPTIONS FOR COMPLETION

OPTION 1: UPPER THIGH

6. Anchor the fan application by using thin elastic tape (Lightplast® or Sheerlight) starting from the mid-calf and ending at the mid-thigh. Enclose all open and exposed areas with the light elastic tape.

Remember that when the light elastic tape is used to "fill in" the exposed areas, do not apply too much tension. This may compromise circulation.

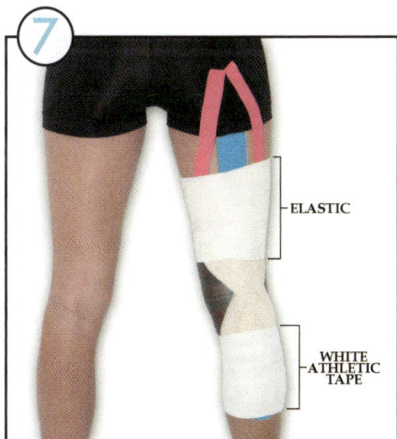

OPTION 2: LOWER THIGH

7. Anchor the fan application by using nonelastic, white athletic tape. If white non-elastic tape is used, only apply ½ circular strips to allow for muscle expansion during activity.

ELASTIC

WHITE ATHLETIC TAPE

Medial/Lateral Collateral Ligament Combination

The use of an elastic tape is not intended to replace an injured ligament or appropriate rehabilitation. It is intended to provide proprioceptive stimuli and psychological assurance. The following description is the combination of the Kinesio ligament corrective technique and prophylactic elastic taping of the injured ligament. It is recommended that the patient wear the Kinesio Tex Tape at all times and only during practice or competition should the prophylactic taping be applied.

At any time the patient indicates that they are not confident and has not been able to demonstrate functionally their ability to perform, participation in activity should not be recommended.

1. Completed application of the Kinesio Ligament Corrective Technique.

   For complete review, see medial collateral ligament application.

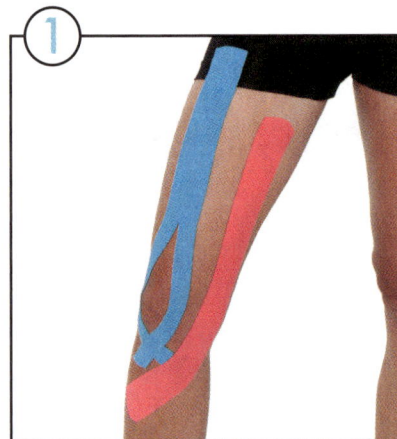

2. The knee should be clean, shaved and cleansed of any oils or lotions, and in approximately 30 degrees of flexion. Lubrication in the popliteal space is advised to limit friction. Spray adherent should be applied to assist in limited migration of the tape. An underwrap (prewrap) may be applied. However, it is highly recommended that the anchors be directly applied to skin. Apply anchors approximately mid-thigh and mid-calf using a thin elastic tape (Sheerlight or Lightplast®).

   If white tape is used, only apply strips in ½ circumference to allow for expansion of muscle tissue during activity.

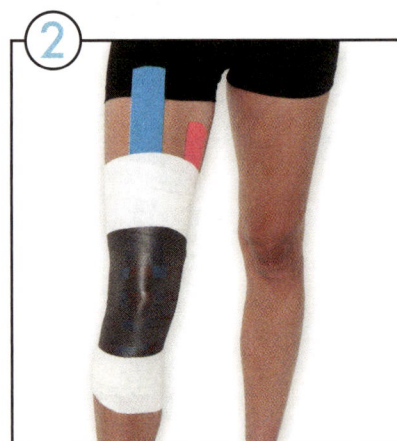

3. Beginning below the knee place the first strip medial and posterior to the tibial tuberosity and directed at the lateral aspect of the mid thigh. An attempt should be made to follow the pathway of the medial collateral ligament so the center of the elastic tape is directly over the MCL. Nearly all of the tension should be removed from the elastic tape over the length of the ligament.

4. The second strip should be placed from the posterior lateral aspect of the calf and directed to the posterior medial aspect of the mid thigh.

5. The third strip should be placed from below the tibial plateau directly below the insertion of the MCL to the superior aspect of the femoral condyle. This pattern should be repeated at least twice. For a larger athlete, the pattern should be repeated three times.

6. Upon completion of support strips, the complete tape application needs to be covered to minimize migration and unraveling during activity. A light elastic tape should be selected (Lighplast® or Sheerlight) and care should be given not to apply tape with too much tension, as to limit circulation and cause cramping. If white non-elastic tape is used to cover, use only ½ strips to limit constriction of tissue.

Begin to apply the elastic tape from the calf region to the mid thigh. This will assist in limiting the possibility of applying the tape too tightly, limiting circulation during activity.

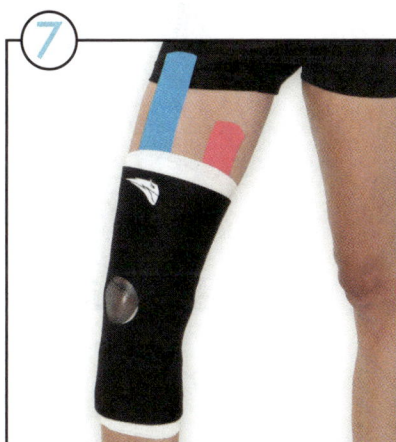

7. The practitioner may want to have the patient also wear a neoprene sleeve or brace over the top of the tape application. If appropriate, the patient may also require a hinged prosthetic device.

Medial/Lateral Collateral Ligament Combination

Medial/Lateral Epicondylitis Combination

The use of an elastic tape is not intended to replace an injured ligament or appropriate rehabilitation. It is intended to provide proprioceptive stimuli and psychological assurance. The following description is the combination of the Kinesio ligament corrective technique and prophylactic elastic taping of the injured ligament. It is recommended that the patient wear the Kinesio Tex Tape at all times and only during practice or competition should the prophylactic taping be applied.

At any time the patient indicates that they are not confident and has not been able to demonstrate functionally their ability to perform, participation in activity should not be recommended.

The practitioner should select one of the Kinesio medial or lateral epicondylitis taping techniques as described.

1. Option 1 of Medial Epicondylitis Kinesio Taping Technique.

2. Option 1 of Lateral Epicondylitis Kinesio Taping Technique.

3. Application of a Cho-Pat® type strap inferior to the medial or lateral epicondyle of the humerus. The use of this strap is believed to act as a "shock absorber" and limit the stress placed upon the common muscle group.

4. This technique may be simulated by using Kinesio Tex Tape, this image is a demonstration as explained in Severs Syndrome. Apply a mechanical correction directly over the area of pain, apply moderate to severe, 50-75% of available tension over the area of pain with downward pressure. Lay down the tails with no tension. This will simulate the Cho-Pat® strap tension of limiting stress on the common muscle group.

5. Application of neoprene knee sleeve over the Kinesio Technique for Epicondylitis. The use of the neoprene sleeve is believed to increase temperature in the region, and decreased pain by pressure applied to the region.

The length of time the Kinesio Technique may remain in place is directly related to the care the patient uses in putting on and taking off the neoprene sleeve.

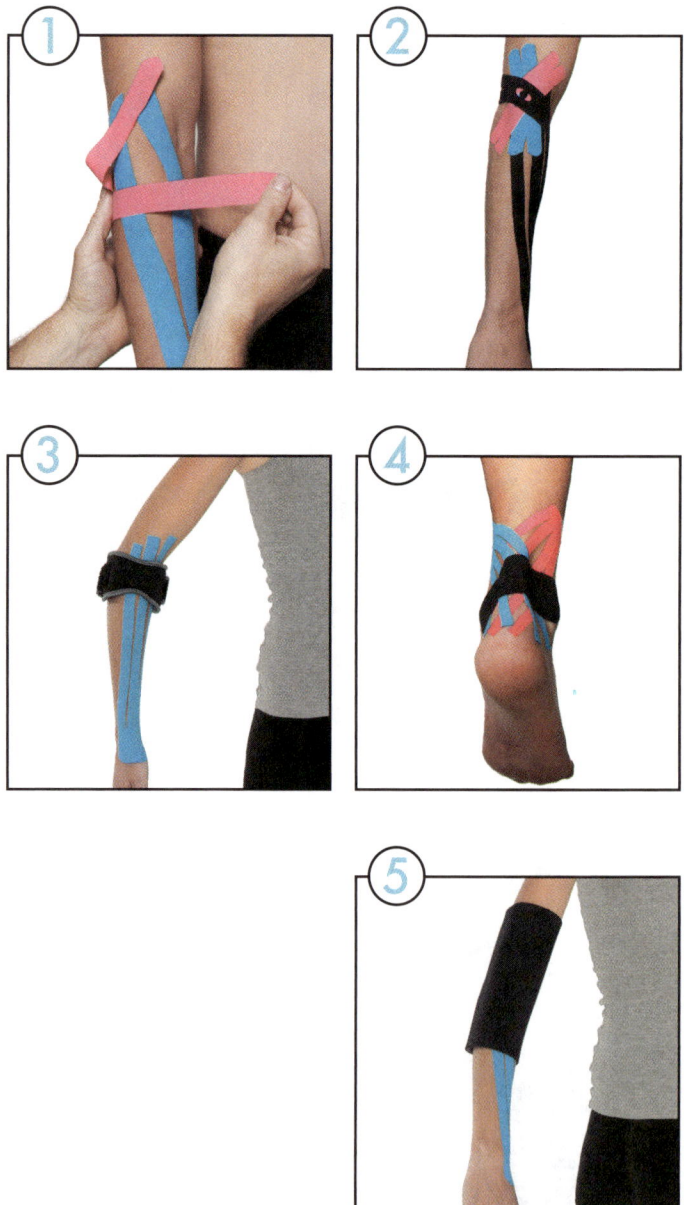

Metatarsal Arch Combination: Low Dye

There are two options for combination taping with the Kinesio Taping Technique. One, combining the Kinesio Metatarsal Arch Technique with a Low Dye Arch Technique. Second, combining the Kinesio Metatarsal Arch Technique with a traditional Metatarsal Arch Taping.

The Low Dye arch support can be used for the medial, lateral, and metatarsal arches located in the plantar surface of the foot. If the practitioner finds this technique successful, they want to investigate the appropriate use of an orthotic to assist in the long term care of the patient.

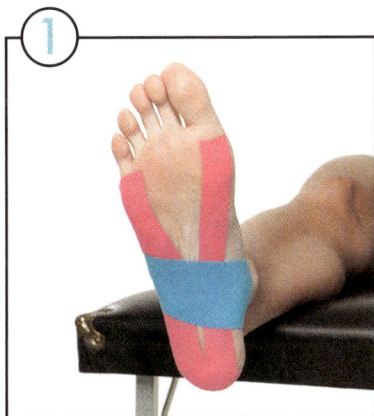

1. Completed Application of the Kinesio metatarsal arch technique. For complete review, see metatarsal arch technique.

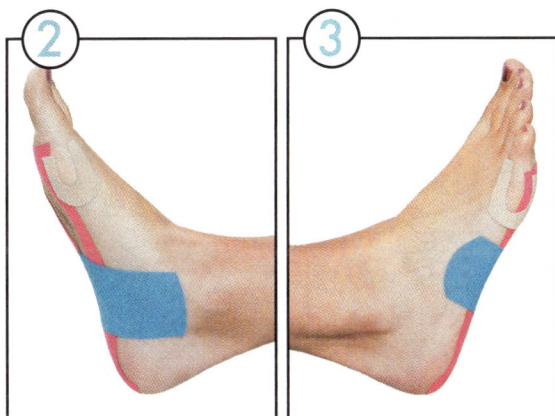

LOW-DYE TECHNIQUE

2-3. To begin, you may place optional pieces of mole skin cut to match the head of the 1st and 5th metatarsal heads, with a strip also on the heel region. These strips are to provide skin protection from multiple tape application.

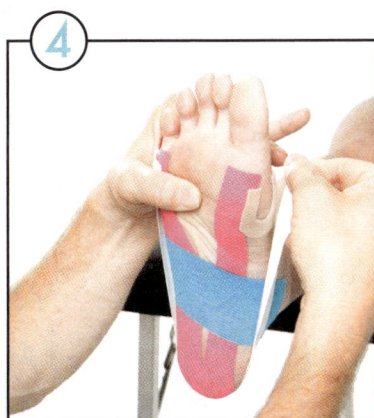

4. Place a 1" strip of non-elastic athletic tape on the distal head of the 5th metatarsal. Bring the strip of tape around the heel. Place the thumb of one hand between the second and third heads of the metatarsal on the plantar surface. Push the thumb up and flatten out the metatarsal arch. Reach around to the dorsal surface with the index and middle finger to the metacarpal phalangeal joint. Apply a downward pressure to the first metatarsal, placing it in a pronated position.

5. Place the free end of the athletic tape onto the distal head of the 1st metacarpal. This process may be repeated depending upon the size of the patient. For smaller patients, one strip is generally enough. For larger patients, two strips may be needed.

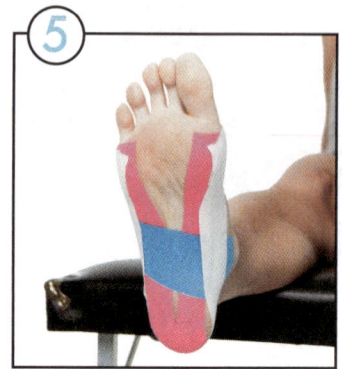

6. Begin on the plantar surface of the 1st metatarsal head, angle the strip at approximately 45 degrees towards the lateral aspect of the heel and return to the 1st metatarsal head along the medial longitudinal arch.

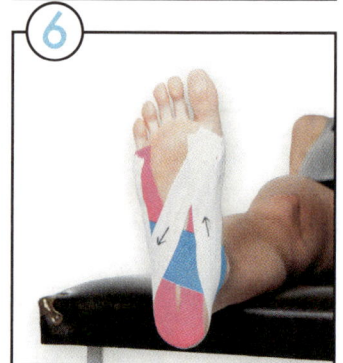

7. Repeat this process until a strip is applied to each metatarsal head, or the metatarsal heads are covered with tape.

   1″ non-elastic tape is used. For a smaller patient only 4 strips may be required. For a larger patient, 5 strips may be needed.

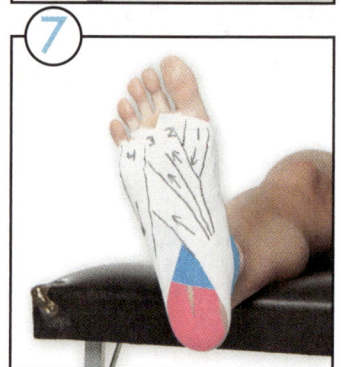

8. Apply anchors to hold the low dye application to the plantar surface. Begin the 1 ½″ strips from the medial aspect of the arch and apply towards the lateral aspect. Being the first strip close to the anterior aspect of the calcaneous. Repeat this process until the complete plantar surface is covered. By beginning at the heel and working distally the white athletic tape has less tendency to "roll" when the patient applies their sock.

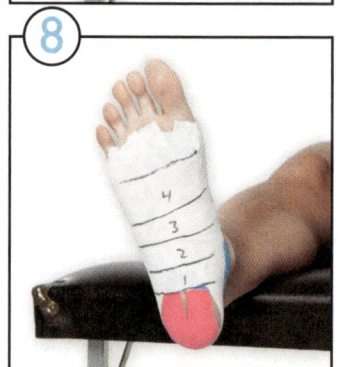

9. Finish the Low Dye by wrapping the arch with a thin elastic tape (Lightplast® or Sheerlight) to secure the completed tape job.

   Completed combination of Kinesio metatarsal arch and Low Dye Technique.

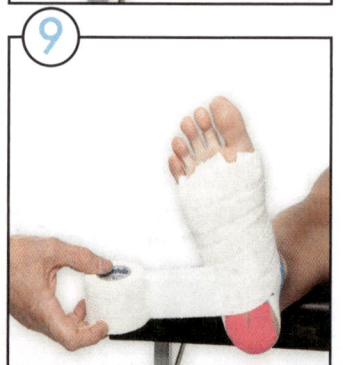

Metatarsal Arch Combination, using the Traditional and Kinesio Taping

The technique will combine the two metatarsal arch tapings previously described. The practitioner may select to apply the Low Dye technique, the Metatarsal Arch technique, or even the Longitudinal Arch Taping technique, as described in the metatarsal arch technique.

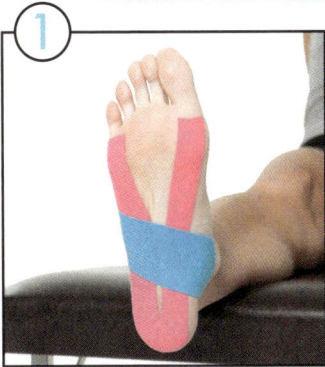

1. Application of the Metatarsal Arch Technique. For complete review see Metatarsal Arch.

METATARSAL ARCH TRADITIONAL

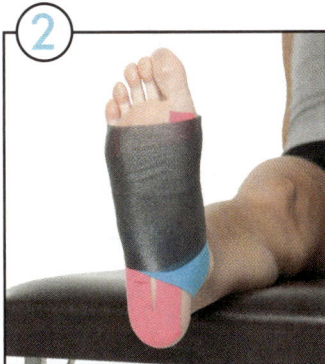

2. Begin by placing an optional layer of protection for the arch area by applying a prewrap or underwrap.

3-4. Begin a series of 1 to 1 ½" non-elastic athletic tape on the medial aspect of the arch. The series of strips should begin at approximately the base of the metacarpal phalangeal joint of the first metatarsal.

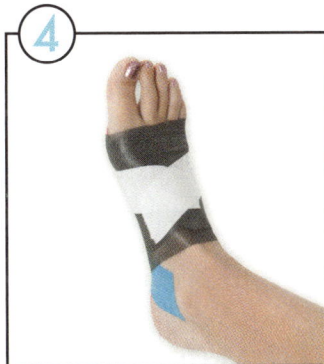

Place a slight tension on the tape, as you cross over the plantar surface of the metatarsal arch region. It should produce a slight crinkling of the skin on the plantar aspect when applied correctly. As you reach the lateral aspect of the 1st ray decrease tension and lay down the tape onto the dorsum of the foot. A "V" should be formed between the 1st and 2nd or 3rd and 4th metatarsals.

Application of too much tension may cause cramping or numbness.

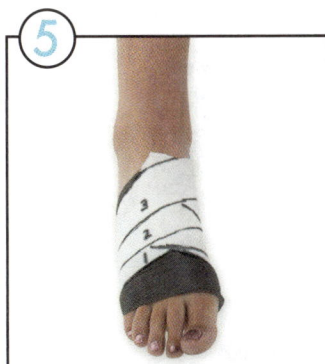

5. Apply a total of 3-4 strips depending upon the size of the patient.

Completed combination taping using Kinesio Metatarsal Arch Taping and Traditional Metatarsal Arch Taping.

Patella Tendonitis Combination Taping/Bracing

The practitioner may desire to use a combination of the Kinesio technique for patella tendonitis and commercially available straps or braces. Some patients may desire additional assistance in the acute inflammation phase or feel a decrease in pain from the external pressure provided by bracing.

The use of the external strapping or bracing may assist the patient during practice or competition. It is recommended that the patient wear the Kinesio technique under any other treatment protocol and when not involved in activity.

At any time the patient indicates they are not confident and has not been able to demonstrate functionally their ability to perform, participation in activity should not be recommended.

1. The practitioner should select one of the Kinesio patella tendonitis taping techniques as described. Image shown is the "U" Technique and Modified Space Correction I strip.

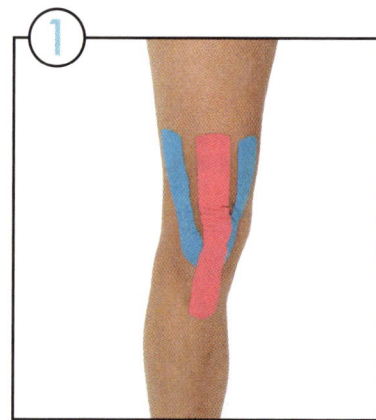

2. Application of a Cho-Pat® type strap over the inferior pole of the patella and directly over the patella ligament. The use of this strap is believed to act as a shock absorber and limit the stress placed upon the patella ligament.

This technique may be simulated by using either Kinesio Tex or an Elastoplast/Elastikon® 1" tape. Take a piece of the tape, measure around the knee and double the length: add an extra 1 to 1 ½". Double the tape over itself, leaving only the extra 1 to 1 ½" exposed. Wrap this strip around the knee just below the patella to simulate the above strap.

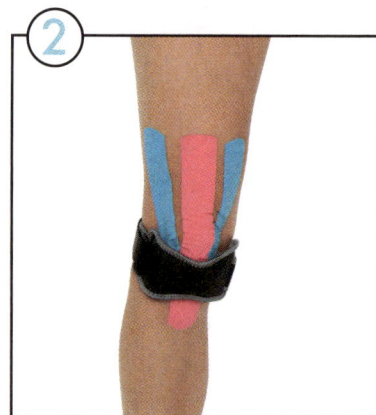

3. Application of a neoprene knee sleeve over the Kinesio technique for patella tendonitis. The use of the neoprene sleeve is believed to increase temperature in the region, and decreased pain by pressure applied to the region.

The length of time the Kinesio technique may remain in place is directly related to the care the patient uses in putting on and taking off the neoprene sleeve.

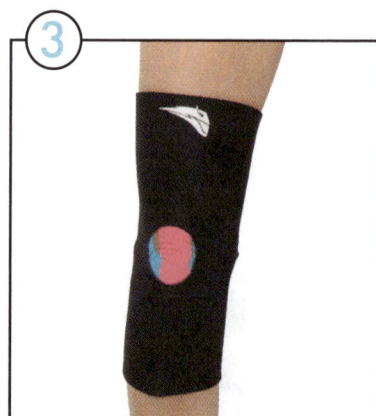

Plantar Fasciitis Combination Technique

The practitioner may find that for acute plantar fasciitis, or with patients that are larger than average, they may need to combine the Kinesio Taping Technique and a plantar fascia mole skin strip or longitudinal arch taping. A third combination could be used, the application of the Low Dye technique as described in the metatarsal arch combination taping technique.

Additional therapies may include the use of a donut placed upon the heel in the region of pain, heel lift to elevate the heel and shorten the Achilles' tendon, and placement of a rigid orthosis in the shoe.

It is recommended that the patient wear the Kinesio Taping Technique under any other treatment protocol.

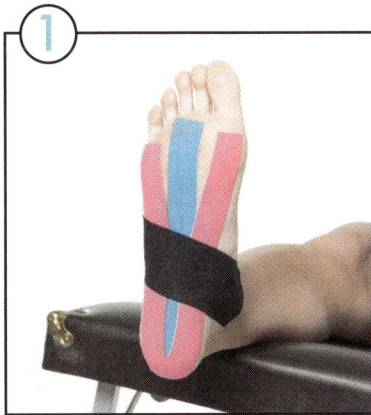

Completed application of the Kinesio plantar fasciitis technique. For review, see Plantar Fasciitis Technique.

TWO OPTIONS WILL BE SHOWN

OPTION 1: PLANTAR FASCIA MOLE SKIN STRIP

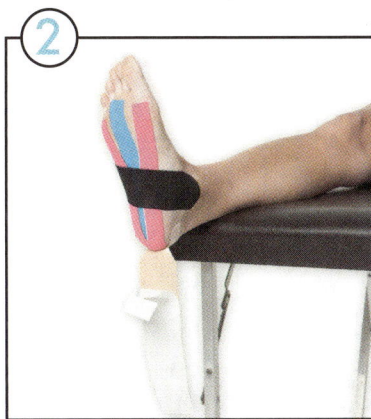

2. The plantar fascia mole skin strip can be purchased commercially, or made from mole skin which comes in a roll. The strip should be 2-3" (5cm to 7.5 cm wide), and length should be from insertion point of Achilles' tendon to metatarsal heads. Each side of the mole strip should have a "V" cut approximately 1" on the head.

   Place the "V" shaped end above the insertion point of the Achilles tendon into the calcaneous.

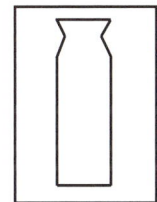

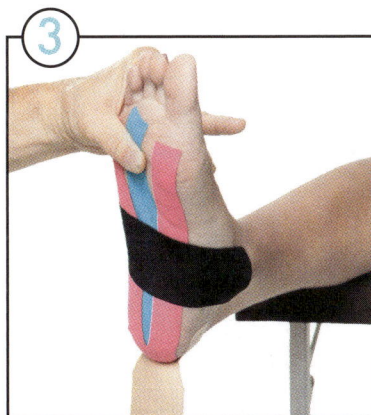

3. Place the thumb of one hand between the second and third heads of the metatarsal on the planar surface. Push the thumb up and flatten out the metatarsal arch. Reach around to the dorsal surface with the index and middle finger to the metacarpal phalangeal joint. Apply a downward pressure to the first metatarsal, placing forefoot in pronated position.

4. Place the plantar fascia mole skin strip along the plantar surface to the heads of the metatarsals, while maintaining forefoot in pronated position. Lay down the remainder of the mole skin strip.

5-6. The mole skin strip will need to be held onto the plantar surface of the foot by using a thin elastic tape (Lightplast® or Sheerlight).

OPTION 2: LONGITUDINAL ARCH TAPING TECHNIQUE

7. Begin by placing an anchor strip using 1″ or 1 ½″ white athletic tape starting from the distal 1st metatarsal phalangeal joint head and ending distally on the 5th metatarsal phalangeal joint. This strip should be applied with minimal or no tension.

8. Using a 1″ athletic tape, begin one strip on the 1st metatarsal phalangeal. The tape should follow directly inferior along the medial longitudinal arch, around the heel of the calcaneous and then angle at approximately a 45 degree angle back to the 1st metatarsal phalangeal joint. Slight tension should be applied to the white athletic tape.

9. Repeat the above description for applying a similar strip on the 5th metatarsal phalangeal joint. This will provide support to the lateral longitudinal arch.

10. Apply a series of 2-3 of the above described strips depending upon the size of the patient. A minimum of 2 strips is recommended.

11. Apply anchors to hold the longitudinal arch application to the plantar surface. Begin the 1 ½″ strips from the medial aspect of the arch and apply towards the lateral aspect. Being the first strip close to the anterior aspect of the calcaneous.

12. Repeat this process until the complete plantar surface is covered. By beginning at the heel and working distally the white athletic tape has less tendency to "roll" when the patient applies their sock.

13. Cover in the longitudinal arch taping with a thin elastic tape, Sheerlight or Lightplast®. Prior to application of the tape, place a small piece of prewrap on the dorsum of the foot. This will assist in protection of a sensitive area and limit irritation and possible blistering. Covering it can also be accomplished by using white non-elastic tape. For review, see metatarsal arch taping.

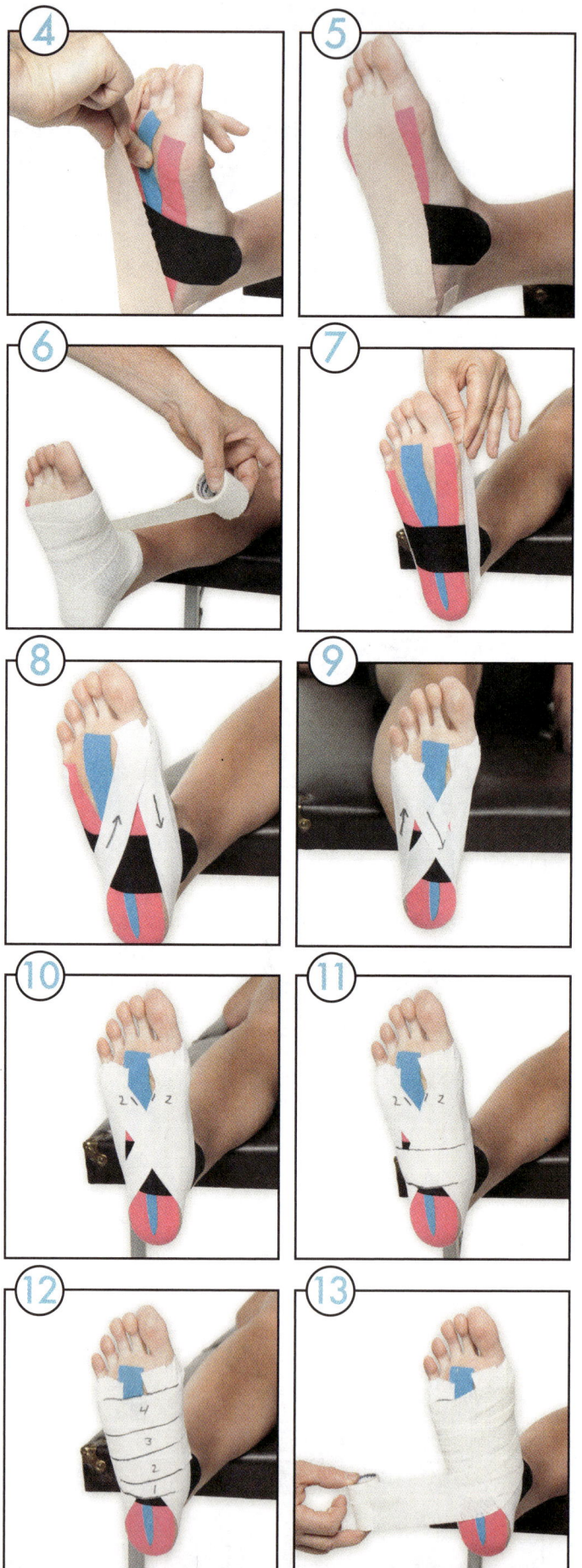

Quadriceps Strain/Contusion Combination

Combination of the Kinesio Taping Technique and use of a neoprene sleeve or elastic wrap may be found to be helpful in both the acute and chronic quadriceps strain/contusion.

A strain to the quadriceps muscle group may result from over-extension or over-contraction of the quadriceps muscle group. If the muscle is acutely inflamed or weakened use the inhibition technique. If the muscle is chronically weakened use the facilitation technique.

A contusion to the quadriceps muscle group needs to be treated with caution, as the largest muscle group in the body, has a significant blood supply and injury may result in bone formation (myositis ossificans).

The use of the neoprene sleeve or elastic wrap may assist in limiting pain due to pressure created by elastic qualities of the products. Pressure around an injury limits pain possibly due to the initiation of the gate control theory of pain. The length of tape application will be directly related to the patient's care during application and removal of the neoprene sleeve or elastic wrap.

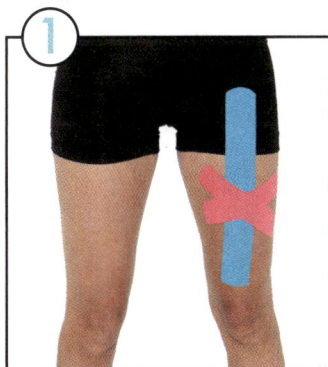

1. Completed application of the Basic Kinesio Taping Application of a quadriceps strain facilitation with space corrective technique. The practitioner may select to use either the basic application, the lymphatic correction, or both. For complete review, see quadriceps contusion/strain.

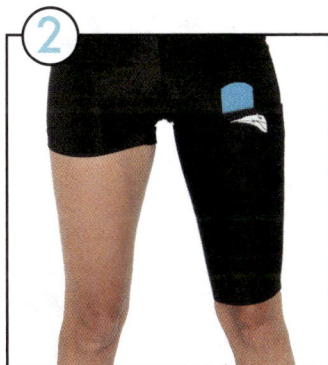

2. Application of neoprene sleeve over the Kinesio Taping Method application.

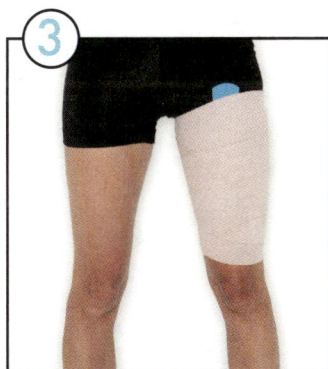

3. Application of elastic wrap over the Kinesio Taping Method application. Use a 6" double length (10 yd.) elastic bandage. Apply a spray adherent to reduce elastic wrap migration. Start application from the farthest point from the heart of the area to be covered. Do not apply with too much tension as to result in compromised circulation.

Shin Splint or Medial Tibial Stress Syndrome Combination

Combining the Kinesio Taping Technique with traditional treatments may provide both acute pain reduction and long term positive benefits for shin splints or medial tibial stress syndrome.

Several examples will be given in which the Kinesio Taping Technique will be combined with traditional treatments; low dye, longitudinal arch, or orthotics. The practitioner will need to evaluate each patient and apply what is in their opinion the best course of treatment. If one method is selected and the results are not as effective as desired, try another method.

1. Completed application of the Kinesio Technique for shin splints. Image shown is a space correction along the medial tibial border (area of pain) and a series of mechanical/space correction combination strips.

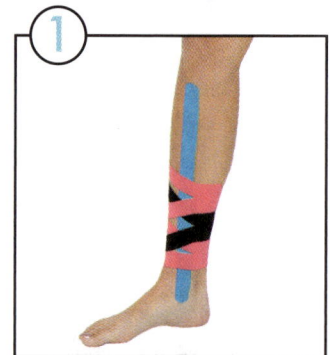

LOW-DYE TECHNIQUE

2. Application of the Kinesio Taping Technique for shin splints in combination with a low dye technique.

   For complete review, see low dye technique, as described in metatarsal arch combination technique.

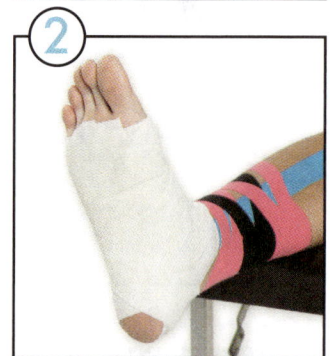

LONGITUDINAL ARCH TECHNIQUE

3. Application of the Kinesio Taping technique for shin splints in combination with the longitudinal arch technique. For complete review, see longitudinal arch technique, as described in plantar fasciitis combination technique.

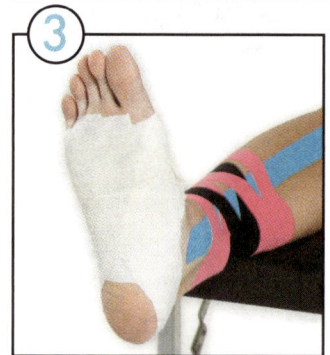

ORTHOTIC COMBINATION

4. Application on the Kinesio Taping technique for shin splints in combination with orthotics.

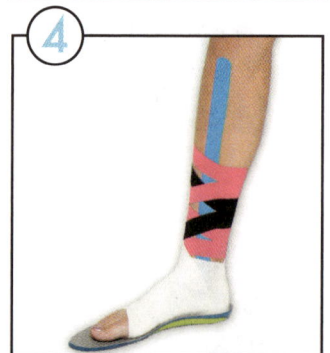

Turf Toe Combination Technique

This technique will combine the Kinesio Turf Toe technique and the use of a moleskin turf toe strap. The mole skin strap is shaped like a "T" and is designed to limit great toe extension. This is accomplished by the non-elastic qualities of the moleskin and the placement of the strap with the toe in a slightly flexed position.

Turf Toe is a very painful condition and return to activity should be based upon the individual's ability to perform functional tasks with minimal or no pain. In addition to the taping techniques the practitioner may want to place a rigid foot insert made of metal or plastic to limit the extension movement of the first MTP joint.

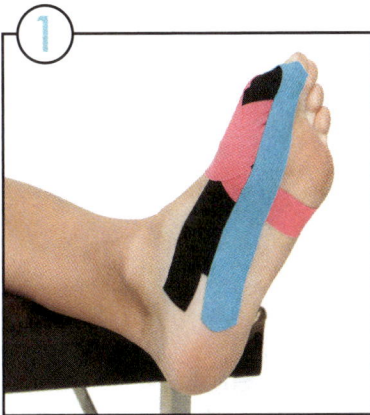

1. Completed application of the Kinesio Turf Toe Technique. For complete review, see turf toe technique.

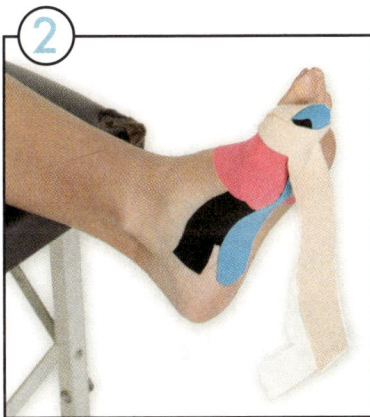

TURF TOE MOLESKIN STRAP

2. The turf toe strap is made of moleskin and can be purchased pre-made or made out of a sheet of moleskin. It should be approximately 8" in length, and 1 to 1 ½" wide depending upon the size of the patient.

Begin by placing the "T" end of the mole skin turf toe strap around the distal phalanx of the great toe.

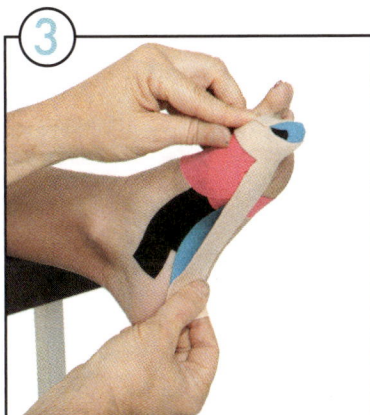

3. Place the patient's great toe in a slightly flexed position which should be prior to the initiation of pain. Place the top of the "T" moleskin strap on the distal end of the great toe.

Place the turf toe moleskin strap down the dorsal aspect of the 1st metatarsal shaft. After the strap has been applied, have the patient move their toe into extension to evaluate whether or not the toe is in the proper position.

Be careful not to place the toe in too much of a flexed position, this may place the toe in a position of risk for a fracture or dislocation due to excessive motion limitation.

4. Upon completion of the moleskin strap application, anchor the strap at both the toe and plantar surface locations. At the toe, an additional Kinesio strip may be used. On the plantar surface, a thin elastic tape, such as Lightplast® and Sheerlight may be used.

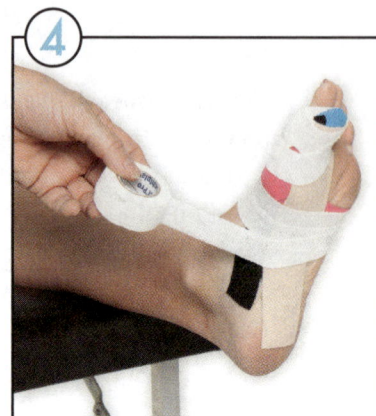

OPTIONAL: SELF ADHESIVE CLOSED CELL FOAM PAD

5. Place a support pad made out of closed cell foam and one which is self adhesive under the 1st metatarsophalangeal joint. The pad should have a "cut out" area for the metatarsophalangeal joint to drop down into. This will assist in decreasing pressure on this joint.

   This pad should be held in place by applying a cover anchor over the pad. First apply a pre-wrap and then cover with an elastic tape.

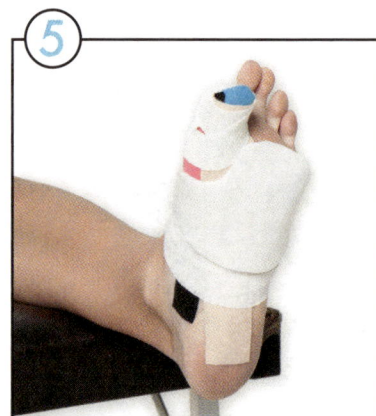

OPTIONAL: METAL/GRAPHITE FORE FOOT PLATE

6. Place a metal plate insert into the forefoot of the patient's shoe. The metal plate will reduce toe extension and limit joint motion. This will assist reducing pain by limiting joint motion.

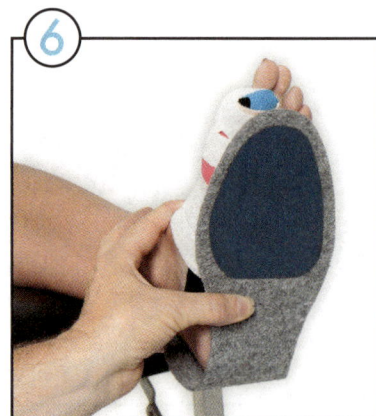

Turf Toe
Combination Technique

Valgus Laxity of the Elbow Combination

A chronic valgus laxity of the elbow may develop from repetitive valgus forces being applied to the elbow during overhead activities. The use of an elastic tape is not intended to replace an injured ligament or appropriate rehabilitation. It is intended to provide proprioceptive stimuli and psychological assurance. The following description is the combination of the Kinesio Ligament Corrective Technique and prophylactic elastic taping of the injured ligament. It is recommended that the patient wear the Kinesio Taping at all times and only during practice or competition should the prophylactic taping be applied.

At any time the patient indicates they are not confident and has not been able to demonstrate functionally their ability to perform, participation should not be recommended.

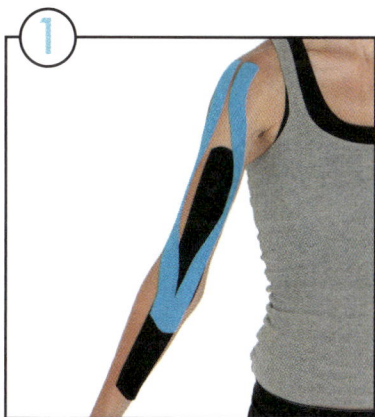

1. Completed application of Valgus Laxity of the Elbow with optional biceps brachii. For complete description of application technique, see valgus laxity elbow.

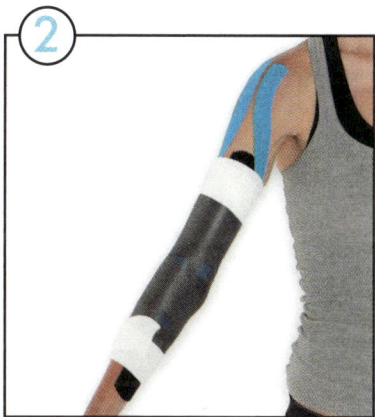

2. The elbow should be clean, shaved, and cleansed of any oils or lotions, and in approximately 30 degrees of flexion. Lubrication in the antecubital space would be appropriate to limit friction. Spray adherent should be applied to assist in limited migration of the tape. An underwrap (prewrap) may be applied, however it is highly recommended that the anchors be directly applied to the skin. Apply anchors approximately mid-forearm and mid-humerus using a thin elastic tape (Sheerlight or Lightplast®). If white tape is used, only apply strips in ½ circumference to allow for expansion of muscle tissue during activity.

3. Place the patients elbow in a flexed position prior to the point of pain. The first elastic strip begins below with the first strip from medial aspect of the mid-anterior forearm and directed over the ligament and continuing the anti-cubital fossa to the lateral aspect of the mid forearm epicondyle of elbow. Nearly all of the tension should be removed from the elastic tape over the length of the ligament.

4. The second strip should be placed from the posterior aspect of the middle forearm and directed over the ligament and continuing the anti-cubital fossa to the lateral mid-forearm of biceps muscle region.

5. The third strip should be placed from mid-forearm inferior to the medial epicondyle superiorly past the medial epicondyle to the mid-humerus region.

   This 3 strip pattern should be repeated at least twice. For a larger athlete, the pattern should be repeated three times.

6. Upon completion of support strips, the complete tape application needs to be covered to minimize migration and unraveling during activity. A light elastic tape should be selected (Lightplast® or Sheerlight) and care should be given to not apply tape with too much tension, as to limit circulation and cause cramping. If white non-elastic tape is used to cover, use only half strips to limit constriction of tissue.

   Begin to apply the elastic tape from the mid-forearm to the mid-humerus. This will assist in avoiding the possibility of applying the tape too tightly limiting circulation during activity.

7. The practitioner may want to have the patient also wear a neoprene sleeve or brace over the top of the tape application. If appropriate, the patient may also require a hinged prosthetic device.

Wrist Sprain Combination Technique

Wrist Combination Taping will combine the Kinesio Wrist Technique with traditional non-elastic white tape. The use of the non-elastic white tape is not intended to replace an injured ligament or appropriate rehabilitation, it is intended to provide proprioceptive stimuli and psychological assurance.

The non-elastic white tape is intended to limit unwanted wrist flexion or extension in a painful range of motion. There are two commonly used traditional techniques used to limit wrist movement: 1) circular strips around the wrist, and 2) use of a fan or check-rein.

With both techniques, have the patient place the injured wrist in slight flexion or extension (opposite position to the limited motion desired), fingers extended and spread to limit compression of the hand resulting in compromise of circulation.

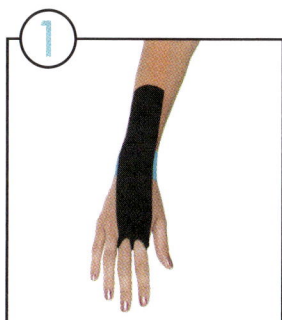

1. Completed application of the Kinesio wrist sprain technique. For complete review of application, see wrist sprain. Image shown has used a "button hole" technique to assist the functional correction strip adhesion.

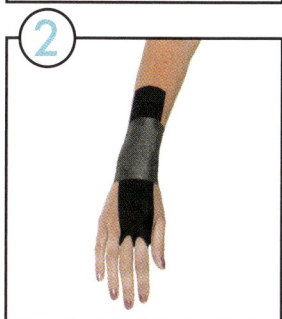

OPTION 1: WRIST ONLY TAPING

2. Hand is placed in neutral or slight flexion with fingers extended and spread. Prewrap (underwrap) is optional.

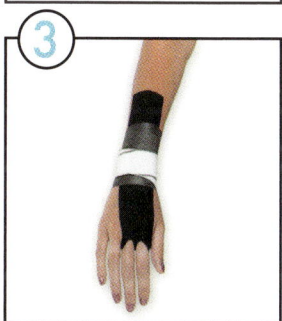

3. Begin the 1 ½" white tape on the dorsum of the hand, wrap tape around the palmar side and return to the dorsum of the wrist. The tape is applied taking in consideration the anatomy of the wrist. The strips should be angled to accommodate the "hour glass" shape of the wrist, the strips must be angled.

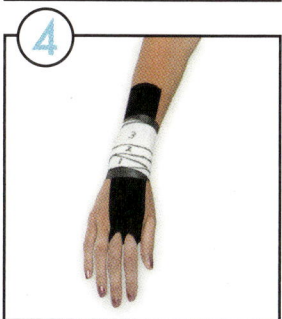

4. Repeat the above procedure 3-5 times as indicated by the size of the patient and restriction desired. The degree of tension is determined by the degree of restricted movement and patient tolerance.

OPTION 2: TAPE THROUGH THE PALM.

5. Begin by applying an optional pre-warp to the palmar surface of the hand and wrist.

6. Place the hand as described in option one. Begin by placing anchors 2-3" below the wrist and mid-palm of spread hand.

7. Place the patient's hand in slight flexion (if desired result is to limit extension). Apply a fan or check-rein strips. As shown, begin strip one at the medial aspect of the wrist at approximately a 45 degree angle and apply to the palm area distal to the thumb.

8. A second strip is applied from the lateral aspect of the wrist at approximately 45 degree angle and apply to the palm area inferior to the little finger.

9. Apply a third fan or check-rein strip starting in the middle region in the wrist to the mid palm area.

   These fans or check-reins can be repeated a minimum of one additional time. If the patient is larger a third series may be appropriate.

10. Finish by applying another series of anchors as described in image 1.

   For more complete description of fan or check-rein application, see elbow or knee hyperextension combination technique.

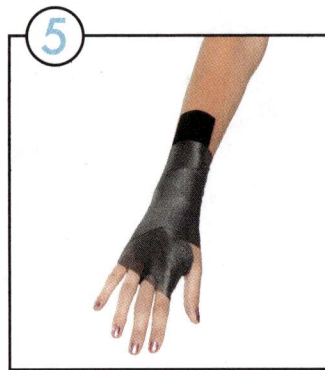

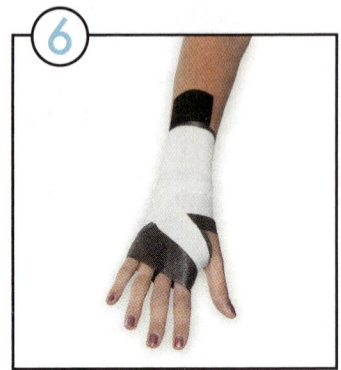

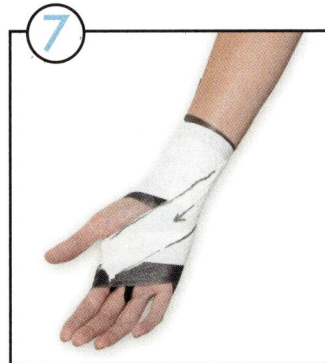

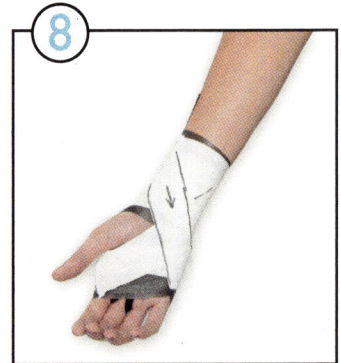

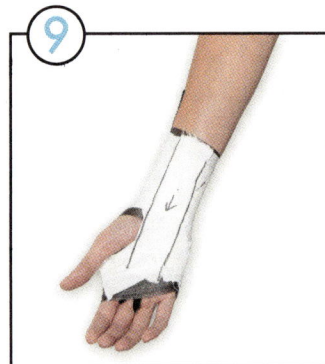

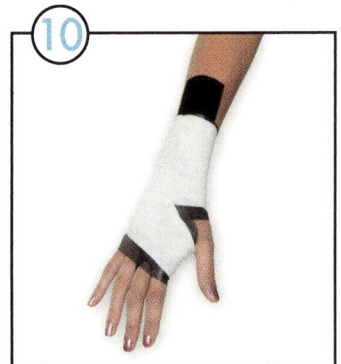